AUGUSTINE

THE
CONFESSIONS

Augustine's fourth-century spiritual autobiography is not only a major document in
the history of Christianity and a classic of
Roman Africa, it also marks a vital moment
in the history of Western culture. As Augustine recounts his life, he probes the great
themes that others were to explore after him
– faith, time, truth, identity, and self-know-
ledge – with a degree of detail unmatched
in ancient literature. Illustrated with vivid
portraits of friends, family, colleagues, and
enemies, *The Confessions* provides a remarkably candid account of the passage from a
life of sensuality and superstition to a genuine spiritual awakening. The result is a
powerful narrative of one man's religious
journey that continues to shape the way we
write and behave today.

EVERYMAN,
I WILL GO WITH THEE,
AND BE THY GUIDE,
IN THY MOST NEED
TO GO BY THY SIDE

AUGUSTINE

The Confessions

Translated and edited by Philip Burton
with an Introduction by Robin Lanc Fox

EVERYMAN'S LIBRARY

Alfred A. Knopf New York Toronto

128

THIS IS A BORZOI BOOK

PUBLISHED BY ALFRED A. KNOPF

First included in Everyman's Library, 1907
This translation first published in Everyman's Library, 2001
Translation, Introduction, Bibliography, and Chronology
Copyright © 2001 by Everyman Publishers plc
Typography by Peter B. Willberg

www.randomhouse.com/everymans

ISBN 0-375-41173-9

Book Design by Barbara de Wilde and Carol Devine Carson

Typeset in the UK by AccComputing, Castle Cary, Somerset

Printed and bound in Germany
by GGP Media, Pössneck

THE CONFESSIONS

CONTENTS

———

THE CONFESSIONS

God's transcendence – life before birth? – tears
before laughter – infant jealousy – language not
taught but learnt – sentenced to school – baptism –
immoral classics – the schoolboy orator – God the
source of being.

'A quagmire of carnal desire' – paternal ambition –
maternal admonition – stealing pears – vice a
parody of virtue – 'a land of famine'.

'In love with love'   why does tragedy give
pleasure? – diabolical students – the reading of
Cicero: the love of wisdom – Manichee delusions –
a vindication of the Patriarchs – Monica's dream.

Rhetoric for sale – Vindicianus on astrology –
Nebridius – an unnamed friend   his baptism and
death – 'half my soul' – the pleasures of friendship
– 'Beauty and Congruence' – the Monad and the
Dyad – the reading of Aristotle – 'our house, your
eternity'.

The gift of confession – religion and science –
waiting for Faustus – Faustus a disappointment –
more student trouble – the flight from Carthage –

Note: The book divisions of the *Confessions* are Augustine's own;
the paragraph numbering follows the conventions of modern
editors.

INTRODUCTION

Augustine's *Confessions* are our most brilliant evidence for the spiritual and intellectual progress of a man in the ancient world. We know his life like nobody else's in that period, but the *Confessions* also challenge us by their paradoxical questioning of everyday life and values and their humble, hard-won submission to what their author believes to be God. 'He saw his own story as that of Everyman', one of his greatest connoisseurs has aptly observed, and yet there is no ordinary limit to the extraordinary range of his mind. He is a fitting study for a lifetime, even for those who do not share the Christian faith which sustained his ceaseless writing and thinking. Apart from the incomparable memories of his past, Augustine is fascinated by the relation of words to things, the force of subconscious memory, the scope of the human will, the notion of understanding through reading, the abstract measurement of time and dozens of other questions of abiding interest. Unlike other biographies of this era, the *Confessions* do not dwell on demons or guardian angels: there is hardly a hint of the Holy Spirit until the final books. They are also a masterpiece of romantic prose. Their Latin resonates with biblical phrases, especially from the Psalms, and includes echoes of philosophy and non-Christian poets. Like most of his other works, the *Confessions* were not written and rewritten in silence. They began by being dictated, the 'oral text' of a professional speaker who could compose spontaneously in this complex style. The dictated version was then worked over and corrected. The *Confessions*, Augustine believed, were overheard by God. But they were first heard by his support-system, staff trained in shorthand.

The *Confessions* are one of the few books to have impressed readers continuously in the sixteen hundred years since their author's lifetime. Some of them have imitated the famous title, whether Rousseau or the modern novelist William Boyd or the literary theorist Derrida in his *Cir-Confessions*. Many more people respect them as a religious classic, although their respect

xiii

is sometimes tempered by denominational prejudice. More than a hundred and fifty Christian communities still live by a monastic rule which is derived from Augustine: his *Confessions* speak directly to their choice of a sexless, self-scrutinizing life. Other Christians are suspicious of what they sometimes miscast as a Catholic classic, a sourcebook for original sin or strong views on the authority of the Church. In fact, this book is not mainly about such themes. Its heart lies elsewhere and individual readers have responded more generously, among them, John Donne and Pascal, Petrarch and the philosopher Wittgenstein.

Nobody had written a book with the title 'Confessions' before and the title may mislead modern readers who are expecting nothing but autobiography. In Latin, 'confessiones' were not simply confessions of doubtful conduct, like de Quincey's 'Confessions of an Opium Eater'. Augustine himself explains in another work that they mean 'accusations of oneself and praises of God'. Since 1990 happy discoveries have returned to us twenty-six sermons by the author, new to us in whole or part. In May 397, the year of the *Confessions*' composition, we now know that Augustine preached on this very topic. He points to the beginning of Psalm 118, what we sing as 'O give thanks unto the Lord'. This Psalm was prescribed for Pentecost, probably the occasion of the sermon, but it was also sung daily and its Latin opening (*Confitemini domino*) caused the congregation to beat their breasts in awareness of their sins. A thunder of pummelled bodies lies behind Augustine's use of the word. But he reminds his audience that 'confession' also entails what we might call 'testifying', praising God as well as admitting human faults. The recurrent praise of God which is woven through the *Confessions*, especially in its final two books, is entirely true to the title. These two aspects are a unifying thread in what may seem, at first sight, a disorderly work.

The Psalms explain the title, but Everyman needs to remember that the author writes from the hypercritical stance of a practised monk. His standards are not ours: the smallest things come under his scrutiny because they are evidence of the misdirected will and build up a subsequent habit. Augustine did not invent the idea of the will: Aristotle, among others, had long anticipated him. But he extended it, even to 'sins' of our flesh. The reason why he dwells at such length on his youthful theft of pears is that he had not even wanted to eat what he stole. The crime mattered so much because he had chosen evil for evil's sake. For eleven years before writing, Augustine had lived a celibate, self-scrutinizing life with a strongly 'monastic' element. Penance, he came to believe, was the necessary antidote against our endemic sins and was to be practised daily by individuals. All the while, the Psalms were the constant companions of his meditations: bits of them were hung up as texts on the wall in the room where he finally died. The *Confessions* are a new form, born from the Psalms and the penitential practice of a long-experienced ascetic.

The *Confessions* were composed in 397, probably in one concentrated burst, although some scholars have argued, unconvincingly, for a process continuing to 401. The first nine books describe Augustine's life until his thirty-third year, from 354 to 387, the same span, coincidentally, as was lived by Alexander the Great. They do not follow a straight chronological course. Augustine's own hindsight often interposes: he draws aside to generalize his experience, to point out that it is a false value for a parent to put worldly education before his son's chastity and spiritual growth (2.3) or to explore why weeping is so dear to people in a time of misery (4.5). He also engages in polemic, against the false views on sin and the universe which were held by his former sect, the Manichees (8.10 is a striking interruption, here) or against the 'pride' and partial insight of Neoplatonist philosophers (7.9 and 7.21). This roundabout progress is sometimes hard for outsiders to follow. Like the rest of his life it is the subject of a brilliant modern biography, the classic work of Peter Brown, first published in 1967. It is the essential companion to enjoyment of the *Confessions* and much else in Augustine's life.

Much of Augustine's early biography has to be based on the *Confessions* themselves. They do not set out to give a full history, let alone a full social history of the many settings which they conjure up. They do not need to tell us that Augustine's north African home in Numidia was in a relatively multi-cultural place, that there were Jews and synagogues in some of its towns, that there were dusky Berbers and people speaking Punic, both of whom had lived there for centuries before Roman rule began. They might, however, have said something about the besetting split in the local Christian churches, the majority being called 'Donatists' by the minority of self-styled 'Catholics', or Universal Christians: it is only in this sense that Augustine calls himself a 'Catholic'. The schism went back to times of persecution c. 308, when the Donatists, or 'Holy' Church, claimed not to have compromised with the pagan inquisitors. Augustine's 'Catholics' were a minority: he does not discuss which sort of Christian his mother had been when baptized, but at the time, in the late 330s, it is highly likely that she had been baptized a Donatist and had later gone over to the Catholics after persecution in the 350s. Augustine's reticence on the entire topic is particularly remarkable because, for three years before writing the *Confessions*, he had been engaged in active manoeuvring against the Donatist churches. In 394, he composed a psalm against them which was to be sung as popular propaganda. It describes the Donatist Christians as having 'handed over' themselves to the devil. Schism, admittedly, was described in the New Testament as the devil's work, and the Donatists were proving every bit as violent as Augustine's 'Catholic' forbears in Africa. But Christians were supposed to forgive and love their enemies. The *Confessions* give no hint of this attack on fellow Christians. To those who know the Sermon on the Mount it will seem a greater sin than many which Augustine confesses in the book.

Most of the 'life' in these books is sufficiently intelligible on a first reading. The most elusive aspects are his various 'conversions' and what they did and did not involve. Augustine is so hypercritical of his past that readers may mistake the scale of his straying: it did not involve a renunciation of Christianity at any point. In all but formal terms he was a Christian throughout. The tremendous scenes in Book 8, culminating in the decision in the Garden, do not involve his decision to 'believe' or 'be a Christian'. They are not a conversion to Christian religion, but a deconversion from sex. A sexless life, he personally decides, is a precondition for baptism.

Only when he has given up sex can he go ahead and be baptized. He dwells on this great drama of the will and the moment of decision: this is what matters, whereas the actual baptism, about eight months later, is described in one brief sentence.

These gradations may well puzzle modern readers. At birth Augustine was exorcized and 'salted' against demons by his Christian mother. Aged five, he was extremely ill with a stomach ache and begged his mother to be baptized. It was not, in fact, unusual for a parent to vow a sick child to total virginity for life before God in return for the child's restoration to health: monasteries thus contained some very unlikely candidates. Augustine's mother, Monica, might have vowed him to virginity at this crisis and simply settled the issue. It is perhaps unlikely that Augustine would have grown up and accepted her vow, without rebelling for good. There would, then, have been no *Confessions* as we know them.

Instead, Monica made him a catechumen, or Christian 'hearer'. Catechumens were a well-recognized group, who would attend church services although they had to leave before the Eucharist. They could call themselves Christians, but not 'seekers' or the 'faithful'. It was expected that in due course they would put their names down for further instruction, become 'seekers' and be baptized. Baptized Christians were the 'faithful'.

There was, however, a snag to baptism. Anyone who took it seriously knew that post-baptismal sins were unforgivable, if they were big ones, although most pre-baptismal sins would be wiped out by baptism itself. There was, then, room for calculation. If you delayed baptism and avoided the most unpardonable sins like murder (some writers included adultery), you could be baptized in old age and be destined for heaven in the life to come. If you were baptized too soon, you might damn yourself to hell by sinning badly later. Those who thought hard could see the attractions of remaining a 'catechumen': Monica saw them, and because she suspected that her son might sow wild oats and be a promiscuous young man, she preferred to keep him as a catechumen.

Augustine's progress was compounded by a further chance:

his exceptional talent. If he was to shine in his worldly career, he needed to marry socially above himself. If he was to attract a rich family, he would have to establish himself and marry quite late, but a delay in marrying increased the chances of his sleeping around. As he would be a late marrier, it was sensible if he was also a late baptismal candidate. In the event, his youth was quite restrained. From sixteen onwards, he stayed faithful to one 'partner' (his *concubina*) and did not do what his mother most feared: sleep adulterously with someone else's wife. This sin meant hell, much as some Catholics still regard the effect of divorce.

In his mother's mind, therefore, it would have been expected, in Book 8, for Augustine to marry the young bride whom she had helped to find and then be baptized and confine his sex to her alone. The surprise was his decision to aim higher, give up sex altogether and be baptized on that first-class basis.

So much for the outcome, real and anticipated. The progress to it is fascinating, but not as inconsistent as we first think. Aged five Augustine was a child catechumen: aged sixteen he still attended the Universal Church in Carthage, aged eighteen he was bowled over by a light-weight exhortation to philosophy, the *Hortensius* by the pagan orator Cicero (written in 46 BC) but because he did not find the name of Christ in it, he tells us, he was not satisfied. This reaction speaks clearly for his Christian alignment at the time, but why then does he go off to join the sect of 'Manichees', a 'lying' group who promise false truth and attack the Old and New Testaments for all their errors (Book 3.6 to 3.10)?

We continue to recover yet more fragmentary texts from Manichaean sects, found between Egypt and Central Asia. They make quite clear what the *Confessions* do not: Manichaeans had their own Gospel, revealed (they believed) by the Holy Spirit, and they regarded themselves as the True Christians. All others were semi-Christians, at best. Manichaeans denied the Incarnation and the Crucifixion; they regarded much of the Gospels as interpolated and too 'Jewish'; they had their own liturgical calendar and psalms and did not accept the usual churches' Eucharist. Christians often helped to persecute them and often obliged their leaders to pronounce anathema on their previous beliefs before accepting them as possible Christians. In mainstream opinion, Manichaeans were obviously heretics. But they themselves disagreed, and so when Augustine was with them, he was actually a True Christian in his own mind.

From Book 5, onwards, in 383/4, his Manichaean faith collapses. It is badly damaged by reading pagan Academic, or 'Sceptical', philosophy which exhorts him to doubt. Even so, he refuses to doubt his inherited allegiance to Christianity. Once again, he tells us, he fights shy of pagan philosophy because it does not base itself on Christ. So he decides, despite his scepticism, to put himself down as a catechumen again in Milan's church.

This entire odyssey, from 354 to 386, is marked more by time than religious distance. Unlike his father, Augustine never went over to paganism. The most finely-balanced moment was in 385/6 when he was given, as a catechumen, some 'Platonist books'. We can identify them as Neoplatonist works by Plotinus (c. 260 AD) and perhaps others, although Augustine only knew them in Latin translations. They fired him, he tells us in other early works, with 'an incredible fire'. In a crucial passage, written in November 386, long before the *Confessions*, he says of this time of new-found fire: 'I looked back only, I confess, as if from a journey, onto that religion implanted in us as children.' More than the *Confessions* implies, he nearly lost touch at this time with his Christian roots. They seemed like a vanishing point on a motorway. One of the excitements was the discovery of these pagan philosophers' inner self-reflection and intense, reasoned meditation. It helped them and him, he believed, to ascend to the very presence of God (recalled at 7.10). But he turned back yet again to the Scriptures and was put back on a Christian track by reading Paul.

By the beginning of Book 8, before the scene in the Garden, he is fully set on a Christian course. One of the threads in the *Confessions* has now been sorted out: his developing idea of God. He had projected his own failings, so he sees with hindsight, onto God at times of loss or crisis; for more than nine years he had accepted the Manichaean idea of a 'Father of

Greatness' in a Kingdom of Light, pitted against a Kingdom of Darkness in a process of cosmic 'Star Wars'. Manichaeans also told him that the 'semi-Christians' believe that God is a person with hair and nails, because their bogus Scripture says that 'man is created in God's image'. In Milan, from the great bishop Ambrose, Augustine discovers that this slander is untrue and that God is a spiritual being. He has no body, but Augustine wonders how He can be infinite and bodiless: for a while he thinks that He surrounds the world and perhaps even permeates it like a giant sponge. Then, with the help of Neoplatonic philosophy, he realizes that God can be unlimited by space or time, transcendent, eternal, uncreated but necessarily related to the universe.

Until late in this process, he had remained most uncertain about the nature of the Incarnation. He is still not alone in this uncertainty. He tended to believe that Jesus was born from a virgin, but did not exist until his birth. This relatively simple view was unorthodox and when he fastened on John's Gospel chapter 1, he must have revised it. 'In the beginning was the Word...' : in my view, he thought this point through only after his meeting with Milan's elderly priest Simplicianus, described at 8.2. The *Confessions* anticipate this by bringing the theology of John 1.1 right up to his first encounter with the Platonic books (7.9).

The brilliant scene in the Garden, therefore, is a wrestle about conduct, not theology. At the end, Augustine decides to give up sex for life and on that basis, to be baptized. He did not have to make such an extreme decision. The sexless option was only one among baptized Christians' possible choices, although it was highly esteemed and, in their opinion, the absolute best. It was not even essential for clergymen. By the 380s, in the Latin-speaking west, the sexless life had found a few takers in Rome and evidently in Milan. Bishop Ambrose was a champion of it, even bringing girls from as far afield as Bologna for a special veiling ceremony as virgins. A small community of celibates was living under his general authority in the suburbs of Milan. A crucial text here was the *Life of Antony*, the Egyptian hermit, which had been written up by Athanasius, bishop of Alexandria, in the 330s. It had been known in Rome since the 340s and by the 380s there were at least two Latin translations of it. Partly in its wake, celibate Christians had become more numerous in the Latin-speaking west. They tended to want the churches to be led by celibates like themselves, but they were still only one voice among many. Some merely believed that married bishops should give up sex if they already had children when appointed. In a region like north Africa, with more than 600 bishops of the two Christian sects, there were simply not enough perfectionists willing to derail their own lives.

Nonetheless, Augustine did it and he was not the only one to think it proper. The man to watch here is Verecundus, the literary teacher in Milan who lent Augustine the sub-alpine villa into which he promptly went into retreat. He regretted not to be able to join Augustine and follow his example, because he still enjoyed sex with his Christian wife: he had accepted, therefore, that he should not be baptized until he gave sex up (9.3). Celibacy in the Latin west was beginning to seem the most meritorious option for those who had not been baptized when young.

Why ever did they think so? They fastened on bits of the Gospels, on 'eunuchs for the sake of the kingdom of heaven', and on a misunderstanding of Paul's cautious advice in I Corinthians 7. When older bishops recruited posses of young virgin heroines, male power, perhaps, came into it. When middle-aged Christian couples gave up sex, perhaps some of them found it easier after a long married innings. Others were spurred on by the promises of high rewards in heaven. In Augustine's case, he had equated the pursuit of wisdom with sexless living at least since reading this same equation in Cicero's *Hortensius*. The inner Elect of the Manichees were celibate; Ambrose was celibate; Ambrose also preached virginity and the priority of soul over body; the Neoplatonic books wasted no time on sex, either. We might wonder, more simply, whether the second *concubina* who replaced Augustine's first one was drearier in bed: the prospect of marriage to a virgin in her early teens was also looming. However, the intriguing *Soliloquies*, which he wrote during the following winter, show Augustine still wrestling with thoughts of sex and a female's lovely embrace. Nor could he stop his wet dreams, which, in turn, emphasized his belief in an inherent sinfulness in humanity.

The important facts are that he was not alone in making this leap and that it was a completely unnecessary selfishness. He could perfectly well have been baptized and ordained without it and he could have continued to mix with women, marry and have more children. He did not 'deconvert' out of guilt or a long-running fear of sex or a dislike for it. Shortly before, he had given Alypius, his great friend, such an enticing account of the delights of sex with a woman that Alypius had been keen to try it again, despite his former bad experience on his first attempt. In the event Alypius deconverted too, and proved his over-achievement by walking barefoot on the north Italian mountain-slopes in winter.

Book 9 ends in 387, but Books 10 to 13 change gear conspicuously. The detailed memories of Augustine's life, friends and family disappear. The books now follow one theme at a time in sequence, but the themes are not what we might anticipate. The factual autobiography disappears and Augustine takes us from an investigation of 'memory' to an extremely austere survey of his continuing sins. Then, we turn to the opening text of Genesis, with a long inquiry into the measurement of time and a wild *tour de force* on meanings supposedly present in Scripture. Yet Augustine has set out to express 'what I still am'. Book 10 attaches to that aim, but the next three books are puzzling to most of their readers.

Modern attempts to discern a unity can be divided into two groups: those which follow Augustine's own overt direction and those which decode patterns, visible only on very close reading, which are then upheld as the unifying structures of the work. Some of those patterns rely on three-fold repetitions, occurring throughout the text: Augustine sometimes picks on three particular virtues, or implies a three-fold focus of the mind (external, internal, superior) or a three-fold scope for concupiscence (the lust of the eyes, the flesh and vainglory) based on one of his favourite texts, 1 John 2.16. The Trinity can also be discerned by those who look faithfully enough: Book 11, on this view, is about God, Book 12 about the Word and Book 13 about the Spirit. These hidden patterns keep scholars busy and are then considered to knit the work together. Whether Augustine considered they did so is another question.

Alternatively, the work has been made to revolve around a pivotal theme of Neoplatonic philosophy: dependence on God and 'return' to him. In this view, the first nine books present the wandering of an individual soul and its return to God through God's grace: the tenth dwells on its present state and Books 11 to 13 apply the same idea to the entire universe. They show how it, too, depends on God and 'turns' to him. The unity here, does not lie in repeated patterns: it lies in a theme which Augustine encountered in Neoplatonic philosophy, the idea of a journey of the soul and of its return.

The trouble is that this scheme omits too much; it does not explain the long sections on the meaning of time or memory or the layers of meaning in Scripture. It makes philosophy the key to the entire structure, whereas it is more like an accompaniment. It is we, nowadays, who value literary works for tight unity or 'closure'. The *Confessions* began by being dictated and although particular Psalms and similar bits of philosophy run through all the books, we should not be uncomfortable if they change gear sometimes or meander. There is, in fact, a general guide to their direction: it is given by Augustine himself.

After following his past down to 387, Augustine declares he will now tell us 'what I still am, and not what I was'. Book 10 is not a later addition. His confessions of this state are addressed to God and fellow Christians, 'your servants, my brethren', present and future. He regards himself hyper-critically in what follows, so as to make others 'conscious of [their] own sickness' and cause them to 'wake up in the love of your mercy and the sweetness of your grace'. With brotherly love we are to give thanks to God for what is good in him and to lament together what is bad. Our thanks and our lamentations will delight God and encourage him to show mercy to Augustine himself. This aim may sound extremely self-centred, but in monastic Christian circles such thanks and lamenting for a Christian brother were common enough. It is with the eye of one such extreme perfectionist that Augustine in Book 10 contemplates himself. He also upholds his ideal for man: the happy life is joy based on truth; truth is God and so happiness is joy based on God. The previous books have concerned the search for a happy life and Book 10 now defines it. To reach it, his sinful nature needs a bridge: the bridge is Christ the Redeemer. The book ends with its fullest praises yet of Christ in this role, as expressed in the Christian Sacraments.

If Augustine had stopped there, we might well question whether his happiness is not in fact a self-feeding misery, but the work would have an obvious unity. He goes on, however, and here 11.2 is a guidepost. It would take too long, he tells God, to go through "all the ways in which you have encouraged me, terrified me, comforted me and guided me, and brought me to preach your word and dispense your Sacrament to your people', that is, to write a biography from 387 to 396, from his years of spiritual retreat to his new public roles as priest and bishop. Instead, he has been 'burning' for some while to 'meditate on your Law', the Scriptures. The task is 'not for my sake alone' but it is also 'to be of use to the brothers I love'. So, he spends the next three books finding the wildest meanings in the opening of Genesis in order to help us too.

I think we can take him at his word here. 'What I still am' is a praiser and a meditator on God's purpose and grace, as discernible in his Scriptures. It is the most important thing in life to him, much as a true scholar, being honest in his autobiography, might simply focus in chapter after chapter on his intellectual research. Augustine, in fact, had already combed through these same biblical chapters in another work, which was slightly more concerned with their literal meaning: his *On 'Genesis' Against the Manichees* (written in 388). He pursues a different line in the *Confessions*, digressing on time and the levels of meaning in Scripture. But even the discourse on time is tied to his purpose: in connection with Genesis 1, he asks, 'What was God doing before he made heaven and earth?' and it is in that context that he discusses the question of time itself. So, too, in Book 12, he digresses, in connection with his scriptural discussion, on the various possible meanings in difficult Scripture. The discussion on time appeals more than anything in the book to philosophers, just as book 10 appeals to psychotherapists and book 12 to literary theorists. But the sections which interest them arise during a carefully signposted progress.

The conclusion of all this praise of God is a completely false reading of Genesis 1, none of which is in the text. It relies on allegory, as others had before Augustine, including Ambrose through whom he first met this way of interpreting Scripture. Like others before him, Augustine is puzzled that the first verse of Genesis mentions a creation of heaven and earth, whereas the second and third verses mention their creation again on successive days. The first verse's creation, he decides, is the 'heaven of heaven', an ideal type which existed in the realms of the intellect only. The second is the creation of the material world. Jewish and Christian Platonists had often argued much the same, but it is a bad start. When Augustine then detects references to the Christian Sacraments and the distinction between the saved Christians and those beyond the pale in other bits of Genesis, he is simply continuing on a spectacularly false trail.

More than any Neoplatonism, the two senses of 'confession' are the overriding unity to the book: confession of sin and praises, like these ones, of God. As for 'what I still am', the answer turns out to be someone still prone to entirely healthy and admirable pleasures which he represses in the name of sin (Book 10), and a meditator on the book of Genesis who has not the slightest clue of its origin and history and the evolutionary truth about the world (Books 11–13).

*

Why, though, did Augustine write such a book at all? Many scholars of Latin cherish the very few allusions to Virgil (perhaps only two, after mentioning his reading of Virgil in school), his quotations from archaic Roman poetry (they were found second-hand) and his allusions to Cicero's late philosophical writings (especially in Book 6) and to his *Hortensius*, now lost to us. There is also a lively industry in identifying allusions to the very difficult philosophy of Plotinus the Neoplatonist (especially to the 'return' of the soul from multiplicity to the One) and possibly Plotinus's anti-Christian pupil

Porphyry. These allusions pale into insignificance beside the book's amazing use of bits of the Psalms. It usually quotes parts of a verse only and so can interweave them with astounding deftness. Book 9.4.8–11 is a brilliant tapestry woven round bits of Psalm 4: Book 3.8 is a multi-coloured tapestry of sixteen bits of Psalms on humans' way of sinning against themselves. Augustine had meditated on the Psalms every day since his sexless retreat in September 386. No other ancient book is so steeped in 'intertextuality', not even Virgil's *Aeneid* in Homer's epics. Augustine quotes from 121 Psalms in all and Psalms 4, 9, 17, 18, 41, 50 and 118 are used 164 times.

In my view, the Psalmist is the driving force behind the form of the book. The driving force behind the writing of it is more arguable. Some have tried to invoke the name of Augustine's contemporary Jerome and see an unacknowledged response to Jerome's views on virginity and on the meaning of Scripture. Others have looked to another sexless Christian contemporary, the aristocratic Paulinus at Nola near Naples, who had encountered some of Augustine's works since 395, wanted to know more about his friend Alypius and might have provoked a self-deprecating show-off from Augustine, a fellow celibate, to reveal who he was and why he had become so. Others have looked to heretical Manichaeism, a sect which included a yearly rite of confession: however, it was long-dead wood to him, still fun to hack at, but now in his past. Others have looked to Neoplatonism and have linked the *Confessions* to the 'fire' for its philosophy as if (on one wrong view) it was his real conversion and as if, eleven years later, it alone could impel him to go over the wanderings of his soul and the created world.

I believe in none of these motives. It is much more relevant that Augustine had just been made a bishop, at first a 'co-bishop' in the harbour town of Hippo and then sole bishop on his partner's death. The date of this event has usually been fixed to 395 in previous scholarship, but the truth, based on hints of Paulinus's letters, is much more likely to be summer 396. This elevation had two known consequences. It was irregular and so it provoked malicious scandal. One Megalius, bishop of Calama, spread stories that Augustine was still a

Manichee and that he had sent a love-drug to the wife of a respected Christian monk, possibly Paulinus himself with whom he had actually exchanged innocent pieces of Eucharistic bread. In north Africa, Augustine had indeed been known as a Manichee in the early 380s. He had been baptized far away in Milan. 'Co-bishops' were strictly illegal; Augustine was too clever by half; some Christians wondered if he was really 'one of us'.

On this view, the *Confessions* were an implicit answer to critics: this is who I am, they say, a humble Christian, conscious of the tiniest sins, certainly no Manichee, nor a Neoplatonist either, and a virtuoso interpreter of the most difficult bits of Scripture. In a further view, Augustine, aged forty-two, was undergoing a mid-life crisis. His early beliefs about the power of reason to ascend to God had faded in his writings since the early 390s. In 395/6, answers to difficult questions in Scripture had forced him to a deeper awareness of God's inexplicable grace and a much deeper engagement with St Paul. Not only had he lived through an 'intellectual landslide' at this point, but he had come out of it and had taken a bishopric with a strong sense of a 'lost future'. His old friends were dead or dispersed; optimism about the vision of God had receded; the early philosophical writings on the soul and the 'happy life' seemed shallow and narrowly rational. Without God's grace, man was capable of nothing: man was ultimately a 'great deep', inexplicable to himself. Plotinus's interest in an 'unconscious' acquired new depth as Augustine brooded on the human will and sin. His new role in life left no scope for the aspirations of his early philosophic interest.

Both these views, I think, can be strengthened by linking them to a new chronology. Augustine, in my view, was ordained co-bishop in late summer 396; Megalius's slanders were real enough and they belonged in the previous months. We do not know when his co-bishop died and left the entire job on Augustine's shoulders. But we do know what an awful burden it brought with it: letter-writing, preaching, acting as a host to strangers and above all, as arbitrator in the endless disputes between members of his diocese. A tidal wave of business would simply sweep him away, bringing the temptations of favour and flattery ('love of praise' was a sin Augustine especially feared), anger and public criticism. It was a 'pack-load', or 'burden', as he and others described it.

During winter 396–7, Augustine was still capable of some short writings, but then a familiar crisis occurred; as so often at other turning-points, Augustine fell ill. We can pick this fact up from one of his surviving letters, our number 38, in which he complains that he cannot walk and is confined to bed; he is praying to use his days there 'temperately', assuming that he does not simply die: he is crippled with piles. In 386, the decision to go celibate had been preceded by trouble with his voice and chest which undermined his career as a speaker. In winter 386–7, he contracted acute toothache and promptly wrote the *Soliloquies*, another novel title, in which his Reason and Soul argue with each other, like a simpler *Confessions* in embryo. In early 397, the same letter 38 records Augustine's reaction to his old enemy Megalius's death three weeks before: the scandals are not forgotten, it shows, nor is the anger which Megalius's past slanders could provoke in him. Bedridden and conscious of God's physical chastisement, he dictated, so I believe, our *Confessions*. In part, they answered what Megalius had so wickedly alleged; in part, they grovelled to God at a time of weakness; in part, they reaffirmed 'what I still am', a perfectionist, a monastic self-critic, a 'burning' meditator on Scripture, who is the product of an errant past and of the grace of a merciful God. This reaffirmation was made on the edge of a job which would sweep perfectionism away, submerging Augustine in disputes, discipline and lengthy polemic and confronting him with sin at every turn. The *Confessions*, made from the sickbed, are like the swansong of a former 'Research Fellow', propelled to be the sole head of a deeply-divided university department.

From May 397 until August 397, we are now able to plot a little of the progress of an Augustine restored to health but fully engaged on his new job. Since 1990, we have recovered, thanks to the brilliance of François Dolbeau, previously unknown sermons by Augustine which are almost certainly dated to these very months. The bishop, we now see, made several preaching tours to Carthage in this period, but in my view the *Confessions* were essentially written. Perhaps they travelled in his kit-bag, ready to be circulated round fellow Christians in Rome, south Italy and Africa. By the happiest of finds, we have in fact been presented with sermons which were the *Confessions*' immediate sequels: Augustine and his mother would thank the grace of God.

*

When the book became known, we cannot help wondering what the first readers made of it. Near the end of his life, Augustine painstakingly reviewed his previous writings and left corrections on points of importance: he recorded the affection with which he himself still read his *Confessions* and the favour which they had found with 'many' Christian contemporaries: the *Confessions*, he wrote, 'praise the just and good God in all my evil and good ways and stir up towards him the minds and feelings of men'. Until recently, the contemporaries whom we knew to have been 'stirred' were not a fair sample. In Rome, Pelagius, Augustine's future Christian opponent, was deeply annoyed on hearing the passage in which Augustine asks God to 'grant what you command' (including sexual continence) and 'command what you will: Pelagius had different ideas about divine grace. Also in Rome, Secundinus, a Manichee, responded artfully to Augustine's chapters on his youthful phase of Manichaean beliefs. Only since 1981, with another happy discovery of twenty-six long-lost letters to and from Augustine, have we been able to hear a simpler contemporary response. From the Balearic Islands, his tiresome old Christian correspondent, Consentius, wrote to tell him how he had come by a copy of the *Confessions* 'twelve years previously' (*c.* 407, within ten years of its completion). It was one of many books which he acquired then but 'oppressed by an incredible torpor, I have owned them as if they were sealed up'. At first Consentius read only 'two or three pages at most' from the first book, but not because he would have endorsed Edward Gibbon's wonderfully sly footnote: Augustine's 'learning is too often borrowed and his arguments too often his own'. Rather, Consentius was put off by 'the annoying splendour of your thoughts'. Eight years later, it appears, Consentius tried again and this time, he read much further, finding directions for many of the questions which were already on his mind. He then treats Augustine to a little account of his own recent progress, showing that the *Confessions* had indeed caught his fancy.

In the winter before his death, in 428–9, Augustine sent out one final copy of the book. The embattled court of the Roman emperors in Italy had sent an agent, Count Darius, to try to negotiate with north Africa's new military master, Boniface, a professional soldier who had once thought of entering a monastery and who had spent his recent life 'waiting for the barbarians' on the edge of the desert in Augustine's own Numidia. Darius wrote courteously to Augustine on arrival and in response to his specific request, Augustine sent this hard careerist a copy of the *Confessions*, perhaps the last which he ever circulated. One year later, north Africa was to be beset by yet more barbarian invaders, the Vandals who started to besiege Augustine's own town of Hippo. With the copy of his book, Augustine wrote to Darius, 'There, look on me, so that you may not praise me beyond what I am; there, believe me, not others, about myself; there, attend to me and see what I have been in myself, through myself. And if anything in me pleases you, praise there with me Him whom I wished to be praised by me; however, do not praise myself, since "He hath made us, and not we ourselves"' (Psalm 119.3).

Soon afterwards, Augustine died, aged seventy-six. We will never know if Darius read the book or what he made of it. It is for us, instead, to act on Augustine's request.

Robin Lane Fox

SELECT BIBLIOGRAPHY

The literature on Augustine is vast. What is offered here is only a selection of the more readily available work in English, covering the historical background to Augustine's age, and those issues specially relevant to the *Confessions*. For academic study, the periodical *Revue des Etudes augustiniennes* offers an invaluable survey of research in learned journals and elsewhere. An Augustine dictionary, the *Augustinus-Lexikon*, is appearing in fascicles under the editorship of C. Mayer *et al.* (Basle); this is in various languages. There are also two machine-readable editions of Augustine: the *Patrologia Latina Database*, and the *CETEDOC Library of Christian Texts*. Useful links (notably to O'Donnell's websites) can also be found through http: //info.ox.ac.uk/ctitext/tchclass.html

BONNER, G., *St Augustine of Hippo. Life and Controversies*, Canterbury Press, Norwich, 1962, revised 1986.
BROWN, P. R. L., *Augustine of Hippo. A biography*, Faber and Faber, London, 1967. A classic work, still highly readable.
—*The World of Late Antiquity*, Thames and Hudson, London, 1971.
—*Religion and Society in the Age of Saint Augustine*, Harper and Row, New York and London, 1972.
—*The Cult of the Saints. Its Rise and Function in Latin Christianity*, SCM Press, London, 1981.
—*The Body and Society. Men, Women, and Sexual Renunciation in Early Christianity*, Columbia University Press, New York, 1988.
—*Power and Persuasion in Late Antiquity. Towards a Christian Empire*, University of Wisconsin Press, Madison, Wisconsin and London, 1988.
CHADWICK, H., *Augustine*, Oxford University Press, Oxford, 1986. A fine short historical and intellectual guide.
CLARK, E. G., *Augustine. The Confessions*, Cambridge University Press, Cambridge, 1993. A excellent short introduction to the work.
CLARK, E. G., ed., *Augustine. Confessions Books I–IV*, Cambridge University Press, Cambridge, 1995. Text with useful introduction and notes.
EVANS, G., *Augustine on Evil*, Cambridge University Press, Cambridge, 1982.
GIBBS, J. and MONTGOMERY, W., eds, *The Confessions of Augustine*, Cambridge University Press, Cambridge. A serviceable one-volume text with running commentary.

KASTER, R., *Guardians of Language. The Grammarian and Society in Late Antiquity*, University of California Press, Berkeley, 1988.

KIRWAN, C., *Augustine*, Routledge, London, 1989. Introduction to Augustine's key ideas.

LIEU, S., *Manichaeism in the Later Roman Empire and Medieval China. A Historical Survey*, 2nd edn, J. C. B. Mohr, Tübingen, 1992.

MACCORMACK, S., *The Shadows of Poetry. Vergil in the Mind of Augustine*, University of California Press, Berkeley, 1998.

MARKUS, R., *The End of Ancient Christianity*, Cambridge University Press, Cambridge, 1990. How Christianity became a mainstream religion, and the social and intellectual causes and consequences of its doing so.

O'DONNELL, J. J., ed., *Augustine. Confessions*, three volumes, Oxford University Press, Oxford, 1992. The indispensable edition for advanced study.

RIST, J., *Augustine. Ancient Thought Baptized*, Cambridge University Press, Cambridge, 1994. How Augustine saw the relationship between classical philosophy and Christian truth.

CHRONOLOGY

DATE	AUTHOR'S LIFE	LITERARY CONTEXT
311		
313		
320		Arius writes *The Banquet*.
324		
325		The Nicene Creed written. Eusebius of Caesarea compiles a list of accepted books of the New Testament.
327		Arius: *Letter to the Emperor Constantine*.
329		Athanasius: *Festal Letters*.
c. 330		Birth of Ammianus Marcellinus, historian, in Antioch.
331		330s: Athanasius working on the *Life of Antony*.
335		
336		
337		Eusebius of Caesarea: *Ecclesiastical History*; *Life of Constantine*.
340		Hilary of Poitiers: *Sermon on the Trinity*.
c. 342–7		
348		Athanasius: *Apologia against the Arians*.
350		Athanasius: *Letter on the Council of Nicaea*.
c. 350		Marius Victorinus translates Neoplatonic works of Plotinus and Porphyry.
354	13 November: Birth of Aurelius Augustinuse, son of Monica, a Christian, and Patricius, a pagan farmer, at Thagaste in the Roman province of Numidia, north Africa.	Hilary: *Commentary on St Matthew*.
355		Lucifer of Cagliari defends Athanasius.

Donatists oppose election of Caecilian as bishop of Carthage. Schism between Donatists and Catholics begins to spread through north Africa. Emperor Constantine's Edict of Milan grants toleration to Christians.

Christianity made the preferred state religion.
General Council of Nicaea.

Constantine transfers capital of Roman Empire to Constantinople.
Arian opponents of Athanasius, bishop of Alexandria, succeed in having him exiled.
Death of Arius.
Death of Constantine.

Birth of Ambrose.

Birth of Jerome.

Birth of John Chrysostom. Birth of Paulinus of Nola.

Death of Donatus in exile.

DATE	AUTHOR'S LIFE	LITERARY CONTEXT
c.356–60		Hilary, in exile in Phrygia, writes *The Trinity*.
357		Athanasius: *Apologia against the Arians*.
		Marius Victorinus: *The Trinity*.
358		Basil and Gregory Nazianzus prepare an anthology of Origen's works (to 359).
		Hilary: *On the Synods*.
360		Hilary: *Hymns*.
c.360		
361		
362		Basil: *Little Asceticon*.
		Oribasius of Pergamon: *Synagogue of Medicine*.
363–5		Basil: *Against Eunomius*.
364		
c.366		Optatus, bishop of Milevis in Numidia, begins *Against Parmenian the Donatist*.
367		
368		
369	Goes to university town of Madaura.	Athanasius: *Synodical Letter to the Africans*.
370	His education interrupted due to lack of funds. Returns to Thagaste.	Ephrem of Syria: *Commentary on Mark*.
		Athanasius: *On Virginity*.
		Gregory of Nyssa: *On Virginity*.
		Ulfila, Arian bishop: Gothic translation of Bible published.
c.370		Birth of the poet Claudian in Alexandria.
371	Goes to Carthage.	Ausonius: *The Moselle*.
372	Death of his father, who is baptized on his deathbed. Augustine begins a liaison with a Carthaginian woman.	
373	Reads Cicero's *Hortensius*. Birth of his son Adeodatus.	Basil: *Liturgy*.
374	Augustine joins the Manichee religion.	
375	Returns to Thagaste to teach literature, rhetoric and dialectic. Becomes a 'Hearer' among the Manichees.	Ambrose: *Paradise*.
		John Chrysostom: works promoting monasticism.
		Basil the Great: *The Holy Spirit*.

CHRONOLOGY

Birth of John Cassian. Birth of Pelagius in Britain.
Julian becomes Emperor (to 363): allows toleration for Donatists.

Succession of Emperors Valentinian I and Valens.

Ausonius, professor of rhetoric, becomes tutor to Gratian, Valentinian's heir.
Basil the Great gives his inheritance to the starving.

Ambrose becomes the provincial governor of Milan. Basil the Great is
consecrated bishop of Caesarea, in Asia Minor. Ostrogoths conquered
by Huns.

Revolt of Firmus, Count of Africa, supported by many Donatists.

Valentinian reimposes laws against Donatists. Death of Athanasius.

Death of Firmus. Ambrose becomes bishop of Milan. He introduces singing
of eastern melodies into liturgy.
Death of Emperor Valentinian I.

DATE	AUTHOR'S LIFE	LITERARY CONTEXT
376	After the death of a friend, returns to Carthage to teach. He is joined by his friends Nebridius and Alypius.	
c. 376		Longus: *Daphnis and Chloe.* Jerome: *Life of St Paul of Thebes.* Epiphanius of Salamis: *Panarion* against heresies. Optatus completes anti-Donatist work.
378		Ambrose: *The Faith.* Ammianus Marcellinus finishes writing *History of Rome.*
379		Jerome begins Latin translations of Eusebius of Caesarea's *History* and Origen's *Homilies.* Gregory of Nyssa: *The Making of Man.* Gregory of Nazianzus writes most of his *Orations.*
380	Writes *Beauty and Congruence.*	Theodore of Mopsuestia: *Against Eunomius.* Tyconius completes *Book of Rules.* Birth of the historian Socrates Scholasticos.
381		Ambrose: *The Holy Spirit.* Gregory of Nyssa: *Catechetical Discourses.*
c. 382		Ambrose: *The Incarnation.* John Chrysostom: *Against the Opponents of the Monastic Life.*
383	Meets the Manichee Faustus of Milevis. Beginning of his disillusionment with Manichaeism. Disobedience of students makes him decide to leave Carthage for Rome, where Alypius is already pursuing career as a lawyer. The students in Rome swindle their teachers.	
384	Symmachus, Prefect of Rome, appoints Augustine Professor of Rhetoric in Milan. Augustine is joined by Nebridius and Alypius.	

CHRONOLOGY

HISTORICAL EVENTS

Valens, last Arian emperor, defeated and killed by Visigoths at Adrianople. Emperor Gratian confirms pre-eminence of bishops of Rome over all others in Catholic Church.
Accession of Theodosius I. Ausonius becomes Consul. Jerome is ordained to the priesthood. Death of Basil the Great.

Theodosius establishes Catholicism as state religion. Vindicianus becomes Proconsul at Carthage. Donatist council at Carthage condemns Tyconius. In Spain, the Council of Saratossa condemns Priscillianism, associated with Manichaeism. Pelagius arrives in Rome.

All church buildings returned to Catholics. The Council of Constantinople reaffirms Nicene Creed and condemns Arianism. Gregory of Nazianzus is consecrated bishop of Constantinople. Rufinus of Aquileia and Melania found double monastery on Mount of Olives.

Revolt of Maximus. Ambrose visits Rome. Famine in Rome. Murder of Gratian.

Symmachus becomes Prefect of Rome. Siricius becomes bishop of Rome, the first to be called Pope.

DATE	AUTHOR'S LIFE	LITERARY CONTEXT
*c.*384		Jerome begins revising old Latin translation of New Testament.
385	Monica joins him in Milan. To further his public career, he renounces his concubine, sends her back to Africa and becomes betrothed to an heiress, selected by his mother.	
*c.*385–90		Optatus: *Seventh Book against the Donatists.*
386	Augustine adopts the scepticism of the Academics and then the Neoplatonism of Plotinus. Joins circle of Manlius Theodorus and other Platonists. July: his conversion to Catholicism in a Milan garden.	John Chrysostom: *The Priesthood*; *Homilies against the Jews.* Ambrose: *Sermon against Auxentius.* Jerome begins revising Old Testament.
*c.*386		
386–7	Retires with friends to Cassicacum. Writes *Against the Academics*, *The Blessed Life*, *Divine Providence* and *Soliloquies.*	
387	24 April: Augustine, Adeodatus and Alypius are baptized in Milan by Ambrose. Evodius becomes a follower. Their journey back to Africa is disrupted by war in Italy. At Ostia, Augustine and Monica share a vision. Death and burial at Ostia of Monica.	Ambrose: *Penitence.* John Chrysostom: sermons *On Statues.*
387–91	*Music.*	
388	He goes to Rome for some months, then returns to Carthage and finally Thagaste where he founds a lay community of his friends.	Libanius: writes in support of pagan temples.
388–9	*The Magnitude of the Soul*; *The Customs of the Catholic Church and the Customs of the Manichees*; *On 'Genesis', Against the Manichees*; begins *The Free Choice of the Will.*	
389	*The Teacher.*	Jerome: *Commentary on Genesis.*

CHRONOLOGY

Theodosius continues suppression of other religions by prohibiting bloody sacrifices. Jerome leaves Rome for the Holy Land. Birth of St Patrick.

Ambrose besieged in his basilica in Milan by Arian supporters of Justina, Emperor Valentinian II's mother. Purge of Manichees at Carthage.

Birth of Julian of Eclanum.

Maximus invades Italy: blockades Rome. Revolt at Antioch.

Jerome settles in Bethlehem.

DATE	AUTHOR'S LIFE	LITERARY CONTEXT
390	Deaths of Adeodatus and Nebridius. Augustine writes *True Religion*.	Gregory of Nyssa: *Not Three Gods*; *The Life of Moses*. Jerome: *Life of Malchus*; translates Didymus of Alexandria's *Holy Spirit*. John Chrysostom: anti-Manichaean *Homilies on St Matthew*.
391	He goes to Hippo to found a monastery. He is ordained priest by Valerius, bishop of Hippo, who encourages him to preach.	Jerome starts to translate Hebrew Bible. John Chrysostom: *Homilies on St John*.
391–2	*The Usefulness of Belief* written as part of an attempt to convert a man to Christianity.	
392	The first of his *Sermons on the Psalms*. Debate with the Manichee Fortunatus and other anti-Manichaean writings. Correspondence with Jerome.	Theodore of Mopsuestia: *Commentary on St Paul*. Jerome: *Commentaries on the Psalms*.
393	Preaches *The Faith and the Creed* at Council of Hippo. Begins active opposition to Donatists.	John Chrysostom: *The Education of Children*. Jerome: *Two books against Jovinian*.
394	*The Sermon on the Mount*; *Psalm against the Donatists*. Alypius made bishop of Thagaste.	Epiphanius of Salamis: *Twelve Jewels*.
*c.*394–8		Publication of Ammianus Marcellinus's *History*.
395	Writes *Celibacy*; *Lying*.	
*c.*395		Claudian: *Panegyric for Stilicho*.
395–9	*Questions Concerning Matthew and Luke*.	
396	Becomes co-bishop of Hippo (later sole bishop on Valerius's death). He and his priests share a monastic life. Writes *The Christian Struggle* against various heresies. Begins *Christian Doctrine* books i–iii.	Jerome debates Origenism: *Against John of Jerusalem*.
397	Debates with Donatist bishop Fortunius. Writes *The Confessions*. Preaching tours to Carthage.	Sulpicius Severus: *Life of St Martin*. John Chrysostom: *Homilies on Epistles of St Paul*.

CHRONOLOGY

Baptism of Paulinus of Nola. Councils at Rome and Milan condemn Jovinian's teaching about the Virgin Mary.

Edict prohibiting pagan ceremonies in Rome and Egypt. Aurelius becomes bishop of Carthage.

Death of Valentinian II. Pagan sympathizer Eugenius elected emperor in the west. Theodosius outlaws pagan worship throughout empire.

Donatist council at Cebarsussa. Optatus becomes bishop of Timgad in Numidia. General council of Africa meets in Hippo.

Donatist council at Bagai: suppression of Maximianist sect. Eugenius defeated by Theodosius. Ordination of Paulinus of Nola. Death of Ausonius.

Revolt of Gildo, Count of Africa, supported by some Donatists, including Optatus, bishop of Timgad, and violent Circumcellions. Death of Theodosius I. The empire divided into eastern and western parts under his sons, Arcadius and Honorius.

Alaric and the Visigoths invade Greece. Paulinus and his wife give up their wealth to form Christian community at Nola, Italy.

Death of Ambrose. Simplicianus succeeds him as bishop of Milan. John Chrysostom appointed archbishop of Constantinople. Council of Carthage discusses the canon of the Scriptures and Donatism. Possidius, follower of Augustine, establishes monastery at Calama in Numidia.

xliii

DATE	AUTHOR'S LIFE	LITERARY CONTEXT
397–8	Writes a series of books against Faustus the Manichee.	
398		Jerome: *Commentary on Matthew.* Claudian: *Epithalamia.* Rufinus: Latin translation of Origen's *Periarchon* and Pamphilus's *Apologia.*
399	More anti-Manichaean writings; *Catechizing the Uninstructed*; *Adnotations to Job.* He preaches in favour of closing pagan shrines and welcoming converts.	John Chrysostom: *Against the Circus and Theatre.*
400	He begins *The Trinity*; anti-Donatist *Against the Letter of Parmenian*; *Holy Virginity.* His follower Evodius becomes bishop of Uzali.	Macrobius: *Saturnalia.* Prudentius: *Psychomachia or The Contest of the Soul.* Palladius: *The Countryside.*
*c.*400		Caelius Aurelianus: *Concerning Acute and Chronic Illnesses.*
401	Begins first of three books refuting Petilian, Donatist bishop of Constantine. Writes *Baptism, against the Donatists*; *The Good of Marriage* and *The Work of Monks.*	Prudentius retires: writes *Peristephanon.* Jerome in literary debate about Origen with Rufinus.
402		
403		Rufinus: Latin translation of Eusebius's *Ecclesiastical History.* Claudian: *War against Gildo.*
404	Debate with Felix the Manichee.	Jerome completes translation of Old Testament from Hebrew. Rufinus completes *Explanation of the Apostle's Creed.* Death of Claudian.
405	Anti-Donatist *Against Cresconius.* He justifies state repression of heretics imposed by Edict of Unity.	Death of Prudentius, Christian poet. Cresconius the Donatist grammarian defends letter of Petilianus.
406		Jerome: *Commentaries on Osee, Joel, Amos, Malachias.*
407		
408		Jerome: *Commentary on Daniel.*

CHRONOLOGY

HISTORICAL EVENTS

Gildo defeated by Honorius. Execution of Optatus.

Pagan shrines in Africa closed. Manlius Theodorus, Neoplatonist friend of Augustine, becomes consul.

Honoratus of Arles founds Lérins monastery.

Election of Pope Innocent I. Crispinus, Donatist bishop of Calama, blamed for attack on Possidius.

Defeat of Goths in Italy. Death of Symmachus. Council of Milevis condemns Pelagius.
Bishop of Bagai attacked by Donatists. John Chrysostom deposed.

Relations between Rome and Constantinople broken off. Bishop of Bagai demands suppression of Donatists.

Imperial Edict of Unity issued against Donatists.

Vandals invade Gaul.

Usurpation of Constantine III. Death of John Chrysostom in exile. Theodosius II becomes emperor in the east. Fall of Stilicho. Alaric, king of the Goths, invades Italy. Pagans riot at Calama.

DATE	AUTHOR'S LIFE	LITERARY CONTEXT
408–12	*The Usefulness of Fasting.*	
409	He opposes the death penalty for heretics.	
410	*Single Baptism, against Petilian*: refutes Donatist ideas. Retires to a villa outside Hippo during the winter.	Hypatia of Alexandria: astronomical works. Theodore of Mopsuestia: biblical commentaries. Synosius of Cyrene: *The Gift of the Astrolabe.* Martianus Capella: *The Marriage of Mercury and Philology.* Death of Rufinus.
411	Attends conference at Carthage where he forms a friendship with Marcellinus, to whom he dedicates his first anti-Pelagian treatise: *The Guilt and Remission of Sins.*	
c.411		Jerome: *Dialogue against the Pelagians.*
412	*Spirit and Letter* and other anti-Pelagian writings.	Pelagius: *Letters.*
413	Writes anti-Pelagian *Faith and Works.* He begins *The City of God*, dedicated to Marcellinus. He tries to save Marcellinus from execution.	
414	Writes *The Excellence of Widowhood. The Trinity* is published.	
415	*The Perfection of Justice in Man*; opposes heresy in Spain in *Against the Priscillianists and Origenists, for Orosius*; *Homilies on St John.*	Paulus Orosius: anti-Pelagian writings.
415–20		Jerome: *Commentary on Jeremiah.*
416	He attends council at Milevis which condemns Pelagius and Caelestius.	Rutilius: *Return from Exile.*
417	To help win the support of Honorius, emperor of the west, in their campaign against Pelaganism, Augustine and his followers present the emperor with eighty stallions.	Orosius: *Universal History.* Death of Orosius. Pelagius: *A Brief Statement of Faith.*

CHRONOLOGY

xlvii

DATE	AUTHOR'S LIFE	LITERARY CONTEXT
418	Augustine takes part in public debate with Emeritus, Donatist bishop of Caesarea. Writes anti-Pelagian *The Grace of Christ and Original Sin*; *Patience*.	
419		Julian of Eclanum: first works opposing Augustine.
419–21	*Seven Questions Concerning the Heptateuch*; discusses original sin in *Marriage and Desire*; *Adulterous Marriages*.	
420		
420–22		Paulinus of Nola: *Life of St Ambrose*.
420–24		John Cassian: *Cenobitic Institutes*; *Conferences*.
421	He writes *The Handbook of Faith, Hope and Love*; *Against Gaudentius, Donatist Bishop of Timgad*; *The Soul and its Origins*.	Julian of Eclanum becomes leader of Pelagian literary opposition to Augustine.
422	*Against Lying*.	
422–3	*Refutation of Two Pelagian Letters*.	
423	Dispute, written in six books, with Julian, Pelagian bishop of Eclanum.	
425		Flavius Vegetius Renatus: first veterinary book (on mules).
426	Completion of *The City of God*; *The Gift of Perseverance*; *Christian Doctrine* book iv; discusses predestination in *Grace and Free Will*. He nominates his successor, the priest Heraclius.	
427	Debate with the Arian bishop Maximinus. Completes *Retractations*, a catalogue of his works.	
428		Letter from Prosper of Aquitaine to Augustine.
429	*The Predestination of the Blessed*. Begins writing further work against Julian, left unfinished at his death. Begins *Answer to the Jews*.	

CHRONOLOGY

Honorius banishes Pelagians from Rome. Zosimus concurs, excommunicates Pelagius and exiles him back to Britain. Death of Zosimus: succeeded by Boniface.

Pelagian bishop Julian of Eclanum exiled from Italy: settles in East. Council of Carthage discusses the claim of Rome to have jurisdiction over North Africa.

Death of Pelagius. Donatists continue to defy policy of repression: Gaudentius of Timgad threatens to burn himself and congregation in his basilica.

Enquiry into Manichees at Carthage.

Celestine elected Pope.

Condemnation of Antonius, bishop of Fussala.

Valentinian III becomes emperor in the west. Foundation of university at Constantinople.

Revolt of Boniface, Count of Africa. Cyril, Patriarch of Alexandria, denounced as heretic by Nestorius, archbishop of Constantinople. Nestorius deposed and his teaching condemned.
Vandals from Spain led by Genseric invade North Africa. Death of Caelestius. Germanus begins mission in Britain.

DATE	AUTHOR'S LIFE	LITERARY CONTEXT
430	28 August: Death of Augustine.	John Cassian: *The Incarnation of the Lord* against Nestorius. Cyril of Alexandria: anti-Nestorian writings. Prosper of Aquitaine: anti-Pelagian writings. Death of Nilus of Ancyra.
c.430–39		Possidius: *Life of St Augustine.*
431	His library escapes damage during the burning of Hippo.	

CHRONOLOGY

THE CONFESSIONS

BOOK ONE

1.1.1 *Great are you, O Lord, and worthy of high praise* (Ps. 48.1 [Ps. 47.2], Ps. 96.4 [Ps. 95.4], Ps. 145.3 [Ps. 144.3]). *Great is your strength, and of your wisdom there is no counting* (Ps. 147.5 [Ps. 146.5]). Even man is, in his way, a part of your creation, and longs to praise you; even man, who *carries in himself his own mortality* (2Cor. 4.19), that testimony of his sin, that testimony also that *you resist the proud* (Prov. 3.34, 1Pet. 5.5, James 4.6); for all that, man is part of your creation, and longs to praise you. You stir us up to take delight in your praise; for you have made us for yourself, and our heart is restless till it finds its rest in you.

Grant me knowledge and understanding, O Lord (Ps. 119.34, 73, 144 [Ps. 118.34, 73, 144]): Can anyone praise you before he calls upon you, or call upon you before he knows you? But surely no one could call upon you if he did not know you, for he might call upon one thing, mistaking it in his ignorance for another. Should we rather call upon you, so as to know you? But how shall any call upon you, if they have not believed in you? And *how shall they believe in you, if no one preaches you?* (Rom. 10.14). *Those who seek the Lord shall praise him* (Ps. 22.26 [Ps. 21.27]). *They will seek and they will find him* (Matt. 7.7–8, Lk 11.10); they will find and they will praise him. I shall seek you, Lord, as I call upon you, and call upon you as I believe in you (Rom. 10.14); for you have been proclaimed to us. My faith, O Lord, calls upon you; the faith that is your gift to me, which you have inspired through the humanity of your Son, and the ministry of him who proclaimed you.

1.2.2 But how shall I call upon God, my Lord and my God? For when I call upon him, I am calling upon him to do nothing less than to come into me – and what place is there in me that my God can enter? He is my God, the *God who made heaven and earth* (Gen. 1.1, Ps. 121.2 [Ps. 120.2]); and shall he enter into me? Is it so, O Lord my God, that there is anything in me that is capable of holding you? *Can the very heaven and earth, which you have made* and in which you have made me, *contain you?* (1Kings 8.27). Is it because nothing that exists could have being without you, that it is possible for anything to contain you?

Seeing, then, as I also exist, why should I ask you to enter me, since I would not exist were you not in me? I am no longer *the depths of the abyss* (Proverbs 9.18), and yet you are there, for *if I go down to the depths, you are present* (Ps. 139.8 [Ps. 138.8]). I would not exist, O God, were you not in me; I would not exist at all.

Or should I say I would not exist if I were not in you, *as all things have their being from you* (Rom. 11.36, 1Cor. 8.6) and through you and in you? Even so, my Lord, even so.

To what place shall I call you? It is in you that I have my being (cf Acts 17.28). Or what place would you leave when you came into me? Is there any place I could withdraw, beyond heaven and earth, so that my God could leave them and come to me? For he is the God who has said, *I fill earth and heaven* (Jeremiah 23.24).

1.3.3 Can heaven and earth, then, contain you, seeing as you fill them? Or when you fill them, is some part of your being left over, as they cannot contain you? And where do you pour it back, this portion of you that remains after you have filled heaven and earth? Or do you not need to be contained in anything, as you yourself contain all things, and in containing them, fill them? For the vessels that contain you do not keep you in one place; even if they were shattered, you would not be poured out. And when you *pour yourself out upon us* (Joel 2.28–9, Acts 2.17–8), you do not sink to the lowest level, but you *raise us up* (cf Lk 13.13); you are not dispersed, but rather you gather us together.

But all that you fill, you fill with your whole being. Or, as nothing can contain your whole being, does each thing contain a part of you? If so, is it the same part that each contains? Or does each individual thing contain an individual part of you, the larger ones containing larger parts of you and the smaller ones smaller parts? In that case, are some parts of you larger and some parts smaller? Or is it that you are wholly present in all places, and no one thing contains your whole being?

1.4.4 What, then, are you, my God? What indeed, if not the Lord God? For who is lord besides the Lord; *who is God besides our God?* (Ps. 18.31 [Ps. 17.32]). Highest and best, most mighty, most almighty; most full of mercy and justice, most hidden and most present with us, most lovely and most strong. You are abiding and unsearchable; you change all things, but are yourself unchanging; you are never new and never old, yet you *renew all things* (Wisdom 7.27) and *bring the proud to their old age unawares* (Job 9.5). You are always at work and always at rest; you gather to yourself, though you lack nothing. You bring together, fulfil and protect; you create, nourish and bring to completion. You seek, when you are short of nothing. You love, without the fever of passion. You are jealous (Joel 2.28, Zechariach 1.14, 8.2, cf Ex. 20.5) and fear no rival. You repent (Gen. 6.6–7, 1Sam. 15.35), but do not regret; you are roused to anger, and remain calm. You change your works, but your counsel is unchanged. You take back what you find, yet you had never lost it. You are never in need, yet you rejoice in riches; never grasping, yet you demand a return from us (cf Matt. 25.27). For you we perform works beyond our duty, to put you in our debt (cf Lk 10.35, Rom. 11.35); but who has anything that is not your own? You repay debts, but are no one's debtor; you remit them, and suffer no loss.

And yet what have we said of you, my God, my life, my holy Sweetness? What can anyone say, in speaking of you? But woe to those who keep silence concerning you – who speak so much, and say so little!

1.5.5 Who shall give me the gift of resting in you? Who will grant me this, that you come into my heart and make it drunk, so that I *forget my evil deeds* (Jer. 44.9) and embrace you, my only Good? What are you to me? Have mercy on me, and let me speak. What, for that matter, am I to you? Why do you command me to love you? And if I do not, why are you moved to anger and threaten me with utter misery? But is my misery any the less, if I fail to love you? Have pity, O Lord! For your own mercies' sake, O Lord my God, tell me what you are to me! Tell my soul: *I am your salvation* (Ps. 35.3 [Ps. 34.3]). Speak, and let me hear your voice. Bend down to my soul's ear, O Lord; open it, and tell my soul: I am your salvation. I shall *run after your voice, and catch you* (Phil. 3.12). Do not hide your face from me. Let me die to see it; for if I do not see it, I shall die.

1.5.6 The house of my soul is narrow, too narrow for you to come into it; enter it, and *make it wider* (2Cor. 6.14). It lies in ruins; rebuild it. There are things about it that will offend your eyes; I know it and confess it. But who will make it clean? To whom but you can I cry: *Cleanse me, O Lord, from my own hidden sins, and from the sins of others spare your servant?* (Ps. 19.13 [Ps. 18.13–4]). *I believe, and therefore I speak* (Ps. 116.10 [Ps. 115.10], 2Cor. 4.13). Lord, you know this (Tobit 8.9, Jn 21.15–6). For have I not declared before you the sins that stand against me? And you, my God, have surely forgiven the *impiety of my heart* (Ps. 32.5 [Ps. 31.5]). I will not go to law against you (Jer. 2.29, cf Matt. 5.40), for *you are the Truth* (Jn 5.6). Nor do I wish to deceive myself, and *let my wickedness lie to itself* (Ps. 27.12 [Ps. 26.12]). Therefore I will not go to law against you. For *if you, Lord, were to keep watch on our transgressions, then who, O Lord, could endure it?* (Ps. 130.3 [Ps. 129.3]).

1.6.7 But let me speak in the presence of your mercy; *dust and ashes* (Gen. 18.27, Job 42.6) as I am, let me speak. For man would *laugh at me* (Ps. 2.4, Ps. 37.13 [Ps. 36.13], Wisdom 4.18); but it is to you I speak, and behold, you are mercy. You too may laugh at me, but you will *turn again, and have mercy upon me* (Jer. 12.15). This, Lord, and nothing else, is what I want to say: I do not know where I came from, when I came here – here, that is, to this mortal life, or living death. I do not know; but your tender mercies received me and comforted me. This much I have heard from my parents after the flesh, the father from whom and the mother in whom you formed me in time; I do not remember it myself. You welcomed me, and comforted me with woman's milk – but it was not of themselves that my mother and my nurses filled their breasts. Rather it was you who through them gave me the right food for my early years; for you have so ordained it that even the least of your creatures should share in your riches. It was your gift too that I was satisfied with the amount you gave me, and that my mother and my nurses were happy to give me what you gave them. And though you had given them milk in abundance, yet they wanted to give it to me only in the quantities you had set for it. For it was good for them to give me what was good for me. Nor was it from them that I received the milk, but through them; for all good things come from you, O God, and *from my God is my whole salvation* (2Sam. 23.5). This I came to realize only later, when you proclaimed it to me through the gifts you bestow upon us both without and within. But in those days, I knew how to suck the breast, and how to fall asleep when my body was comfortable and cry when it was not; and beyond this, I knew nothing.

1.6.8 Later on I learnt to laugh, at first in my sleep, then when I was awake. I have been told that I did this, and I believe it, as we can see other children do the same; but I do not remember my own early tears and smiles. And by and by I came to perceive my surroundings, and conceived the wish to make my wishes known to others, so that they could fulfil them. But in this I was frustrated, for my wishes were within me, while the bystanders were outside, and none of their senses enabled them to enter my soul. So I would thrash around with my arms and legs, and make noises, which I intended to be signs bearing some resemblance to my wishes; but such few poor signs I could make bore no true resemblance to them. And when my wishes were not granted, either because those around me could not understand me or because what I wanted would not have been good for me, I grew indignant to find that my elders were not slaves, only there to wait upon children; and I revenged myself upon them by fits of tears. My own experience of babies has been enough to teach me that this is typical behaviour. Without ever having known me, these babies have taught me that I too was like that – more so even than the nurses who did know me.

1.6.9 My childhood has died once and for all, and yet I live on. But you, Lord, who live for ever, in whom nothing ever dies, from the beginning of the ages, before anything that can even be called 'before', you exist. You are God and Lord of all your creation. In you stand unmoved the causes of all things transient;

in you remain unchanged the sources of all things that know change; in you lives the eternal Reason behind all things irrational and bounded by time. Have mercy on me, O God, I pray, and in your loving-kindness speak to this unhappy creature of yours. Tell me this: Did my childhood itself follow on from some previous time in my life, already dead when my childhood began? Was that stage of my life the time that I spent in my mother's womb? I have been told something of that time, and I know how women look when they are expecting; but what came even before that, O God my Sweetness? Did I exist, in some form and in some place? There is no one else who can tell me this; my father and my mother cannot tell me, and I cannot rely on the experiences of others, or on my own memory. Or do you *laugh at me* (Ps. 2.4, Ps. 37.13 [Ps. 36.13], Wisdom 4.18) when I ask such questions, and bid me praise you and confess myself before you for what I do know?

1.6.10 And I do confess to you, O Lord of heaven and earth; I praise you both for my hidden beginnings, and for my infancy, though I do not remember either. But through your gifts a man can gain from the example of other babies some idea of what he himself was like, and can even take the word of ordinary serving-women on many details of his childhood. For even at that age, I existed; I was alive; and, as my infancy drew to its close, I tried to find signs in which to convey my feelings to others. From where could such a living creature come, if not from you, O Lord? For who could be the craftsman of his own creation? Is there some source from which we can draw the power to exist and to live, apart from your creative power at work in us? For to you, Lord, there is no difference between life and existence. Your supreme existence and supreme life are one and the Same.[1] You are *supreme and unchanging* (cf Malachi 3.6). 'Today' is never completed in you, and yet is completed in you, for in you exist all these things also; they would have no way of passing on, were they not contained within you. And since *your years are unfailing* (Ps.102.28 [Ps. 101.28], Heb. 1.12), your years

---

1 '... one and the Same'. Sameness, or identity, will be a key theme in the theology of the *Confessions*. See especially 9.4.11.

are this 'today'. Many days, of our life and of our fathers', have passed through this 'today' of yours, receiving from it their due measure and their very being. But there are yet as many more still to pass the same way, having their being and their end within it. But *you are the same* (Ps. 102.28 [Ps. 101.28], Heb. 1.12); in this 'today' you have made all things that happened yesterday and ever before, and will make all things that will happen tomorrow and ever after. Does it matter to me if someone fails to understand? Let him rejoice to ask, *What is this?* (Ex. 13.14, 16.15, Ecclesiasticus 39.26). Let him rejoice even so, and let him love to discover you and not discover this, rather than to discover this and not discover you.

1.7.11 *Hear my prayer, O God* (Ps. 55.1 [Ps. 54.2]). *Woe to the sins of man!* (Isaiah 1.4). It is man who says this, and you have pity upon him, for you yourself made him, but not the sin that is in him. Who will recall to me the sins I committed while yet an infant? For *there is none that is free from sin in your sight, not even a baby whose life upon earth has lasted but one day* (Job 14.4–5). Who will recall my sins? Is there any child now living, however tiny, in whom I do not see the things I did myself, yet cannot remember? How then did I sin at that age? Was it by clinging to the breast and wailing? For if I did that now – not, that is, clinging to the breast, but clinging in the same way to food more appropriate to my years – people would quite rightly laugh at me and take me to task for it. Likewise I deserved a scolding for the things I did at that age, but as I could not have understood if someone had given me a scolding, both custom and reason forbade it. For as we grow up, we weed such habits out of ourselves and throw them away; but I have never known any wise farmer, when weeding his plot, to throw good plants out with the bad. But perhaps it was actually good, for a while, that I should cry and seek even things that it would have been dangerous to give me; it was good that I should be outraged to find that adults were not there to wait upon children, and that I should thrash out and do all I could to hurt my elders, both my own parents and many others who were so much wiser than I, when they did not obey my orders, knowing it would not be at all safe to do so. Children are innocent only because they do not yet have any physical strength; their minds are not innocent. I know for myself what a jealous child is like; I have seen one who was too young to speak, but as he watched another baby being fed at the same breast, his face turned white with resentment. This is all common knowledge. Mothers and nurses claim to have all sorts of remedies to cure their charges of these faults. But is it really innocence, for one child to begrudge another the rich stream of milk that is their one shared source of life, on which they both depend utterly for their food? We smile tolerantly at such actions; not because they are not faults, or because they are only minor faults, but because they will pass with the passing of the years. All well and good – but we would not put up with them so philosophically, were we to detect them in an older person.

1.7.12 You then, O Lord my God, who gave me my infant life and body, who equipped that body with senses, who fastened together its limbs, who moulded its fair form, who instilled in it all the impulses a living creature needs to maintain and preserve its oneness – you, O God Most High, bid me praise you in these things, and confess before you, and make music to your Name. For you are God the Almighty and Good, and would be so if this were all you had done – although no one else can do even these things. You are the one God, from whom all things receive their allotted end; God most lovely, who shape all things in loveliness; and by your Law you set all things in their due place. I do not remember my infancy; I can only take other people at their word, and make some guess as to how I spent it from looking at other children. And though this guesswork is quite reliable, I would be none the less reluctant to consider that life to be of a piece with the one I now live in this world. Rather it is like the life I led while still in my mother's womb, for both are now wrapped in the mists of oblivion. But if *I was conceived in iniquity, and my mother fed me on sin in her womb* [Ps. 51.5 (Ps. 50.7)], then, Lord, at what time or what place was I, your servant, ever innocent? But I will say no more of my infancy. What does it matter to me now, seeing as I cannot recall any traces of it?

1.8.13 For from babyhood I advanced to boyhood. Or should I rather say that my boyhood came over me and took over from my babyhood? But my babyhood did not take its leave of me; if so, where did it go to? And yet I was now a baby no more. I was no longer an 'infant', that is, one who cannot speak; I was now a boy, and I could talk. I remember this; and in after years I have been able to recall how I learnt to speak. I was not taught according to some educational system, with grown-ups showing me the words, in the way that I later learnt to read. Instead I learnt by using my own mind, the mind you gave me, my God. At first I tried to express my inmost wishes through squalling and making different noises, and thrashing about with my arms and legs, in the hope of getting people to do what I wanted. But I found that I could not in this way communicate everything I wanted to everyone I wanted. So whenever they referred to something by name, and in mentioning the name made some gesture towards the object in question, I took a firm hold of it with my memory. I would watch them, and I remembered that the sound they made when they wished to refer to something was the name they gave to it. That they were referring to this or that object was clear from the gestures they made; they were, so to speak, the natural language of all peoples. It is by these gestures – facial expressions, winks, movements of the arm, tones of voice – that we signify our attitude towards things; whether we want to acquire something, or hold on to it, or refuse it, or avoid it altogether. I would listen to the words, and immediately I would work out from their position in different sentences what they meant; and, as soon as I had learnt to get my tongue around them, I began to string them together in sentences of my own, in order to convey my own desires. And so it was I came to share with those around me the signs we use to convey our wishes; I entered deeper into the troubled waters of human society, still subject to the authority of my parents and the whims of my elders.

1.9.14 What unhappiness, what humiliation I suffered at their hands, O God my God. It was right and proper, they would tell me, for a boy to pay attention to those who advised him to get ahead in this world, and enjoy pre-eminence in the verbal arts – though these arts are no more than the slaves of human ambition, and of the desire for what is falsely called 'riches'! So I was packed off to school, and set to learning to read and write. I was miserable there, and had no idea what use these skills were; but nevertheless, if I was slow to learn them, I was beaten. This is the system that my elders recommended; and there have been many who living this life before us have built for us those highways of woe by which we were compelled to pass. Truly you have *multiplied the toil and grief* [Gen. 3.16] of the children of Adam!

But I found there were men and women who have called out to you; and from them I learnt to perceive you, so far as I could, as some great Being, who, without being visible to our senses, could hear our prayers and help us. For while still a boy I began to call out to you, my Help and my Refuge; tongue-tied as I was, I still found a voice and called upon you. And though I was just a little boy, it was with no little emotion that I asked you not to let me be beaten at school. And when you did not hear and answer my prayer (or so I thought in my foolish way), older people would laugh at me. Even my parents, who had no wish that anything bad should happen to me, would laugh off the beatings I received, though they were bad enough and heavy enough for me at the time.

1.9.15 Is there anyone, Lord, of such a noble spirit, of such a fervent affection and devotion to you, that they would make light of the rack and the hook and other such instruments of torture, from which people throughout the earth pray to you for deliverance, while still loving those who live in terror of them? Is there anyone – even someone not quite in their senses – of such faith, such affection and such devotion to you? And yet this was how our parents laughed at the torments that our teachers inflicted upon us boys. We were no less terrified of such punishments than any victim of the rack; we were no less importunate in our prayers for deliverance. And yet we did sin. We made mistakes in our reading and writing. We paid less attention to our books than was expected of us. It was not, Lord, that we lacked the memory or the mental powers, for by your will we had the right amount of them for children our age. We were simply too fond of our fun and games; but those who exacted retribution from us for these misdemeanours were doing precisely the same sort of thing themselves. Adults have their games, which they dignify by the name of 'business'. But when boys play around, adults punish them for it, and no one has any sympathy either for boys, for adults, or for both. Would any impartial observer judge it a good thing that I was punished because my fondness for ball games was keeping me back in learning to read and write – when it was these skills that would enable me, as a man, to play a game more dishonourable still? But the man who beat me would do exactly the same as me; if he happened to be outwitted on some academic question by a fellow-teacher, he would suffer worse agonies of anger and jealousy than I would, if one of my playmates beat me at ball.

1.10.16 And yet, O Lord God, who has created all things in nature and set them in their allotted place – but not the creator of sins, which you have only set in their place[2] – and yet, I did sin. I sinned in acting against the instructions of my parents and the teachers of whom I have spoken. For in later life I would be able to put to good use these skills of reading and writing, which they would have me learn, willing or unwilling, I did not disobey them out of a preference for something more worthwhile. I liked rather to have my fun and games, my moments of glory when I won in our contests. I loved to hear the tales of myth and legend, which would *make my ears tingle and burn for more* [2Tim. 4.5]; and this ardent fascination increasingly drew my eyes towards the theatrical pageants,[3] those games that adults play. But those who stage these games receive such public

2 '... sins ... set in their place'. Augustine's former Manichee associates (of whom more in Books 3–6) held that a truly good God could not be the creator of the world, because of the evil and imperfections in it. Augustine here asserts the supremacy of the Creator-God, rejecting the notion that the existence of sin compromises God's goodness in favour of his own doctrine of 'order', by which all things in creation are set in their due place. The goodness of things in creation depends on their remaining in their allotted place.

3 *(See next page.)*

recognition that everyone hopes their little boys will one day do the same – although they would have no objection to their children being flogged, if they were distracted by the games from the studies that will, they hope, enable them to give similar shows themselves. Look upon these things with pity, O Lord. Set us free, we who already call upon you; free also those who do not yet call upon you, that they may call upon you, and you may set them free.

1.11.17 While I was still a boy I had already heard of the eternal life promised to us through our Lord God, who in his humility descended to us in our pride. From the moment I left my mother's womb (for she hoped deeply in you) I had been signed with the sign of his cross, and seasoned with his salt.[4] One day, when I was still a boy, I was seized with a severe attack of stomach cramp, and hovered on the verge of death. But you, O Lord, were my guardian even then; you saw the distress and the faith with which I begged my pious mother, and your Church, the mother of all your people, to have me baptized into your son, Christ our God and Lord. My mother in the flesh was distraught; in her heart, pure and faithful to you, she travailed for my eternal even more than my temporal well-being. Immediately she hurried off and would have seen that I was initiated

3 'theatrical pageants'. It is important to dissociate the Roman theatre from the modern. Ancient theatres were venues for mass entertainment including not only plays but spectacles of other kinds, such as gladiatorial games. Leading families would vie with each other to put on bigger and better shows. In his critique of them Augustine belongs to a long tradition, including notably Tertullian on the Christian side and Seneca on the pagan. Julius Caesar is said to have demonstrated his contempt for the games by ostentatiously dealing with his correspondence during them. While ancient writers, both pagan and Christian, do criticize the cruelty towards the contestants that was an intrinsic part of many 'games', they are no less criticized for the irrational passions they arouse in the spectators; see also Augustine's account of his young friend Alypius's experiences (6.8.13). Here Augustine focuses rather on the false values involved in the staging of the games.

4 'seasoned with his salt'. Signing with the cross and seasoning with salt (a symbol of the purification of an offering to God) was a rite administered to catechumens in the Catholic Church, before baptism, which might be postponed till just before the believer's death, as nearly happens to Augustine. Unlike baptism, the rite could be administered repeatedly.

and washed clean in your healing sacraments, confessing you, Lord Jesus, for the forgiveness of my sins – had I not suddenly recovered. My cleansing in the waters of baptism was thus delayed, on the grounds that if I lived, I ought still to remain unclean, as my guilt would be all the greater and more perilous if having been washed in that font I continued to wallow in my sins. So it was that my mother, myself and our whole household were now believers in you. Only my father did not believe in Christ, but he did not succeed in overthrowing the rule my mother's piety held over me, and in making me an unbeliever, as he still was himself. For her part, my mother was anxious that you, my God, rather than he, should be my father; and you helped her, and saw that her influence prevailed over her husband's – though she served him all the better, since even in so doing she was obeying your orders, and so serving you.

1.11.18 O Lord, I would know, if you would have me know it, what design lay behind the postponement of my baptism on that occasion? Was it for my own good that the reins keeping me from sin were loosened? Or were they not loosened? To this day from all quarters we hear some people say: 'Leave him alone, let him do it; he is not baptized yet.' But if someone's physical health is in danger, we do not say: 'Let him suffer a little more; he has not recovered yet.' It would have been better, far better, that I should have been healed, and that my family and I should have spared no effort to see that it was done straight away; that *my soul's health* (Ps. 35.3 [Ps. 34.3]), once recovered, should have been safe in the safe-keeping of you, the health-giver. But my mother, being the woman she was, knew what mighty waves of temptation threatened to break over me once my boyhood was past; and she would have me launched into them not as a figure already formed, but as a lump of clay, to be moulded into shape thereafter.

1.12.19 My family were less concerned about what I was as a boy than about what I would be as an adolescent; but even as a boy I had no love for my lessons, and I hated being pressed into learning them. But pressed I was, and it did me good, though I did not do my lessons well; I would not learn, unless forced to do so. No one does anything well if he does it against his will, even if it is something good that he is doing. Nor were those who forced me to learn doing me any good; the good that was done to me came from you, my God. For they did not consider the use to which I would put what they were forcing me to learn. They thought only of satisfying our insatiable longings for the poverty which is called riches and the ignominy that is called glory. But you, to whom *our hairs are numbered*[5] (Matt. 10.30), used to my advantage the misguided notions of all those people who insisted I learn my lessons, while my misguided reluctance to learn, you used to my own punishment; and one I well deserved, for I was a great sinner for such a little boy. So it was that you did me good through those who were doing no good, and through my own sin you exacted from me a just penalty. For you have decreed and so it stands, that every undisciplined soul is its own punishment.

1.13.20 As for the reason why I hated the Greek literature in which I was steeped as a boy – for that I have still found no satisfactory explanation. I had fallen in love with Latin literature – not, that is, with the texts taught by my earliest teachers, but the literature taught by the so-called 'grammarians'. My primers of reading, writing and arithmetic I found more of a burden and a punishment than the whole of Greek literature put together. And what reason was there for this, if not my sin and the emptiness of my life, seeing as I was *a breath that goes its way and returns not again* (Ps. 78.39 [Ps. 77.39])? But it was through those books that I gradually acquired the ability to read any piece of writing that I came across, and to write myself anything that I wished to write; which ability, once gained, I still possess. Those books were in every respect more dependable, and therefore better for me, than the ones through which I was made to memorize the wanderings of Aeneas, whoever he may be, and

5 '*our hairs are numbered*'. The reference looks back to the opening sentence of the *Confessions*, where the infinity or uncountability of God's wisdom is stressed; there is also an implied contrast between Augustine's reluctance to learn to count (one of the 'three Rs', see 1.13.20) and the fact that God has already 'counted' him completely.

to weep for the death of Dido, who killed herself for love. And all the while I did not give a thought to my own wanderings, and though I was myself dying separated from you, O God my Life (cf Jn 11.25, 14.6), in the midst of my literary pursuits, yet I never shed a tear over it. What a wretch I was!

1.13.21 For who could be more wretched than I was – a wretch who had no pity for himself? I would weep for the death of Dido, caused by her love for Aeneas, but not for my own death, caused by my lack of love for you. Yet you, O God, are the light of my heart, the bread that feeds my soul within, the strength that weds my mind and the meditation of my heart. I did not love you. *I was unfaithful to you* (Ps. 73.26 [Ps. 72.27]) and all around I heard voices saying, '*Well done! Well done!*' (Ps. 35.21 [Ps. 34.21], Ps. 40.16 [Ps. 39.16], Ps. 70.4 [Ps. 69.4]) For *the friendship of this world* (James 4.4) is unfaithfulness to you; the cry 'Well done!' is meant to make a man ashamed, if he is not like the rest. These things I did not weep for; but I did weep for Dido, her 'life cut short' when she 'sought by the sword the lower world',[6] while I had myself abandoned you and was seeking the lowest things in your creation; I was *dust to dust returning* (Gen. 3.19). And I was unhappy if prevented from reading these stories, because I had nothing to read to make me unhappy! Such is the madness in which those books are held to be nobler and more profitable than the ones through which I learnt to read and write.

1.13.22 But now let my God cry out within my soul. Let your Truth tell me over and over again that this is not so, and that my earlier teaching was by far the better. For I would rather forget all about the 'wanderings of Aeneas' and so forth than I would forget how to read and write. It is true that the portals of the grammar school are hung with veils, but these are less a mark of respect for the mysteries taught within than a curtain to hide the errors. Do not let my schoolteachers raise their voice against me (no longer am I afraid of them), as I confess to you what my soul desires, and find rest in reproving *my own evil*

6 ' "sought by the sword the lower world" '. Cf Virgil, *Aeneid* 6.456–7.

ways (Ps. 119. 101 [Ps. 118.101], Jer. 18. 11), that I may love your
good ways. Do not let those grammar-mongers raise their voice
against me, nor their customers. For if I ask them whether it is
true, as the poets say, that Aeneas once upon a time came to
Carthage, the less educated will say they do not know, but the
more educated will admit that it is false. But if I ask how the
name 'Aeneas' is spelt, all my teachers would give the answer
that is true according to the established convention that men
have agreed among themselves, by which these signs are given
their set values. And if I ask whether it would be a greater
disadvantage to someone to forget how to read and write, or to
forget the stories the poets tell, is it not obvious what anyone
would reply – anyone, that is, who had not completely forgotten
what he is himself? I sinned, then, as a boy, in placing these
vain conceits higher in my affections than those more useful
skills; or rather in hating the one, and loving the other. 'One
and one is two, two and two are four' – this was a chant I hated.
But the sight of the Wooden Horse full of warriors, of Troy in
flames, and 'the shade of Creusa herself'[7] – nothing was sweeter
than this pageant of vanity.

1.14.23 Why, then, did I hate Greek literature, seeing as it too
had poems of this sort? For Homer also is a skilled spinner of
tales, and though his stories too are but vanity, he tells them very
sweetly. But when I was a boy Homer left a sour taste in my
mouth. I suppose Greek boys feel much the same about Virgil,
when they are forced to learn him as I was made to learn Homer.
It was the sheer difficulty of gaining a thorough grasp of a foreign language that cast gall, so to speak, over the sweet allurements of Greek myth and epic. I knew none of the words, and
was under constant threat of dire punishments to make me learn
them. Previously, as a baby, I had been just as ignorant of Latin
words, but I had learnt by paying attention to those around me,
and not through the fear of punishment. Indeed, my nurses had
encouraged me gently, had made jokes and laughed, and played
with me and teased me. I learnt Latin not under pressure from

7 ' "the shade of Creusa herself" '. Virgil, *Aeneid* 2.772. The other scenes that
Augustine mentions are also from the second book of the *Aeneid*.

others, on pain of being punished; my own heart pressed me to bring to light the ideas it had conceived, which would not have been possible if I had not learnt at least some words. I did not, however, learn them from Latin teachers but from speakers; and I in turn learnt to express all my feelings in their ears. This is proof enough that unbridled curiosity is a more effective way of learning a language than constraint and compulsion. But it is in accordance with your laws, O God, the compulsion that keeps in check the flow of curiosity; all the way from the school-teacher's cane to trials of the martyrs, it is in accordance with your laws. It is your laws that have power to add a health-giving admixture of bitterness that calls us back to you and away from the malady of pleasure which has caused us to stray from you.

1.15.24 *Hear my prayer, O Lord* (Ps. 61.1 [Ps. 60.2]) *and let not my soul grow weary* (Ps. 84.2 [Ps. 83.3], Ps. 119.81 [Ps. 118.81]) under your instruction. Let me not weary of *confessing your mercies* (Ps. 107.8, 15, 21, 31 [Ps. 106.8, 15, 21, 31]). You have rescued me from all the evil roads I have trodden, and given me a sweetness surpassing all the pleasant by-paths I used to pursue. Let me have a mighty love for you; in my inmost being let me hold tight to your hand, so that you may deliver me from every temptation to the very end. For you, O Lord, *are my King and my God* (Ps. 5.2 [Ps. 5.3], Ps. 44.2 [Ps. 43.5]). Whatever useful skills I acquired as a boy, I place at your service. Speaking, writing, reading, counting – let all of these skills serve you. As for those vain literary studies, it was you who were disciplining me when I learnt them; and vain as they were, through them you forgave me the sinful delights I took in them. In them too I learnt many useful words, but these can also be learnt through things that are not vain; and that is the safe path for boys to walk.

1.16.25 Woe to you, river of human custom! *Who shall withstand you?* (Ps. 76.6 [Ps. 75.8]). How long will you roll on and not run dry, sweeping the children of Eve to a great sea of terrors, that can scarce be crossed by those who clamber on to the ark of the Cross? Was it not in you that I read of Jove the Thunderer – and Jove the Adulterer? He could scarcely be both, but so, in the play, he was. Thus his fictitious thundering acted as a pimp, providing a precedent for those who wished to imitate his adultery – for that was real enough. None, however, of these schoolteachers in their rhetoricians' gowns lends a sober ear when another man, one of their own, speaks up: 'These things are all Homer's invention,' says Cicero. 'He conferred upon the gods attributes that are properly human; I would rather he had ascribed divine qualities to us men.'[8] But it would be truer to say that Homer did indeed make up the stories he tells, but ascribed divine attributes to depraved humans. In this way he hoped that their depraved doings would be thought no depravity at all, and that whoever did the same would be seen as imitating not a pack of bandits, but the heavenly gods!

1.16.26 But you, River of Hell,[9] sweep away the children of men, who pay to learn these things – and education is a big business, seeing as it is conducted in public, in the town square, in full view of the laws that award teachers a living allowance on top of their fees. As the waters crash over your boulders, your voice rings out: 'This is the way to learn to read and write; this is the way to get the eloquence you need to make your point and win over your hearers.' I would not even recognize the words 'shower of gold' and 'lap' and 'deceive' and 'vaults of heaven' and so on, were it not for that scene of Terence's, where the young rake admires a wall painting of Jupiter deceiving Danae by sending the shower of gold into her lap, and follows the god's example in forcing his own attentions on a girl. 'What a god!' he says, seizing on Jupiter's action as a divine sanction for his own sordid passion. 'Is this the one "whose thunder shakes the vaults of heaven"? And what am I? A mere mortal. Thundering's no job for me. But I did the other thing cheerfully enough!'[10] It is not that the words are

8 ' "These things ... to us men" '. Cicero, *Tusculan Disputations* 1.61.
9 'River of Hell'. Literally 'River of Tartaros', the Greek Underworld. This is an unusual instance where Augustine uses the language of Greek mythology in connection with the Underworld; presumably to be explained first by the fact that this is a poetic word and hence appropriate to a discussion of poetry, and second as a rather extended and loose sense of the word.
10 ' "What a god ... cheerfully enough" '. Quoted from Terence, *The Eunuch* 584–91. The passage contains a parody of a description of Jupiter by Ennius, 'Father of Roman Poetry', (239–169 B.C.).

more conveniently learnt because of this immoral episode, but rather that the immorality is more confidently committed because of the words. I do not hold the words responsible; they are just the choice and *costly vessels* (Acts 9.15, Proverbs 20.15) that contain the wine of error. Our teachers had imbibed that wine too well, and used the words to serve it to us also. If we refused to drink, out came the cane; and we were given no right of appeal to any sober judge. But yet, my God, in whose sight I may remember without fear, I confess that I was eager to learn these books, for they were the joy of my wretched life. This eagerness earned me the reputation of being a promising pupil.

1.17.27 Let me, my God, speak a little of the mental powers you have given me, and how I frittered them away on mere delusions. Our teacher set us the task of retelling the story of Juno's 'anger and resentment' that she could not 'turn back from Italy the Trojan king'.[11] The rewards promised for this were enough to make my soul restless: praise on the one hand, humiliation and the threat of beatings on the other. I had heard that no Juno ever made any such speech; but we were made to trace the poet's tale step by wandering step, and to give a prose rendering of his verses, reproducing the speech as closely as possible. The prize went to the boy who made a show of 'anger and resentment' most in keeping with the dignity of his assumed character, while clothing her thoughts in the most appropriate words. But what good did it do me, my True Life, to hear my recitation acclaimed above those of all my contemporaries and school-fellows? Was it not all so much smoke and wind? And was there no other way of training my mind and tongue? Would that my heart had been trained on your praises, O Lord, as they are found in the Scriptures; would that it had been trained on your praises, like a young vine on a trellis. Then it would not have been blighted by the empty conceits of the poets and left a prey to be torn up by the birds of heaven.[12] For we have more ways than one of sacrificing to the rebel angels.

11 '"Anger and resentment . . . the Trojan king"'. Virgil, *Aeneid* 1.38.
12 'left a prey . . . birds of heaven'. A fusion of classical and Biblical allusions: Virgil, *Georgics* 2.60 and Matt. 13.4.

1.18.28 But it is not surprising that I was drifting off towards these vanities, and away from you, my God, considering what sort of men were held up to me as examples to imitate. These men would be filled with embarrassment if they were caught out in some lapse of grammar or pronunciation in describing some deed of theirs, even if the deed itself was not evil. If, however, they could tell an admiring audience of their immoral passions in suitably elegant and refined language, with a smooth flow of pure Latinity, they would be full of pride. You, O Lord, see all these things, and are silent, for you are *long-suffering and full of mercy and truth* (Ps. 86.15 [85.15]). But *will you keep silent for ever?* (Is. 42.14). Even now you are *rescuing from the horrors of the abyss* (Ps. 86.13 [Ps. 85.15]) some soul that searches for you, and *thirsts to taste your joys* (Ps. 42.2 [Ps. 41.3], Ps. 63.2 [Ps. 62.2]); whose heart says to you, *Your face, O Lord, have I sought; your face will I seek again* (Ps. 27.8 [Ps. 26.8]). For my mind is clouded by darkness and is far from your face. The road that leads us from you and back to you again is not one that we can measure, or tread with our feet. The younger son in your story did not need horses or chariots or ships when he set out to squander his wealth in a far country; he did not grow wings and fly off in view of all, or go striding on his way. But you, his father, who had been kind in giving him his inheritance when he set out, were kinder still when he came home empty-handed. The far country into which he departed was a state of mind; ruled by lusts, full of darkness, and cut off from your face.

1.18.29 Look upon us, Lord God, with patience; and see how carefully the children of men observe the rules of spelling and pronunciation they have received from previous speakers of the language, while neglecting the eternal rules that lead to everlasting salvation, which they have received from you. If some speaker or teacher of the received pronunciation drops the 'h' in the first syllable of 'human being', in contravention of the rules laid down by the grammarians, see how his fellow-humans look askance at him – more so than if he were to hate one of his fellow-men, in contravention of the laws laid down by you! It is as if he thought that any enemy could be more dangerous to him than the actual hatred he felt towards that enemy, or that by pursuing a feud with his enemy, he could harm him more than he would harm his own heart by his feelings of enmity. The knowledge of how to read and write does not go deeper than the guilty knowledge that we *are doing to others what we would not have done to ourselves* (Tobit 4.16, cf Matt. 7.12, Lk 6.31): for that is written in our nature.

You are hidden from us, O God the only great one, *dwelling on high* (Is. 33.5) in silence; and by your unrelenting Law you cast blindness as a punishment over our illicit desires. A man seeking to make a name for himself as an orator might attack his enemy in a speech full of hatred and malice; but even though the judge was a man like himself, even though the crowds of spectators were men like himself, he would take great care to ask them 'justly to condemn' rather than 'to justly condemn' their fellow-man. This would be a mere slip of the tongue; but as for the fact that the madness into which his mind had fallen might lead to his fellow-man's being removed from among men, he would not care a jot!

1.19.30 It was on the threshold of this moral world that it was my unhappy lot to lie as a boy. This was the arena in which I was to fight; and I was more afraid of committing an error of grammar or pronunciation than I was of the feelings of jealousy that would arise in me if I made such a mistake and the others did not. I acknowledge and confess to you, my God, the ways in which I earned the praise of those around me, for in those days my notion of a good life was to win the approval of these people. I did not see the whirlpool of immorality into which *I was cast out from your sight* (Ps. 31. 24 [Ps. 30.23]). For what in that moral world was more loathsome than I was, seeing as I incurred the disapproval even of my human spectators, deceiving with countless falsehoods my family tutor, my teachers and my parents; with my love of playing games, my passion for the empty pageantry of the theatre, and my restless desire to imitate the scenes I had seen enacted. I even stole from my parents' larder and table, sometimes prompted by sheer greed, sometimes in order to have something to bribe the other boys to let me win in their games, despite the fact that they enjoyed them no less than I did. Even then, I was so much a slave of my vain desire to win that I often claimed victory by cheating. But what was it that I was so unwilling to have done to me, and denounced so fiercely if I detected it in others – and did the same just as willingly to others? If I was caught cheating and denounced by my friends, I would strike out sooner than give way. Is this the innocence of childhood? No, Lord; it is not, so it please you, my God. From tutors and schoolmasters, nuts, balls and pet sparrows, to magistrates and kings, money, estates and slaves, it is all the same. We grow up, and one set of cares is replaced by another; the schoolmaster's cane is replaced by punishments more severe. It was the humility symbolized by children's low physical stature that you, our King, enjoined when you declared, *Of such is the Kingdom of Heaven* (Matt. 19.14).

1.20.31 But thanks be to you, O Lord, our God; most high and mighty, creator and ruler of the universe, even if it had been your will that I should be no more than a boy. For even then I had being and life and feeling. My wholeness, the imprint of that most hidden Oneness from which I took my being, I guarded; and by an inner sense I watched over the integrity of my senses. My thoughts were small and of small things; yet I delighted in the truth, I shunned error, I grew in memory. I learnt to use language and found pleasure in friendship; pain, sorrow and ignorance I fled.

What was there in such a creature that was not worthy of wonder and praise? But all these things were my God's gifts to me. I did not give them to myself, but they are all good and together they are what I am. Good is my Maker; he is my Good, and I *rejoice before him* (Ps. 2.11) in the good things he has given me, which made up my being even when I was a boy. My sin lay in this, that I sought pleasures, distinctions and truths within myself and in the other objects of your creation; and in doing so I fell headlong into pain, disgrace and error. Thanks be to you, my God, my Sweetness, my Glory and my Trust, for all the gifts you have given me. Preserve, I pray, these gifts; for thus you will preserve me. The things you have given me will grow and reach perfection, and I myself will be with you; for it is you who have given me my very being.

BOOK TWO

2.1.1 It is not because I am still in love with my shameful past that I wish to recall the deeds I committed then, the sins of my body which corrupted my soul. Rather it is so that I may love you, my God. Out of love for your love I do this. With bitter regretfulness do I retrace the evil and unprofitable paths I have trodden, that you may fill me with your sweetness, O God my Sweetness, never deceiving, blessed and serene; that you may gather together the members that were torn apart and scattered piecemeal when I turned away from you, the One, and wasted myself in my pursuit of the Many. More than once in my youth I burnt to satisfy myself with the lowest things; with reckless daring I ran wild, overgrown and overshadowed by my various loves. And all the time I pleased myself and sought to be pleasing in the sight of men, *my beauty wasted away and I was foul* (Dan. 10.8) in your sight.

2.2.2 And what pleasure did I know except loving and being loved? But my love did not keep within the bounds marked out by the shining border of friendship, the affection of one mind for another. Around me lay the quagmire of carnal desire,[1] bubbling with the springs of pubescence, and breathing a mist that left my heart fog-bound and benighted; I could no longer tell the clear skies of love from the dark clouds of lust. The two swirled around me in confusion; and in my youthful ignorance I was quickly drawn over the cliffs of desire and sucked down by the eddying currents of vice. Your anger was heavy upon me, though I did not know it. I was deafened by the clanking chain of my mortality, the punishment for my soul's pride; I was straying further and further from you, and you let me. I was seething

1 '... carnal desire'. Cf 1Jn 2.16. This is a key verse for Augustine's meditation on the false priorities of human life, and deserves to be quoted in full: 'For all that is in the world, the lust of the flesh and the lust of the eyes, and the pride of life, is not of the Father but is of the world.' Augustine discusses this verse at length in 10.30.41.

with fornications; overflowing, spilling out, boiling over. O my Joy at last! You said nothing then, as I wandered further and further from you, sowing more and more seeds that would yield no harvest but sorrows. I was haughty despite my humiliation; restless, yet listless.

2.2.3 But there was no one to temper the sufferings I endured, to turn to my advantage the fleeting beauties I found in the lowest things, and to set a limit to the pleasures I had from them; to see that, if it were impossible for the waves of my youthful passion to be stilled and constrained within the bounds of procreation, then at least they broke upon the shores of marriage. For this is what your Law prescribes, O Lord; you shape even our mortal progeny, and put forth a mighty but gentle hand to check the thorns that you have shut out of your Garden. In your omnipotence *you are not far from us* (Acts 17.27), even when we are far from you. I might at least have paid more attention to the rolling thunder of your clouds:[2] *They that marry will have affliction in their flesh, but I would spare you* (1Cor. 7.28), and: *It is good for a man to have no contact with a woman* (1Cor. 7.1), and: *The unmarried man considers the things of God, and seeks to please him; but the man under the yoke of matrimony considers worldly things, and seeks to please his wife* (1Cor. 7.32–3). If I had listened, I would have *made myself a eunuch for the sake of the kingdom of Heaven* (Matt. 19.12), and would have known a truer happiness as I waited for your embrace.

2.2.4 But I was wretched and seething with passion. I had abandoned you, and was drifting wherever the tide of my own desire took me. I had gone beyond all the limits set by your Law, and I did not escape your lash; for who among mortals can? You were always present with me, striking me in your mercy, and smearing the bitterest pains over all my illicit pleasures. This you did to the end that I should seek pleasure without pain; and where I found this, I should find nothing but you, O Lord; you, who *fashion pain in your instruction*,[3] and *smite us, that you may*

2 'your clouds'. Those who preached God's word. Cf 13.15.18.
3 *'fashion pain in your instruction'*. Vulgate Ps. 93.20, based on the Septuagint Greek, itself here a mistranslation of the Hebrew.

make us whole (Hosea 6.2); who *slay us, that we die not apart from you* (Deut. 32.39). Where was I in that sixteenth year of my fleshly life, how far was I *exiled from the joys of your house* (Micah 2.9), when I gladly surrendered myself to the rule of lust – a madness which man, even in his disgraced condition, regards as excessive, and which your laws regard as illegal? My family were not concerned to keep me from plunging headlong by marrying me off; they were concerned only that I should learn how to speak as well as possible, and to carry an audience with my eloquence.

2.3.5 It was in that year that my studies were interrupted. I was recalled from the nearby town of Madaura, where I had gone to study literature and rhetoric, while the necessary funds were assembled to send me to Carthage, a greater distance away. This project was more in keeping with my father's paternal pride than with his resources; for though he was a citizen of Thagaste, he was not a wealthy man. – To whom am I telling all this? It is not to you, my God; rather it is from within you that I speak to my own kind, to my fellow-men, however few may come to read these words of mine. And why do I do so? So that I and any reader of mine may reflect upon the depths from which we must call upon you. For what is closer to your ears than a heart that confesses you, and a life *lived by faith* (Habakkuk 2.4, Rom. 1 17, Gal. 3.11). Everyone heaped praise upon my father because he spent beyond our family's resources to ensure that his son had everything he would need when he was pursuing his studies far from home. There were many citizens far wealthier than we were who took no such trouble on behalf of their children. My father, for his part, was not so worried about what sort of man I was growing up to be in your sight, or how I kept my chastity. He was interested only to see that my rhetorical powers bore fruit, while instead I grew rank and untended by you, O God, the one true and good *Lord of your field* (Matt. 13.24–30), my heart.

2.3.6 So it was that in my sixteenth year a period of leisure intervened. I was compelled by my family circumstances to take a holiday from all my studies, and to stay with my parents; and meanwhile the brambles of lust grew up over my head, and there was no hand to uproot them. Indeed, when my proud father saw in the public baths that I was reaching puberty and had put on the restlessness of youth, he was as pleased as if I had already made him a grandfather; and, drunk with joy, he announced the news to my mother. Such is the way in which the world forgets its Creator and *loves your creation instead of you* (Rom. 1.24), drunk on the invisible wine of its own will, perverse as it is and bent on lower things. But within my mother's heart you had already *established your Temple, and laid the foundations of your holy dwelling-place* (1Cor. 1.16–17, Ecclesiasticus 24.14), while my father was still under instruction in the faith, and indeed had only recently begun it. My mother was full of holy *fear and trembling* (2Cor. 7.15); and though I was not yet a believer, she was afraid that I had already strayed into the tortuous paths walked by those who turn their back towards you and not their face (cf Jer. 2.27).

2.3.7 Do I venture to say that you, my God, kept silence all the time I was wandering further and further from you? Woe to me if I do. Was it thus that you were silent at that time? Whose words were they but yours that you whispered to me through your faithful servant, my mother? None of these counsels, however, sunk into my heart; I did not follow them. For she wanted me to avoid fornication, and most of all – and in some corner of my heart I remember how anxiously she admonished me – not to commit adultery. These warnings seemed to me just women's words, and I would have been ashamed to obey them. But they came from you, though in my ignorance I thought that you were silent, and it was my mother talking. You were speaking to me through her, and not keeping silent; and in despising my mother and *your maidservant*, I was despising you, *my Master* (Ps. 116.14 [Ps. 115.16]). But I did not know that it was your voice. So blind was I, and so precipitate was my fall, that when I heard my contemporaries boasting of their exploits, I felt ashamed that I had less to be ashamed of. The more immoral their actions, the more they would brag about them. They lusted for such acts, and not for the act alone; they lusted also for glory. What is worthy of censure, if not vice? I, however, was becoming more

vicious in order to avoid censure. And when my actions were
not enough to put me on a level with these hardened delinquents, I would pretend to have done things that I had not.
I was afraid that the more innocent I was, the more of a coward
I would seem; and that the more chaste I was, the more contemptible I would be considered.

2.3.8 These were my companions as I roamed the squares of
Babylon, rolling in its dirt as if it were *cinnamon and costly ointments* (Song of Songs 4.14). The unseen Enemy was mocking
me, and thereby making me cleave more closely to the heart of
that city; I was ripe to be misled, and he misled me. For her
part, my mother, who had already *fled from the midst of Babylon*
(Jer. 51.6), though she was going more slowly now she had
reached the outlying parts – my mother after the flesh did not
show the same concern to confine within the bounds of marriage
(if it could not be cut back to the quick) that part of me of
which she had heard from her husband, as she had done to urge
chastity upon me. She perceived that it was already a peril to
me, which might in future prove fatal, but she was afraid that
the shackles of matrimony would be an impediment to my
aspirations – not her aspirations for the world to come (for those
she reposed in you), but rather my own literary aspirations; for
both my parents were determined that I should be grounded in
literature. My father, however, had no thought for you, and for
me he had only vain ambitions. My mother, for her part,
thought that the usual course of studies would not only be no
hindrance to my reaching you, but might even be a help. So
I surmise, recalling as best I can my parents' characters. The
reins that held me were loosened; instead of being restrained
by parental discipline, I was let loose to follow every random
inclination. But, my God, wherever my inclinations took me, a
dark cloud came between me and the clear skies of your truth;
and *out of my abundance came forth my wickedness* (Ps. 73.7
[Ps. 72.7]).

2.4.9 Theft, O Lord, is certainly punishable under both your
Law and under the law that is written on the human heart, that
sin itself cannot erase. No thief can endure another thief with

equanimity, even if one is wealthy and the other is driven by poverty to crime. But it was not poverty that drove me to conceive the desire to steal, and to act upon that desire. I lacked only righteousness, and my stomach turned at it; I had grown fat on wickedness. What I stole, I already had in abundance, and of much better quality too. I did not steal so as to enjoy the fruits of my crime, but rather to enjoy the theft itself, and the sin.

There was a pear tree in the orchard next to ours, laden with pears, but not ones especially appealing either to the eye or the tongue. At dead of night, after messing around on some empty plots in our usual insalubrious manner, a group of us young delinquents set out, our plan being to shake the tree and make off with the pears. We carried off a vast haul of them – but not in order to feast on them ourselves; instead, we meant to throw them to the pigs. And though we did eat some of them, we did so only for the pleasure we had in tasting forbidden fruit. Such was my heart, O God; such was my heart, on which you showed your pity in the depths of the abyss. Let my heart now tell you what its purpose was; why I was gratuitously evil, and why there was no reason for my evil save evil itself. My evil was loathsome, and I loved it; I was in love with my own ruin and rebellion. I did not love what I hoped to gain by rebellion; it was rebellion itself that I loved. Depraved in soul, I had leapt away from my firm foothold in you and cast myself to my destruction, seeking to gain nothing through my disgrace but disgrace alone.

2.5.10 For there is indeed beauty in physical objects; in gold, silver, in all things. Where physical contact is concerned, harmony of form counts for much; the other senses, too, each derive their own sort of pleasure when they perceive something harmonious and well-proportioned. Temporal honour, the power to command and to dominate, also has its own glory, and for this same reason men are so avid for freedom. But in striving after these things, we must not depart from you, nor stray from the path of your Law. Even the life we live here has its own charm, proportionate to its own limited glory and in accordance with lower beauties it possesses. Human friendship too is sweet, binding in a bond of affection many souls into one. But all such things may be occasions for sin, when we incline towards them more than we ought; when, seeing that these lower things are good, we abandon the things that are higher and more excellent – you, O Lord God, and *your truth and your Law* (Ps. 119.142 [Ps. 118.142]). It is true that these lesser things have their delights, but none like my God, the maker of all things; for *in him the righteous delights, and he is the joy of the upright in heart* (Ps. 64.10 [Ps. 63.11]).

2.5.11 When we investigate a crime and ask for what reason was it committed, it is generally thought that there must be some obvious motive; either the hope of gaining or the fear of losing one of those things that we have set down in the class of lower goods. These things are indeed beautiful and fair, though lowly and slight compared to the ones that are higher and more blessed. – Let us suppose that someone has committed a murder. We may then ask: why? Perhaps it was because he coveted his victim's wife, or his land; perhaps he hoped to steal something, and to live on the proceeds of his crime. Perhaps he was afraid that his victim would deprive him of something of this sort; perhaps he had suffered some injury, and was burning for revenge. But who would believe that the murderer had killed without a cause, just for the joy of killing? It has been said of a man utterly savage and inhumane that he 'preferred to be wicked and immoderately cruel for no purpose';[4] but the writer does first give a reason – 'lest hand or courage be dulled by disuse'. If we ask again, why? there is an answer: so that once Rome was in his power, his training in vice should enable him to amass titles, offices and riches, unhindered by the fear of the law or by the financial embarrassment occasioned by his 'straitened domestic circumstances and the guilty awareness of his crimes'. Not even Catiline himself, then, loved the crimes he committed, but the things he hoped to gain by them; which is something else entirely.

4 ' "preferred to be wicked ... dulled by disuse" '. The description of Catiline, Roman politician and failed revolutionary opposed by Cicero, given by his contemporary biographer Sallust (*Catilinarian Conspiracy* 16.3); a very common school text in late antiquity.

2.6.12 But you, my theft, the crime I committed that night of my sixteenth year – what was there in you that I was so wretched as to love? You had no beauty, being a theft. Are you indeed anything at all, that I can address you in this way?[5] The pears that I stole were indeed beautiful, for you, O God, had created them; you, the creator of all things and of all things the most beautiful, the good God, the highest Good, my true Good. The pears were beautiful; but it was not them that my soul so pitiably desired. I had plenty of pears, and better ones too; the ones I picked, I picked only in order to steal. Once I had picked them, I threw them away; I feasted only on the wickedness that was the fruit of my theft. If any morsel of pear entered my mouth, it was the crime of stealing that gave it spice. And now, O Lord God, I would know what it was about the theft that gave me such delight. There was no beauty in it; not the beauty that we find in justice or in wisdom, nor the sort we find in the human mind, in our memory, our senses, or in the very pulse of life; not even such as we see in the stars, each shining in its proper place, or in the earth or sea, teeming with life that is reborn as each generation passes. There was not even the appearance of beauty that vices possess, imperfect and shadow-like as it is; for vice always falls short of its aim.

2.6.13 Pride imitates exalted status, whereas you alone are exalted as God above all things. Ambition seeks nothing but honours and glory, whereas you alone are worthy of honour above all things, and your glory endures for ever. The savagery that waits on power seeks to be feared; but who should be feared save God alone, and who or what can ever strip him of his power or detract from it in any way? The sensualist seeks the charms of love; but there is no charm greater than your love, nor anything that we may more profitably love than your Truth, more lovely and radiant than all things. A shallow and inquisitive nature affects a desire for knowledge, but your knowledge of all

5 'Are you indeed ... in this way'. The first appearance in the *Confessions* of a key Augustinian teaching. God is both supreme Good and supreme Being; in so far as something is evil, it ceases to participate in goodness, and hence also in being. Thus pure evil is non-existent.

things is supreme. Ignorance and stupidity would shield themselves with names of simplicity and harmlessness; but what simpler than you may be found, or more harmless, inasmuch as it is their own works that are the enemy of the wicked? Idleness, too, aims for a kind of repose, but what true Rest is there beside the Lord? Extravagance would be called sufficiency and plenty, but you are the fullness and unfailing source of pleasure incorruptible. Profligacy makes a pretence of generosity, whereas you of your great riches bestow upon us all good things. Avarice desires a multitude of possessions, but you possess all things. Envy vies for supremacy; what is supreme over you? Anger seeks revenge; what Avenger is more just than you? A timorous disposition shies away from circumstances unfamiliar or unforeseen or unfavourable to the things it loves, and seeks to anticipate any threat to its security. But what is unfamiliar to you, what circumstance unforeseen? *Who can separate you from what you love?* (Rom. 8.35). And where is there any lasting security, if not in you? A sullen nature is consumed with resentment, if it loses the things on which it had set its heart; it wishes to have nothing taken from it, just as nothing can be taken from you.

2.6.14 Thus the soul is unfaithful to you, when it turns away from you and seeks outside you the things it cannot find in pure and unmixed form until it returns to you. All who forsake you and set themselves up against you, are acting in perverse imitation of you; but by their very imitation they confess that you are the creator of all that is, and hence that there is nowhere at all where they can go from you. What was it, then, in my theft that I loved? In what way was the theft of the pears an imitation of my Lord – even the most perverse and vicious kind of imitation? Did I take pleasure in breaking your Law by deceit, since I could not do it by my own authority? Did I find a dim reflection of your omnipotence in doing with impunity what was forbidden? So might a prisoner aspire to an illusion of liberty, or *a slave escape his master to gain a shadow!* (Job 7.2). What a hideous distortion of a life! What an abyss of death! Could I indeed have found pleasure in tasting forbidden fruit, for no other reason than that it was forbidden?

2.7.15 My soul can recall these things and yet not be afraid; but *how shall I repay the Lord* (Ps. 116.12 [Ps. 115.12]) for this? I shall love you, O Lord, and give you thanks; *I shall confess your Name* (Ps. 54.6 [Ps. 53.8]), for you have forgiven my many sins and shameful deeds. You have *made my sins melt away like ice* (Ecclesiasticus 3.17), and this I ascribe to your grace and your mercy. To your grace I ascribe also all the evil deeds I have not done; for if I could love to sin even without a cause, what might I not have done? All these things I confess that you have put far from me; both the evil deeds I did at my own behest, and those that with you as my guide I did not do. Who indeed, after reflecting upon his own weakness, would venture to attribute his purity and integrity to his own strength? Whoever did so you would love the less, as if he had less need of the mercy in which you forgive the sins of those who turn to you (Ps. 51.13 [Ps. 50.15]). I now make an open account and confession of my sins; if my reader is one whom you have called, who has followed your voice and avoided the same sins, let them not laugh at me as they read my account. I have been healed by the same Physician whose care has kept them from falling ill at all, or at least not so severely. Let them love you not less, but more. Let them see that it is through you, who have saved me from the sickness of my sins, that they too do not suffer to the same degree from the sickness of their own.

2.8.16 But *what profit did I ever have* (Rom. 6.21) from the sins I now blush to recall, and least of all that theft of mine? Wretch that I was! I loved nothing about it save the theft itself, and that too was a nothing – and moreover made me more wretched still. If, however, I remember clearly my state of mind at the time, I am sure I would never have done it had I been by myself. Was it, then, the company of my partners in crime that I loved? Is it true, after all, that I loved nothing but the theft? No; it is all the more true, for their company too was nothing. What is the truth of this? Who can explain this to me? Only the one who *sheds light on my heart* (Ecclesiasticus 2.10), whose eye can pierce its shadows. What is it that gives me the notion of enquiring into my actions, of debating and pondering them in this way? If

I had stolen the pears because I loved them and wanted to enjoy them, I could have done so by myself. If that had been all, I could have committed my crime alone, and so have obtained the pleasure I sought. I did not need to scratch the itch of my desire by having other minds to share my secret. But my real pleasure did not lie in eating the pears but in stealing them. This was the pleasure that the company of my fellow-sinners gave me.

2.9.17 What was my state of mind that night? Certainly nothing to be proud of, and woe to me for having it. But what was it? *Who understands his own offences?* (Ps. 19.12 [Ps. 18.13]). It was a joke to us; it tickled our fancy to think of the people we were tricking – the parents, teachers, the owner of the fruit – who had no idea what we were doing, and would have been most displeased if they had known. Why, then, did I enjoy the fact that I was not doing it by myself? Is it because no one laughs when they are alone? No one, that is, laughs readily on their own; though it is possible for some individuals to be overcome with laughter, if they see or think of something eminently laughable, even though there is no one else present. But I would never have stolen those pears had I been on my own. *Behold, my God, the living recollection of my soul is before you* (Num. 10.19). I would not have stolen them by myself, and it was not what I was stealing that enticed me, but the fact that I was stealing. What hateful friendship, leading my mind astray along paths I cannot retrace! What had started as mere fun and games became an appetite for destruction, a desire for another's loss not driven by a passion for my own gain, or for revenge for some injury; but when my friends said, 'Let's go and do it,' I would have blushed to appear unblushing.

2.10.18 Who can unravel this twisted bundle of knots and tangles? It is repugnant; I do not wish to see it or think of it. It is you that I want, O God, Righteousness and Integrity, fair and lovely, a beacon of goodness. You satisfy our longing, and we long for you still. In you there is rest and life untroubled. Those who enter into you, *enter their master's joy* (Matt. 25.21); all is perfect for them in you, the Perfect One. I abandoned you, my God, and went astray; in my youthfulness I wandered from your upholding arms and became to myself a *land of famine* (Lk 15.14).

BOOK THREE

3.1.1 I came to Carthage, and a frying pan of sinful loves was spitting all about me.[1] I was not yet in love, but I was in love with love; such was my inner need that I hated myself for not being more in need. I was looking for something to love, in love with love and hating the safety of a path free from pitfalls; for inside I was starving for lack of inner food – you, my God – and yet starving as I was, I felt no hunger. I felt no lack of the foods that do not perish (cf Jn 6.19), not because I was full of them, but because the more empty I was, the more nauseating I found them. For this reason my soul was sick; covered with sores (cf Lk 16.20), it turned itself outwards, pathetically eager to scratch itself with the touch of sensible objects. But if these objects had no soul, they would not be loveable. Loving and being loved was sweeter to me if I could also enjoy my lover's body. So it was that I defiled the well of friendship with the filth of concupiscence, and clouded its clear light with the infernal fog of lust; crude and boorish as I was, my vanity was so excessive that I longed to be smart and sophisticated. I rushed headlong into love, seeking to be swallowed up in it. *O God ever merciful to me* (Ps. 59.19 [Ps. 58.18]), what gall you in your goodness smeared over my sophisticated pleasures; for I was loved in return, and came secretly to know the chains of carnal enjoyment. Gladly I was enmeshed in those bonds of woe, and let myself be beaten with *iron rods blazing with jealousy and suspicions* (Ps. 2.9, Ps. 79.4 [Ps. 78.5]), with fears, *anger and quarrels* (Gal. 5.20).

3.2.1 I was carried away by the pageantry of the theatre, full of reflections of my own miseries and of kindling for the fire that was consuming me. Why is it that a man at the theatre wants to suffer as he watches those tales of tragedy and woe – woes which, however, he would not wish to undergo himself? He is,

1 'I came to Carthage ... all about me'. Augustine puns here on *Carthago* (Carthage) and *sartago* (frying pan).

however, willing to undergo the suffering he derives from them as a spectator, and this suffering is itself a pleasure. What is all this but the most spectacular madness? The less free each spectator is of these emotions, the more he is moved to pity them in others; although when he himself undergoes these sufferings, his plight is said to be pathetic, but when he shares those of others, he is said to be sympathetic. But what sympathy can a man have with the fictitious productions of the stage? As a member of the audience, he is not called on to help the characters, but merely invited to suffer; the more he suffers, the more he applauds the actor who has undergone these imaginary troubles. And if those tales of human woe are acted in such a way that the spectator does not suffer, perhaps because they are old-fashioned or untrue, then he leaves the show in disgust, criticizing the performance; but if he does suffer, then he stays in rapt attention, and rejoices amid his tears.

3.2.3 Are sufferings, then, objects of love? It is certain, at all events, that every man wishes to be happy. Or is it that although no one enjoys being pitiable, nevertheless everyone enjoys being sympathetic, which is impossible without suffering; for which reason, and no other, sufferings are objects of love? This, too, springs from the well of friendship that I have spoken of. But where does it go? Where does it flow? Why does it become, as it runs down, a torrent of boiling pitch, a loathsome broil of foul lusts, into which it is changed and transformed by its own will, warped and cast down from the clear skies of heaven? Are we, then, to reject sympathy? Far be it. Are we, then, to love sufferings? Sometimes. But beware, my soul, of impurity; under the watchful care of my God, the *God of our fathers, praised and exalted on high throughout all ages* (Dan. 3.52–5), beware of impurity. It is not that I do not pity now, but in those days, at the theatre, I rejoiced with the lovers, when they had sinful enjoyment of each other, notwithstanding the fact that their deeds were imaginary and all part of the show; and when they lost each other, I grieved with them, as if in sympathy. But in both joy and grief there was pleasure. Now, however, I pity more one who rejoices in sin than one who, enduring hardship, is bereft of the pleasure that leads to destruction and loses the happiness that leads to misery. This, surely, is truer sympathy, but there is no pleasure in it. For even if we commend one who grieves for another's suffering and say that he performs a duty of friendship, nevertheless he who shows true brotherly sympathy would rather have no cause to grieve. If there is such a thing as ill-willed goodwill (which is impossible), then it is possible for one who truly and sincerely feels pity to wish that others may suffer, so that he can pity them. Some sorts of suffering, then, are to be commended; but none is to be loved. For in this respect you, Lord God, lover of souls, show pity that is far purer than ours, far more incorruptible: you are assailed by no suffering. *And who is capable of these things?* (2Cor. 2.16).

3.2.4 But I, pitiable as I then was, loved suffering, and sought causes for it; the more tears an actor shook out of me, the better I liked him and the more I admired his performance – albeit the troubles he enacted were none of my own, unreal and mere pantomime! What, however, is surprising in this, seeing as I was an unhappy sheep, straying from your flock,[2] impatient of your safe-keeping, and afflicted with a loathsome mange? That was the source of my love of sorrows – not the kind that pierced me at all deeply, for I did not love to endure the sort of things I loved to watch, but the fictitious kind, that I loved to hear, which only grazed me skin-deep; but like the scratches of nails, they led to burning inflammation, infection and foul purulence. Was such a life life at all, my God?

3.3.5 And all the while your faithful compassion hovered over me from afar. In what iniquities did I waste away, and how sacrilegious was the curiosity that I pursued; so much so that, as I deserted you, it led me down to the depths of faithlessness, to the covert service of the *demons to whom I offered up* (Deut. 32.17, 1Cor. 10.20) my evil deeds, and in all of these deeds *you struck me with your lash* (Ps. 73.14 [Ps. 72.14]). I even ventured within the walls of your house, and during the celebration of your rites,

---

2 'unhappy sheep ... your flock'. A conflation of allusions to Virgil, *Eclogues* 3.3, Ps. 119.176 [Ps. 118.176], Matt. 18.22, Lk 15.4–6, 2Pet. 2.15.

to lust after women, and to do business for them – though what profit did I hope to gain but my own death (cf Rom. 7.5)! For this you chastised me with heavy punishments, but they availed nothing to prevent my guilt, O you my great Mercy, my God and my Refuge (cf Ps. 59.18 [Ps. 58.18]), from the terrible sins in which I wandered, stiff-necked and forsaking you, in love with the liberty of a runaway slave (cf Job 7.2, and 2.6.14).

3.3.6 My studies, too – 'the liberal arts', as they were called – were leading me in a direction of their own; they led me towards 'the brawling law courts',[3] intending me to excel in them; for the better I could deceive, the more I would be praised. Such is the blindness of men that they boast even of their own blindness. I was now a senior pupil in the school of my teacher of rhetoric, rejoicing in my pride, puffed up with my conceit – though much more subdued, *Lord, you know* (Tobit 8.9, Jn 21.15–16), than the Destroyers, and wholly absent from their destructive activities. It was among these Destroyers (an inauspicious, diabolical name that they wore as if it were a badge of sophistication) that I spent all my time, ashamed, in a shameless way, that I was not like them. I would pass my time with them, and enjoy, at times, the pleasure of their friendship, though their deeds – their destructive activities – always filled me with abhorrence, for they took a reckless delight in affronting the modesty of perfect strangers, harassing them and mocking them without provocation, and so satisfying their greed for the pleasures that come from malice. Nothing is more typically demonic than this activity. What truer name, therefore, could they have than 'Destroyers', seeing as it is they whom the spirits that deceive in secret had plainly twisted and destroyed first of all, mocking them and seducing them through their very love of mockery and deceit?

3.4.7 It was among these people that I, at that tender age, was studying the classics of rhetoric, an art in which I was eager to distinguish myself – a damnable end, as empty as wind, urged on us by the delight men take in vanity. In the regular course of study I came to a book by a certain Cicero, whose eloquence, if

3 ' "the brawling law courts" '. An allusion to Ovid, *Fasti* 4.188.

not his thought, is admired by all. But this book of his contains an exhortation to philosophy; it is called the *Hortensius*. It was this book that changed my outlook, that changed my prayers and turned them to you, O Lord, and made my aspirations and desires other than they had been. Suddenly all my vain hope seemed cheap, and I began to lust with a passion scarcely to be believed after the immortality conferred by philosophy; I *arose and began to return to you* (Lk 15.18–20). I took up that book not as a means to hone my tongue, the skill which I was ostensibly purchasing with my mother's money (I was now eighteen years old, and my father had been dead for two years). It was not in order to hone my tongue that I took it up, nor was it Cicero's manner of speech that swayed me, but what he was saying.

3.4.8 How ardently, my God, I burned to fly from earthly things back to you, though I did not know how you were dealing with me! For *with you is wisdom* (Job 12.13, 16). The love of wisdom has the Greek name 'philosophy',[4] and it was with this name that that book set me ablaze. There are some who seduce others by means of philosophy, using that great and noble name, which can offend no one, as a front and a pretext for their own errors; most, if not all, such people, both of Cicero's own day and in previous generations, are singled out and exposed in that book. The truth is made clear of that salutary admonition given by your Holy Spirit through the mouth of your good and pious servant: *See that none deceive you by means of philosophy and vain seduction, according to the tradition of men, according to the elements of this world, and not according to Christ; for in him dwells in bodily form the whole fullness of the Godhead* (Colossians 2.8–9). As for me, you know, O Lord, that at that time I did not yet know the Apostle's words; but in Cicero's exhortation to philosophy there was one thing that I loved especially, namely that his words aroused me and set me on fire not to be a lover of this or that sect, but of wisdom itself, whatever it may be; to love it and seek it and gain it and keep it, to embrace it with all my strength. And there was one thing that damped my ardour, namely that the name of Christ was not in that book. For that

4 'The love of wisdom … "philosophy" '. 'Philo-sophia' – the 'love of wisdom'.

name, *according to your mercy, O Lord* (Ps. 25.5 [Ps. 24.7]), the name of my saviour, your Son, my young heart had piously drunk in with my mother's milk, and kept deep within; and nothing without this name, however literate and refined, however truly it spoke, could carry me away completely.

3.5.9 I applied my mind, therefore, to the Holy Scriptures, to see what manner of books they were. There I saw a thing not discovered by the wise, nor revealed to the little ones.[5] Low is the entrance to it, but where it issues it is lofty and veiled in mysteries; and I was not such as could enter it, or bend my neck to its path. For when I first turned my mind to the Scriptures, I did not think what I am saying now; they seemed to me unworthy of comparison with the majesty of Ciceronian rhetoric. My pride shunned their modest style, and my eyes could not penetrate their inner secrets. It was the same Scripture which grows up with the little children; but I disdained to be a little child, and, swollen with my pride, fancied myself an adult.

3.6.10 So it was I fell among men proud to the point of madness,[6] wholly carnal, full of words, in whose mouths were *the*

5 'a thing not discovered ... to the little ones'. Indirect references to James 4.6, 1Pet. 5.5, and perhaps also to Matt. 11.25, Lk 10.21.
6 'men proud to the point of madness'. Augustine's first explicit allusion to the Manichees. It is worthwhile considering the terms in which he first describes them. They are proud, i.e. seeking a place in the order of things higher than that allotted to them; perhaps the main aspect of their pride is their identification of physical matter, symbolized by the 'Prince of Darkness', with evil, whereas Augustine repeatedly asserts God as Creator, and the *Confessions* conclude with an exegesis of the Creation story in Genesis. Pride is, of course, the primal sin of the Devil. They are mad, irrational (Book 4 is taken up with a critique of their bad science). They are carnal-minded; that is, they criticize the Old Testament deity by means of a literal interpretation of the anthropomorphic language used of him, being unable, in Augustine's view, to see the spiritual truth. On the score of carnality, Manichees would no doubt return the compliment. They are full of words – that is, they 'speak so much, and say so little' (1.4.4). Language is, for Augustine, a distinguishing feature of humanity, but not its final purpose; his own trade of rhetoric he comes to see as attaching an excessive value to mere skill with words. Their appeal lies in the pseudo-Christian elements of their teaching. Humans are naturally drawn towards the truth, and the Manichee emphasis on truth and on Christianizing language is the basis of their appeal.

snares of the devil (1Tim. 3.7, 2Tim. 2.26), a birdlime compounded of the syllables of your name, of the name of our Lord Jesus Christ, and of the Paraclete, our Comforter, the Holy Spirit (cf Jn 14.6). These names were never absent from their lips; but they went only as deep as the sound, the noise made by the tongue; their heart was empty of truth. They would say 'truth, truth', and spoke much of it to me, but it was nowhere in them. They spoke falsehoods not only of you, who are in truth the Truth, but even the *elements of this world* (Col. 2.8), your creation, concerning which I ought, for love of you, my Father supremely Good, Beauty of all things beautiful, to have passed over even those philosophers who spoke truly on these elements.

O Truth, Truth, how deeply, even then, the depths of my heart were sighing for you, as those companions of mine uttered your name so many times and in so many ways – but only with their voice, and in all those huge tomes of theirs! I was hungry for you, and those books were the dishes on which they served up to me not you, but the sun and the moon in your place.[7] The sun and moon are your works, and beautiful indeed; but they are your works and not you, nor the earliest of your works; for your spiritual works came before your physical ones, however radiant and heavenly they may be. But I was *hungry and thirsty* (Matt. 5.6); not for your created works, even the earliest of them, but for you, the very Truth, *in whom there is no changing, who are never cast into shadow by your motion* (James 1.17). Yet all the while they kept setting before me those serving dishes of theirs,

---

7 '...served up to me ... in your place'. The extended food metaphor here reminds us of Augustine as the Prodigal Son, 'longing to satisfy himself with the husks the swine ate' (Lk 15.16, cf 3.6.11); by the end of Book Two, Augustine has 'become to myself a land of famine' (2.10.18). It also hints at the Manichee concern with dietary habits; the inner circle of Manichee 'Elect' were held to release particles of the divine from their food (cf 3.10.18). The repeated references to the 'illusory' nature of Manichee teaching deserves comment. Augustine uses a Greek word (often a bad sign) *phantasma*, denoting a thing not truly or correctly perceived. O'Donnell notes that the Manichees themselves believed that Jesus's death was in fact an illusion (as the truly divine could not suffer); that Augustine believed that the Manichees did not worship God in their own way, but did not worship God at all (cf 1.2.2 and 4.7.12); and that he came to use this term to describe their doctrines in general.

piled high with those glorious illusions of theirs, though even then it would have been better to love the sun, which is at least real to the eyes, than those illusions of theirs, which are unreal and deceive the soul through the eyes. But as I thought that they were you, I ate them; not eagerly, since they left not the least taste of you in my mouth (for you were not such empty fictions). Nor did I derive any sustenance from them, but rather they sapped my strength. The food we eat in a dream is like in every way to the food we eat when awake, but in eating it we are not fed, for we are asleep. The foodstuffs they offered me were not in any way like you as you have now spoken to me, for they were bodily illusions, unreal bodies. The real bodies that we see with our carnal sight, whether in heaven or on earth, have a more certain existence; we and the beasts and the birds can see them, more surely than when we picture them in our minds. And again, these mental pictures we have of them are surer than the great and infinite things whose existence we infer from them, but which do not exist at all.

Such were the empty shadows on which I then fed, and was not fed. But you, my Love, for whom *I faint to grow strong* (Ps. 119.81 [Ps. 118.81], 2Cor. 12.10) are not those physical objects. You are not the physical things which are visible to us, although they be in the heavens. Nor are you the things which we do not see in the heavens; for you have established them, but you dwell not even in the highest of the things you have established. How far, therefore, are you from those illusions of mine – illusions of bodies which do not exist at all. Surer than these are the mental images we have of bodies which exist, and surer than them are the bodies themselves – but you are not even the bodies. You are not even the soul, the life of the body – and the life of the body is better and surer than the body itself – but you are the life of the soul, the life of life, yourself living and unchanging, the *life of my soul* (Prov. 3.22).

3.6.11 Tell me then: where were you at that time, and how far from me? I, for my part, was far away from you, cut off even from the husks the swine ate, the husks that I fed them. How much better than those snares are the tales the schoolteachers and the poets tell! Poetry and verse, 'Medea winging on her way',[8] – all these things are surely more worth knowing than the Five Elements,[9] with the various shadows cast on them by the Five Caves of Darkness – things which do not exist at all, and which are deadly to those who believe in them. Poetry and verse I could turn to a true form of sustenance. Even when I recited 'Medea winging on her way', I was not asserting that she had indeed done so. When I heard others reciting the same passage, I did not believe that it was true; but I did believe in the Five Elements. Woe to me! By what steps was I led down to the depths of hell, sick and feverish from being starved of truth, seeking you, my God – for it is to you that I confess this, you who pitied me even when I did not confess – seeking you not according to the intellectual faculty by which you willed it that I should be superior to the brute beasts, but according to my carnal perception. But you were within what was deepest in me, and higher than what was highest. I stumbled across the brazen woman, bereft of wisdom, that Solomon uses as a parable; the one who sits on her chair at her house door and says: *Eat and enjoy the hidden bread; drink the sweet water of theft* (Prov. 9.17). She it was who seduced me, for she found me living outwardly, in the eye of my flesh, and ruminating in my mind only such things as I had devoured through that eye.

3.7.12 I knew nothing else that truly is; and I was often needled into throwing in my lot with those foolish deceivers, when they asked me: 'Where does evil come from? Is God confined within a bodily form? Does he have hair? Or nails? Should we suppose the Patriarchs righteous, seeing as they practised polygamy, killed men, and offered animal sacrifice?' In my ignorance of the

8 ' "Medea winging on her way" '. A quotation from the tragedy *Medea* by the early Latin poet Pacuvius (220–c. 130 B.C.) (fragment 397).

9 'Five Caves of Darkness'. The Manichee doctrine of the Five Elements is summarized by Augustine, *de Haeresibus* 46.7: 'The Five Elements ... they call by these names: Smoke, Darkness, Fire, Water, Wind ... To defeat these Five Elements, they say, another Five were sent from the kingdom and substance of God, and in that conflict Aër was mingled with Smoke, Light with Darkness, Good Fire with Evil Fire, Good Water with Evil Water, Good Wind with Evil Wind' (cited by O'Donnell).

true state of things, I was put out by these questions; it seemed to me that I was entering into the truth, while in fact I was departing from it. I did not know that evil is deficiency of good to the point where there is no good at all. How could I see it, since my eyes could see only as far as the body, and my mind only as far as illusions? I did not know that *God is spirit* (Jn 4.24), and, as such, does not have limbs with length and breadth, nor does he have mass. For mass is less in any part than it is the whole, and if it is infinite, is less in any given part with specific spatial extension than it is throughout the infinity; it is not everywhere the whole, as spirit is, as God is. As for the question of what it is in us, according to which we exist and are rightly called in Scripture 'fashioned in the image of God' (Gen. 1.27) – about this I was utterly ignorant.

3.7.13 Nor did I know the true and inner righteousness that judges not according to convention, but according to the Law of God Almighty, that most perfect Rule of all. It is according to this Law that the customs of different times and places are shaped to fit their time and place; but the Law itself is everywhere and always, not one thing in one place and another in another. It is according to this Law that Abraham, Isaac, Jacob, Moses, David, and all those who were praised by the mouth of God, were righteous. It is the naïve who judge them unrighteous, judging them in accordance with their brief place in human time, and measuring the moral character of the human race from the direction of their own moral character. It is as if someone ignorant of armoury and not knowing which piece fitted which part of the body should wish the head to be protected by a greave and the shin with a helmet, and grumble that it did not fit properly; or as if, when, on one and the same day a cessation of all public business had been announced from midday onwards, someone should be indignant that he was not allowed to set out his stall in the afternoon when he had been allowed to do so in the morning. It is as if, in one and the same house, someone should see one slave handling something that the cup-bearer was not allowed to touch, or something being done behind the stables that was forbidden in front of the dining table, and be indignant that in one and the same house and household, the same tasks were not allotted to all persons and places.

Such are those who are indignant when they hear that the righteous were allowed to do something in one generation that they were not allowed to do in another, and that God commanded one generation to do one thing and another to do another, in accordance with the rationale of different times, though it was the same righteousness that the righteous of both generations were obeying – when they can see that in one and the same man, different pieces of armour fit different limbs; in one and the same day, something may have been permitted up to a certain hour but be forbidden thereafter; and in one and the same house, something may be allowed or ordered to be done in one corner that is forbidden and punishable in another right next to it.

Is righteousness, then, something 'fickle and changeable'?[10] No; but the periods of time over which it presides, do not all proceed alike; they are time. Men, however, whose *life on earth is short* (Wisdom 15.9), are unable to conceive with their own minds the reasoning processes of earlier generations and of other races whom they have not known for themselves, whereas in the generations they do know, they can easily see what is appropriate within one and the same body or day or house, to each limb or hour or part and person. They are scandalized by the past, and enslaved to the present.

3.7.14 These things I did not then know, nor did I observe; they were battering my eyes from every direction, and I did not see them. When I composed poetry, I was not allowed to put any foot in any position; the rules were different in different metres, and even in any given line I could not put a given foot in every position. The art of composition itself did not have different rules at different times, but all these rules at the same time. Yet I did not have the insight to see that the righteousness to which those good and holy Patriarchs were enslaved (cf Rom. 6.16–18), like the art of poetry but far more supremely and sublimely, had

10 'fickle and changeable'. Virgil, *Aeneid* 4.569, 'Woman's a fickle and a changeable thing.'

all its rules at the same time; in no part did it vary, yet at various times it did not have all the same rules, but distributed the appropriate commandments to each age. In my blindness I held reprehensible the pious Patriarchs, who not only lived, as God bade and inspired them, in the present, but also foretold, as God revealed, the future.

3.8.15 Is there any time or place in which it is unrighteous to *love God with all your heart and all your soul and all your mind, and to love your neighbour as yourself* (Deut. 6.5, Matt. 22.34, Mk 12.30, Lk 10.27)? Sins against nature, such as those of Sodom, are always and everywhere to be abominated and punished. Even if all nations committed them, the law of God would hold them all alike guilty of the same crime; for that law did not make them so that they could use themselves thus; inasmuch as the bond of fellowship which ought to exist between us and God is violated when that nature of which he is the Maker is defiled by lust and perversion. Sins against human morality, on the other hand, are to be avoided on account of the diversity of those morals; no one, citizen or foreigner, should by their lust violate the social contract that exists within a state or people, whether it is ratified by law or by convention; for loathsome is every part that does not fit into its whole. But when God orders something against the existing morality or social contract of any body of men, even if it has never been done in that place, it must be done. If the custom has lapsed, it must be restored, and if there never was such a custom, then one should be established. If it is permissible for a king, within the state he rules, to issue a commandment which neither he nor any before him has ever issued; and if it is not injurious to the social harmony of that state for that commandment to be obeyed – indeed, it would be contrary to social harmony for it not to be obeyed, inasmuch as it is a general agreement of human society that kings must be obeyed – how much more, then, ought God's whole creation obey without hesitation whatsoever its Ruler commands! For just as, where the authority of human society is concerned, the greater power is set over the lesser and must be obeyed by it, so God is set over all powers.

3.8.16   Likewise in the case of crimes against others, which arise from a lust to hurt others whether by word or deed. They might be committed out of a desire for revenge, as in a feud between two mutual enemies, or in order to gain some outward benefit, as when a brigand waylays a traveller. They might be committed out of a desire to avoid some stroke of misfortune, as a man might do to someone whom he fears. They might be committed out of envy, as a poor man may do to a richer one, or a man successful in some aspect of life may do to someone whom he fears may come to be his equal, or whose rise to equal status he resents. They might be committed out of mere pleasure in others' misfortune, like spectators at gladiatorial games, or those who mock and scoff at others in general. These are the types of wickedness; they breed from the lust for dominance, the lust for seeing, and the lust for touching, from any one or two of these, or from all together. It is thus that men live wicked lives, in defiance of the Three and the Seven, the *ten-stringed instrument* (Ps. 33.2 [Ps. 32.2], Ps. 144.9 [Ps. 143.9]), your Ten Commandments, O God Most High and Most Sweet.

But what sins can be committed against you? For you are incorruptible. Or what crimes can be committed against you? For you are invulnerable. But you punish the sins men commit against themselves, for even when they sin against you, they are acting impiously against their own souls, and *their wickedness lies to itself* (Ps. 27.14 [Ps. 26.12]), either by corrupting and perverting their own nature, which you have made and ordained, or by using the things you have declared permissible beyond the bounds you have permitted, or by burning with desire for the things you have declared forbidden, and *using them in ways against nature* (Rom. 1.26). They are guilty of violence in thought and word against you, and of *kicking against the goads* (Acts 9.5, 26.14), when, according to their several likes and dislikes, they break through the bounds of man's fellowship with man and take a wilful delight in their private cliques and factions. These things come about when *men abandon you, the source of life* (Jer. 2.13), the one and true Creator and Ruler of the universe, and in their private arrogance love only a part of the universe, a false unity. Therefore with humble piety we return to you, and you strip us of our evil customs, and *are merciful to the sins* (Ps. 78.38 [Ps. 77.38], Ps. 79.9 [Ps. 78.9]) of those who confess. You *hear the groaning of the prisoners shackled in iron* (Ps. 102.20 [Ps. 101.19]), and release us from the chains we have fashioned for ourselves, if we *lift not up against you the horn* (Ps. 75.4–5 [Ps. 74.4–5]) of a spurious liberty, losing all in our greed to gain all, loving our own good more than you, the Good of all things.

3.9.17 But in between sins against you and crimes against one's fellow-man, and all the many sorts of wickedness, are the sins committed in youth,[11] which right-thinking people both condemn when measured against the yardstick of perfection, and extol as the green blade that gives promise of the harvest. There are also some things that are like sins and crimes but are not sins, since they offend neither you, O Lord our God, nor the bond of society; as when a man stores up goods to be used in a manner appropriate to his situation and time, or in his zeal to set matters straight uses the power duly vested in him to punish others. It is uncertain in the former case whether he is acting out of lust for possession, or in the latter out of lust for hurting others. There are many actions, therefore, that have seemed culpable to men, but which according to your testimony are worthy of approval. You are our witness also that many actions praised by men are worthy of censure, seeing as the appearance of a deed is often one thing, while the mind of the doer and the mystic juncture of time is quite another. But when you suddenly command something unusual or unprecedented, then even though you have previously forbidden it, even though you conceal for the time being the reason for this command, even though it is contrary to the social convention of this or that group of men, who would doubt that it must be done, inasmuch as the just human society is the one that serves you? But blessed are those who know that you have given the commandment; for

11 'the sins committed in youth'. Augustine is speaking literally of the sort of behaviour winked at in children and adolescents (cf *Sermon* 302.1.1), but perhaps also of the 'youth of mankind'. For the theory of the 'ages of mankind', parallel to the ages of an individual's life, cf *City of God* 10.14.

all that your servants do is done either as an example of what is to be done in the present, or a prophecy of what is to come in the future.

3.10.18 It was in my ignorance of these things that I mocked those holy servants and prophets of yours. But as I mocked them, what was I doing but being mocked by you, in being led little by little, a step at a time, to believe in the silly stories of the Manichees – such as that a fig, when picked, weeps, and its mother tree sheds milky tears? If, however, one of their saints ate the aforementioned fig (not, of course, having incurred the guilt of picking it, but leaving that to another) – then, I believed, he would churn it in his guts, and breathe out angels, and more; he would breathe out very particles of God, groaning and belching them forth in prayer. These particles of the supreme and true God would have been imprisoned within the fig, had their holy Elect not released them with their tooth and their stomach. In my miserable state I even believed that mercy should be shown to the fruits of the earth rather than to mankind for whose sake they grew; for if a hungry man who was not a Manichee were to ask for a mouthful, then that mouthful, once given to him, seemed to me to risk being condemned to lose its divine status.

3.11.19 And you *put forth your hand from on high* (Ps. 144.7 [Ps. 143.7]) and *rescued my soul* (Ps. 144.7 [Ps. 143.7]) from this deep darkness, for my mother, your faithful servant, wept for me to you, more than mothers weep for the bodily death of their children. She saw that I was dead to *the faith and the Spirit* (Galatians 5.5) that she had from you, and you heard her prayers, O Lord; you heard her prayers, and did not despise her tears, which flowed out and watered the ground beneath her eyes in every place that she prayed. You heard her prayer. For what was the source of that dream with which you consoled her, telling her that she would go and live with me, and have one table in her house with me? This she began to hope would not happen, loathing and abominating as she did the blasphemies into which I had strayed. In her dream, she saw herself standing on a kind of wooden measuring rule, and coming towards her she saw a young man, radiant and joyful and smiling at her. She, for her part, was grieving, and *exhausted with grief* (Lamentations 1.13) The young man asked her – not in order to learn, but, as is his wont, in order to teach – the reasons for her grief and her daily tears. She replied that she was bewailing my perdition; and he bade her not to be troubled, and admonished her to *take heed and see* (Lamentations 1.12) that where she was, I was also. As soon as she took heed, she saw me standing beside her on the same measuring rule. And why was this – if not because *your ears hearkened to her heart* (Ps. 10.17), Good and Almighty One, who care for each of us as if you had no other to care for, and all of us as you care for each alone?

3.11.20 And how too was it that when she had related to me the vision as it happened, and I endeavoured to twist it to mean rather that she should not despair of being where I was, she immediately and without any hesitation said, 'No, I was not told: "Where he is, you shall be also," but: "Where you are, he shall be also."'

To you, O Lord, I confess my recollection; I have often acknowledged my whole memory of this matter. My mother with her watchful mind was unperturbed by my false if plausible interpretation of your prophetic oracle, and saw quickly what was to be seen – which I, for my part, had not seen before she spoke. I was, I confess, more disturbed by that prophetic utterance than by the dream itself, with its prediction of future joy long before it happened, as a comfort for a pious lady in her present distress. For some nine years followed, in which I wallowed in *the mire of the abyss* (Ps. 69.2 [Ps. 68.3]) and darkness of falsehood, often attempting to rise up only to be struck down deeper than before. Meanwhile, for her part, my mother, that chaste, pious and sober widow, such as you love, did not cease to weep for me to you at all her hours of prayer. She was now all the more insistent because of the hope she had, but no slower in her tears and groaning; and *her prayers came before your face* (Ps. 88.1 [Ps. 87.3]), but you allowed me to roll and wallow in that darkness yet.

3.12.21 Meanwhile, you gave one more prophetic utterance that

I recall here (for I pass over much, in my haste to reach the things that urged me most to confess you, and many things I cannot remember). This second oracle, then, you gave through a priest of yours, a bishop brought up in the Church and trained on your Scriptures. When my mother asked him if he would deign to speak to me, refute my errors, unteach me the bad I had learnt and teach me the good – as he would do this to all such as he found suitable – he refused, and wisely, as I later realized. His response was that I was as yet unteachable, as I was puffed up with the novelty of this heresy, and, as she had told him, I had upset many simple folk with a handful of quibbles. 'But,' he said, 'let him be where he is. Just pray the Lord for him; he will find out for himself from his reading the nature of his mistake and the extent of his impiety.' Thereupon he also told her that, as a small boy, he too had been given over to the Manichees by his mother, who had been seduced by them, and had not only read all their literature (or near enough), but had even copied it out; and it had become clear to him, with none to oppose him in debate or to refute him, how far that sect was to be shunned; and therefore he had shunned them. When he had told her this, and she would not agree, but was all the more insistent, weeping copiously and beseeching him to see me and debate with me, he grew weary and a trifle irritated. 'Leave me alone,' he said. 'As you live, it is impossible that the son of these tears should perish.' In her conversations with me, she would often recall how she had welcomed these words as if they had been spoken from heaven.

BOOK FOUR

4.1.1 Throughout that period of nine years, from the age of eighteen to the age of twenty-seven, I was seduced, and seduced others; I was misled, and misled others, through all manner of desires: both openly, through my teaching of the so-called 'liberal arts', and in secret, through what was falsely called 'religion'. Ambition me drove into the one, superstition into the other, and vanity into both. Down one path I pursued the vanity that is popular acclaim; eager for the applause of the theatre, the prizes for poetry, the contests for crowns of grass, the empty show of the public pageants, the intemperance of my lusts. Down the other I sought to be cleansed from those stains, by bringing food to those so-called 'Saints' and 'Elect', so that they could fashion for me in the workshop of their bowels angels and gods, who would set me free. These were the things I pursued; this is what I did, I and those friends of mine who were deceived through me and with me. Let the proud laugh at me, those whom you have not yet humbled and laid low for their salvation; I will confess to you my backslidings *to your praise*. Allow and grant me, I pray, to retrace with present memory the circuitous ways I wandered in the past, and to *offer unto you the sacrifice of rejoicing* (Ps. 27.7 [Ps. 26.6]). For without you what am I to myself except my own guide over the precipice? And what am I now that it is well with me, if not a child sucking on your milk, gaining strength from you, the *food that perishes not* (Jn 6.27)? And what is a man, any man, being as he is a man? But let the strong and mighty laugh at me; weak and helpless as I am, I shall confess to you.

4.2.2 Throughout those years I taught rhetoric; conquered by my own cupidity, I sold the all-conquering art of loquacity. But *you know, O Lord* (Tobit 8.9, Jn 21.15–16), that I preferred to have good students (good, as they are called), and in all honesty I taught them trickery – not so that they could employ these tricks to have an innocent man condemned, but so that, when the occasion required, they could act on behalf of a guilty man. And you, O God, saw from afar the good faith I showed in teaching duties towards those *lovers of vanity and seekers after falsehood* (Ps. 4.2 [Ps. 4.3]), being myself one of them; you saw how it was sliding on the slippery path, and guttering out amid much smoke. Throughout those years I had one woman; not joined to her by the bond that is called lawful wedlock, but hunted out by my roving ardour, bereft of wisdom. Nevertheless, I had but one woman, and was faithful to her bed. Surely this was so I could learn from my own example how different are the bounds of wedlock, entered into by due consent of the parties, from the bargain struck by two lovers out of lust. The former compact is made for the sake of procreation, whereas in the latter it is against the wishes of the couple that children are born; though once born, they make themselves loved.

4.2.3 I recall, too, that on one occasion, when I had decided to enter a poetry competition, to be staged in the theatre, some soothsayer sent word to me, asking me what reward I was willing to give him to make me win. I replied that I utterly abjured and abominated such loathsome offerings; not if the crown were one of imperishable gold would I allow even a fly to be killed to procure my victory. He was prepared to kill living things in his sacrificial rites, and, it seemed to me, to canvass demons through these acts of worship to support my entry. But it was not from respect for your purity, *O God of my heart* (Ps. 73.26 [Ps. 72.26]), that I repudiated this evil deed. I did not know how to love you, knowing no better than to think of you as something radiant indeed – but physical.[1] For was not my soul *unfaithful to you* (Ps. 73.27 [Ps. 72.27]), *trusting in lies and feeding the winds*,[2] in sighing over such fictitious inventions? But I was unwilling to sacrifice to demons on my own behalf, when all the time I was sacrificing myself to them through that superstitious nonsense! For what does it mean 'to feed the winds', if not to feed the

1 'something radiant indeed ... but physical'. The Manichee ascription of divinity to the heavenly bodies.
2 '*trusting in lies and feeding the winds*'. A combination of Prov. 10.4 (as found in the Vulgate translation) and Hosea 12.1.

demons, that is, to be their delight and laughing stock through one's wandering steps?

4.3.4 For this same reason I did not altogether give up consulting those charlatans who are known as 'astrologers' – namely, that they offered no sacrifice, nor did they direct their prayers to any spirit for the purposes of divination. This, however, is held repellent and damnable by true, Christian piety. For *it is good to confess you, O Lord* (Ps. 92.1 [Ps. 91.2]), and to say, *have mercy upon me; heal my soul, for I have sinned against you* (Ps. 41.4 [Ps. 40.5]), not to abuse your indulgence as a licence to sin, but to remember the words of the Lord: *Behold, you are made whole; now do not sin, lest something worse befall you* (Jn 5.14). It is this state of complete well-being that the astrologers endeavour to destroy, when they say: 'The cause of your sin comes from heaven; it is inevitable,' and: 'It was Venus (or Saturn, or Mars) who did this.' Their aim is to exculpate man, *flesh and blood* (Matt. 16.17, 1Cor. 15.50), that proud putrefaction, and to blame him who created and ordained the sky and the stars. And who is that but you, our God, Sweetness and Fount of Justice, who will *repay each man according to his works* (Ps. 62.12 [Ps. 61.13], Matt. 16.27, Rom. 2.6), and *do not despise a heart crushed and laid low* (Ps. 51.17 [Ps. 50.19])?

4.3.5 There was at that time a knowing man, most learned and indeed renowned in the art of medicine, who had with his own hand set the crown of victory in the aforementioned poetry contest on my sick head – not as physician, but as Proconsul. It was you, who *resist the proud, and give grace to the humble* (James 4.6, 1Pet. 5.5), who were the healer of that illness. But, even by means of that old man, did you ever abandon me, or cease to tend my soul? I became one of his more intimate companions, and would listen to him talk with unflagging attention; for without rhetorical artifice, his words were attractive and worth hearing for the pungency with which he expressed his views. When he learnt from our conversations that I was devoted to the literature of horoscopology, he gave me some kind and fatherly advice: to cast it aside, and not squander the effort and attention required for profitable affairs on such vain pursuits. He had himself, he said, studied them to the point where, at an early stage in life, he had been prepared to enter it as his profession and livelihood; if he had understood Hippocrates, he thought he could easily understand the literature of astrology too. But later on, he told me, he had abandoned astrology and taken up medicine, for the sole reason that he had discovered his astrological texts to be wholly fallacious, and, being a respectable man, had no wish to get his living by deceiving others. 'You', he said, 'have your rhetoric; you can keep yourself alive with that. As for that misguided astrological stuff, you pursue it in your spare time; your family fortunes don't depend on it. All the more reason why you should believe what I say about it, seeing as I took such pains to learn it properly, and was ready to live by it alone.' When I asked him how, if this were so, it often happened that the predictions of the astrologers came true, he gave what reply he could. This, according to him, was the result of a capacity for sortilege which permeated the whole universe. Suppose, he said, a man consults the work of a poet, any poet. The poem may deal with some subject far removed from his situation; but often, as he consults it, a line leaps off the page that corresponds miraculously to it. It was, he insisted, no miracle, if, as a result of some kind of higher instinct unconscious of what is happening within itself, the human spirit produces some kind of resonance which chimes in with the circumstances and activities of the enquirer; not as the result of any skill on his part, but of sortilege.

4.3.6 So it was that, by or through means of this man, you tended me at a distance, and sketched out in my memory the questions I would later ask for myself. But at that time, I could not be persuaded, either by him or by my dear friend Nebridius, still a very young man, but very good and very sceptical, who laughed at the whole business of divination, to cast my astrological pursuits aside. I was more influenced by the authority of the writers themselves; and as yet had no such certain proof as I sought, that would make it clear beyond doubt that when these astrologers, in answer to a consultation, predict something that comes true, it is the result of chance or coincidence, not of their skill in scanning the stars.

4.4.7 It was during those years, when I had first begun to teach in my home town, that I made a friendship. My friend shared in my studies, and was very dear to me; we were contemporaries, both blooming in the flower of youth. He had grown up with me as a boy; we had been to school together, and played together. But at that time he was not such a friend of mine – although not even at the time I am speaking of was he a friend in the true sense, for it is only true friendship when you glue together those who cleave to you by *diffusing your love in our hearts through the Holy Spirit* (Rom. 5.5), which you have given us. Nevertheless, it was indeed a sweet friendship, fired in the heat of our shared studies. While he was still a schoolboy, I had turned him away from the true faith, which by reason of his years he did not cling to truly or with any depth, and towards the superstitious and pernicious tales which made my mother weep for me. Now, as a man, he strayed in spirit with me, and my soul could not be without him. And behold, you stood over the backs of these fugitives from you, *O God of vengeance* (Ps. 94.1 [Ps. 93.1]) and fount of mercy alike, who *turn us again to you* (Ps. 51.15 [Ps. 50.15]) in wondrous ways; and behold, when he had reached manhood you took him from this life, when he had been my friend for barely a year – a friendship sweeter to me than all the sweetnesses of my life, as it then was.

4.3.8 Who can alone *tell all your praises* (Ps. 106.2 [Ps. 105.2]), all the works of yours that he has known in himself alone? What did you then do for me, my God, and how unsearchable are the *depths of your judgements* (Ps. 36.6 [Ps. 35.7]; cf Rom. 11.13)? My friend fell ill with a fever, and for a long time lay unconscious in a mortal sweating fit. When those around him had abandoned hope of his recovery, he was baptized without his knowing. I was indifferent to this, confident that his soul would retain what he had learnt from me, not what was done to his body without his knowing. But the truth was far different. My friend rallied and recovered, and as soon as I could talk to him – and that was not long, no longer than it took for him to be able to talk to me, since I would not leave his side, and we were inseparable from one another – I tried to tease him about it, thinking that he would join with me in laughing at a baptism he had received while wholly unconscious and insensible. He, however, had learnt beforehand of the baptism he had received, and shrank from me as if from an enemy. In a remarkable and sudden burst of plain speaking he warned me that if I wanted to be his friend, I would have to stop talking to him like that. For my part, I was astonished and upset at this, and put all my own feelings on one side until he had recovered and had regained the full vigour of health; then, I thought, I would be able to deal with him as I wished. But he was rescued from my madness, so that in you he might be reserved for my consolation; a few days later, when I was away, the fever struck again, and he died.

4.4.9 *What pain darkened my heart!* (Lam. 5.17). All that I saw was death. My home town was a torment to me, my home strangely cursed; all the things I had shared with him were, without him, transformed into grievous tortures. My eyes looked expectantly for him everywhere, but he was denied to their sight. I hated everything, because it did not contain him; nor could anything now say to me, 'Look, he is coming,' as they could when he had been absent during his life. I became the object of my own investigation, and asked my soul repeatedly *why it was sorrowful, and why did it trouble me so deeply*; and it did not know what to say in return. And if I said, *Hope in God* (Ps. 42.5, 11, Ps. 43.5 [Ps. 41.6, 12, Ps. 42.5]), it would not obey, and rightly; for the friend I had lost was, though a man, a thing more real and better than the illusion in which I bade my soul trust. Weeping alone was sweet to me, and took the place of my friend among the pleasures of my mind.

4.5.10 Now, O Lord, all this has passed; the pain of my wound has been assuaged with time. Can I now listen to you, the Truth (Jn 14.6), and place my heart's ear by your lips, so you can tell me why weeping is sweet to the wretched? Is it because, although you are everywhere present, you have put away our wretchedness from you, and *remain in yourself* (Wisdom 7.27), while we wallow in our own experiences? But if it were not to your ears that we cried out, we would have no hope left at all. Why is it, then, that from the bitterness of life we pluck this sweet fruit of groaning and weeping, of sighs and lamentation? Is it sweet inasmuch as we hope that you will hearken to us? In the case of prayers this is indeed so, because prayers long to reach their destination. But what when we mourn and grieve for something lost, as I was wrapped in grief at that time? I did not hope to see him come back to life, nor when I wept did I pray that he might do so; I only mourned and wept. I was wretched; I had lost my source of gladness. Or is weeping too a bitter thing, whose pleasure lies in the loathing we feel for things we enjoyed previously, and now abhor?

4.6.11 But why do I say all this? It is not now time for questions, but time to confess to you. I was wretched; my whole mind was wretched, bound by its friendship with things mortal, and torn in pieces when it lost them. It was then that I felt the wretchedness which had afflicted me even before I lost them. Such I was at that time; I kept weeping bitterly, and in bitterness I lay down to rest. I was wretched — but I still loved my wretched life more than I had loved my friend. However much I wished to change my life, I would not have preferred to lose it rather than to lose my friend. I am not even sure that I would have been willing to die in his stead, like Orestes and Pylades in the story (if it is any more than a story), who, it is said, were prepared to die for each other or to die together, since it would have been worse for them if both were not alive together. In me there arose completely the opposite feeling; I was oppressed with both a weariness of life and a dread of death. I think that the more I loved my friend, the more I hated and feared death as my most implacable enemy, supposing that if it could devour him, it might suddenly swallow up all mankind. Such, I remember, was my condition throughout. Look on my heart, O God, look within. See me as I remember; you, *my Hope* (Ps. 71.4 [Ps. 70.5]), who cleanse me from the taint of such feelings, who direct my eyes towards yourself, who *draw my feet out of the snare* (Ps. 25.14 [Ps. 24.15]). I was astonished that other mortals lived, since he, whom I had loved as if he were immortal, was dead, and even more astonished that though he was dead, I, his other self, lived. He spoke rightly who said that his friend was 'half his soul'.[3] I felt that my soul and my friend's were one soul in two bodies, and life filled me with horror, as I had no wish to live on, a mere half of myself. Perhaps, too, I dreaded death for this same reason, fearing that he whom I had loved so much would die utterly.

4.7.12 What madness it is that men do not know how to love their fellow-men as men! What a fool is man, indulging in excessive grief over the lot of mankind! This is what I then was. Thus I was borne to and fro on the tide of my feelings, sighing, weeping, grieving, knowing no rest, taking no counsel. I hauled around a soul cut in two and bloody, weary of my hauling, and I found no place to lay it down. Nowhere would it rest; not in the greenness of the woods, not among the music of the theatre, not amid the sweet scents of nature, not in the sumptuousness of the banqueting hall, not the pleasures of bedroom and bed, not even in books and poetry. All these things filled me with horror; the very light of day, anything that was not the same as him, battered me relentlessly, and was loathsome to me beyond the reach of tears and groans. In these alone did I find what little rest I did. But as soon as my soul was taken away from these solaces, it weighed me down with a huge burden of misery. I knew that its relief and cure lay with you, O Lord, but I had neither the will nor the strength, all the more so since, when I thought of you, you were nothing solid and reliable to me. For it was not you, but an empty illusion; and my misapprehension was my god. If I tried to lay down my burden with that god, it would slip through the void and fall back on me, and I remained to myself a barren land, in which I could not exist and from which I could not retire. For where could I flee from my heart? Where could I flee from myself? Where would I not follow myself? But nevertheless, I fled from my home town. My eyes sought my friend less where they were not used to see him; and from the town of Thagaste I came to Carthage.

4.8.13 Time is not empty, nor does it wash over our senses without effect; it works wonders on the mind. From day to day it

3 '"half his soul"'. Horace, *Odes*. 1.3.8. The friend in question was Virgil.

came and went, and coming and going engrafted other hopes and other memories within me. Little by little it restored me to my former kinds of pleasure, and my grief gave way before them. But in its place came not fresh griefs, but the seeds of them. For why had my former grief been able to pierce me so easily and so deeply, if not because I had, as the saying goes, 'spilt my soul on the sand' by loving a mortal as if he were immortal? What refreshed and renewed me most of all was the solace I derived from other friends, who shared my love for the thing I loved instead of you – that great myth, that long lie which entered my mind as it itched to be tickled through my ears, and rubbed it as an adulteress strokes her lover. That myth of mine did not die if one of my friends did, and in my friends I found other pleasures, which captivated my mind even more: shared talk, shared laughter, mutual acts of kindness, the shared reading of good literature, of moments of levity and seriousness; occasional disagreements that were without ill-feeling, as a man can disagree with himself, which gave a relish to our more usual concord; teaching and learning from each other, longing impatiently for each other when absent, welcoming our absent friends with joy when they returned. These and other such tokens, which proceed from the hearts of those who love each other and express themselves in the face, the speech, the eyes, and a thousand gestures of goodwill, are, so to speak, the kindling of the fire which melds minds together, making one out of many.

4.9.14 This is what we cherish in our friends, to the extent that a man's conscience feels guilty, if he does not love one who loves him in return, or love in return one who loves him, seeking nothing from his lover's body except these tokens of goodwill. This is the source of our grief if someone dies; this is why we are darkened with sorrow, why sweetness is turned to bitterness, why the heart streams with tears. It is the dead who have lost their life, but the living experience death. *Blessed is he who loves you* (Tobit 13.18), who loves his friend in you and his enemy for your sake. Only he to whom all are dear in Him who cannot be lost, can lose no one that he loves. And who is that but our God, *the God who made heaven and earth* (Gen. 1.1, Ps. 146.5–6

[Ps. 145.5–6]) and who fills them, since *by filling them he made them* (Jer. 23.24)? None can lose you, unless he so chooses; and if he so chooses, *where will he go or flee* (Ps. 139. 7 [Ps. 138.7]) but from your tranquillity to your anger? Where will he not find your Law to punish him? For *your law is truth* (Ps. 119.142 [Ps. 118.142]), and the Truth is you (cf Jn 14.6).

4.10.15   *O God of hosts, turn us around and show us your face, and we shall be saved* (Ps. 80.7 [Ps. 79.8]). For in whichever direction the soul of man turns, unless it turns to you, it is transfixed on things that cause pain − even if it is fixed on things that are beautiful but outside you and outside itself. But even these things would be nothing were they not from you. They are born and die. At birth they begin (so to speak) to be; they grow towards full stature, and having reached full stature they grow old and perish.[4] Not all grow old, but all die. When they are born and begin their journey towards being, the more swiftly they grow into being, the more they hasten into unbeing. Such is their allotted limit. This is the space you have given them, for they are the parts of things that do not all exist at the same time, but in passing away and succeeding to each other they all go to make the whole of which they are the parts. It is in just such a way that human language is made up of audible signs. It would not be a whole language if a word did not pass away when its constituent parts had been made audible, so that another could take its place. *Let my soul praise you* (Ps. 146.1 [Ps. 145.2]) by means of these transient things, *O God, Creator of all things*,[5] but let it not become fixed and glued on to them with its love of physical senses. They go where they were going, into unbeing, and rend the soul with perilous longings, for she wishes to be, and loves to rest in the things she loves. In them, however, there is no resting place, for they are impermanent. They fly away, and who can follow them by means of his physical perception? Or who can hold on to them, even when they are at hand? Our

4 '... having reached full stature they grow old and perish'. Based on Sallust's description of the human lot, *Jugurthine War* 2.3
5 '*O God, Creator of all things*'. 2Macchabees 1.24, cf Ambrose of Milan, *Hymns* 1.2.1 (a translation is given at 9.12.32).

physical perception is slow, being physical; it is its own limit. It is sufficient for the task for which it was made, but it is not sufficient for the task of holding on to the things that pass it by as they hasten from their due beginning to their due end. For in your Word, through whom they are created, they hear the words: 'This shall be your beginning, and this your end' (cf Job 38.11).

4.11.16 Do not be vain, my soul, and do not let the ears of your heart be deafened by the tumult of your vanity. You too must listen: it is the Word himself that summons you to return. With him is the place of rest untroubled, where love is not abandoned, if it does not itself abandon him. Those transitory things pass on, so that others may take their place, and so that the parts of this lower universe should together constitute a whole. 'But will I pass on and go to some other place?' asks the Word of God. Fix in him your dwelling place; entrust to him all that you have from him, O my soul, weary as you are of things that prove false. Entrust to the Truth all that you have from the Truth, and you shall lose nothing. The parts of you that are withered shall bloom again, and *all your illnesses shall be healed* (Matt. 2.23). The parts of you that hang limp will be restored to their proper form, made new, and bound up against you. They will not take you down to the place to which they tend, but will stand fast with you, and abide *the God that stands fast and abides for ever* (Ps. 102.12, 26 [Ps. 101.13, 27], Hebr. 1.11, 1Pet. 1.23).

4.11.17 Why do you perversely follow your flesh? Turn back, and let your flesh follow you. Whatever you perceive through her, you perceive in part (cf 1Cor. 13.9). You do not know the whole, of which these are the parts; nevertheless, the parts give you pleasure. But if your fleshly sense were capable of comprehending the whole, and had not, being itself a part of the whole, been confined within its right and proper limit – that being a punishment proportionate to your crime – you would wish all that exists in the present to pass away, so that you could derive still more pleasure from the totality of things. The very words we speak you hear by means of the same carnal sense, and you do not wish the syllables to stand still but to pass away swiftly, so that others may come and you may hear the whole. Likewise all the constituent parts that make up one thing (even though they do not all simultaneously constitute it) give more pleasure as a totality than they do individually, if it is possible to perceive them as a totality. But he who made them is better by far than them all, and *it is he that is our God* (Ps. 100.3 [Ps. 99.3]), who does not pass away, nor does anything take his place.

4.12.18 If you take pleasure in corporeal objects, use them to praise God, and turn your love back towards their Artificer, so that you do not, in the things that give you pleasure, incur his displeasure. If you take pleasure in souls, love them in God, for they too suffer change, and stand fast only when fixed in him; otherwise, they pass on and perish. Love them in him, therefore, and take such as you can to him without delay. Tell them: 'This is he whom we should love; it is he that has made all these things, and *he is not far off* (Acts 17.27). For he did not make them and depart; they are from him and in him. And where is he? Where you taste truth. He is within the depths of the heart, but the heart has strayed from him. *Return, sinners, to your heart* (Is. 46.8), and cleave to him who made you. Stand with him, and you will stand fast. Rest in him and you will be rested. Why do you go off on to the rough paths? Where will you go? The good that you love is from him, but it is good and pleasing only so far as it is considered in relation to him. But if you abandon him, the love you direct towards anything that is from him will be unrighteous, and the object of your love will righteously be bitter to the taste. Why do you still persist in *walking the toilsome and laborious ways* (Wisdom 5.7)? There is no rest where you seek it. Seek what you seek, but it is not where you seek it. You seek a life of blessedness in *the land of death* (Is. 9.2, Matt. 4.16); it is not there. How can there be a blessed life in a place where there is not even life itself?

4.12.19 'This Life of ours descended here,[6] and took our death upon him and slew it with the abundance of his life. With a

6 ' "This Life of ours descended here" '. A conflation of Jn 14.6 ('I am the Way, the Truth, and the Life') with Jn 6.33 ('The bread of God is that which comes down from Heaven'), 6.41 ('I am the bread which came down from Heaven').

voice like thunder he called on us to return from here to him, into that hidden place from which he came forth to us, into the original virgin's womb, where our human and created nature was wedded to him, and mortal flesh was joined to him, lest it should remain for ever mortal. From thence he *came forth like a bridegroom from his wedding chamber, and exulted like a giant to run his course* (Ps. 19.5 [Ps. 18.6]). He did not tarry, but ran forth calling on us – with his words, his deeds, his life, his death, his descent, his ascension – that we should return to him. He *departed from our sight* (Lk 24.51, Acts 1.9), so that we would "return to our heart" and find him. He took himself off, and behold, he is here. He would not be with us long (cf Jn 16.16), yet he has not deserted us. For the place to which he took himself off is the one from which he never departed, since *the world was made by him, and he was in the world* (Jn 1.10), and *he came into this world to save sinners* (1Tim. 1.15). Him it is my soul confesses, and he *heals my soul, for it has sinned against him* (Ps. 41.4 [Ps. 40.5]). *Children of men, how long will you be heavy of heart?* (Ps. 4.2 [Ps. 4.3]). Our Life has descended to us; do you refuse to rise up and live? But where can you rise up, seeing as you are *exalted on high, and have set your face in heaven* (Ps. 73.9 [Ps. 72.9]). Come down, so that you may rise up, and rise up to God; for in rising up against God you have fallen.' Tell this to the souls you love, that they may weep in *the valley of weeping* (Ps. 84. 6 [Ps. 83.7]), and with these words take those souls with you swiftly to God, for it is by his Spirit that you tell them this, if you speak to them blazing with the fire of love.

4.13.20 I did not know this then. I was in love with lesser beauties, and heading for the abyss, as I told my friends: 'What is it that we love except what is beautiful? What, then, is "beautiful"? And what is beauty? What is there in the things we love that charms and attracts us? They could not draw us to themselves unless there were some internal harmony and beauty of form about them.' I looked around and saw that within physical objects there is one sort of beauty that comes, so to speak, from the totality, and another which gives a sense of harmony through the congruence with which it fits in with another object, as part of a body fits in with the whole, or as a shoe fits a foot, and so forth. This thought welled up in the depths of my heart and filled my mind, and I wrote a work called *Beauty and Congruence*. I think it was two or three books long; *you know, O God* (Ps. 69.5 [Ps. 68.6]), but it escapes me, for I do not have a copy. It has wandered off from me somehow or other.

4.14.21 But what induced me to dedicate those books of mine to Hierius, the City Orator at Rome? I did not know him by sight, but was in love with him on account of the great reputation for learning that he possessed. I had, moreover, heard a few words of his quoted, and liked what I heard. More importantly, I liked him because other people liked him. They were astonished that a man from Syria, whose first training was in 'Greekish eloquence',[7] had later become a remarkably fine speaker in the Latin tradition too, and they heaped praise upon him. Moreover, they said, he was wholly cognizant of matters pertaining to the study of philosophy, the 'pursuit of wisdom'. This man inspired praise and love even in his absence. Did that love come from the mouths of those who praised him, and enter the hearts of their hearers?[8] Far be it; but one lover is aroused to love by another. Thus it is that he who inspires praise inspires love, so long as it is taken on trust that his praiser spreads his fame in all sincerity of heart; that is, so long as it is a lover who praises him.

4.14.22 Such was the way in which at that time I loved my fellow-men; according to the standards of other men, and not, my God, according to your standard, by which no one is deceived. Why, however, did I not admire Hierius in the way that the populace admires a famous charioteer or well-known

7 ' "Greekish eloquence" '. A derogatory phrase taken from Sallust's *Jugurthine War*, 63.3, illustrating the traditional Roman attitude towards Greek rhetoric.
8 '... from the mouths ... of their hearers'. Cf Matt. 15. 17–18, Mk 7.18–19. Augustine is picking up on Jesus's words that what goes into a man's mouth does not enter his heart, but what comes out of his mouth comes from his heart. In Augustine's version, what comes out of one man's mouth does not enter another man's heart, but it does carry credibility if it truly comes from the speaker's heart.

beast-fighter, but in a way far different and much deeper – the way that *I* wanted to be admired? Not that I had any wish to inspire the sort of praise and love that actors inspire, even though I myself joined in this praise and love; I would rather choose to remain unknown than to enjoy that sort of fame, or even to be hated rather than loved in that way. How are the weights of our various and several loves distributed within a single soul? How is it that there was something in another man that I loved – but had I not hated it in equal measure, I would not have abjured and kept at a distance from myself, even though we were both human? It was not like the way that one may love a good horse even though one has no wish to be a horse oneself, this is something which can be said also of an actor, who shares our human nature. Did I, then, love in a man what I would have hated to be myself, though I too am a man? Man is himself a great mystery. The *hairs of his head are numbered* (Matt. 10.30) to you, and none of them is lost in you; but his hairs are more easily numbered than his feelings, and the emotions of his heart.

4.14.23 The great orator Hierius, however, belonged to the class of men that I loved to the point where I wished to be such as he was. Puffed up with pride, I went astray and was *borne around by every wind* (Eph. 4.14), but in your hidden depths you steered my course. How is it that I know and confess with confidence to you that I fell in love with Hierius more on account of the love his admirers accorded him than on account of the things for which they admired him? For if, instead of praising him they had criticized him, and in this spirit of criticism and contempt they had told me of his accomplishments, then even though both they and his accomplishments were the same, I would not have been inflamed with love or aroused with admiration for him. To be sure, neither his accomplishments nor the man himself would be different; only the attitude of my informants would be different. Such is the way the soul lies sick and indecisive, not yet holding fast to the wholeness of truth. The opinions of men are like winds, coming from their hearts through their tongues, and as they blow, our souls are carried away, twisting and turning, now in one direction, now in the other. The light of day is blocked out from them by clouds, and they cannot discern the truth; and behold, it is before us. It mattered much to me that my words and thoughts should become known to Hierius. If he found them good, I would be all the more ardent in my enthusiasm; if not, my heart would be wounded, vain as it was and empty of your wholeness. But even so, I was no less pleased to turn over in my mind my treatise *Beauty and Congruence*, on which matters I had despatched my thoughts to him, and to read it through in my mind's eye. I admired it, even in the absence of any fellow-admirer.

4.15.24 What I did not yet see was that this great question turned upon your craftsmanship, O Almighty, who *alone work wonders* (Ps. 72.18 [Ps. 71.18], Ps. 136.4 [Ps. 135.4]). My mind was proceeding by means of corporeal forms; I defined the beautiful as being that which is harmonious in itself, and the congruent as being that which is harmonious through the way it fits in with some other object. Thus I distinguished between these terms, illustrating my distinction with a whole heap of examples drawn from the corporeal world. I then turned my attention to the nature of the mind, but the false opinion that I held about spiritual matters did not permit me to see the truth. The force of the truth was battering my eyes, but I turned my trembling mind away from an entity that was incorporeal towards the outward features, towards colours and bloated magnitudes, and, not seeing them in the mind, I thought I could not see the mind. Since I loved peace as being in the class of virtue, and hated discord as being in the class of vice, I set down unity as being in the former class and disunity as being in the latter. And within the class of unity, it seemed to me that a rational mind was the origin of truth and of the highest good, while in the class of disunity I was so wretched as to think that the irrational mind possessed a kind of substance, that was the origin of the highest evil. This thing was not merely a substance, but was a living thing, and yet did not come from you, my God, *from whom are all things* (Rom. 11.36, 1Cor. 8.6). Unity I called 'the Monad', it being, so to speak, a mind with no division of gender; disunity

I called 'the Dyad', being anger that leads to crimes, lust that leads to sins. I babbled away in ignorance, not as yet having known or learnt that evil is no substance, and that our mind is not the supreme and immutable Good.

4.15.25 For just as crimes occur if the mind's driving emotion is vitiated, and it sets itself up to disturb the usual order, and just as sins occur if the soul's disposition to derive carnal pleasures exceeds its due limits, so also a living thing is polluted by errors and false opinions, if its rational mind is itself vitiated. Such was my mind at that time. I did not know that in order to participate in the truth, the mind must be enlightened by another light, since it is not itself the nature of truth; for *it is you, Lord, who light my lantern, and you, my God, who lighten my darkness* (Ps. 18.28 [Ps. 17.29]), and *of your fulness have we all received* (Jn 1.16). For *you are the true Light, that lightens every man that comes into this world* (Jn 1.9), for in you *there is no changing, nor are you cast into shadow by your motion* (James 1.17).

4.15.26 Thus I endeavoured to reach you and *you drove me from you* (Ps. 43.2 [Ps. 42.2]) to *taste death* (Matt. 16.28, Mk 8.39), for you *resist the proud* (James 4.6, 1Pet. 5.5); and who could be more proud than I was, in falling into the strange madness of asserting that I was by nature the same as you are? For although I was mutable, and this was clear to me from the fact that I wished to be wise, so as to change from a worse to a better condition, I nevertheless preferred to hold that you were mutable rather than that I was not what you are. Therefore I was driven back, and you resisted me, stiff-necked and inconstant as I was. I deluded myself with thoughts of corporeal forms; I blamed the flesh, being myself flesh. And being *a breath that goes its way* (Ps. 78.40 [Ps. 77.39]) I did not yet return to you, but in going my way I went after things that are not – things that are neither in you nor in me, nor in any physical thing. It was not your Truth that created them for me, but my vanity that fashioned them out of what is physical. I would say to the little ones, your faithful people, my fellow-citizens, though I was exiled from them and knew it not – I would parrot away with my impertinent questions: 'Why does the soul err, if God made it?' But

I would not say to myself, 'Why does God err?' I preferred to contend that your immutable substance was compelled to err than to confess that my mutable substance had gone astray of its own free will, and that its errors were its punishment.

4.15.27 I was some twenty-six or twenty-seven years old when I wrote those volumes, turning over in my mind those fictitious physical objects whose noise deafened the ears of my heart, as I stretched them out to hear your inner melody, sweet Truth. I pondered on beauty and congruence, longing to stand firm, to listen to you and to *rejoice and be glad because I heard the bridegroom's voice* (Jn 3.29), and I could not, because the voices of my own error took me towards outer things, and the weight of my pride caused me to fall towards the lowest things. You did not *make me hear of joy and gladness*, nor did my *bones rejoice*, for they had not been *laid low* (Ps. 51.8 [Ps. 50.10]).

4.16.28 And what good did it do me that when I was some twenty years old, one of Aristotle's works came into my hands, namely the *Ten Categories* – a name that caused the Professor of Rhetoric at Carthage, my teacher, along with the other so-called intellectuals, to puff out his cheeks with pride whenever he mentioned the work, and when he did so, I was filled with suspense and anticipation; this book, I felt, would be something great, something divinely inspired. But what good did it do me that I read and understood this work all by myself? I have discussed it with men who say they could scarcely understand it even though they had the most erudite teachers not merely talking it through with them but also drawing copious diagrams in the dust; and they have been able to tell me nothing but what I understood by myself from my own reading of it. The *Categories* seemed to me to speak quite plainly about 'substances', such as a man, and the things in them, such as a man's shape: 'quality'[9] and 'size'[10] (how many feet tall he is); 'relationship' (whose brother he is); 'whereness and whenness' (where he is in place, and when he was born); 'position' (whether he is standing or

9 '"quality"'. The usual technical term is 'predicates'.
10 '"size"'. The usual technical term is 'quantity'.

sitting); 'habit' (whether he is wearing shoes, or armour); and 'activity and passivity' (whether he is doing anything or having anything done to him). All the things that fall into these nine categories, a few of which I have listed by way of example, may be found in countless number in the category of 'substance' alone.

4.16.29 What good did all this do me? Rather, it did me harm; for, thinking that whatever existed could be completely contained within these ten categories of predicate, I attempted to understand you in the same way, my God, wondrously simple and immutable as you are. I supposed that you too were subject to your magnitude or beauty (they being in you and you being, so to speak, the subject, like a physical body) – when in fact you are your own magnitude and beauty, and a body is not large or beautiful because it is a body, since even if it were less large and less beautiful, it would still be nevertheless a body. It was a falsehood that I believed about you, not the truth; mere fictions fashioned from my wretchedness, not the sure support that comes from your blessedness. For you had ordered that *the earth should bring forth thorns and thistles for me, and with toil I should get my bread* (Gen. 3.18–19), and so it came true in me.

4.16.30 And what good did it do me that I read by myself all the books on the so-called liberal arts, and understood all that I read – when I was myself the *unprofitable servant* (Matt. 18.32, 25.26, Lk 19.22) of my evil desires? I rejoiced in these books, not knowing from whence came all that was true and certain in them. For I had turned my back on the light, and my face to the things that it enlightened, and hence my face, as I beheld the things that were enlightened, was not enlightened. Whatever I learnt without great difficulty and with no human teacher, whether it was on the art of speaking and rhetoric, on the measurement of figures, on music and numbers – all these things *you know, O Lord my God* (Tobit 3.16, Ps. 69.5 [Ps. 68.6]), since both swiftness of understanding and acuteness of perception are your gifts. But I did not offer sacrifice to you from among these gifts. Therefore it was no use to me but rather to my peril that I was so eager to have such a good part of my substance in my own power, and did not *ascribe my strength for you* (Ps. 59.9 [Ps. 58.10]). Instead I *set off from you into a far country, to squander my substance* (Lk 15.13, 15.30) on pleasures that can be hired for cash. For what good did it do me to have a good thing and not make good use of it? I realized that these arts are very difficult even for the studious and talented to understand, only when I tried to expound them to them, and found that the very best of them could only follow my exposition without flagging too much.

4.16.31 But what good did all this do me, seeing as I thought that you, O Truth, Lord God, were an immense, radiant body, and I was a fragment of that body? What perversity! Such, however, I was, nor do I blush, my God, to *confess to you your mercies towards me* (Ps. 107.8, 15, 21, 31 [Ps. 106.8, 15, 21, 31]), since I did not blush at that time to profess before men my blasphemies, and to *bark like a dog at you* (Judith 11.15). What good did it do me to have quick wits, able to skip through Aristotle's teachings, to read all those books and unravel their tangled skeins of thought without the help of any human teacher, when all the while I was wandering in error with respect to the teaching of true piety, lamed and blighted by my own sacrilege? Or what harm did it do to your little ones that they were so much slower-witted, so long as they did not depart from you, but remained safe in the nest of your Church while their feathers grew and the wings of charity were fed with the food of sound faith? O Lord our God, *let us hope beneath the shadow of your wings* (Ps. 17.8, Ps. 36.7, Ps. 57.1, Ps. 61.4, Ps. 63.8 [Ps. 16.8, Ps. 35.8, Ps. 56.2, Ps. 60.5, Ps. 62.8]). Cover us under those wings, and bear us up. It is you who *will bear up the little ones, and bear them till their hairs are grey* (Is. 46.4, Ecclesiasticus 6.18); when you are our strength, we are strong indeed, and when we are our own strength, we are weak. With you lives our Good for ever, and we are perverse in that we have turned away from it. Let us return now, O Lord, lest we be ruined, for with you lives our Good without any defect. You are this Good, nor do we fear that we will have nowhere to return to, for it is from this Good that we have fallen; but not so does our home fall down while we are away, and that home is your eternity.

BOOK FIVE

5.1.1 *Accept the sacrifice* (Malachi 1.10) of my confessions from *the hand of my tongue* (Prov. 18.21), the tongue you have fashioned and stirred up to *confess your name* (Ps. 54.6 [Ps. 53.8]). *Heal all my bones,* and let them say, *'Lord, who is like unto you?'* (Ps. 6.2 [Ps. 6.3], Ps. 35. 9–10 [Ps. 34.9–10]). He that confesses to you does not inform you of what is happening within him; for a heart that is shut cannot shut out your eyes, nor can the hardness of man's heart repel your hand, for when you choose you soften it, either by pitying it or by punishing it; *there is none that can hide himself from your heat* (Ps. 19.6 [Ps. 18.7]). But *let my soul praise you* (Ps. 119.175 [118.175]), that it may love you, and *confess your mercies* (Ps. 107.8, 15, 21, 31 [Ps. 106.8, 15, 21, 31]) before you, that it may praise you. Without pause or ceasing, all your creation tells forth your praise. *Everything that has breath* (Ps. 150.6) *turns its lips to you and praises you* (Ps. 51. 15 [50.15], Tobit 3.14), and all things animate or inanimate praise you through the lips of those who contemplate them. So may our soul rouse itself from its slothfulness and rise up into you, and from leaning on the things you have made, may it pass over to you, who have made these things so wonderfully. And with you there is renewal and true strength.

5.2.2 Let the wicked depart from hence; let them *flee from you* (Ps. 68.1 [Ps. 67.2]), those restless evil-doers. You see them, and you shade them into your picture; and behold, everything in your picture is fair with them to set it off, though they themselves are foul. And what hurt could they have done you? How could they have diminished the glory of your empire, righteous and complete from the heavens to the least of your creatures? Where could they flee, when they *fled from your face* (Ps. 139.7 [Ps. 138.7])? Or where would you not find them? But flee they did, so that they should not see you as you see them; that in their blindness they might stumble against you (for you abandon nothing that you have made); and that having stumbled against

87

you in their unrighteousness, they might righteously be punished. They have withdrawn from your tenderness, stumbled against your righteousness, and fallen into your wrath. They do not know that you are everywhere; that you are circumscribed by no place; and that you alone are present even with those who forsake you. Let them turn again, therefore, and seek you; for you do not abandon your creatures as they abandon their Creator. Let them turn again, and behold, you are there in their hearts; in the hearts of those who confess you, cast themselves upon you, and weep on your bosom after the *hardships of their journey* (Wisdom 5.7). You deal gently with them, and *wipe away their tears* (Rev. 7.17, 21.4), and they weep all the more, and rejoice in their weeping; for you, O Lord, are not a man, *flesh and blood* (Matt. 16.17, 1Cor. 15.50), but you, O Lord, their Maker, make them anew and comfort them. Where indeed was I, when I sought you? You were there before me, but I had taken leave of myself, and could not find myself; much less could I find you.

5.3.3 In the presence of my God I shall unfold what happened that year when I was twenty-nine. A Manichee bishop, Faustus by name, had come to Carthage. He was a great *snare of the Devil* (1Tim. 3.7, 2Tim. 2.26), and many people were drawn to him by the charm of his voice, and so were enmeshed in that snare. I too spoke highly of his rhetorical ability; but I knew that rhetoric was not the same as truth – the truth of the matters that I was so eager to learn. I was not concerned with the language he used – that was, so to speak, only the serving dish – but with what sort of knowledge their so-called Faustus, Favourite of Heaven,[1] was serving up to me. I had heard of his reputation before I met him; he was, I was told, a brilliant scholar, outstandingly erudite in the liberal arts. Having read deeply in the philosophers, and committed much of their teaching to memory, I compared some of their doctrines to the mythologies taught by the Manichees; and the philosophers' teachings seemed to me more plausible, inasmuch as they had *prevailed to measure the universe, although they had not discovered*

1 'Favourite of Heaven'. The name Faustus suggests in Latin divine favour.

its Lord (Wisdom 13.9). For *great are you, O Lord* (Ps. 145.3 [Ps. 144.3]), *and you look kindly on the humble; but the proud you know from far off* (Ps. 138.6 [Ps. 137.6]). You *draw nigh only to those that are crushed in heart* (Ps. 34.18 [Ps. 33.19]), and the arrogant cannot find you, even if in their zeal for their art they number the stars and the sand and measure out the regions of the heavens and trace the paths of the stars.

5.3.4 For when these philosophers enquire into these things, they use their own intellect and understanding, which you have given them. With these they have made many discoveries, and predicted many things years before they happened. They have foretold eclipses of the sun and moon to the day and the hour, and how great the eclipse will be, nor have their calculations failed them – the eclipses have occurred as predicted. They have, moreover, committed to writing the intricate rules which others read to this day and use to predict the month, day, hour and extent of solar and lunar eclipses; and everything will come about as they have predicted. Men who are ignorant of these arts are amazed and awestruck at this, while those who do know them are proud and boastful. In their pride and impiety they forsake you, and cut themselves off from your light; they can foresee at what future date the light of the sun will be cut off, but they cannot likewise see that they are even now cut off from your light. They do not ask, as in good conscience they might, whence they have the intellect by which they conduct their astronomical investigations; and even if they do find you, they do not give themselves up to you, so that you may save what you have created. They do not sacrifice to you what they have made of themselves, slaughtering their overweening pride as if it were the *birds of the air*, nor their zeal for knowledge, that leads them to *walk the hidden paths of the deep*, as if it were *the fishes of the sea*, nor their lusts as if they were *the beasts of the field*.[2] If they

2 '*birds of the air ... consuming fire*'. A fusion of 1Jn 2.16 ('For all that is in the world, the lust of the flesh and the lust of the eyes, and the pride of life, is not of the Father but is of the world') with an allegorical interpretation of Ps. 8.6–8 ('Thou hast given [man] dominion over the works of thy hands ... all sheep and oxen, and also the beasts of the field; the fish of the sea ...').

did these things, then you, O God, the *consuming fire* (Deut. 4.24, Hebr. 12.29), would burn off their mortal concerns, and fashion them anew for immortality.

5.3.5 But they have not known the Way, your Word, through whom you have made the things they count, and those who count them, and the sense by which they perceive what they count, and the mind with which they count them; and *your wisdom is beyond counting* (Ps. 147.5 [Ps. 146.5]). Your only-begotten Son himself *became wisdom and righteousness and sanctification for us* (1Cor. 1.30), and *was counted among us* (Is. 53.12), and paid his taxes to Caesar. This Way they have not known – the Way by which they might descend from themselves to him, and through him rise up to him. This Way they have not known; they think they are radiant and exalted as the stars of heaven, when all the while they have fallen headlong to earth, and *their heart is darkened in its folly*. They have indeed uttered many truths about your creation; but the Truth itself, the craftsman of creation, they do not seek with proper piety, and hence do not find; or if they do find him, then *having known God they honour him not as God, nor do they give thanks to him, and in their own conceits they have dwindled away to nought. They say that they are wise, ascribing to themselves the things that are yours, and in their blindness and perversity they do not stop at ascribing to you what is theirs*, that is to say, attributing their lies to you who are the Truth, and *exchanging the glory of the incorruptible God for the likeness of a corruptible man, of birds, of four-footed beasts, and of creeping things. They turn your truth into a lie, and worship and serve the creature rather than the creator* (Rom. 1.21–5).

5.3.6 As, however, I studied the many truths that these astronomers have uttered about your creation, it seemed to me that their account added up; it was shown to be true both by mathematics and by the visible testimony of the sequence of the seasons and of the celestial bodies. When I compared their teachings to the sayings of Mani, who also wrote, with all the eloquence of madness, on the same subjects, it seemed to me that his account did not add up. There was nothing in it – nothing on solstices, equinoxes or solar or lunar eclipses – to compare with what I had learnt from the books of the *wisdom of this world* (1Cor. 1.20). I was told that I must put my trust in Mani's teaching; but so far from concurring with the accounts that were proven both by mathematics and by the evidence of the eyes, it was far removed from them.

5.4.7 Can it be true, *Lord God of truth* (Ps. 31.5 [Ps. 30.6]), that whoever possesses this mathematical and astronomical knowledge is already pleasing in your sight? Unhappy indeed is the man who has this knowledge, but does not know you; blessed is the man who knows you, even if he does not have this knowledge. But blessed indeed is he who knows you and who knows also mathematics and astronomy. He is not more blessed on their account; he is blessed on account of you alone, if *having known you he honours you as God, and gives thanks to you, and does not dwindle away to nought in his own conceits* (Rom. 1.21). A man who knows he possesses a tree, and gives thanks to you for the use he has of it, is better off, even if he does not know how high this tree is or how wide it spreads, than a man who measures it and counts all its branches, and yet neither possesses it, nor knows you or loves you, its Creator. In the same way, only a fool would doubt that a believer, even though he does not know the wheeling track of the Great Bear, yet *owns the earth in all its riches* and *though poor, yet possesses all things* (2Cor. 6.10) through his faith in you, whom *all things serve* (Ps. 119.91 [Ps. 118.91]), is better off than one who measures the heavens and numbers the stars and weighs the elements, yet ignores you, who have *appointed all things in their measure, their number, and their weight* (Wisdom 11.21).

5.5.8 But who asked this Mani to write even on mathematics and astronomy – things in which one can be quite unversed, and yet learn a proper piety? For you have said to man, *Behold, piety is wisdom* (Job 28.28). Mani might indeed have known this astronomical lore to perfection and yet been ignorant of such piety. But since he knew nothing of such matters, and yet had the audacity to teach them, it is plain that he could not have known this piety. It is but vanity to make a profession of these earthly things, even if one does know them; but it is piety to make confession to you. Mani departed from this path, in speaking so much on these matters; to the end that his opinions on them should be shown to be false by the true practitioners of these arts, and that the value of his opinion on other, more recondite matters should be plain for all to see. Not wishing to be thought a nobody, he endeavoured to persuade others that the Holy Spirit, the comforter and enricher of your faithful people, dwelt personally and with plenary authority in himself; and when the falsity of his teaching on the heavens and the stars and the movements of the sun and the moon was exposed, it became clear to all how sacrilegious his endeavours were. Not that his astronomical views were relevant to his religious teaching; but so vain was he and so greedy of glory that he strove to have these views – not merely ill-informed but false – ascribed to him as if to a person of the Deity.

5.5.9 When I hear some Christian brother expressing similarly ignorant views and believing things to be other than they are, I can look on him with patience. I know that his opinions are no hindrance to him, even if he is ignorant of the position and condition of your physical creation, so long as he believes nothing unworthy of you, *O Lord, Creator of all things*.[3] It is a hindrance to him if he supposes that this is pertinent to the sort of learning that belongs to true piety, and if he persists in venturing to assert his views on matters of which he knows nothing. Mother Charity may, however, tolerate such weakness in a believer, as long as he is in the cradle, until the *new man* rises up *in perfect manhood, and cannot be blown around by every wind of doctrine* (Eph. 4.13–14. 24). But what of Mani? To those on whom he urged his astronomical lore, he was their supreme authority, their teacher, their guide, their ruler. With such a show of audacity did he teach that his followers believed him to be no mere man, but your Holy Spirit. Who would not regard this as sheer madness, fit only for anathema and utter rejection, if his teachings were shown to be false on only one point? But

3 '*O Lord, Creator of all things*'. Based on 2Macc. 1.24, as paraphrased by Ambrose, *Hymns* 1.2.1 (a translation of which is given at 9.12.32). Augustine's friendship with Ambrose is described later in Book 5.

I had not yet discovered for certain whether it was possible to explain according to Mani's account the alternation of longer and shorter days and nights, of day and night itself, and all the things I had read in other writers; and, if they could indeed be explained thus, I was still uncertain whose explanation was correct, his or theirs. But because of the sacrosanctity accorded to him, I let my belief be ruled by his authority.

5.6.10 So it was that throughout the time (some nine years in all) that I was a Hearer[4] of that sect and a wanderer in my spirit, I longed for the day when their great man Faustus would arrive. All the rest of them had proved, when pressed, unable to answer the questions I raised on matters of astronomy and mathematics; but when Faustus came, they assured me, we could discuss these points, and he would have no difficulty unravelling them and any bigger ones I wished to raise. When he did come, I found him an agreeable man with a pleasant way with words. He could parrot off the same things that the others always said, albeit with much more sophistication. But what good is it to a thirsty man, such as I was, to be served from precious goblets by a smart wine steward? My ears had had enough of such things by now; they did not seem better, because they were better put, or true, because they were couched in fine words. Nor did Faustus seem to be a philosopher at heart, merely because he looked the part and had the eloquence to match. As for those who assured me that Faustus had the answer to all my questions, they were no judges of things; they thought he was a philosopher and sage merely because he had charmed them with his rhetoric. For my part, I have come to know that there is another class of person again, who is suspicious and ill-content with the truth itself, if it comes tricked out in elegant and high-flown diction. But even at that time I had been taught by my God in strange and secret ways; and I believe what you teach me because it is true, and because there is no other teacher of truth beside you, wherever he may come from or however widespread his fame. I had now been taught by you that nothing should be thought true merely

4 'Hearer'. The main class or outer circle of Manichees. The inner circle were the 'Elect'. See ch. 18.

because it was eloquently put, or false because the signs uttered by the lips had a rough ring to them; and likewise that nothing should be thought true because it was pronounced in homely fashion, nor false because it was wrapped in lofty phrases. Moreover, I had learnt that there was wisdom and folly, just as there was good food and bad; and that they could be served up in plain or fancy language, just as either sort of food could be served in coarse or fine dishes.

5.6.11 This, then, was the man I had wished so long and so eagerly to meet. When I met him, I was impressed with the intensity and the earnestness with which he debated, and by the effortless ease with which he found apt words to dress up his thoughts. I, like many others, was impressed; I praised and extolled him with the rest, and perhaps more. But I was annoyed that among the crowds that gathered to hear him I was not allowed to push myself upon him; I had no chance to share with him my questions and concerns in friendly dialogue. But when, with a few friends, I did get his ear, and found an opportunity for an exchange of opinions, I put forward some of the questions that were troubling me; and I discovered that this erstwhile master of the liberal arts knew only literature – and had no special knowledge even of that. He had read some of Cicero's speeches, a few books by Seneca, some odds and ends of poetry, and the more literate of the Latin works of his own sect. This, combined with his daily practice of public disputation, was the source of his rhetorical skill, which was all the more attractive and seductive when allied to his equable disposition and natural charm. Is it not so, even as I recall it, O Lord my God, judge of my conscience? *My heart and my recollection lie open before you* (Num. 10.9), even then you were dealing with me in some secret corner of your providence, and *setting before my face* (Ps. 50.21 [Ps. 49.21]) those inglorious wanderings of mine, so that I should see them and hate them.

5.7.12 When it became clear to me that he was a novice in the arts in which I had thought him a master, I despaired of his being able to explain and resolve the questions that were troubling me. He might indeed have known nothing of those arts and

yet have held on to true piety – but only if he had not been a
Manichee. The scriptures of that sect are replete with lengthy
myths about the sun, the moon and the stars; and on comparing
them with the accounts given by the mathematicians, which
I had read elsewhere, I was eager to know whether the contents
of the Manichee scriptures were true instead, or at least whether
they gave an account to match that of the mathematicians. But
by now I no longer thought that Faustus could give me a subtle
explanation of these questions. When I put them before him for
consideration and asked him to discuss them, he knew his own
limits, and did not venture to take up the burden. He knew that
he did not know such things, and was not ashamed to admit it.
He was not like all those talkers I had endured, who tried to
teach me and said nothing all the while. Faustus had a heart,
and if it was not *turned towards you* (Ps. 78.37 [Ps. 88.37], Acts
8.21), nor was it over-confident in himself. He was not wholly
ignorant of his own ignorance, and was not so rash as to let
himself be trapped in a corner, with no way out and no easy way
back. I liked him all the better for it. The modesty of a heart
that confesses its weakness is more lovely than all the things
I was so eager to know. Such I found Faustus to be on all harder
and more subtle questions.

5.7.13 So it was that the zeal with which I had applied myself to
the study of Mani's writings was checked; while I had even less
confidence in the other Manichee teachers, seeing as their so-
called 'Favourite of Heaven'[5] had turned out the way he had on
all the many questions that were troubling me. I began to spend
much of my time with him, in keeping with his own ardent
enthusiasm for the literature which I was teaching to my young
students, being by now employed as Professor of Rhetoric at
Carthage. With him I began to read through the works that he
knew only by reputation and of which he wanted to know more,
or which I myself judged appropriate to his abilities. But all the
effort I had resolved to expend in the service of that sect fell
away as I came to know the man. I did not reach the point of
cutting myself off from them completely; it was rather that

5 ' "Favourite of Heaven" '. Faustus; see note on 5.3.3.

I could find nothing better than the beliefs into which I had so recklessly flung myself, and had decided in the meanwhile to be content with them, unless something preferable should show itself. Thus Faustus, who had been *a deadly snare* (Ps. 18.5 [Ps. 18.6], Prov. 21.6) to many, had now begun, unwilling and unknowing, to release the snare in which I myself was caught. For according to your hidden providence, my God, your hands did not desert my soul. Day and night my mother through her tears offered sacrifice of her heart's blood to you for my sake, and you *dealt wondrously with me* (Joel 2.26). It was you who did this, O God; *it is the Lord that guides a man's steps, and the Lord will choose out a path for him* (Ps. 37.23 [Ps. 36.23]). For what is there that can gain our salvation except your hand making anew what you have made?

5.8.14 It was through your dealings with me that I was per-suaded to set out for Rome, and teach there what I was already teaching at Carthage. Nor shall I fail to confess how I was persuaded to do this, since in this too I must contemplate and proclaim your hidden depths and your ever-present mercy towards us. I did not decide to head for Rome because of the higher earnings and status which, I was assured by the friends who urged me to go, would be mine – though these considera-tions did weigh on my mind as it then was. The main, almost the sole reason was that I had heard that the young students at Rome were quieter and better-disciplined. If they were not studying under a particular teacher, they did not constantly invade his lecture rooms and indulge in wild antics; they were allowed in only by his permission. At Carthage the students enjoyed a licence that knew no bounds; it was a disgrace. They would burst in and break up completely the discipline that each teacher had imposed for the benefit of his students, quite shamelessly – indeed, with a boldness that verged on the insane. For sheer loutishness they were a wonder to behold; they would commit many outrages that would be punishable by law, were they not protected by custom. Hence it can be seen that the more these students did things that your Law will never permit, as if they were even now permissible, and thought that they did so with impunity, the more wretched they were; inasmuch as they were being punished all the while by the very blindness with which they did them, and suffering retribution incomparably worse than what they wrought. So it was that I now endured as a teacher the sort of behaviour in others that as a student I had rejected in myself. I decided, therefore, to go to a place where all those who knew informed me that it did not take place. But it was you, *my hope and my portion in the land of the living* (Ps. 142.5 [Ps. 141.6]), who urged me for the sake of my soul's welfare to move to a new land. At Carthage you wielded the stick that drove me out, and at Rome you set out the enticements that drew me on. This you did through human agency, through men who love this mortal life; through the mad conduct of my students on the one hand, and the empty promises of my friends on the other. You secretly used both their perversity and my own to *guide my steps into the right path* (Ps. 40.2 [Ps. 39.3]). For the students who disturbed the peace of my lecture hall were blind with their own shameful frenzy, and those who urged me to regain it at Rome had *their minds set on earthly things* (Phil. 3.19). For my own part, I loathed the misery I had experienced at Carthage, and was eager for the happiness of Rome. My misery had been real, but my happiness was to prove false.

5.8.15 Why I was leaving Carthage and going to Rome, you knew, O Lord, but you revealed neither to me nor my mother. She wept grievously at my departure, and followed me to the edge of the sea, holding on to me violently, so as either to call me back or to set out with me. But I deceived her, pretending there was a friend I did not want to leave until the wind rose and I could sail. I lied to my mother (and to her, of all mothers), and slipped away from her; and in your mercy you gave me leave to do this, saving me from the waters of the sea of accursed filth, and bringing me to the waters of your grace. The tears that streamed from my mother's eyes, with which she daily watered the ground beneath her face for my sake, would be dried when I was washed in those waters. She refused to go back without me, but with difficulty I persuaded her to stay the night at the Shrine of St Cyprian, which was hard by our ship. But that night I set out in secret, and she did not; she stayed behind, praying and weeping. And what was she begging of you, my God, if not that you should not allow me to sail? But in your deep counsels you hearkened to her true wish, and did not attend to what she prayed at that time, so as to make me what she prayed I should be always. The wind blew and filled our sails, and took from our sight the shore on which she stood, wild with grief and filling your ears with cries and reproaches. You stood aloof from her complaints, both because through my desires you were carrying me off to make an end of those same desires, and because you were chastising her with the whip of her sorrows, a just punishment for her fleshly longing. She loved to have me present with her, as mothers do, but much more than most mothers, not knowing what joys you would bring her out of my absence. Not knowing this, she wept and wailed, and by her torments she was convicted of having in her the remnant of Eve, as she sought with groaning what *with groaning she had brought forth* (cf Gen. 3.16). Yet even so, after charging me with deceit and cruelty, she turned back to praying to you for me. Then she went back to her usual life, while I sailed for Rome.

5.9.16 At Rome I was greeted – with the scourge of physical illness, and was on the way *down to the depths of hell* (Job 7.9), bearing all the evil deeds I had done, against you, against myself, against others. There were many such deeds, and weighty ones too – and all this on top of the chain of original sin, by which *all we in Adam die* (1Cor. 15.22). You had not yet forgiven me any of them in Christ, nor had he *broken down on the cross the enmity with you that I had incurred through my sins* (Eph. 2.14–16). How could he break it down, when, as I believed, it was a phantasm of him that had been crucified? Accordingly, my spiritual death was as true as his physical death seemed false, and my spiritual life was as false as his physical death (in which my soul disbelieved) was true. As my fever grew worse, I began to slip away and perish; but had I departed this life then, where would I have gone, if not to the flames and the torments that, in accordance with the truth in which you have ordered the world, my deeds had merited?

My mother knew nothing of this, yet she prayed for me from afar. You were everywhere present with her, and heard her prayer, and present with me, and took pity upon me, and I began to recover my physical health. But my heart was still not cured of its impiety; for even when my life was in danger, I felt no need of your baptism. I was in a better plight when, as a boy, I had begged my pious mother to have me baptized, as I have recalled and confessed before. But the man did no credit to the child; in my madness I scoffed when your medicines were counselled. But you did not allow me to die unbaptized the twofold death.[6] Had my mother's heart been smitten with that blow, she would never have recovered. I cannot express what concern she had for me, or how much more anxiously she *travailed for me* (Gal. 4.19) in spirit than she had done in the flesh.

5.9.17 Had I died in that state, the blow would have run clean through her loving heart. I do not see how she could have been healed. And where did all her prayers go, so unremitting and unceasing? Nowhere but to you. And would you, *O God of mercies* (2Cor. 1.3), spurn the *heart crushed and laid low* (Ps. 51.17 [Ps. 50.19]) of a widow constant in almsgiving, obedient and *ministering to the saints* (Hebr. 6.10), letting no day go by without bringing her offering to the altar, but coming without fail twice a day, morning and evening, to your church; not to listen to gossip and old women's chatter, but so that she could hear you in your Word, and that you would hear her in her prayers? It was not gold or silver nor any thing transient or passing that she was seeking with those tears, but the salvation of her son; and would you, by whose gift she was what she was, despise her tears and cut her off from your help? No, Lord. You were there; you heard her prayer, and worked according to the order in which you had foreordained to work. Far be it from you to have deceived her in those visions and oracles I have mentioned before, or in those I have not mentioned. These she kept in her faithful heart, and would press them upon you in her prayers as

6 'the twofold death'. Physical death, then hellfire.

if they were so many promissory notes. For you, whose *mercy is everlasting* (Ps. 118.1 [Ps. 117.1], Ps. 138.8 [Ps. 137.8]), deign even to become by your promises the debtor of those whose *debts you have forgiven* (Matt. 18.32).

5.10.18 So it was you restored me from my illness, and for the time being you *saved the son of your handmaid* (Ps. 86.16 [Ps. 85.16]) in the body, so that he might be one to whom you could give a better and a surer salvation. Even so, I was still an adherent of those deceivers who were wrongly called 'saints'. During my illness and convalescence, I had stayed with one of their 'Hearers'; but I now attached myself to their so-called 'Elect'. For it still seemed to me that it is not we ourselves who sin, but some other nature within us; in my arrogance I was pleased to think myself blameless when I had committed some misdeed, and not to confess what I had done, so that you might *heal my soul, for it sinned against you* (Ps. 41.4 [Ps. 40.5]). I loved to exculpate myself and lay the blame on that something that was with me but not me. But it was all me. In my impiety I was *divided against myself* (Matt. 12.26), and my sin was all the more incurable in that I did not consider myself a sinner. What heretical wickedness it was, O God Almighty, for me to prefer to risk damnation by supposing that you could be overcome within me, than to gain salvation by letting myself be overcome by you. You had not yet *set a guard over my mouth, and placed a door of restraint over my lips, lest my heart incline to speak evil, to excuse the sins of men that work wickedness*; and therefore I still *joined together with their Elect* (Ps. 141.3–4 [Ps. 140.3–4]), though now I despaired of making any progress with their false doctrine. I had decided to be content with their teachings, so long as I found nothing better, and I still held on to them; but more carelessly and negligently than before.

5.10.19 For now the thought grew on me that the wisest philosophers were those called the Academics, in that they were convinced that judgement should be reserved on all questions, and adamant that no truth can be apprehended by man. In this, I, like many, deemed that they judged rightly – which is proof that I did not understand even the basic premise of their teaching.

I did not hesitate to reprimand even my host for the excessive trust I saw that he reposed in those mythologies of which the Manichee scriptures are full. Nevertheless, I was on more intimate terms with them than other men who were not members of that sect. I no longer defended them as vigorously as before, though my intimacy with them – for many a Manichee lurks at Rome – made me slower to look for some other doctrine. Above all, *O Lord of heaven and earth* (Gen. 24.3), maker of all things visible and invisible, I despaired of finding the truth in your Church. The Manichees had turned me against it; and it seemed to me outrageous to believe you had the form of human flesh, and were confined within the physical outline of our limbs. And when I wished to think of my God, I did not know how to think of him except as some physical mass – for I thought there was nothing that was not physical – and, inevitably, this was the main and almost the sole cause of my error.

5.10.20 For this same reason I believed that evil too had a sort of substance, of similar nature, having a foul and misshapen mass that was either dense, in which case the Manichaeans called it 'Earth', or refined and subtle, like the body of air. This evil 'Mind' they pictured as creeping through the aforementioned Earth. And since some pious instinct forbade me to believe that a good God had created anything evil, I posited two mutually opposed masses, both infinite, but the evil mass infinite in fewer directions than the good. From this pernicious premise the rest of my impiety followed. For when my heart endeavoured to take refuge in the Catholic faith, I was beaten back, since the Catholic faith was not what I thought it was. It seemed less impious to me, my God, to whom I *confess these your mercies* (Ps. 107.8, 15, 21, 31 [Ps. 106.8, 15, 21, 31]), to believe that you were infinite in all other directions, even though I was compelled to acknowledge that you were finite in the one direction in which you came up against the mass of evil, than to suppose that you were finite and bounded in all directions within the form of a human body. It seemed better to me to believe that you had created no evil nature – which in my ignorance I supposed was not only something substantial, but also something corporeal, for I did not know how to think of Mind except as some sort of subtle body, albeit one diffused over space – than to believe that any evil nature (such as I supposed it) could come from you. Our Saviour himself, your only-begotten Son, I supposed to be something forged from your supremely radiant mass, and stretched out for our salvation. So convinced was I of this that I had no other belief about him except the vainest possible imaginings.[7] Being of such a nature, he could not, I thought, be born of the Virgin Mary without being fused with the flesh. But I did not see how the sort of nature I envisaged could be fused with the flesh and not corrupted by it. For this reason, I was afraid to believe that he was born in the flesh, in case I should be forced to believe that he was corrupted by the flesh. Let those of your followers who are spiritual laugh at me now, if they should read these confessions of mine; but that is how I was.

5.11.21 Moreover, I thought indefensible those points of your Scriptures that the Manichees had criticized. But I still longed from time to time to discuss each question with some scholar versed in those Scriptures, and to discover what he thought. Even at Carthage, I had been moved by words of a certain Elpidius, who had publicly conducted anti-Manichee debates and lectures. He had produced arguments in favour of the Scriptures that could not easily be countered. The Manichee response – which they would not put about openly, but communicated to us in secret – seemed to me a feeble one; the New Testament writings, they said, had been tampered with by certain individuals who wished to graft the Jewish law on to the Christian faith; but they could produce no copies of the unadulterated text. But my mind was set on things corporeal; I was utterly deceived by their 'masses', which were, so to speak, dragging me down and drowning me. I gasped for breath beneath them, and could not breathe in the pure and simple air of your truth.

7 'something forged ... vainest possible imaginings'. Manichees believed that Jesus had three forms. In one of these forms, he was stretched out from the earth to the moon. They also believed that the figure who was crucified on the cross was an empty image or 'phantasm' or 'illusion' of Jesus. The rather obscure nature of Augustine's allusions here probably reflects the illogicality and self-contradiction that he sees as characterizing Manichee views.

5.12.22 So it was I set hard at work about the business for which
I had come to Rome, namely to teach rhetoric. But first I
gathered to my home a circle of men among whom and through
whom my reputation had begun to spread. Then I learnt that
some things went on at Rome that I had not had to endure
at Carthage. My friends confirmed that there were no young
hooligans who indulged in wrecking activities, as there were at
Carthage; 'but', they told me, 'a whole group of students will
contrive to avoid paying one teacher by transferring to another.
They will renege on their contract, and count honest dealing as
nothing compared to their love of money.' My heart hated these
students too, though not *with a perfect hatred* (Ps. 139.22
[Ps. 138.22]); for I hated them more, perhaps, because I was
going to suffer their actions than because they would act in the
same dishonest fashion towards anyone. None the less, such
people are indeed repellent. *They are unfaithful to you* (Ps. 73.27
[Ps. 72.27]). They love the fleeting pleasures of the moment, the
sordid getting of money, which soils the hand that holds it; they
embrace this passing world and despise you, the Abiding One,
who call the human soul back to you and forgive it when it
returns from its harlotry. To this day I hate such warped and
twisted people; but now I will love them, in the hope of
straightening them out, so that they put education before money
– and put you before that, O God, who are the Truth and wealth
of goodness unfailing, whose Contract is most inviolate. But in
those days I was more reluctant for my own sake to endure
such wicked men than desirous for your sake that they should
become good.

5.13.23 It was then that word came from Milan to the City Prefect at Rome, ordering that a professor of rhetoric should be
provided for that city, whose removal expenses were to be paid
by the State. I began to canvass for the post, using as my agents
none other than the Manichees, drunk as they were on their
vanities. Neither of us knew at the time that it was so as to be
rid of them that I would leave Rome. I made a speech on a set
theme; the City Prefect of the day, Symmachus, approved of
my speech, and despatched me to Milan. On arrival, I went to

Ambrose, the bishop, known throughout the world as one of the great, a pious worshipper of yours, who by the eloquence he then possessed administered to the populace *the finest wheat, the oil of rejoicing, and the wine that makes men merry and sober.*[8] It was by you that I was brought to him without my knowing, so that through him I might be brought knowing to you. He, a man of God, welcomed me as a father and showed me the love a bishop should show to one far from home. I too came to love him, not as a teacher of the truth (which I despaired of finding in your Church) but as a man who was kind to me. I listened keenly to his public debates, if not for the right reasons; my purpose was to test out his rhetorical skills, and see if they lived up to their reputation, or were more or less fluent than report made them. I had no curiosity about the subject of his speech, and in that respect was a contemptuous bystander, enjoying the pleasant flow of his language; which, though more learned, was less stirring and less seductive than Faustus's had been, so far as the manner of his speech was concerned. But in the subject matter itself there was no comparison. Faustus, misled by the Manichees, was far astray; Ambrose taught the health-giving doctrine of salvation. But *salvation is far from sinners* (Ps. 119.155 [Ps. 118.155]), such as I then was. Yet gradually and unknowingly, I was growing nearer to it.

5.14.24 For though I was in no hurry to learn what he was saying, but only how he was saying it (and idle as it was, that preoccupation had remained with me, even though I had now abandoned hope that any path to you lay open to man), nevertheless along with his words there came into my mind also the things of which he spoke. I loved to hear the words and cared nothing for the content; but as I opened my heart to hear the eloquence with which he spoke, there entered into my heart also (albeit only by degrees) the truth which he spoke. What he

8 '*the finest wheat ... merry and sober*'. Cf Ps. 104.15 (Ps.103.15). Augustine's quotation here is based on the paraphrase of this verse by Ambrose himself, *Hymn* 1.7.23–6, 'Let Christ be our food, and faith our drink; let us be merry and drink the sober intoxication of the Spirit'; there are also oblique allusions to Ps. 81.16 [Ps. 80.17], Ps. 147.17, Ps. 4.7 [Ps. 4.8], Ps. 45.7 [Ps. 44.8].

said seemed to me for the first time to be defensible. Even the Catholic faith, which I had thought indefensible in the face of the Manichee onslaught, I no longer thought merely an impudent assertion. This feeling grew as Ambrose solved one riddle after another from the Old Testament, which, as long as I had interpreted to the letter, had been fatal to me (cf 2Cor. 3.6). But when Ambrose had expounded many passages from the Law and the Prophets in their spiritual sense, I began to rebuke myself for my despair in believing that those books were incapable of withstanding the anathemas and mockeries heaped on them by the Manichees. I did not, however, now feel that the Catholic faith should be embraced merely because it too had learned men to assert its claims and refute eloquently and without self-contradiction the charges levelled at it; nor that the faith I already held should be condemned merely because its attacks had met with a defence equal to them. The Catholic faith seemed to me not to be defeated – nor yet triumphant.

5.14.25 Then I applied my mind strenuously to seeing if I there were any firm grounds on which I could convict the Manichees of falsehood. Had I only been able to conceive of a spiritual substance, all their cunning ploys would immediately have been undone, and I would have cast them from my mind; but I could not. Nevertheless, as I pondered and compared their opinions concerning the material of this world and of the universe as a whole with those of various philosophers, the views of the philosophers seemed to me much more plausible, so far as our carnal sense can reach. Therefore I followed what is believed to be the Academic practice; reserving judgement on all questions and wavering between all points of view, I resolved that I should at all events abandon the Manichees, and not remain in their sect while I doubted, seeing as I now regarded various philosophers as preferable to them; while reluctant to commit the care of my sick soul to these philosophers outright, because they lacked the saving name of Christ. I resolved, therefore, to be a catechumen of the Catholic Church that my parents had urged upon me, until some definite landmark emerged, towards which I could steer my course.

BOOK SIX

6.1.1 You who have been *my hope from my youth up* (Ps. 71.4 [Ps. 70.5]), tell me where you were, and *where you had gone from me* (Ps. 10.1 [Ps. 9.22]). Was it not you who had made me, had *set me apart from the four-footed beasts, and made me wiser than the birds of the air* (Job 35.10–11)? I was *walking through the darkness* (Is. 50.10) along *the slippery path* (Ps. 35.6 [Ps. 34.6]), seeking you outside myself and not finding *the God of my heart* (Ps. 73.25 [Ps. 72.26]). I had entered *the depths of the sea* (Ps. 68.22 [Ps. 67.23]),[1] and had lost faith or hope of discovering the truth. By this time my mother had come to me, strengthened by her piety, *following me by land and sea*[2] and confident in you through all her dangers. Even amid the perils of the deep she had reassured the sailors, themselves more accustomed to reassure nervous travellers unused to the sea. You had promised her in a vision a safe landfall, and this is what she promised them. When she found me, I too was in grave peril, through my despair of ever tracking down the truth; but when I told her that I was, at any rate, no longer a Manichee, even if I was not a Catholic Christian, she did not jump for joy as if she had heard something unexpected. She was, however, no longer anxious so far as that part of my misery was concerned. In her mind it had been like a bier, on which she, a widow, had carried me to you, weeping, in the hope that you could tell her son: *Young man, I tell you, arise* (cf Lk 7.12–15), and that he would revive and begin to speak, and you would give him back to his mother. It was, then, with no turbulent exultation that her heart trembled when she

1 'I had entered *the depths of the sea*'. Literally true, in that Augustine had taken ship to Italy; but the sea has wider symbolic meaning. In the Old Testament, the sea is sometimes seen as the enemy of Yahweh/God. Augustine picks up this negative sense early on in the *Confessions* (e.g. 1.8.13, 2.2.3). For him, the sea is characterized by bitterness (contrasted with the sweetness of God) and instability.
2 Virgil, *Aeneid* 9.492–3. The words are spoken by a mother over the body of her dead son.

heard that what she prayed every day would happen had happened, at least in part: I had not yet attained the truth, but had now been rescued from falsehood. Indeed, in her confidence that you, who had promised to grant all her prayer, would also grant what remained, she told me in complete calmness and with a heart full of trust that she believed in Christ that, before she left this life, she would see me a believer and a Catholic.

This much she told me. To you, however, fount of mercies, she poured out prayers and tears more constantly than ever, begging you to send down your help more quickly, and she hastened to the church and hung on Ambrose's words, the *fount of water that springs up to eternal life* (Jn 4.14) even more zealously. She loved Ambrose *as if he were an angel of God* (Gal. 4.4), as she had learnt that it was through him that I had been brought to my present state of wavering on the tide of uncertainty. She took it for granted that this condition would be a strait that, with peril, I would cross, like what doctors call the crisis of an illness; and that I would pass over from sickness to health. Such was her confidence.

6.2.2 It was for this reason that, when a beadle prohibited her from bringing offerings of corn, bread and unmixed wine to the shrines of the saints (as she was used to doing in Africa), she embraced this prohibition so devoutly and so obediently, when she learnt that it came from the bishop, that even I was surprised how much more ready she was to blame her own habit than to criticize Ambrose. Her spirit was not the prisoner of a fondness for drink, nor did a love of wine arouse in her a hatred of truth, as is the way with many people, men and women – the sort of drunkards who find a sober hymn as nauseating as watered wine. When my mother brought her basket of food oblations to be tasted and then offered around, she never set down more than one little cup to pay her respects, and that was enough for her taste, completely sober as it was. Even if there was more than one shrine to the departed to be honoured (as it was accounted) in this way, she would carry the same cup around with her to set down at each of them. This cup, not only heavily watered down but also lukewarm, she would share with those present, all taking only the smallest of sips; for her object was piety, not pleasure.

When, therefore, she learnt that it was a command of that great preacher and pious priest that these rites should not be practised even by those who did so in all sobriety, so as not to give the drinkers an opportunity to tipsify themselves, and because they were too much like the pagan rite of the Parentalia, she abstained from them with all alacrity; instead of a basket full of the fruits of the earth, she learnt to bring to the shrines of the martyrs a heart full of purer prayers. In this way she could give what she had to the poor; and what she shared at the shrines was the Body of the Lord, in imitation of whose Passion the martyrs were sacrificed and crowned. But it seems to me, O Lord my God (for my heart is before you in this matter) that perhaps my mother would not have given way so easily on the breaking of her custom had it been forbidden by someone whom she did not love as she loved Ambrose. She loved him deeply, on account of my spiritual welfare. For his part, he loved her on account of her most devout conduct, both *in good works* (1 Tim. 5.10, 6.18) and in constantly attending church *with a fervent spirit* (Acts 18.25, Rom. 12.11). Often, when he saw me, he would break off in the middle of his sermon, congratulating me on having such a mother; not knowing what sort of son she had in me, who doubted on all matters, and thought the *path of life* (Ps. 16.11 [Ps. 15.11], Acts 2.28, Prov. 6.23) wholly impossible to find.

6.3.3 Nor yet in my prayers did I groan for you to help me; rather, my mind was intent on its search, and restless in my rhetorical career. Even Ambrose I judged to be a happy man by worldly standards, seeing as he held such offices and commanded so much respect; only his celibacy seemed to me to be at all irksome. As for what hope he had, what struggle he had against the temptations that his very elevation brought on, what consolation he had in adversity, what sweet joys the hidden mouth of his heart had from feeding on your bread – these things I could neither guess, nor had I experienced. He, for his part, did not know the tide of uncertainty on which I hung, nor the pit of peril into which I had fallen; for I could not ask him what I wanted to ask in the way I wanted to ask it, since I was cut off from his ear by the crowds of tiresome people to whose weaknesses he ministered. When he was not with them (a very small amount of time), he refreshed either his body with the necessary sustenances, or his mind with reading. But when he read, his eyes ran over the page and his heart sought out the sense, while his voice and tongue were resting. Often when I was present (for no one was denied access to him, but it was customary for no one to be announced to him when they came) I saw him reading in this way, silently; never otherwise. I would sit in silence for a long time – for who would venture to impose himself on one so intent on his reading? – then go away, trying to guess why he read in this way. Perhaps it was because in the little time he managed to get for intellectual refreshment, free from the clamour of other people's affairs, he would not want to be distracted by another noise. Perhaps, too, I thought, Ambrose was afraid that his hearer would be straining his ears expectantly to hear whether the author whom he had been reading had raised any particularly obscure points, and that he would have to explain them, or give an exposition of some other particularly difficult questions. He might be afraid, I thought, that if he spent his time on this task, he would be able to get through fewer of his scrolls than he wanted. Perhaps, too, he had better reason for reading silently in that he wanted to preserve his voice, which was apt to become hoarse. But whatever his reason for acting thus, Ambrose was surely acting for the good.

6.3.4 At all events, no opportunity was given me of asking the things I longed to know from that sacred oracle of yours, his heart, except when there was some brief remark of his to be heard. But for him to turn back the tides of uncertainty on which I drifted, I needed to find him completely at leisure, which I never did. I would at least listen to him every Sunday addressing the people, *handling the word of truth in all integrity* (2Tim. 2.15), and had ever more proof that it was possible to undo the mesh of cunning slanders that the deceivers of my sect would weave to entrap the sacred scriptures. When, however, I found out that your spiritual children, those whom you have begotten again of the Mother Catholic Church, do not take the statement that you *fashioned man in your own image* (Gen. 1.26–7, 9.6) to mean that they should believe and hold that you are limited to the form of a human body, I blushed and rejoiced that what I had been 'barking against' for all those years was not the Catholic faith, but mere fictions of the carnal-minded – even though I had not the slightest or dimmest notion of how a spiritual substance could exist. I had, indeed, been hasty and impious, inasmuch as I had said by way of accusation what I should have said by way of question. For you, most high and most near, most secret and most present, do not have some limbs that are larger and others that are smaller, but are everywhere whole, and are in no place. You are not in the physical form of a man, but *made man in your own image*, and he occupies his due place from his head to his feet.

6.4.5 Since, therefore, I did not know how this image of yours could exist, I ought to have *knocked at the door* (Matt. 7.7) and asked how it was to be believed in and not jumped at it with both feet, complaining that the Church believed it in such and such a way. Anxiety over what I should hold on to as a certainty ate away at my innermost being, and all the more so the more I was ashamed that I had been so long deceived and deluded with the promise of certainties, and that, in my childish and misguided zeal, I had pattered off so many uncertainties as if they were certainties. That they were, indeed, false, became clear to me later. It was, however, certain that they were uncertainties, and that I had long considered them certainties, seeing as I was arraigning your Catholic Church with such ill-informed accusations, when it did not teach the things for which I arraigned it so heavily – though I had not yet found that what it taught was true. Therefore I was put to confusion, and turned back and rejoiced, my God. I rejoiced to find that *the one Church, the body of your only Son* (Col. 1.18, 1.24) in which the name of Christ had been set on me as an infant, did not have the flavour of children's stories about it, nor, in its salubrious doctrine, did it teach that you, the *Creator of all things*,[3] were constrained on all sides by the form of a human body, nor that you were confined within any space, however exalted or extensive.

6.4.6 I rejoiced, too, that the Old Testament writings, the Law and the Prophets, were no longer put before me to be read with the same eyes as before, when they had seemed so full of inconsistencies – as when I had taken your holy ones to task for holding such and such beliefs, when in fact they did not. Moreover, I was glad to hear Ambrose repeating in his sermons a rule that he was most anxious to enjoin upon his congregation: namely that *the letter slays, but the spirit gives life* (2Cor. 3.6). In so doing, he took away the mystic veil and exposed the spiritual meaning of things which, taken literally, had seemed to me perverse in their doctrine. He said nothing that could be a stumbling block to me, even though I still did not know whether what he said was true. I kept my heart from assenting to any proposition; frightened of falling head first, I was hanging myself to death instead. I wished to be as certain of the things I could not see as I was that Seven and Three are Ten.[4] I was not so mad as to think that not even this truth could be apprehended; but I wanted all other things to be like this, whether they were corporeal but not present before my senses, or spiritual – which I did not know how to think of except in corporeal terms. I could, indeed, have been healed by believing. Then my mental sight would be cleared of the things that clouded it, and directed in some way towards your truth, ever abiding and lacking in no part. But, just as it often happens, that when a man has had experience of a bad doctor, he is afraid to put himself under a good one, so my soul, whose sickness could be healed only by believing, refused treatment for fear that it should fall into false beliefs. It *resisted your hands* (Dan. 4.35 [Dan. 4.32]), but it is you who have prepared the remedies of faith, have

---

3 Based on 2Macc. 1.24, as paraphrased by Ambrose, *Hymns* 1.21. (a translation of which is given at 9.12.32).
4 'Seven and Three are Ten'. Augustine's formula for the Ten Commandments. The first three Commandments refer to human duty towards God, the remaining seven to duties to one's neighbour.

spread them over our earthly sicknesses, and conferred so much power upon them.

6.5.7 From now on, however, I preferred Catholic to Manichee doctrine. I felt that the Catholics' requirement that one should believe on trust something for which no proof was given (whether proof existed but happened not to be present before one, or whether it did not exist at all), was more moderate and less likely to mislead than the way the Manichees mocked one's credulity with their rash promise of knowledge, and then told one to believe all their teachings, with all their mythological fantasies and inconsistencies, on trust – precisely because no proof could be given. Then, O Lord, you slowly softened and composed my heart, as I considered how many countless things I believed on trust even though I had never seen, or been present when they happened – all the events in world history, all the facts about places and cities I had not seen, all the things I believed because I had been told by my friends, by doctors, by various people of one sort or another. If we did not trust these people at their word, we would do nothing in this life. Most of all, it was by faith that I was unshakeably convinced who my parents were; which I could not know, unless I believed what there was for me to hear. Thus you persuaded me that I should criticize not those who believed your Bible, which you have established with such authority among all nations (or near enough), but those who did not believe; and that I should not listen to any who said to me, 'How do you know that these books were given to mankind by the Spirit of the one true and truthful God?' That fact was to be believed above all; for no amount of fighting talk, name-calling, or ruthless questioning on the part of the various conflicting philosophers I had read, had ever forced me not to believe that you were what you are (cf Ex. 3.14) (though I did not know what you were), or that 'the governance of human affairs'[5] was not your concern.

6.5.8 This I believed at some times more strongly than at others; but I always believed both that you existed and that you cared

5 ' "the governance of human affairs" '. Cicero, *On the Nature of the Gods* 2.3.

for us, even though I did not know what I should believe about your substance, or which road led (or led back) to you. Seeing, therefore, that *we are too weak* (Rom. 5.6) to discover the truth by pure reason, and hence need the authoritative word of Holy Writ, I now believed that you would never have accorded the Scriptures such surpassing authority throughout all lands, if you had not willed that through them men should believe in you and seek you. As for the 'inconsistency' in the Scriptures that had so often been a stumbling block to me, I had now heard a credible explanation of many of these points, and ascribed this 'inconsistency' to the deepness of the mysteries concerned. Indeed, the authority of Scripture seemed all the more worthy of veneration and inviolable trust, since it was available for all to read, yet preserved the dignity of its secret in the depths of its meaning. It offered itself to all in the plainness of its words and its low manner of speech, but exercised the attention of those who were not *light of heart* (Ecclesiasticus 19.4). It welcomed all manner of people to its breast, and drew a few through the *narrow doors* (Matt. 7.13–14) to you; but many more than it would had its authority not loomed so high, or if it had not drawn the great masses to the bosom of its sacred humility. These were my thoughts, and you were with me. I sighed and you heard me; I was tossed on the waves, and you guided me; I was walking along the world's broad path, and you did not desert me.

6.6.9 I was greedy for preferment, profit, marriage, and *you laughed at me* (Ps. 2.4, Ps. 37.13 [Ps. 2.4, Ps. 36.13], Wisdom 4.18). Through my desires I suffered the most bitter struggles, and you looked mercifully upon me – all the more so in that you did not allow me to find sweetness in anything that was not you. *Look, O Lord* (Lam. 1.11) on my heart; for it is you who willed that I should call to my heart all these things, and confess you. Now *let my soul cling to you* (Ps. 63.9 [Ps. 62.9]), for you have drawn it from the lime of death that held it so tightly. How unhappy it was! You made my wound sting me more, so that I would leave everything and *turn back to you* ([Ps. 21.28, Ps. 50.15]), *who are above all things* (Rom. 9.5), and without whom everything would be nothing; so that I should *turn back to you, and be healed* (Is. 6.10, Matt. 13.15).

How unhappy, then, was I! And how you dealt with me, and made me conscious of my unhappiness one day! I was preparing to recite a panegyric to the Emperor. In that panegyric I would tell many lies, and be applauded for my pains by many who knew that they were lies. These thoughts made my heart breathless and feverish, tossed by a wasting sickness of anxieties. As I passed through a street in Milan, I noticed a pauper begging. I suppose he had already had a skinful, and was now in a happy mood, full of jokes. I groaned, and observed to the friends who were with me how many were the sufferings our own madness inflicted upon us. In all our strivings, such as those under which I was then labouring as I dragged my burden of unhappiness, driven by the lash of my own desires, making it heavier as I dragged it, we had but one wish: to arrive at a state of happiness and confidence. But that beggar, I said, had beaten us to it, and we would perhaps never reach it. What he had attained with the aid of a few small coins, and begged ones at that, I was approaching by a circuitous route, with many painful twists and turns: namely, the happiness that comes from earthly felicity. It was no true joy that he had; but the joy that I was seeking through my ambitions was far falser. He, at any rate, was cheerful, while I was anxious; he was carefree, while I was full of trepidation. If someone had asked me whether I would rather be happy or fearful, I would have said, 'Happy'. If they had asked again, whether I would rather be like the beggar, or as I then was, I would have chosen to be myself, exhausted though I was with worries and fears. But this is a perverse choice; what of the truth? I should not have regarded my condition as preferable to his because I was more educated, for I had no joy of my education. Instead, I sought to please men with it; not to teach them, but only to please them. For this reason, you *broke my bones* (Ps. 51.8 [Ps. 50.9]) with the rod of your discipline.

6.6.10 *Let them depart, therefore, from my soul* (Jer. 6.8), who say to it: 'It matters why a person is happy. That beggar was happy because of his taste for wine, while you were endeavouring to be happy by gaining glory.' But what glory, O Lord? Not the glory that is in you. Just as the beggar had no true joy, so I had no true glory – but my glory had turned my head more than his joy. That night he would sleep off his wine that had made him drunk, but I had slept and woken up drunk, and would sleep and wake up drunk – and for how many days! It does matter, I know, why one is happy; the happiness that comes from faithful hope is incomparably different from my vanity. But even then, there was a difference between us: he was the happier, not only in that he was drenched with high spirits, whereas I was eaten up inside with anxieties, but also in that he had got his wine by wishing people good day, whereas I sought to get my vain glory by lying.

I said many things in this vein to my friends on that occasion; and in saying them, I repeatedly took cognizance of how matters stood with me. I found that they stood badly, and I was grieved, and made my state twice as bad; and if some favourable circumstance smiled on me, I was reluctant to hold on to it, for almost before I gained a grip on it, it flew away.

6.7.11 My complaint was shared by all of us who were living together on friendly terms, and I discussed these matters most of all and with the greatest familiarity with Alypius and Nebridius. Alypius was born in the same town as me. His parents were prominent citizens of the town. He was younger than I, and had been a student of mine when I began to teach in our home town, and later at Carthage. He loved me, because I seemed to him a good and learned man; I loved him for his great disposition towards virtue, which was fully apparent even when he was no great age. But the moral whirlpool of Carthage, with its seething passion for the frivolities of the theatre, had sucked him down, and made him a mad follower of the games. But while he was being spun round most pitiably in that whirlpool, I, as Professor of Rhetoric, had rented for my classes a lecture theatre that was open to the public. Alypius was not yet attending my lectures, as the result of a disagreement that had arisen between me and his father. When I discovered that he was desperately in love with the circus, I was deeply disturbed, afraid that all the hope I had placed in him would prove wasted, if it were not indeed wasted already. But I had no opportunity to warn him, or to use any compulsion to call him back, either in accordance with my good wishes for him as a friend, or my rights as his teacher. I thought that he thought the same about me as his father did, whereas in fact he was not like that. For this reason, he set aside his father's wishes, and began to come into my lecture hall to pay his courtesy greeting, to listen for a while, and then go away.

6.7.12 But it very nearly slipped my mind to have a word with him, to keep his excellent character from perishing through his blind and precipitate enthusiasm for the vanity of the Games. You, however, O Lord, who preside over the direction of all the things you have created, did not forget that he would be a priest of your sacrament among your children; and you worked through me – but without my knowledge, so that his amendment would be ascribed to yourself. For one day, when I was sitting in my usual place and my pupils were present, he entered, greeted me, sat down, and put his mind to the matter in hand. It happened that this was an expository reading. As I gave my exposition of the page, it occurred to me that I could illustrate it with a happy comparison to the Circus Games, and that way the point I was trying to impress would be made more clearly and amusingly, while at the same time I could take a biting laugh at those who had been captivated by its madness. *You know, O Lord* (Ps. 69.5 [Ps. 68.6]), that I was not concerned at the time to heal Alypius of the sickness that had seized him. He, however, took it to himself, and believed I had spoken only on his account; and what another person might take as grounds for being angry with me, he, being the upright young man that he was, took as grounds for anger with himself, and for loving me all the more ardently. For you have once given the word, that is woven into the web of your Scriptures: *Rebuke a wise man, and he will love you* (Prov. 9.8).[6] I had not rebuked Alypius, but

6 '*Rebuke a wise man, and he will love you*'. The word translated 'a wise man' could be translated 'a philosopher', and the word translated 'he will love you' could be translated 'he will thank you'.

you use all things, knowing or unknowing, according to the order which you know (and righteous is that order). From my heart and my tongue you made *burning coals* (Ezek. 1.13), to sear the mind that had promised so well and was wasting away, and to heal it. Let him refuse to praise you who does not consider your mercies, which praise you from the depths of my being. For Alypius, when he heard those words, rescued himself from the deep well in which he was willingly drowning and taking strange pleasure in being blinded. With mighty self-control he gave his mind a good shaking; all the dirt of the circus fell away from him, and he went there no more. Then he convinced his reluctant father that he should study under me; his father gave in, and agreed. But when he began to attend my lectures again, he became enmired with me in the Manichee superstition, in love with their show of continence, which he thought was true and genuine, when it was silly and seductive; it *trapped precious souls* (Prov. 6.26) who did not yet know how to attain the depths of virtue, and could readily be deceived by a superficial appearance of it – but even so, it is an adumbration and likeness of virtue that captures them.

6.8.13 He did not, however, abandon the earthly path that his parents had bewitched him into following, and went to Rome before I did, to study law. There he was carried away by a well-nigh incredible hunger for the gladiatorial games, and in a way that almost defied belief. Although he regarded such games with loathing and abomination, some of his friends and fellow-students took him with good-natured force into the amphitheatre (which happened to be on their way back from lunch) during the days when those cruel and deadly games were being celebrated. He protested vehemently, struggling and saying, 'If you drag my body off to that place and set it down there, do you think you can make my mind or my eyes pay any attention to the games? I shall be there and not be there, and thus prove myself stronger than you or they.' On hearing these words, his friends took him off with them just the same, perhaps wanting to find out whether he could manage to do what he said. When they arrived and had sat down in what seats they could, the whole place was boiling with pleasures of the most savage kind. Alypius closed the doors of his eyes, and forbade his mind to pay any attention to all this wickedness. Would that he had stopped his ears! For at one moment in the fight, a gladiator fell, and a great clamour arose from the whole populace, and beat against him; and, overcome by curiosity and ready, as it were, to despise whatever the cause, even when he had seen it, and to prove stronger, he opened his eyes, and was more severely wounded in his soul than the gladiator whom he longed to see had been in his body, and suffered a more pitiable fall than his whose fall had been the cause of all the clamour. The noise had entered his ears and unlocked his eyes, to make a path by which his mind could be assailed and overthrown, being as yet more daring than strong, and all the weaker as it *presumed to trust itself, when it ought to trust you* (Judith 6.15). When it saw the blood, it drank in the savagery; nor did it turn away, but fixed its gaze and glutted itself on the fury, unknowingly taking pleasure in the wickedness of the fight, and becoming drunk on its bloody pleasure. He was no longer the man he had come, but one of the crowd to whom he had come, a true companion of those who had brought him. What more is there to say? He watched, he cheered, he burnt; he took his madness away with him, to stir him up to come again − not just with the friends who had dragged him there previously, but more enthusiastically than they, even dragging others along with him. Even from that state, however, you rescued him with your most strong and most merciful hand, and taught him to *have confidence in you, not in himself* (Prov. 3.5, Is. 57.13). But that was long afterwards.

6.9.14 But for the time being, this incident was stored up in his memory, for his future healing. There was another incident also: one afternoon, while he was still studying under me at Carthage, he was in the Market Square, running over the recitation he was to give (the usual student exercise), and you allowed him to be apprehended by the Market Wardens as a thief − for no other reason, I suppose, our God, than because you wanted someone who was to be such an important person to begin at an early age to learn how reluctant one human being should be to condemn

another out of rash credulity. It happened like this: he was strolling about in front of the Courthouse with his writing tablets
and pencil, when a youth, one of the student body and the
real thief, entered the Courthouse without Alypius's knowing,
carrying a concealed axe, and went to the leaden railings that
overhang the Silversmiths' Street, and began to hack away at
the lead. The silversmiths underneath, however, hearing the
noise of the axe, put their heads together, and sent out a party
to apprehend anyone they might find up there. The thief, hearing their voices, abandoned his axe and made off, afraid of being
caught with it. Alypius, however, who had not seen him going
in, noticed him coming out and saw him making off in a hurry;
and, wondering why, entered the Courthouse and found the axe.
As he stood looking at it in puzzlement, the party despatched
by the silversmiths arrived, and found him by himself, carrying
the axe whose sound had aroused them to come. They seized
him, dragged him off, and in front of a crowd of Market Square
regulars they boasted of having caught a thief in the act. From
there they took him to be presented before the Court.

6.9.15 But that was as far as his lesson was to go. You, O Lord,
the sole witness of his innocence, immediately came to his aid.
As he was being taken off, either to prison or to corporal
punishment, his party happened to encounter a certain architect, the curator-in-chief of public works. The arrest party were
especially pleased to have met him, because they were often
suspected by him of the theft of items which had disappeared
from the Market Square. Now at last he would know who had
done it! But the architect had often seen Alypius at the house of
one of the Senators, to whom he used to go every morning to
make his courtesy greeting, and recognized him straight away.
Grabbing him by the hand, he took him aside from the crowd
and asked him what had caused all this unpleasant business. On
hearing what had happened, he ordered those present, who were
all in a state of uproar and threatening violence against him, to
come with him. They came to the house of the youth who had
committed the crime. There was a slave boy in front of the door,
but so young that he would not be afraid on his master's behalf

of their questions, and could easily reveal all, having, in fact, been his master's attendant in the Market Square. Alypius remembered him, and immediately indicated as much to the architect, who then showed the boy the axe and asked whose it was. Without hesitation, the boy said 'Ours.' On further questioning, he disclosed the remaining details. Thus, while the investigations were concentrated on that house instead, and the crowds, who had prematurely begun to celebrate Alypius's capture, were put to confusion, Alypius himself, the future steward of your Word and arbiter of so many cases in your Church, departed a more experienced man, and better prepared for his task.

6.10.16 So it was that I found him at Rome, and he attached himself to me with the strongest of bonds, and left Rome for Milan with me, both so as not to desert me, and to gain some experience in the practice of the law which he had studied, though more in accordance with his parents' wishes than his own. Three times he acted as Clerk to the Justice, and behaved with a self-restraint which others found remarkable – whereas he found more remarkable those who put gold before innocence. Even his character was tested, and not only by the lure of greed but by the impulse of fear. At Rome he was acting as Court Clerk to the Count of the Italian Largesse.[7] There was at that time a very powerful Senator, who had many men indebted to him for his good offices towards them, and subject to their terror of him. He, as is customary with the powerful, wanted permission for something not permitted by law. Alypius resisted him. A reward was offered; Alypius laughed at it in his heart. Threats were made; Alypius despised them, and all were amazed at this extraordinary soul, which neither sought as a friend nor feared as an enemy a man so powerful, with so many countless means of assisting him or injuring him, and with such an enormous reputation. The judge to whom Alypius was acting as Clerk, although he too was reluctant to grant the permission sought, did not refuse openly, but laid the blame on Alypius, saying that

7 'Count of the Italian Largesse'. An official responsible for the monetary taxes in Italy.

he would not let him grant the permission. And quite rightly; for had he done so, Alypius would have left the Court.

Only one thing came close to enticing Alypius, and that was his enthusiasm for literature; he could have had codices copied out for himself at Palace expense. But on considering where justice lay, he turned his mind to higher things, adjudging equity, which forbade him to do so, better than the authority which allowed him. This is a small matter, but *he who is faithful in a small matter will be faithful in a great matter also*; nor will *the word that proceeds from the mouth of your Truth be proved empty* (Jn 1.14, 8.40, 14.6). *If you are not faithful in unrighteous mammon, who will give you true mammon? And if you are unfaithful in another's property, who will give you what is your own?* (Lk 16.10–12).

Such was he who attached himself to me at that time, and agreed with me when we took counsel on what manner of life we should keep.

6.10.17 Nebridius, too, had abandoned his home town near Carthage, had abandoned Carthage itself, where he was a very frequent visitor, had abandoned his fine ancestral estate, had abandoned his home and his mother, who would not follow him, and had come to Milan for the sole purpose of sharing with me a life of burning zeal for truth and wisdom. He sighed no less than Alypius and I, and, no less than we did, wavered in uncertainty, ardent seeker though he was for the blessed life, and keenest investigator of the most difficult questions. There were three of us, three hungry mouths sighing to each other over their scant resources, and *looking to you to give them food in due season* (Ps. 104.27 [Ps. 103.28]) And in every bitterness that, in accordance with your mercy, pursued our worldly actions, when we considered the end for which we suffered all these things, we were confronted with darkness; and we turned away, groaning and saying, 'How long will all this last?' This we said often, but in so saying we did not abandon the things that made us suffer; for no certain object had emerged, which, having abandoned the rest, we might hold on to.

6.11.18 I was, moreover, in a state of complete bemusement as

I reviewed with agitation how much time had elapsed since, in my nineteenth year, I had begun my fervent quest for wisdom, making it my purpose to discover it and abandon all the empty hopes, all the deceitful delusions that my vain desires awoke in me. I was now some thirty years old, and still 'stuck in the same mud'[8] in my avid desire to enjoy things present, even though they tore me in so many directions; and all the time I said, 'Wisdom? I will discover it tomorrow. It will appear before my eyes, and I will lay hold on it.' – 'Faustus will come, and will explain everything.' – 'What heroes the Academics are! Is it true that "nothing pertaining to the blessed life be apprehended as a certainty"?'[9] – 'No; rather, let us seek more diligently, and not despair.' – 'The apparent inconsistencies in the Church's sacred books are not inconsistent after all; another decent explanation can be given. I shall set my feet in the upward path on which my parents set me as a boy, until the truth be found in all its transparency.' – 'But where shall I seek it? When shall I seek it? Ambrose has no time to spare, and I have no time to read. And the books themselves – where will I seek them? Where and when shall I buy them? From whom shall I get them?' – 'I will set aside time, and allot certain hours to my soul's welfare.' – 'A great hope has dawned on me. The Catholic faith does not teach what I thought it taught, and vainly accused it of teaching. Its scholars hold it impious to believe that God is confined within the figure of a human body. Will I, then, hesitate to knock on the door where the rest will be laid open?' (cf Matt. 7.7–8, Lk 11.9–10) – 'My mornings are taken up with my students; what do I do with the rest of my time? Why do I not make that my business?' – 'But when will I pay my greeting to my powerful friends, whose backing I need? When will I prepare new merchandise for my students? What time will I find for my own refreshment and relaxation, after giving my mind to all these concerns?'

6.11.19 'Let them all go hang! Let us cast them away, vain and

8 ' "stuck in the same mud" '. Terence, *Phormio* 780.
9 ' "nothing pertaining to the blessed life be apprehended as a certainty" '. Cicero, *Academica* 2.18, 2.31.

hollow as they are. Let us betake ourselves to the quest for truth, and nothing else!' – 'Life is unhappy, death uncertain; it creeps up on us unexpectedly, and how can we escape it? Or where will we learn what we have neglected here? Will we not rather pay the penalty for our negligence?' – 'Suppose death itself cuts short and puts an end to all our senses, and all our cares with them? This question, too, must be asked.' – 'But far be it that this should be so. It is not for nothing, not in vain that the authority of the Christian faith should stand so high, and be diffused throughout the whole world. Never would the divine power work so many or such great things for us, if the life of the soul were extinguished in the death of the body. Why, then, do we hesitate to abandon our worldly hope and betake ourselves to the search for God, and for the blessed life?' – 'But wait. Worldly things too are pleasant, and have no little charm of their own. It is no easy matter to cut short our striving for them, for it would be ridiculous to go back to them afterwards.' – 'Look what a great thing it is to gain preferment; what more among worldly things do you need? You have enough powerful friends; let us not waste our time, and we may be given a minor governorship at least. You must also marry a woman with a certain amount of money, so as not to add to the burden of our expenses; that will be the limit of my desires. Many great men, worthy models for imitation, have combined matrimony with a dedicated pursuit of wisdom.'

6.12.20 While I said all this, and while the winds shifted to and fro and drove my heart this way and that, time was passing; and I *was slow to turn back to the Lord, and postponed from day to day* (Ecclesiasticus 5.8) my living in him, though I did not postpone the way I was daily dying in myself. I was in love with the blessed life, but feared it even in its own home, and sought it even as I fled from it. I thought I would be unhappy beyond endurance if I were deprived of a woman's embraces, and I did not contemplate the medicine of your mercy as *a cure for my infirmity* (Ps. 103.3 [Ps. 102.3], Matt. 4.23), for I had not known it; I thought that continence was a matter of my own strength, which I was not conscious of possessing; for I was so foolish that I did not know that, as it is written, *no one can be continent unless you grant it to them* (Wisdom 8.21). And you would have granted it, had I knocked at the door of your ears with my inner groans, and *cast my healing upon you* (Ps. 55.23 [Ps. 54.23]) in sure faith.

6.12.21 Alypius, it is true, kept warning me off marriage. His burden was that if I married, we could not live together in untroubled retirement, pursuing a love of wisdom, as we had long desired. He himself was even then wholly chaste in this respect, indeed remarkably so – perhaps because he had had sexual experience early in his adolescence, but had not become limed in it, regarding it rather as a source of suffering, and despising it, and thenceforth living a life of complete continence. For my part, I countered his arguments with the examples of men who, though married, had cultivated wisdom and *found favour with God* (Hebr. 13.16), and been faithful and loving to their friends. I, however, fell far short of them in greatness of soul; bound to my carnal disease by the bond of deadly pleasure, I dragged my chain around, fearing to be released from it, and rejecting Alypius's words of good advice as though my wound had been exacerbated by the hands of my rescuer. And moreover, *the serpent was speaking* (Gen. 3.1) through me to Alypius, using my tongue to weave his alluring snares and set them in Alypius's path, to trap the feet that had always been honourable and unfettered.

6.12.22 Alypius, then, was amazed that I, of whom he thought so highly, was so tightly caught in the snare of sexual pleasure that whenever we debated the question I could state that I could in no way live a life of continence, and, seeing his amazement, could defend myself by saying that there was a big difference between his hasty and furtive experience, which by now he could hardly even remember and for that reason had no trouble in despising, and the pleasures that with me had become a matter of habit; and if these pleasures were endowed with the honourable name of 'marriage', he ought not to be amazed that I could not reject that manner of living. He, too, began to feel the need for sexual congress – not that he was in the least overcome by a lust for sexual pleasure, but for knowledge of hidden things. He said that he wanted to know what it was without which my life, which seemed to him so desirable, seemed to me not life but a form of torture. His own mind being free from the shackles of sexual pleasure, it was unable to comprehend my servitude; and being thus unable, he drifted towards the desire to experience it for himself. From this he advanced to the experience itself, and might perhaps have fallen into the same servitude that he had been unable to comprehend. Alypius *wished to make an covenant with death* (Is. 28.18), and *he who loves peril will fall into it* (Ecclesiasticus 3.27). Neither of us took any but the slightest thought of what honour was due to the union of a man and a woman in its proper function – the living of an ordered married life, and the bringing up of children. I was for the most part tortured severely by the habit of satisfying the insatiable concupiscence that had made me its captive, whereas Alypius was drawn towards captivity by his curiosity. Such we were, until you, Most High, who do not desert us, dust as we are, had mercy on our unhappiness, and came to our aid in strange and hidden ways.

6.13.23 In the meantime, I was under unrelenting pressure to marry. I was already in the process of seeking and being granted espousal to a girl, my mother being especially concerned that once married I could be washed clean in the saving waters of baptism, and rejoicing more each day that I was being made fit for it, and observing that both her prayers and your promises were being fulfilled in my faith. Indeed, in accordance both with my request and her own desire she besought you daily with great and heartfelt cries that you would show her through a vision something of my future marriage, but you refused. She did see some empty illusions of the mind, driven to them by the momentum of her own human spirit and its agitation over this matter; but she related them to me without the confidence she usually had when you showed her something, instead looking on them with contempt. For she used to say that she could tell, as it were, by a 'taste' not explicable in words, the difference between your revelations and the imaginings of her own soul.

Nevertheless, pressure was put on me, and betrothal sought with a girl some two years under marriageable age; and, as she was pronounced satisfactory, a period of waiting ensued.

6.14.24 There were several of us friends who pondered and debated the troubles that vex our human life, and regarded them as anathema; to the point where we had all but made firm our resolve to remove ourselves from its troubles, and live in cultured retirement. This retirement we had arranged thus: whatever we could procure, we would offer to the general good, and of all our possessions we would make one common property. Through the sincerity of our friendship, there would be no mine and thine, but the common property, contributed by all of us, would belong in full to each of us; everyone would own everything. There could, we thought, be perhaps ten of us in one community, among us some that were extremely wealthy, most notably Romanianus, my fellow-townsman and close friend from an early age, who was drawn to court by the great ebb and flow of his business affairs. He was most insistent on this point, and had the most authority in putting his case, because the amount of his property far excelled the rest. We had also decided that two officers every year should see to all our needs, while the others led a quiet life. But when we began to consider whether this life would be possible if our womenfolk were present (some of us already being married, and others, myself included, hoping to be), all our noble plans fell to pieces in our hands, and lay utterly shattered on the ground. From then on we returned to our sighing and groaning, toiling up the wide and well-trodden paths of the world; for *many were the cares in our heart, but your counsel abides for ever* (Ps. 33.11 [Ps. 32.11]). Of your good counsel you laughed at our plans and prepared your own, making ready to *give us food in due season, and to open your hand and fill our souls with blessing* (Ps. 145.15–16 [Ps. 144.15–16]).

6.15.25 In the meantime, *my sins were multiplied* (Ecclesiasticus 23.3). My familiar bedfellow was torn from my side as being an impediment to my marriage; and my heart, to which she had fixed herself, was torn and wounded, and left a trail of blood. She returned to Africa, vowing to you that she would never know another man, and leaving behind the natural son she had borne me. But in my misery I could not even imitate her, a woman; although after two years I was to receive in marriage the girl for whom I had made my suit, I was impatient of the delay, and, being not a lover of marriage but a slave of lust, I got myself another − and not a wife − so as to maintain my soul's sickness as it was, or if possible to make it worse, and convey it, with an escort of enduring habit, into the realm of matrimony. Nor did I find any healing for the wound caused by the severance from my previous partner, but after the inflammation and the grievous pain, gangrene set in; it was as if the wound were numbed, but that it was even more incurably painful.

6.16.26 *Praise and glory be to you, O fount of mercies!* (1Chron. 29.11−12). I became more needing of mercy, and you became nearer. Your right hand was even now present, ready to rescue me from the mire and wash me clean, and I did not know it. I was called back from plunging even more deeply into the whirlpool of carnal pleasures only by the fear of death and your coming judgement, a fear which among all the various opinions I entertained, never departed from my heart. As I debated the nature of good and evil[10] with my friends Alypius and Nebridius, I came close in my heart to awarding the palm to Epicurus, except that I believed that there remained to the soul life after death, and recompense according to one's deserving, which Epicurus declined to believe. Moreover, I asked, if we were immortal and lived lives of unbroken physical pleasure, without fearing any loss to our state, why were we not happy? What else did we seek? I did not know that this too was part of our great unhappiness, since I was so sunk in misery and so blind that I could not contemplate the light of open dealing and beauty that may be freely embraced, which the eye of the flesh cannot see, but which is apparent in our inmost being. Nor, in my unhappiness, did I consider from what source flowed the sweetness that I derived from discussing even those unlovely matters

10 '... the nature of good and evil'. *The Nature of Good and Evil* (*de finibus bonorum et malorum*) is a philosophical tract by Cicero, which Augustine and his friends were reading together.

with my friends, or the fact that I could not be happy without my friends even according to the perception which in those days I knew in the midst of all my carnal pleasures. These friends I loved freely, and perceived that they in turn freely loved me. What tortuous paths! *Woe to my reckless soul* (Is. 3.9), which hoped, if it departed from you, to gain something better! It tossed and turned on to its back, its sides, its stomach, but the bed was hard throughout, and you alone are rest. Behold, you are present, and deliver us from our miserable wanderings, and establish us *in your way*, consoling us and saying: *Run, and I will bear you up; I will convey you, and bear you up* (Is. 46.4).

BOOK SEVEN

7.1.1 By now my youth, evil and shameful as it had been, was dead, and I was entering my full manhood; and the older I was in years, the more riddled I was with vanity, inasmuch as I could not conceive of a substance except as the sort visible to our bodily eyes. I had not conceived of you, O God, in the figure of a human body, since I first gave heed to wisdom. This conception I always shunned, and I now rejoiced that I found that this was the teaching of our spiritual Mother, your Catholic Church; but it was not immediately apparent how else I should conceive of you. I, a man (and what manner of man!) attempted to form a conception of you, the highest and *one true God* (Jn 17.3), and in my deepest being I believed on trust that you were incorruptible, inviolable and unchangeable, as I did not know how or why. This, however, I saw clearly and did not doubt: that the corruptible is worse than the incorruptible. Without hesitation I held that the inviolable was preferable to the violable, and that what suffered no change was better than that which could be changed. My heart cried out violently against all my illusions, and I endeavoured with one blow to drive from my mind's sight the buzzing crowd of impurity that hovered around me. But scarcely had it been dispersed when *in the twinkling of an eye* (1Cor. 15.52) it gathered again, and assailed my vision and clouded it, so that although I did not conceive of you in the figure of a human body, I was none the less compelled to think of you as something corporeal, with spatial extension, either infused through the universe, or diffused even outside the universe through infinite space; something, indeed, incorruptible, inviolable and unchangeable, which I regarded as better than one corruptible, violable and changeable, but still a something. For whatever I deprived of this sort of spatial extension seemed to me to be a nothing – a complete nothing, not even a void, such as when a body is removed from a place and the place remains evacuate of all body, earthly, moist, aerial or heavenly, but there is, nevertheless, a place that is void, as it were a nothing but with spatial extension.

7.1.2 So it was that I had *grown dense-hearted* (Matt. 13.15, Acts 28.27) and hidden even from myself, thinking that whatever did not have some degree of spatial extension or diffusion or densification or tumescence or some such, was a complete nothing. My heart was proceeding through images of the same sort as the forms through which my eyes were accustomed to proceed; nor did I see that the mental focus, by which I formed those images, was itself not something of the same sort, even though I believed that it could not form these images were it not a something with magnitude.

Thus I conceived even of you, Life of my life, as permeating through infinite space in every direction the whole fabric of the universe; and outside it as extending through measureless distances without end. Earth, I thought, contained you, heaven contained you; all things contained you and had their end in you, but you had no end anywhere. Just as the physical mass of the air above the earth does not obstruct the sunlight and prevent it crossing it and penetrating it – not that the sunlight pushes or shears through the air, but fills it completely – so, I thought, the mass not only of heaven and air and sea but even of earth were permeable to you and penetrable from their greatest parts to their least, so as to contain your presence; within, through your hidden inspiration, and without, through your governance of all your creation. This was my surmise, for I could make no other conception; and it was false. For in that way, a greater part of the earth would contain a greater part of you and a lesser part a lesser; although all things would be full of you, more of you would be contained in the body of an elephant than of a sparrow, in proportion as it was bigger and occupied a bigger place. According to this theory, you would make the parts of you present bit by bit, with large parts of you in large parts of the universe, and small in small. This is not so; but you had not yet *lightened my darkness* (Ps. 18.28 [Ps. 17.29]).

7.2.3 What I found enough, O Lord, to refute those deceivers who are themselves deceived, who speak so much and say so little, seeing as they do not speak your Word – what I found enough was a question that Nebridius had asked many times, ever since we were in Carthage, shaking to the core all of us who heard it. What, he asked, of the 'race of darkness', derived from the Opposing Mass, which the Manichees habitually pit against you? What would they do to you if you declined to fight them? If the Manichees replied that they would inflict harm upon you, then you would be violable and corruptible. If, however, they said that they could not inflict any harm upon you, they could offer no reason why you should fight them – and fight them in such a way that a portion of you, a limb of yours, or an offspring of your very substance should become involved with these hostile powers, these beings not created by you, and be so much corrupted and changed for the worse by them, that from a state of blessed happiness it should pass to misery, needing help in order to be rescued and made clean. This 'offspring', say the Manichees, is the soul, whom your Logos, free, pure, and incorrupt, succours in its servitude, pollution, and corruption; but the Logos too is corruptible, being of one and the same substance. If, therefore, they say that you, whatever you are – that is to say, your substance, through which you exist – are incorruptible, then all of what they say is false and execrable. If, however, they say that you are corruptible, that is itself false and should be abjured as soon as it is uttered. This question, then, was enough against the Manichees, fit as they were in every way to be spewed out of my overcharged stomach; they had no way of escaping that question without committing a horrible sacrilege of the heart and tongue, thinking such things about you, and speaking them.

7.3.4 But even then, although I declared and firmly believed that you are incapable of pollution or transformation, and unchangeable in any part, our God, the true God, who have made not only our souls but also our bodies, and not only our bodies and souls but all bodies and all souls, I did not consider that I had unravelled and solved the question of the origin of evil. I saw, however, that whatever its origin, I would have to approach the question in such a way as not to be constrained to believe that the unchangeable God was changeable; in asking what was the origin of evil, I would have to be careful not to become evil myself. Thus I asked the question without anxiety, certain that what the Manichees said was not true; for in my heart I was in full flight from them, seeing that when they enquired into the origin of evil, they were themselves *full of evil thoughts* (Ecclesiasticus 9.3, Rom. 1.29), inasmuch as they supposed that your substance was more likely to suffer evil than their own to commit it.

7.3.5 I applied my mind to understanding what I was hearing: namely, that free will was the reason why we commit evil, and *your righteous judgement* (Ps. 119.37 [Ps. 118.37]) the reason why we suffer it; but I could not understand it as it was. Therefore as I endeavoured to raise my mental sight from the depths, I was drawn down again; and often as I tried, I was drawn down again and again. What raised me up towards your light was the fact that I knew that I had a will just as much as I knew I was alive. Thus, when I willed or did not will something, I was wholly certain that it was I and no one else who was willing it or not willing it; and I was now on the point of perceiving that therein lay the reason for my own sin. As for the evil I did against my will, I saw that I was suffering it rather than committing it, and adjudged it not so much my guilt as my punishment; conceiving of you as being just, I was swift to acknowledge that I was not being punished unjustly. But once again, I said: 'Who made me? Was it not my God, and is he not only good, but the Good itself? What, then, is the origin of my willing bad deeds and not willing good ones – why I should justly pay the penalty for my deeds? Who was it that set and planted this *bitter plant* (Heb. 12.15) in me, seeing as I came into being entirely from my God, the supreme Sweetness? If the Devil is responsible, what is *his* origin? But if the Devil himself changed by his perverse will from being a good angel to being the Devil, what is the origin of the evil will by which he became the Devil, seeing as he was made wholly an angel by the supremely good Creator?' These anxious thoughts dragged me down and choked me again and again, but I was never brought to that abyss of error in which *no one confesses you* (Ps. 6.5 [Ps. 6.6]), of thinking that you suffer evil rather than that man commits it.

7.4.6 Thus I struggled to discover the rest, just as I had already discovered that the incorruptible is better than the corruptible, and for that reason I confessed that you, whatever you were, were incorruptible. Nor could any soul ever conceive or have conceived anything that could be better than you, the highest and best Good. For although it is most true and most certain that the incorruptible should be regarded as better than the corruptible, just as I by this time regarded it, I might still have conceived of something better than my God, were you not incorruptible. When, therefore, I saw that the incorruptible should be preferred to the corruptible, I was bound to seek you, and then to consider the origin of evil; that is, the origin of that corruption by which your substance can in no way be violated. For there is no way at all in which our God is violated by corruption; neither through will, nor through necessity, nor through circumstance unforeseen. He himself is God; what he wills is good, and he is himself the Good. Nor are you, O God, compelled to do anything against your will, since your will is not greater than your power. It would be greater, if you were greater than your own self; for the will of God and the power of God is God himself. And what is unforeseen to you, who know everything? There is nothing in creation, but it exists because you know it. And why should I say at length why the substance that is God is not corruptible, seeing as if it were, it would not be God?

7.5.7 I sought to know the origin of evil, but I sought in an evil way; and I did not see the evil in my very searching. *In the sight of my spirit* (Ps. 16.8 [Ps. 15.8]) I set out the whole of creation – whatever we can see in it, such as the land, the sea, the air, the stars, trees, mortal living creatures, and whatever we cannot see, such as the firmament of heaven above us, all its angels and spiritual beings; but these too I ordered according to their several places, as if they were corporeal objects. And I made of your creation one big mass, divided into different kinds of body, whether these bodies did indeed exist, or whether they were what I had made up for myself by way of spirits. I made it big; not as big as it was, which I could not know, but as big as I chose, though still finite in all directions. You, however, O Lord, I supposed to surround and permeate the universe, but you were infinite in every direction: as if there were a sea, and that sea and nothing else were infinite in every direction through unmeasured space; and within it the sea had a sponge, of any magnitude whatsoever, but finite; and the sponge were full in every part of the sea, which was unmeasured. In the same way, I thought your creation, finite as it was, was full of you, the infinite; and I said again and again: 'Behold God, and behold the things that God has created. God is good, and more excellent than his creation by far; but being good, he created good things. Behold, too, how he surrounds and fulfils his creation; where, then, is evil? From where and by what route did it worm its way into his creation? What is its root and its seed? Or does it not exist at all? Why, then, do we fear and guard against that which does not exist? If our fears are in vain, what of the fear that goads and torments the heart for nothing – is that not itself an evil, and all the more grievous an evil, in that what we fear does not exist for us to fear it? Therefore, either there is evil, and we fear it, or the very fact that we fear it is itself an evil. What, then, is its origin, seeing as all things that the good God made are good? (cf Gen. 1.31) It is true that a greater Good, indeed the highest Good, made the lesser goods; but both the creator and the things created are all good. What is the origin of evil? Or was there some kind of evil matter, out of which he made his created works, shaping it and ordering it, but leaving in it something untransformed into good? Why, then, did he do this? Did he, the Omnipotent, lack the power to transform and change the whole, so that no evil remained? Why, indeed, did he will to make something out of this matter, and not rather use this omnipotence to make it not exist at all? Could it have existed against his will? Or if it was eternal, why did he allow it to exist for so long, through the infinite spaces of previous time, and then so much later decide to make something out of it? Or if he suddenly willed to perform some action, would he, the Almighty, not act to see that the evil matter should not exist, and that he should be alone, the whole, true, supreme and infinite Good? Or if it was not good that he, the good, should not fashion and create something good, why did he not abolish and bring to nothing the evil matter, and decree that there should be good matter from which he could create everything? For he would not be omnipotent if he could not create something good without the help of matter that he had not created.'

These thoughts I turned around in my heart, unhappy and burdened as it was with its consuming preoccupations with the fear of death and with my failure to discover the truth; but in my heart there remained firmly fixed the faith in your Christ, our Lord and Saviour, that I had found in the Catholic Church. This faith was in many respects still unformed, and ebbed and flowed around the fixed point of Catholic teaching; but my soul did not abandon it, but rather drank it in more and more every day.

7.6.8 By this time too I had rejected the fallacious divinations and impious delusions practised by the astrologers. And for this also *let your mercies confess you* (Ps. 107.8, 15, 31 [Ps. 106.8, 15, 31]) from the bowels of my soul! It was you and wholly you who did this, for who else brings us back from the death caused by every error, if not the Life which knows no death, and the Wisdom that enlightens the minds of those who need it, which itself need no light; by which the world is governed, down to the leaves that blow off the trees? It was you who, through others, cured the obstinacy with which I resisted that old wiseacre Vindicianus, and Nebridius, that young man of remarkable character. These two told me – Vindicianus as a round assertion, Nebridius with some hesitation, but none the less very frequently – that human powers of reckoning often had a force amounting to that of sortilege. When much was said, they told me, much of what was said would come true; not that the speakers knew that it would, but they happened upon it simply by not being quiet. You cured me, too, through the agency of a friend of mine, who was himself a not infrequent consultor of astrologers. Nor was he a true scholar of astrological literature, but, as I have said, he consulted them out of curiosity, and did have some knowledge of astrology, which he said he had learnt from his father. What he did not know was how far his knowledge went towards undermining the reputation of that art. This gentleman, then, by name Firminus, a man of liberal education and thorough rhetorical training, consulted me on one occasion as a close friend on certain affairs of his, in which he had good hope of worldly success, and asked me what I thought in the light of his birth sign (as it is called). I, who was by now coming round to Nebridius's point of view on this subject, did not refuse to make an astrological reckoning or, despite my hesitation, to tell him the result of my computation; but I added as an afterthought that I was now almost convinced that such horoscopes were ridiculous and that there was nothing in them. Firminus then told me that his father had been very curious about the literature of astrology, and had had a friend no less enthusiastic, with whom he pursued his enquiries. The two of them, by their shared interest and discussion of the subject, had blown up the fire of their hearts into such a blaze for these frivolities that they even observed the exact instant and the position of the heavens at the time of birth of any dumb animal that happened to be born in their house, so as to plot their horoscopes as a means of testing out that so-called science. So it was, Firminus told me, that when his mother had been pregnant with him, his father's friend had had a slave woman who was also great with child. This fact could hardly escape her master's notice, seeing as he took such scrupulous pains to determine the time when even his bitches gave birth. So it came about that when his father had calculated the day, hour and minute of his wife's pregnancy with the most careful observation, and his friend had done likewise for his slave woman, both women gave birth at the same time; so much so that the two men were compelled to make exactly the same birth sign for each child, one for his son, one for his slave boy. For when the women went into labour, each man informed the other of what was happening at his house, and they prepared messengers to send to each other as soon as the child that was being delivered should be born; and being, so to speak, in their own kingdom, they had no trouble ensuring that the messages were sent by a direct route. So it was that the messengers sent out by each man met up exactly halfway between the two houses, making it impossible for either man to record any difference in the position of the stars or in the smallest particulars of the moment of birth. Yet Firminus was born to high place in his household, and walked the high roads of the world; he was furnished abundantly with riches and exalted with high offices, whereas the slave served his masters with no remission at all to his servile condition, as Firminus, who knew him, could attest.

7.6.9 I heard this account and, in view of the narrator, believed it; and all my resistance gave way and collapsed, and first of all I endeavoured to recall Firminus from his curiosity about astrological affairs, telling him that, having inspected his birth signs, if I wished to tell the truth, I would have to say that I saw in them that his parents were masters in their own home, that theirs was a noble family, possessing citizen rights, that the children were free-born and received a gentleman's education in the liberal arts; but if the aforementioned slave had consulted me about his birth signs (these being identical for him too), if I were to tell him also the truth, I would have to say instead that in them I saw a most humble family, in a servile state, and so forth − all quite remote and quite distant from the first family. How, then, I asked, could it be that if I considered the same horoscopes, I would have to give different answers if I were to speak truly; but if I give the same answers, I would be speaking falsely. From this I concluded as a certainty that the truths which are told out of a consideration of birth signs are not spoken out of skill but out of sortilege; whereas the falsehoods are not spoken from ignorance of the art but from the lying nature of the sortilege.

7.7.10 Having made this my starting point, I went on to ponder the matter for myself, not wishing any of those dupes who made their living from astrology to resist me on the grounds that Firminus had told me (or his father had told him) a false story; for by now I could almost want to turn on them, laugh at them, and prove them wrong. I focused my thoughts on the question of twins, who generally speaking emerge from the womb after each other with only a short interval between them − so short that whatever force the astrologers attribute to it in the scheme of the universe, it cannot be registered by human observation, nor can it be distinguished by the manuals that an astrologer must inspect, if he would make a true prediction. But his prediction would certainly not be true; for if he inspected his manuals, he would have to make the same prediction about Esau and Jacob, whereas what befell each of them was not the same. His prophecy would, therefore, be false; or if he were to make a true prediction, he could not make the same prediction. But the books he would consult would be the same. If, then, the prediction he made were to be true, it would be a matter of sortilege, not of skill. For you, O Lord, most righteous Moderator of the universe, *out of the depth of your judgement* (Ps. 36.6 [Ps. 35.7]), bring it about that by some hidden instinct, without the knowledge either of consultor or consulted, every consultor hears what it is right that he should hear, according to his soul's hidden deservings. Let no man say to him, 'What is this?' or 'Why is this?' Let him not say it. Let him not say it. He is a man.

7.7.11 So it was that you, *my Helper* (Ps. 18.1, Ps. 19.15, Ps. 59.17 [Ps. 17.3, Ps. 18.15, Ps. 58.18]), had now freed me from my bonds. I sought to know the origin of evil, but found no way out. But you did not allow any wave of anxious thought to carry me away from my faith. By that faith I believed both that you exist and that your substance is unchangeable; that you care for and judge mankind; and that in Christ, your Son, our Lord, and in the Holy Scriptures that are upheld by the authority of your Catholic Church, you have laid the way of salvation for mankind – the way that leads to the life which is to come after this death. These beliefs remained firm and unshakeably buttressed in my heart, even though I wavered as I enquired into the origin of evil. What birth pangs my heart knew then, and what groans it gave! But even then your ears were near, though I did not know it. When I sought valiantly in silence, the unuttered tribulations of my heart rang like great voices calling out to your mercy. What I was suffering, you knew, but no man knew. How much of this did I share through my tongue with the ears of my most intimate friends! All the tumult of my soul, for which I had neither time nor speech enough, resounded around them. But it all came into your hearing: the way I *roared with the groaning of my heart*, and *my desire was before you*, and *the light of my eyes was not with me* (Ps. 38.9–11 [Ps. 37.9–11]). That light was within, but I was without. Nor was that light in any place; but I was applying myself to things that are contained within place, and found in them no place to rest. Nor was there room for me in those places, to let me say, 'I am satisfied; all is well'; but nor did they let me return to where all would be well, and I would be satisfied. For I was higher than those things, but lower than you. You would have been my true joy, had I made myself your subject, and you would have put into subjection to me all you had created to be lower than me. This would have been the proper mean, the straight middle way to my salvation: to remain *fashioned in your image* (Gen. 1.28), and, being slave to you, to be master of the corporeal. But since I rose up and *ran against the Lord with the thick boss of my shield* (Job 15.26), even those lowest things became higher than me, and pushed me down, giving me no respite and no breathing space. These lower things assailed my senses from all sides in great heaps and masses, and when I contemplated them, the very images of their corporeality blocked my return to you, saying, as it were: 'Where are you going, unworthy and soiled one?' All this stemmed from my wounded condition; for *you have laid low the proud as if smitten with a wound* (Ps. 89.11 [Ps. 88.11]). I was separated from you by my pride, and my face was so puffed up that my eyes were closed.

7.8.12 But you, O Lord, *abide for ever* (Ps. 102.12 [Ps. 101.13]), but are not *angry with us for ever* (Ps. 85.5 [Ps. 84.6]), for you had mercy upon our *earth and us* (Ecclesiasticus 17.31), and it was pleasing in your sight to restore my moral deformities to their proper form. You drove me on by inward goadings to be impatient until with my inner sight I gained certain knowledge of you. The swelling of my pride began to subside under the treatment of your hidden hand, and my mental sight, which had been troubled and darkened, was restored from day to day by the astringent salve of the sufferings that brought me health.

7.9.13 First, however, wishing to show me how you *resist the proud, and give grace to the humble* (Prov. 3.34, James 4.6, 1Pet. 5.5), and with what mercy you have shown to mankind the path of humility, in that your *Word was made flesh, and dwelt among men*, you obtained for me through the agency of a man swollen with pride of the most monstrous sort certain books of the Platonists, translated from Greek into Latin. In them I read – not, it is true, in these same words, but the very same message, argued with many intricate chains of reasoning – that *in the beginning was the Word, and the Word was with God, and the Word was God. He was in the beginning with God. Through him all things were made, and without him was not anything made that was made. In him was life, and the life was the light of men; and the light shines in the darkness, and the darkness has not comprehended it.* I read, too, that the human soul, although it *bears witness to the light*, is not itself that light; but the Word – God – is the *true light, that lightens every man that comes into this world*; and that *he was in the world, and the world was made through him, and the world did not recognize him.* But as for the fact that *he came to his own, and his own did not receive him; but as many as received him, to them he gave authority to become children of God, to those that believed in his name* (Jn 1.1–14) – that I did not read in the Platonists.

7.9.14 Likewise I read in them that *the Word*, that is God, *was born not of the blood nor of the will of man nor of the will of the flesh, but of God*; but as for the fact that *the Word was made flesh and dwelt among us* (Jn 1.13–14), that I did not read. But in those books I did find it said in many and various ways that the Son, *being in the form of God did not consider equality with God a thing to be grasped at* – being by nature the very Same[1] – but that *he emptied himself, taking on the form of a slave, and was made in the likeness of mankind; and being found in fashion as a man, he humbled himself, becoming obedient all the way to death, even death on a cross; wherefore God raised him up* from the dead *and gave him the name that is above all names, that at the name of Jesus*

1 '. . . the Same'. On the significance of identity in Augustine's theology, see 9.4.11.

*every knee should bow, of things heavenly, earthly, and of things
beneath; and that every tongue should confess that Jesus is Lord, to
the glory of God the Father* – that is not contained in the Platonists' books (Phil. 2.6–11). As for the fact that your only-begotten
Son abides coeternally with you before all time and above all
time, and that souls *receive from his fulness* (Jn 1.16) in order to
obtain blessedness, and that they are renewed by participation
in *the Wisdom that abides in itself* (Wisdom 7.27) in order to be
wise, that is there; but as for the fact that *in due time he died for
the impious*, and that *you did not spare your only Son, but gave him
over for us all* – that is not there. For *you have hidden these things
from the wise and revealed them to the little children* (Matt. 11.25),
so that they should *come to him weary and heavy-laden, and he
would refresh them, for he is meek and humble in heart* (Matt.
11.28–9); *he will direct the meek in judgement, and teach the gentle
his ways* (Ps. 25.8 [Ps. 24.9]); *you see our humility and our labours,
and forgive all our sins* (Ps. 25.17 [Ps. 24.18]). But those who strut
around on the high boots[2] of their so-called higher doctrine do
not listen to him who says, '*Learn from me, for I am meek and
humble in heart, and you will find rest for your souls*' (Matt. 11.29).
Although they recognize God, *they honour him not as God, nor
do they give thanks to him, and in their own conceits they have
dwindled away to nought. Their foolish heart is darkened; saying
that they are wise, they have become fools* (Rom. 1.21–2).

7.9.15 Thus I read in those books how *they have exchanged the
glory of the incorruptible God for the likeness of a corruptible man,
of birds, of four-footed beasts, and of creeping things* (Rom. 1.23),
that is to say, the food of the Egyptians, for which Esau lost his
rights as first-born; for your first-born people honoured the
head of a four-footed beast, instead of you (cf Ex. 32.1–6), and
turned back in heart towards Egypt (Acts 7.39), and twisted your
image, its own soul, into *the likeness of the bullock that eats hay*
(Ps. 106.20 [Ps. 105.20]). These things I found there, but I did
not eat of them. For it pleased you, O Lord, to *take away the
reproach* (Ps. 119.22 [Ps. 118.22]), of being the younger son from

---

2 'high boots'. The *cothurnus* or buskin worn by tragic actors, also a byword for
high-flown literary style.

Jacob, and to make *the elder serve the younger* (Gen. 25.23, Rom. 9.23), and you *called the nations into your inheritance* (Ps. 79.1 [Ps. 78.1]). I too had come to you from out of the nations, and I applied myself to the gold which by your will your people took from Egypt,[3] for it was your own, wherever it was. Through your apostle you told the Athenians that *in you we live and move and have our being*, as some of their own poets have said (Acts 17.28), and it was from Athens that these books came. I gave no attention to the idols of the Egyptians, to which those who *turn God's truth into a lie, and worship and serve the creature rather than the creator* (Rom. 1.25), use your gold to minister.

7.10.16 And being admonished to return from there (cf Matt. 2.22) to myself, I entered my own deepest being. You were my guide, and I could do it because you *became my helper* (Ps. 30.11 [Ps. 29.11]), I entered, and I saw with my soul's eye, such as it is, an unchangeable light, a light above my soul's eye, above my mind; not the ordinary light that is visible to all flesh, nor something of the same sort but greater, as if daylight were to shine brighter and brighter and fill the totality of things with its magnitude. This light was not that, but something different, far different from all such things. It was not above my mind in the way that oil floats above water, or that heaven is above the earth, but higher because it made me, and I was lower because I was made by it. He who knows the truth, knows this light, and he who knows this light knows eternity. Love knows this light. O eternal truth, true love, and beloved eternity! *You are my God* (Ps. 43.2 [Ps 42.1]), and for you I sigh day and night. When I first recognized you, it was you who took me up so that I could see that there existed something for me to see, and that I who saw it, did not yet exist. You beat against the weakness of my sight, shining with brilliant radiance, and I shook with love and trembling; and I found that I was far from you, in a land of unlikeness (cf Lk 15.13). It was as if I heard your *voice from on*

3 '... gold ... from Egypt'. Cf Ex. 3.22, 11.2. The 'spoiling of the Egyptians' (when Yahweh ordered the fleeing Israelites to strip the Egyptians of their gold and silver) is used by Augustine as an image for the correct Christian use of pagan culture.

high (Jer. 31.15), saying: 'I am the food of grown adults; grow, and you will eat me. Nor will you change me within yourself, as you change the food of your flesh, but you will be changed within me.' And I acknowledged that *according to his iniquity do you teach a man, and you have made my soul to waste away like a cobweb* (Ps. 39.12 [Ps. 38.12]), and I said, 'Is truth a nothing, seeing as it is diffused neither through finite nor through infinite space?' And you shouted out from afar, 'No indeed! *I am who I am*' (Ex. 3.14). I heard these words as one hears in the heart, and there were no grounds at all for doubting; I could more easily have doubted that I was alive than that there was no truth, which is perceived and glimpsed through created things.

7.11.17 I considered too the remaining things, those that are beneath you, and I saw that they did not entirely exist or not exist. They existed, inasmuch as they were from you, but they did not exist, inasmuch as they were not what you are. The truly existent is that which abides unchangeable. *For me it is good to cleave to God* (Ps. 73.27 [Ps. 72.28]), since if I do not *abide in him* (Jn 15.4), I cannot abide in myself. But he *abides in himself and makes all things new* (Wisdom 7.27), and *you are my Lord, for you need none of my goods* (Ps. 16.2 [Ps. 15.2]).

7.12.18 It was revealed to me also that it is good things that are corrupted. They could not be corrupted if they were supreme goods, nor unless they were good. If they were supreme goods, they would be incorruptible, whereas if they were not good at all, there would be nothing in them to be corrupted. Corruption damages; and it would not damage if the good were not diminished. Therefore, either corruption does not damage at all (which is impossible), or all things that are corrupted are deprived of good (which is most certain). But if they are deprived of all good, they surely do not exist at all. Things that exist and are incapable of corruption are assuredly better things, for they will remain incorruptible. And what could be more impious than to say that things become better when they have lost all good? All that is, then, is good. As for evil, whose origin I was seeking, it is not a substance, since if it were a substance, it would be good. For as a substance it would either be incorruptible (in which case it would be a great good), or corruptible; but it could not be corrupted if it were not good. Thus I saw and thus it was revealed to me that it is you who have made all good things, and that there are no substances at all that you have not made. The reason why they *all* exist is that you have not made them all the same. Individually they are good, and all together they are very good; for our God *made all things to be very good* (Gen. 1.31, Ecclesiasticus 39.21).

7.13.19 For you there is no evil at all; and not for you only, but for all your creation, for outside you there is nothing which could irrupt upon and corrupt the order you have set on creation. In parts of creation, however, there are some things that are not appropriate to those parts, and for that reason are thought evil; but these same things are themselves appropriate to other parts, and are good both in that respect and in themselves. And all these things that are not appropriate to each other, are appropriate to that lower part of the universe that we call 'earth' – earth, that has its own sky, full as it is of clouds and wind, but fitting to itself. Far be it from me to say now, 'Would that these things did not exist.' For if I were to contemplate them alone, I would indeed long for better things, but as it is, I am bound to praise you even for these. *Dragons and all deeps, fire, hail, snow, ice, stormy winds that do your word, mountains and all hills, fruitful trees and all cedars, all beasts wild and tame, creeping things and winged birds* proclaim on earth your praiseworthiness; *kings of the earth and all peoples, princes and all judges of the world, young men and maidens, old men and children praise your name*. But in heaven also may you, our God, be praised. *Let all your angels praise you in the highest; let all your hosts, the sun and the moon, all stars and light, the heaven of heavens and the waters that are above the heavens, praise your name* (Ps. 148.1–12). I did not now long for better things, for I pondered on all things, and I now considered the better things to be higher indeed than the lower ones, but with my judgement somewhat healed I held the whole to be better than the higher things alone.

7.14.20 But *there is no healing* (Ps. 38.3, 7 [Ps. 27.4, 8]) for those who are displeased at some part of your creation, just as there was none for me as long as I was displeased at many of the things you have made. And since my soul did not venture to be displeased at my God, it refused to believe that anything that displeased it was of you. Hence it strayed into its theory of the two substances, found no rest, and spoke other men's words. On its way back from there it had fashioned for itself a God with infinite spatial extension, supposed that deity to be you, and set up in its heart, becoming once again the *temple of its own idol* (2Cor. 6.16), an abomination before you. But when, without my knowledge, you stroked my head and closed my *eyes lest they see vanity* (Ps. 119.37 [Ps. 118.37]), I stood back from myself for a short while; my madness *slept, and I awoke* (Ps. 3.5 [Ps. 3.4]) in you, and I saw that you were infinite in a different sense, and this vision did not come to me through the flesh.

7.15.21 I turned my sight to other things, and saw that they owe their being to you, and that in you all things are finite, but in a different sense; not finite in place, but because you hold all things in your hand, they are bounded by truth; all things are true, in so far as they exist, nor is there any falsehood, except when something is thought to exist that does not. I saw, too, that everything is appropriate not only to its place but to its time, and that you, who alone are eternal, did not begin to work after an unmeasurable space of time, for all spaces of time, both those that have passed by and those that will pass by, would neither come nor go were you not working and abiding.

7.16.22 I realized, too, from my own experience, that bread is a torture to a sick palate but a pleasure to a healthy one, and that weak eyes hate the light that sound eyes love. To the wicked, even your justice is displeasing; much more so the viper and the worm, the good things that you have created, which are well fitted to the lower parts of your creation, to which the wicked themselves are well fitted in proportion as they are unlike you – whereas they are fitted to the higher parts, in proportion as they become more like to you. I sought to know what wickedness was, and found it was no substance, but a perverse distortion of the will away from the highest substance and towards the lowest things; the will *casts forth its innermost part* (Ecclesiasticus 10.10), and swells outwards.

7.17.23 I was full of wonder that I now loved you, not some illusion instead of you. I did not, however, stand fast in the enjoyment of my God, but was borne up to you by your harmonious beauty, and soon borne down away from you by my own weight, and fell back to these lower things with a groan; and this weight was that of my carnal habits. But the memory of you remained with me, nor did I have any doubt that you existed for me to cleave to; rather I thought that I did not exist in such a state as to cleave to you, for *the body, being corruptible, weighs down the soul, and the earthly dwelling place overwhelms the mind that thinks on many things* (Wisdom 9.15). I was wholly certain that *from the foundation of the world your invisible nature has been apprehended and perceived through the things you have made, both your eternal strength and your divinity* (Rom. 1.20). I sought to know why I thought good the beauty of physical objects, whether in the heavens or on earth, and what it was that helped me judge correctly when I said of mutable objects, 'This thing ought to be such and such, but that thing so and so.' As I asked the question of why I judged thus (seeing that I did judge thus) I had found an eternity of truth, unchangeable and true, that was above my changeable mind. So it was that gradually I was led from bodily objects to the soul that through the body perceives them, and thence to the inner faculty of the soul to which the body's senses report what is outside. Thus far the beasts also can comprehend; but from there I proceeded further, to the ratiocinative power to which the soul brings for judgement what it receives from the bodily senses. This ratiocinative power, finding that within me it was itself changeable, lifted itself up to the level of its own understanding, and removed my thoughts from their usual path. It took itself away from the crowd of contradictory illusions, to find what light was cast upon it when it unhesitatingly proclaimed that the unchangeable was to be preferred to the changeable, and how it knew the unchangeable itself; for if it did not know the unchangeable at least to some degree, there was no way in which it could with certainty prefer the unchangeable to the changeable. My soul went on and *in the twinkling of an eye* (1Cor. 15.52) attained to that which is. Then at last I *apprehended and perceived your invisible nature through the things you have made* (Rom. 1.20), but I could not fix my gaze on them. My weakness was driven back from it, and I was returned to familiar things, and I carried in me only a loving memory of it, like the desire for things I had smelt but did not yet have the strength to eat.

7.18.24 I sought the way to get the strength to be able to enjoy you, but I did not find it until I embraced the *mediator between God and men, the man Christ Jesus* (1Tim. 2.5), who *is above all things, God for ever blessed* (Rom. 9.5); he who cries out and says, *I am the way and the truth and the life* (Jn 14.6); who mixes with flesh the food that I was too weak to receive – for *the Word became flesh* (Jn 1.14) so that your Wisdom, *through which you have created all things* (Col. 1.16) might nourish us in our infancy like milk. I did not humbly hold on to my God, Jesus the humble, nor did I know what his weakness had to teach me. For your Word, eternal Truth, towers over the highest parts of your creation and lifts up to himself those that submit to him; but in the lower parts of it he has *built for himself a house* (Prov. 9.1) of our clay, through which to bring men down from themselves and draw them to him to be brought into submission. He heals the swelling of their pride and nurses their love, so that they should not trust in themselves and depart from him, but seeing before their feet the weakness of the Godhead who shares in our *clothing of skin* (Gen. 3.21) might themselves be made weak, and cast themselves in exhaustion upon him; and he, rising, might raise them up.

7.19.25 I, however, thought otherwise, and thought of my Lord Christ only as much as I would of a man of outstanding wisdom, to whom none could be compared. Most of all, I thought his miraculous virgin birth to be an example of how things temporal are to be despised for the sake of gaining immortality; and that through his divine care for us he had earned his great authority as a teacher. But as for the mystery of the *Word made flesh* (Jn 1.1), at that I could not even guess. From what the Scriptures record about him – that he ate and drank, slept, walked, rejoiced, was sad, talked among us – I learnt that not without a human soul and mind did that flesh cleave to your Word.

This much is known to all who know the unchangeability of your Word, which by now I knew, as far as I could, and had no doubt about any part of it. The fact that he could will at one moment to move the limbs of his body and at another not to move them, that at one moment he felt one emotion and at another did not, that through linguistic signs he could impart his wise sayings at one moment, and at another be silent – these are properties of changeability of soul and mind. If what was written about him in these respects were false, the whole thing would risk being a lie, nor would there remain any salvation for the human race by trusting in the Scriptures. But as these Scriptures are true, I recognized in Christ a whole man, not just a human body or an animating soul allied to a body but without a mind. I judged that as a very human being he was to be preferred to all others; not as a personification of truth, but for the surpassing excellence of his human nature, and his more perfect participation in wisdom.

Alypius, however, thought that Catholics believed the Word to be God clothed in flesh, such that there was nothing in him except God and flesh; Catholics, he thought, taught that there was in him no human soul or mind. And being well assured that the things recorded about Christ could come about only in a living and rational creature, he was accordingly more reluctant to move towards the Christian faith. But on learning that this was an error taught by the Apollinarist heretics, he rejoiced and was reconciled to the Catholic faith. I, for my part, admit that I learnt rather later what a gulf lay between the Catholic truth and the Photinian falsehood in the matter of how *the Word was made flesh* (Jn 1.14). It is the slander of heretics that makes it stand out what your Church believes and what sound doctrine teaches. For *it is right that heresies too should exist, so that those who are found good should be made plain* (1Cor. 11.19) to the weak.

7.20.26 But at that time, having read the Platonist literature and been admonished by them to seek the incorporeal truth,

I *apprehended and perceived your invisible nature through the things you have made* (Rom. 1.20), and though driven back, I sensed what through the darkness of my soul I was not permitted to contemplate. I was certain that you existed, that you were infinite and not diffused over finite space, and that you existed in truth, in that you had always been yourself and the Same, neither anyone or anything else in any part or in any motion, and that all other things were from you – there being one proof of this, and that the strongest of all, namely that they exist. I was certain of all these things, but too weak to enjoy you. I could patter away about these matters as if quite learned in them; but if I had not sought your Way *in Christ our Saviour* (Tit. 1.4), I would not have been learned but lurching towards destruction. I had now begun to wish to be thought wise, being full of my own punishment; nor did I weep, but rather was puffed up with my knowledge. Where was *the love that builds on the foundation of humility, which is Christ Jesus* (1Cor. 8.1, 3.11)? When did the Platonist books teach that? I believe you wished me to encounter them before I considered your Scriptures, to the end that it should be impressed on my memory how I was affected by them, and, later, when I had been made docile towards your Scriptures, and my wounds were being treated by your healing fingers, I could discern and distinguish the difference between presumption and confession; between those who saw where they should go, but not how, and the Way that leads to our blessed Homeland, which we will not only descry but in which we shall dwell. Had I been educated in your Holy Scriptures first, and had you cast your sweetness over me by my familiarity with them, then perhaps either the Platonist literature would have cut me adrift from my mooring of piety, or, if I had stood firm in the health-giving attitude I had imbibed, I would have thought that that attitude could be conceived from a reading of the Platonist literature alone, if one had read nothing else.

7.21.27 So I seized avidly upon the venerable idiom of your Spirit, and most of all on the Apostle Paul, and all my quibbling came to an end. At one time it had seemed to me that the texture of his language was self-contradictory and inconsistent with the testimonies of the Law and the Prophets, but now it was clear to me that the holy oracles had all one tenor, and I learnt to *rejoice and tremble* (Ps. 2.11). I found, too, that all the truths I found spoken there were ascribed to your grace. This was done so that whoever saw these truths should not boast, as if he had been given not only the truths he saw, but even the very power of seeing them – for *what does a man have that has not been given to him* (1Cor. 4.7)? It was done also so that such a person should not only be admonished to see you, who are for ever the same, but also to be healed, so that he can hold on to you; and that he who cannot see you from afar, should nevertheless walk in the way by which he may come and see and hold on to you. For although a man *rejoices in the law of God according to the inner man*, what shall he do about *the other law in his members that fights against the law in his mind, and leads him captive into the law of sin that is in his members* (Rom. 7.22–3).

Righteous are you, O Lord (Ps. 119.137 [Ps. 118.137], Tobit 3.2), but *we have sinned, and done wrong* (1Kings 8.47). We have acted impiously, and *your hand has been heavy upon us* (Ps. 32.4 [Ps. 31.4]), and justly have you handed us over to the ancient sinner, the Lord of Death, since he has persuaded our will to take on the likeness of his will; and he has willed not to *stand fast in your truth* (Jn 8.44). *What is a wretched man to do? Who will deliver him from the body that is leading him to this death, if not your grace shown through Jesus Christ our Lord* (Rom. 7.24–5), whom you begat as your coeternal, and created *in the beginning of your ways* (Prov. 8.22), in whom the *prince of this world* (Jn 14.30), *found nothing deserving of death* (Lk 23.14–15), and killed him; and *the record of our debt was made void* (Col. 2.14)? These things are not contained in the books of the Platonists. They do not have this countenance of piety, that is, the tears of confession, nor *the sacrifice acceptable to you*, that is, a *broken spirit, and a heart crushed and laid low* (Ps. 51.17 [Ps. 50.19]) nor the salvation of your people, the *betrothed city* (Rev. 21.2), the *pledge of your Holy Spirit* (2Cor. 5.5), the cup by which our price is paid. No one in the Platonist books chants the words: *Surely my soul will be subdued to God; for he is my God and my salvation, and he that lifts me up so that I shall be moved no longer* (Ps. 62.1–2 [Ps. 61.1–

2]). No one hears in them the voice that calls out: *Come to me, you who labour.* The Platonists disdain to *learn from him, for he is meek and humble in heart. You have hidden these things from the wise, and revealed them to the little ones* (Matt. 11.28–9). It is one thing to see the Homeland of Peace from a wild mountain top (cf Deut. 34.1–4) and not to find the road that leads to it, and to attempt in vain to enter it by trackless and circuitous routes, beset by renegade deserters who lie in ambush, and with them their prince, *the lion and the dragon* (Ps. 91.13 [Ps. 90.13]). It is another thing to hold on to the Way that leads there, that is paved by the care of the Emperor of Heaven, where there are no ambuscades set by deserters from the heavenly soldiery; for they avoid that Way like torture. These things lodged in my vitals in wondrous ways, as I read *the least of your Apostles* (1Cor. 15.9), considered *your works, and was afraid* (Habakkuk 3.2).

BOOK EIGHT

8.1.1 My God, may I recall with thanksgiving and confess to you *your mercies towards me* (Ps. 86.12–13 [Ps. 85.13]). *Let my bones be steeped in your love* and let them say: *Lord, who is like unto you?* (Ps. 35.10 [Ps. 34.10]). *You have burst my bonds*, and I would *offer to you the sacrifice of praise* (Ps. 116.16–17 [Ps. 117.16–17]). How you burst them, I shall tell; and all who worship you, when they hear it, shall say: *Blessed be the Lord God in heaven and on earth; great and marvellous is his name.*[1] Your words had lodged deep in my being, and *you hemmed me in on every side* (Is. 29.2). Concerning your eternal life I was certain, even though I saw it *in a glass darkly* (1Cor. 13.12). As for the incorruptibility of your substance, all my uncertainty on that score had been taken from me, since I saw that every substance comes from your substance. I desired not to be more certain about you, but to stand more firmly in you. But concerning my temporal life, all was uncertain; my heart was yet to be cleansed of the old leaven (1Cor. 13.12). I had chosen the Way, who is our Saviour, but was still reluctant to pass through the narrow places of that Way (cf Matt. 7.14).

Then you put a thought into my mind, and it seemed good in my sight to go straight to Simplicianus. It was clear to me that he was a good servant of yours; in him your grace shone out. I had heard that from his youth he had lived a life of complete devotion to you. He was now an old man; and, given his great age, and the devout zeal with which he followed your Way, I was sure he had experienced much and had learnt much. And so it was. I wanted, therefore, to share with him the ebb and flow of my uncertainties, and to hear from him what was the proper middle course for one affected as I was, so that I could *walk in your Way* (Ps. 128.1 [Ps. 127.1]).

1 '*Blessed be the Lord . . . is his name*'. An agglomeration of references to Ps. 72.19 [Ps. 71.18], Ps. 135.6 [Ps. 134.6], Ps. 75.1 [Ps. 74.1]).

8.1.2 I could see that the Church was full of people, each according to their own sort.[2] I had no pleasure in my worldly business,
and it was now a great burden on me, for I was no longer set on
fire by my familiar desires – the hope of high office or of wealth
– to endure such heavy servitude. Such things held no delight
for me compared with your sweetness and *the beauty of your
house*, which I loved (Ps. 26.8 [Ps. 25.8]). But I was still caught
fast in my entanglement with womankind. Your Apostle did not
forbid me to marry, but he urged me to better things and *would
have all men to be as he was* (1Cor. 7.7–8). In my weakness,
I chose a more comfortable spot; and for this one reason I was
tossed around with sickness in all other matters, consumed and
wasting away with anxieties. Being bound over to the conjugal
life, I was forced to conform to it even in respect of things I had
no wish to undergo. I had heard from the mouth of truth that
there are *eunuchs who have made themselves so for the sake of the
Kingdom of Heaven*, but *let him receive this who can receive it*
(Matt. 12.9). It is certain that *all men are vain in whom there is
no knowledge of God, nor from among the things that seem good
have they been able to find him who is* (Wisdom 13.1). I was not
now in that state of vanity; I had transcended it, and by the
universal testimony of all creation had found you, our Creator,
and your Word, who is with you, and with you is one God,
through whom you have created all things (Jn 1.1–3). And there
is another sort of impiety – that of those who *knowing God have
not worshipped him as God, nor given thanks* (Rom. 1.22). Into
this error, too, I had fallen; but your right hand raised me up,
took me from it, and set me in a place where I could recover; for
you have said to man: *Behold, piety is wisdom* (Job 28.28), and *do
not wish to appear wise* (Prov. 26.5), for *saying they are wise they
have made themselves fools* (Rom. 1.22). I had now found the great
pearl. It remained for me to *sell all I had and buy it* (Matt. 19.21),
and that I could not do.

8.2.3 Therefore I went directly to Simplicianus, who was the
father of the current Bishop, Ambrose, by virtue of baptism,

2 '. . . each according to their own sort'. Based on 1Cor. 7.7, where the division
is between married and unmarried Christians.

and whom Ambrose indeed loved as a father. I told him of the circuitous paths in which I had strayed. But when I mentioned the fact that I had read various books of the Platonist persuasion, translated into Latin by Victorinus, the sometime City Orator at Rome, who, as I had heard, had died a Christian, Simplicianus congratulated me on not having stumbled on the literature of other philosophers; they were, he said, *full of fallacies and deceits, according to the elements of this world* (Col. 2.8), whereas the Platonist literature hinted in every way at God and his Word. Then, by way of exhorting me to the humility of Christ which is *hidden from the wise and revealed to the little children* (Matt. 11.25), he gave me his own recollections of Victorinus himself, whom he had known very well when he was at Rome; and he told me a story about him that I will not keep to myself. For I am bound to confess and offer great praise to your grace for Victorinus's action. He was an old man of great learning, most skilled in every liberal art, who had read and evaluated the works of so many philosophers. He had taught a great many noble Senators, and, in reward for his distinguished discharge of his office as teacher, had been granted what the citizens of this world deem the highest honour of all, namely a statue in the Forum at Rome. He had until his old age been a worshipper of idols and a participant in the sacrilegious rites with which, at that time, the vast majority of the Roman nobility were full – the rites in which they sighed for the Infant Osiris, for

> ... those monstrous deities, mongrel-gods begot
> Of every breed, barking Anubis – who against
> Neptune and Venus and Minerva once
> Wielded their weapons.[3]

3 'those monstrous deities ... weapons'. Taken from Virgil, *Aeneid* 8.698–700, a description of the prophetic representation on the Shield of Aeneas of the Battle of Actium. Anubis and Osiris are Egyptian deities revered by Cleopatra, opposed to the traditional Roman gods; the mystery cult of Osiris enjoyed some popularity under the Roman Empire. Here Augustine pokes fun at the Roman aristocracy for resenting the innovation of Christianity, when at least some of them were devotees of the foreign cults vilified in Rome's great patriotic poem.

These were the gods whom Rome had once conquered, and whose aid she now implored; and for many years old Victorinus had defended them with thunderous eloquence. But he was not ashamed to become a child of Christ, an infant at your font, *bending his neck to the yoke of humility* (Ecclesiasticus 51.34, Jer. 27.12, Matt. 11.29) and conquering his pride before the *reproach of the Cross* (Gal. 5.11).

8.2.4 O Lord, Lord, who *bowed down the heavens and descended, who touched the mountains and they smoked* (Ps. 144.5 [Ps. 143.5]), by what means did you steal into Victorinus's heart? He was reading (according to Simplicianus) the Holy Scriptures and making a most thorough inspection and scrutiny of the whole of Christian literature, and would say to Simplicianus – not openly, but as between friends – 'Rest assured that I am now a Christian.' Simplicianus would reply, 'I shall not believe it, or set you down as a Christian, until I see you in the church of Christ.' And Victorinus would laugh at him and say, 'Is it, then, walls that make a Christian?' He would often say the same thing, that he was now a Christian, and Simplicianus would make the same reply, and get the same jibe about walls in return. Victorinus was afraid of offending his friends, those proud worshippers of demons, thinking that enmity would come crashing down upon him from the heights of their Babylonian elevation, as if from the *cedars of Lebanon, which the Lord has not yet laid low* (Ps 29.5 [Ps. 28.5]).

But having read and drunk in the Scriptures and accepted their trustworthiness, he became afraid of being denied by Christ before the holy angels, if he was afraid to confess him before men (cf Matt. 10.32–3, Mk 8.38, Lk 12.8–9); and it became apparent to him that he was guilty of a great crime in being ashamed of the mysteries of your humility but not of the sacrilegious rites of the proud demons, which he had received by tradition and proudly imitated. Accordingly, he put off his shame for vanity, and blushed for the truth; and suddenly and unexpectedly he said to Simplicianus, 'Let us go to church. I want to become a Christian.' Unable to contain himself for joy, Simplicianus set off with him. Not long after he had been steeped in the first mysteries of instruction, he also enrolled for regeneration through baptism. Rome wondered, the Church rejoiced. The proud *saw it and were wroth; they gnashed with their teeth, and were consumed away* (Ps. 112.10 [Ps. 111.10]). But to your servant, *the Lord God was his hope, nor did he give heed to vanities and lying follies* (Ps. 40.4 [Ps. 39.5]).

8.2.5 When at last the moment came for him to make his profession of faith, which at Rome it is customary for all who are to proceed to your grace to repeat according to a form of words that they have learnt by heart, from a prominent position in sight of the faithful, Simplicianus told me that the priests offered Victorinus the opportunity to repeat it in a more private setting – an offer usually made to those who are likely to hesitate out of shyness. Victorinus, however, preferred to profess his salvation in the sight of the saintly multitude. For it was not salvation that he taught in his duties as Professor of Rhetoric; but he had made a public profession of that! How much less, then, ought he to fear to pronounce your word before your tame flock, having been unafraid to address the mad crowds in his own words! So he went up to repeat the profession; and as each one present recognized him, all whispered his name to each other in a hubbub of mutual delight. And who there did not recognize him? A hushed cheer of shared joy rang through the mouth of all: 'Victorinus! Victorinus!' Suddenly they cheered in exultation at seeing him, then at once fell silent in anticipation of hearing him. He made his pronouncement of the true faith with the plainest assurance, and all wished to take him into their heart. This they did with love and rejoicing; these were the hands that took him in.

8.3.6 O good God, what is it within man that makes him rejoice more over the salvation of a soul given up for dead and his deliverance from a greater peril, than if that soul had never been given up, or the peril had been less? You also, merciful Father, *rejoice more over one penitent than over the ninety-nine righteous who have no need of repentance.* We too listen with great joy, when we hear how the shepherd exults to carry the lost sheep back on his shoulders, and how the neighbours of the woman who found the coin rejoice with her when it is put back in your treasury (cf Lk 15.4–7), and the *joyful solemnities of your house* (Ps. 26.8 [Ps. 25.8]) drive out our tears when the lesson of the Prodigal Son is read there; how he *was dead, and lives again, was lost, and is found* (Lk 15.32). It is in us, therefore, and in your angels, sanctified by your sacred love, that you rejoice. For *you are the same for ever* (Ps. 102.27 [Ps. 101.28], Hebr. 1.12), since you have ever known in the same way the things that do not exist for ever, or do not always exist in the same way.

8.3.7 What is it, then, in a soul, that it delights in finding or having returned to it the things that it loves more than if it had always held on to them? All things bear witness to this, and all things cry aloud in testimony that this is so. The victorious general celebrates his triumph; but had he not fought, he would not be victorious, and the greater the danger in battle, the greater the joy of his triumph. Sailors tossed by a storm and threatened with shipwreck grow pale at the prospect of death; sky and sea fall calm, and, having been greatly afraid, they are greatly exultant. A loved one lies sick, and his pulse gives evidence of his sickness; all who wish him well are likewise sick at heart. He recovers, and before he can walk with his former vigour, there is joy such as there was not beforehand, when he could walk with perfect health and strength. The very pleasures of human life come to men by means of unpleasurable sensations that do not befall them unexpectedly or against their will, but in accordance with their designs and wishes. There is no pleasure in eating or drinking if there has not been a previous unpleasant sensation of hunger or thirst. Drinkers sometimes eat salty foods to set up an unpleasant feeling of burning, for the quenching of this fire with drink gives enjoyment. It is customary not to hand brides over immediately upon betrothal, lest the man, once married, think cheap a girl he did not sigh for impatiently when betrothed.

8.3.8 This holds good in the case of joys that are shameful and damnable, and in those that are legitimate and lawful. It holds good in the most sincere and honourable friendships. It holds good in the case of one who *was dead, and lives again, who was lost, and is found* (Lk 15.24, 32). In all cases, the more unpleasant the previous condition, the greater the joy. Why, O Lord my God, seeing as you are yourself your own eternal joy, and there are certain things, of you and around you, that rejoice for ever – why is it that this part of the universe alternates between wax and wane, repulsion and attraction? Could it be that this is the limit and measure that you have given it, seeing as you set all manner of good things and all your righteous works in their proper place and proper time, from the heights of heaven to the depths of the earth, from the beginning to the end of ages, from angel down to worm, from the first motion to the last? Oh, how much higher are you than the heights, and how much deeper than the depths! You never depart from us, yet we can scarce return to you.

8.4.9 Come, O Lord, I pray. Stir us up and call us back; kindle us and take us to yourself. Set us ablaze, and cast your sweetness over us. Let us love you and run to you. Are there not many who return to you from a pit of blindness deeper than Victorinus's; who *draw near to you and are enlightened* (Ps. 34.5 [Ps. 33.6]), when they receive the light? All who receive that light, receive from you *authority to become your children* (Jn 1.23). But if they are less well known to the populace, there is less rejoicing over them even among those who do know them; whereas when many people rejoice together, there is a richer joy even among the individuals in that multitude, as each rouses and fires up the fervour of the other. Moreover, because the converts are known to many, they become a precedent for many, showing how salvation may be gained. They lead the way, and many will follow; and there is much rejoicing, both over the followers and those that have shown the way, since it is not over isolated individuals. Far be it that the *persons of the rich be accepted in your tabernacle before the poor* (Deut. 1.17, 16.19, Ecclesiasticus 42.1, James 2.1–9), seeing as you have chosen *the weak things of the world, to confound the strong, and the inglorious and contemptible things, and have chosen the things that are not as if they were, to make void the things that are* (1Cor. 1.27–8, Rom. 4.17). Even the *very least of your apostles* (1Cor. 15.9), by whose mouth you spoke these

words, having *warred down the pride*[4] of the proconsul Sergius
Paulus by his soldiership, and forced him to submit to the *gentle
yoke* (Matt. 12.29) of Christ and become a mere provincial of the
great King, loved to be called Paul instead of his previous name
of Saul, as a token of that great victory. The more tightly the
Enemy has had someone captive, and the more he holds captive
because of that one, the more beaten he is; and the proud he
holds all the more tightly with the word 'nobility', and through
them he holds many more with the word 'precedent'. The
greater the esteem, therefore, in which Victorinus was held for
his powers of mind, which the Devil had seized and was holding
as if it were some fastness impregnable to assault, the more right
it was for your children to rejoice in his powers of tongue, that
great sharp spear with which the Devil had slain so many. For
our King had *bound the strong man* (Matt. 12.29), and they could
see how the vessels he had rescued were being *cleansed and made
fit for your honour, and serviceable to their Lord for every good work*
(2Tim. 2.21).

8.5.10 But by the time your servant Simplicianus told me this
story of Victorinus, I was all ablaze to follow his example. It
was, indeed, for this that he had told me it. Then, however,
Simplicianus added that when in the reign of the Emperor Julian a law had been promulgated forbidding Christians to teach
literature or rhetoric, Victorinus had welcomed that law with
open arms, and had chosen to abandon the verbiage of the
schools rather than abandon your Word, by which you *make
eloquent the mouths of infants* (Wisdom 10.21, cf Ps. 8.2 [Ps. 8.3]);
and it seemed to me that Victorinus was a man as fortunate as
he was courageous, inasmuch as he had found an opportunity to
leave himself open to you. This was the very thing that I was
sighing for, being loaded with irons not loaded on me by others,
but my own iron will. The Enemy kept his hold on my powers
of willing, and had made of it a chain for me, and bound me
with it. My will was perverted, and became a lust; I obeyed my
lust as a slave, and it became a habit; I failed to resist my habit,

---

4 '*warred down the pride*'. Based on Virgil, *Aeneid* 6.853; in its original form, a
statement of Rome's imperial mission.

and it became a need. It was with this series of interconnected links — for which reason I have called it a chain — that I was constrained in harsh servitude. But the new will which had sprung up within me — the will to worship you without seeking a return, and to enjoy you, O God, my only certain pleasure — was not yet capable of overcoming the former one, buttressed as it was by its very oldness. My *two wills, the old, carnal will, and the new, spiritual will* (cf Eph. 4.22, 24, Col. 3.9–10), were *at war with one another* (Rom. 7.16–17), and in their discord rent my soul in pieces.

8.5.11 From my own experience I realized that what I had read was true in myself: the *flesh lusted against the spirit, and the spirit against the flesh* (Gal. 5.17). I was in both the flesh and the spirit, but I was more myself in that which I approved in myself, than in that which I disapproved in myself. By now it was rather not I who was in the flesh, since for the most part I was an unwilling sufferer rather than a willing doer. But it was my own doing that habit gripped me so fiercely, since I had arrived willingly at a place to which I had no wish to come. And who could rightly object, when the sinner is pursued by a righteous judgement? Nor did I now have the excuse I was accustomed to make for not yet despising the world and serving you, namely that I had no certain perception of the truth; that too was now certain. I was still bound to the earth, and refused to serve in your army. I was as afraid to be rid of all that hindered me as I should have been of being hindered.

8.5.12 So it was that the burden of the world overwhelmed me with its sweetness, like sleep; and my thoughts, when I meditated upon you, were like the efforts of a sleeper who wants to wake up, but is overcome by the depths of sleep, and is drowned in it once more. And just as there is no one who wishes to sleep all the time, and all sane people agree that it is better to be awake, nevertheless a man will generally postpone the shaking off of sleep when drowsiness lies heavily upon his limbs. Even though it is no longer his purpose to sleep, he does so willingly enough — even though the time has now come to get up. Likewise I was certain that it was better to entrust myself to your love than to yield to my own desire; but I was persuaded and convinced of the one, and charmed and chained by the other. I had no reply to give to you when you said to me: *Wake up, sleeper, and rise up from the dead, and Christ will enlighten you* (Eph. 5.14), and when you demonstrated to me from every angle that you spoke the truth. I was convinced of the truth, but had no reply to give – only sleepy and drowsy words: 'Just a minute,' 'A minute more,' 'Let me be for a little while.' But my 'minute' had no limit, and my 'little while' was becoming a long while. It was in vain that I *delighted in your Law according to the inner man, when another law in my members was at war with the law of my mind, and led me captive in the law of sin, which was in my members* (Rom. 7.22–3). For the 'law of sin' is the violent force of habit, by which the mind is held fast and dragged along as punishment for slipping willingly into it. *Wretch that I am! Who will deliver me from this body of death, except your grace through Jesus Christ, our Lord?* (Rom. 7.24–5])

8.6.13 How you released me from the bonds of sexual desire which held me so tightly, and from my slavery to the affairs of the world, I shall relate and *confess to your name, O Lord* (Ps. 52.9 [Ps. 51.8]), *my Helper and my Redeemer* (Ps. 19.14 [Ps. 18.15]). My habitual anxiety increased as I went about my business; I sighed daily for you, and haunted your church as much I was permitted by the affairs under whose weight I groaned. With me was Alypius, now resting from his legal work after his third term as Clerk to the Court and looking out for new customers for his legal opinions, as I had customers to whom I would sell an easy way with words, so far as that can be passed on by teaching. Nebridius, for his part, had given way to the claims of friendship and was acting as assistant master to Verecundus, a citizen and grammarian of Milan and close friend of us all, who had been in great need of a faithful assistant, and in the name of friendship had requested the help he so much needed from among our number. It was not, therefore, the desire for wealth that induced him to teach – he was capable of far greater literary activity, if he wished – but, being the sweet-tempered and gentle friend that he was, he refused to scorn our entreaties. He conducted his work, however, with the greatest caution, taking care not to make a name for himself among persons great *according to this world* (Eph. 2.2), and avoiding in his teaching all that might disturb the quiet of his mind; for that he wished to keep free and unoccupied for as many hours of the day as possible, while he sought to read or hear something concerning wisdom.

8.6.14 One day – I cannot remember the reason why Nebridius was not present – one Ponticianus came to our house to visit Alypius and myself. He was a fellow-citizen of mine, inasmuch as he was an African, and was performing distinguished service in the Palace Guard, and had some business or other with us. We all sat down and began talking. Ponticianus happened to notice a book which was lying on the gaming table in front of us. He picked it up, opened it, and found that it was the works of the Apostle Paul. This was something he had not expected; he had supposed it was one of the books whose profession was wearing me out. He smiled and looked at me, full of joy on my behalf, and amazed to find these books and no others before my eyes. He was a Christian and baptized, and prostrated himself before you in church many times, with constant, daily prayers. When I told him I was giving close attention to those Scriptures, the conversation took a turn: Ponticianus told us about Antony, the Egyptian monk, whose name was well known among your servants but unknown among us until that hour. When Ponticianus discovered this fact, he persisted on that topic of conversation, giving us to understand what a great man Antony was, and amazed at our ignorance. We were dumbfounded to hear of your *mighty works* (Ps. 145.5 [Ps. 144.5]), which you had wrought through the orthodox faith of the Catholic Church. There was the strongest attestation for them; they had occurred within living memory, and almost, indeed, within our own life-times. We were all amazed: Alypius and I at the greatness of these wonders, Ponticianus at our ignorance of them.

8.6.15 Then the conversation turned to the vast numbers of monasteries, to the moral life that is a sweet savour to you, to the waste places of the wilderness and the abundant riches they contain.[5] There was, indeed, a monastery at Milan, outside the city wall, full of good brothers and under the tutelage of Ambrose; but we had not known this. Ponticianus pressed on and kept talking, and we listened in rapt silence. So it came about that he told us how on one occasion he and three fellow-officers of his at Trier[6] had gone for a walk in the market gardens adjacent to the city walls, while the Emperor was engaged at the morning show at the Games. They were strolling along in pairs, he with one companion and the other two some way apart. The two pairs, he said, went their separate ways; but the second pair, wandering in no particular direction, stumbled upon a little hovel where lived some servants of yours, *poor in spirit, of such as is the Kingdom of Heaven* (Matt. 5.3). There they found a book containing the *Life of Antony*.[7] One of them began to read the *Life*, and was set on fire with wonder; and even as he read it, he began to contemplate laying hold of such a life for himself, leaving the Imperial Service (both of them happened to be Officers of Public Affairs),[8] and serving you. Then, filled all of a sudden with holy love and sober shame, and angry at himself, he cast his eyes on his friend and said: 'Tell me this: all these tasks we endure – where are they taking us? What is it we are looking for? For what reason are we in the Imperial Service? Can we have any greater hope at Court than that of becoming Friends of the Emperor? And if we do, what will we then have that is not frail and beset with perils? How many perils must we

5 '... vast numbers ... they contain'. Christian monasticism has its roots in fourth-century Egypt. The original monks lived outside towns and villages, in the waste country. In western Europe, the 'wilderness' was as much conceptual as local. The monks that Ponticianus and his friends encounter live just outside the city walls. Small islands were another favourite setting.

6 'Trier'. After Milan, the most important Roman administrative centre in the West in late antiquity.

7 *Life of Antony*. By the theologian Athanasius of Alexandria; the first real example of the genre of hagiography. It is preserved in Greek and in two Latin translations.

8 'Officers of Public Affairs'. A division of the Imperial Court whose members were often marked down for rapid promotion to provincial governorships. Among their court duties was the gathering of intelligence. Ponticianus and his colleagues thus enjoyed access to the inner circles of power, and could look forward to high office.

endure to arrive at a greater peril? And when will we do so? But if I wish to become a *friend of God, behold, I can become one now!*' (James 2.23, Judith 8.22).

So saying, he cast his eyes back on the page, troubled by the birth pangs of a new life. He read, and was changed within, where you could see; and, as became apparent soon afterwards, his mind began to put off the world. For as he read the *Life* and pondered the shifting tides of his heart, groaning intermittently, he discerned the better course, and resolved upon it.

Now he was yours, he said to his friend: 'I have now cut myself off from the hope we shared, and decided to serve God. This choice I undertake in this place and from this hour. If you will not be like me, do not be against me.' His friend replied that he would stand by him and share with him in this great reward and great service.

Now both were yours; they had begun to build their tower, having paid the requisite cost (cf Lk 14.28) – that of *abandoning all that was theirs and following you* (Matt. 19.27, Lk 5.11, 28). Then Ponticianus and his companion on his walk through the other parts of the garden came to the same place, looking for them. On finding them, they suggested that they should go back, as the sun had now begun to set (cf Lk 9.12, 24.29). Their friends, however, told them of their resolve and purpose, and how the will to do this had arisen and been confirmed in them; and they asked Ponticianus and his companion, if they refused to join them, not to obstruct them. For their part, Ponticianus told us, he and his companion were not at all changed from their former selves, but nevertheless wept for themselves; they joined piously in their friends' joy, commended themselves to their prayers, and went off towards the Palace, trailing their hearts on the ground, while their friends remained in the hovel, setting their hearts in heaven. Both men, moreover, were engaged; but when their brides heard their story, they too dedicated their virginity to you.

8.7.16 This much Ponticianus told us, but it was you who through his words turned me back to myself. You took me from behind my own back, where I had placed myself so long as

I refused to attend to myself, and you *set me before my own face* (Ps. 50.21 [Ps. 49.21]), where I could see how foul I was: twisted and dirty, full of stains and sores. I saw and was horrified, and *there was nowhere I could flee from myself* (cf Ps. 139.7 [Ps. 138.7]). Even if I tried to avert my gaze from myself, Ponticianus was saying what he was saying, and again you confronted me with myself and painted a picture of me on my eyes, so that I might *discover my iniquity and loathe it* (Ps. 36.2 [Ps. 35.3]). I knew my iniquity; but I hid it away and hushed it up and tried to forget it.

8.7.17 But as Ponticianus told his story, the more ardent the love I felt for those men who, as I was hearing, had been moved to such a wholesome frame of mind, in that they had entrusted themselves wholly to you for their healing, the more I loathed and execrated myself in comparison with them. Many years – perhaps twelve – had flowed away (and my life with them) since in my nineteenth year I had read Cicero's *Hortensius* and been stirred up to a zeal for wisdom, and all that time I had postponed the decision to despise earthly happiness and leave myself free to hunt for wisdom instead. Merely to seek this wisdom, even if I did not find it, now seemed preferable to finding treasure houses or kingships of the nations, or an abundance of bodily pleasures that surpassed all my wishes. But I had spent my young manhood in extreme misery; in such misery I had besought you, on the very brink of manhood, to give me chastity: 'Grant me chastity and continence,' I had said, 'but please, not yet.' I was afraid that you would swiftly answer my prayer and swiftly heal me from the sickness of concupiscence, which I would rather have satiated than extinguished. Moreover, I had walked the crooked paths of an impious superstition; not indeed certain of it, but holding it preferable to other things, which I did not seek with due piety, but had fought as an enemy.

8.7.18 I had thought that I was postponing from day to day the decision to despise my worldly hope and follow you alone on the grounds that no certain landmark had emerged, to which I could steer my course. The day had now come to stand naked before myself, and within me my conscience rebuked me: 'Where is your tongue? Was it not you who used to say that you were reluctant to cast off the burden of vanity because the truth was uncertain? Now it is certain, but you are still weighed down by your burden. Those who most readily gain wings on their shoulders[9] are not those who have worn themselves out in seeking and spent ten years or more pondering these matters.' Thus my conscience gnawed me within, and I was put to shame and confusion most horribly as Ponticianus related his tale. Our conversation concluded, he went off on the errand for which he had come, and I went back to myself. What accusations did I not bring against myself? With what mental whips did I not lash my soul into following me as I endeavoured to come after you? My soul resisted. She refused, and did not excuse herself; all her arguments were used up and shown to be false. There remained to her a mute trepidation; she feared like death to be released from habit, that haemorrhage which was causing her to waste away to death (cf Matt. 9.20, Mk 5.25, Lk 8.43).

8.8.19 As I stirred up my soul in the privacy of my chamber (cf Matt. 6.6), that is, my heart, I stirred up a great quarrel in the house of my inner being. Troubled both in my looks and my mind, I burst in on Alypius, and exclaimed: 'What is it we are enduring? What is it? What have you heard? The untaught arise and *lay hold of heaven* (Matt. 11.12) while we, for all our learning, have no heart – see where we wallow in flesh and blood! Are we ashamed to follow them, merely because they have gone first? Should we not rather be ashamed not to follow them?' These or some such words I spoke, then I was swept away from Alypius by the surging tide of my hesitation, even as he stared at me in silent astonishment. This was not my usual tone. My brow, cheeks, eyes, colour, the pitch of my voice – all these bespoke my thoughts more than any words I uttered.

There was attached to our lodgings a little garden; we had the use of it, along with the whole house, for our landlord, the householder, did not live there. It was to this garden that the tumult of my heart bore me; there would be no one there to

9 '... wings on their shoulders ...'. A reference to Plato's story in the *Phaedrus* 249–50 that the souls of philosophers grow wings more quickly than those of others.

hinder my blazing indictment of myself, until it reached an outcome – what outcome, you knew, O Lord, but I did not. I was
sick with a frenzy that was my cure, dying to gain life. I knew
what evil I was, but not what good I would soon be. So I went
off to the garden, with Alypius hard on my heels, for his presence would not deprive me of privacy, and when would he ever
abandon me in that frame of mind? We sat down as far from
the house as possible. I *groaned in spirit* (Jn 11.33), full of the
most turbulent anger that I was not *entering a covenant and
compact with you* (Ezek. 16.8), that state of being for which *all
my bones* (Ps. 35.10 [Ps. 34.10]) cried out and extolled to the
heavens. But neither by ship nor chariot nor on foot had I pro-
gressed any nearer to it than I had gone from the house to the
place where we were sitting. To progress towards it – indeed, to
attain it – was nothing other than the will to progress, but with
a will that was strong and whole throughout; not a will that was
twisted and tossed around, wounded in part, caught in a struggle
between rising and falling factions.

8.8.20 Moreover, despite the tides of hesitation on which
I drifted, I was physically able to do many things which people
may at times have the will to do and yet be unable; if, for
example, they do not have the limbs, or if they are constrained
with bonds or enervated by sickness, or hindered in some other
way. If I tore my hair, if I beat my brow, if I knitted my fingers
and clasped my knee, I did so because I willed it. It was possible,
however, for me to have willed it and not done it, if my limbs
did not move in obedience. There were, therefore, many things
that I did, in the case of which the will to do them was not the
same as the ability. Yet I did not do what was both incomparably
more in keeping with my purpose, and which I could do as
soon as I willed it, since as soon as I willed it, I would will it
wholeheartedly. My body more readily obeyed the slightest will
of my soul and moved its limbs when ordered, than my soul
itself performed its own will, however great that will might be,
if it only willed to do so.

8.9.21 Whence is this strange situation? and why is it so? Let
your mercy shine out, and let me enquire – if the hidden snares

that are man's punishment and the deep-shadowed tribulations of the children of Adam can respond. Whence is this strange situation? and why is it so? The mind orders the body, and the body obeys; the mind orders itself, and it resists. The mind orders a hand to be moved, and this is accomplished with such ease that its authority can scarcely be discerned from that of a master over his slave. The mind orders the mind to will; it is only one mind, but it does not do as ordered. Whence is this strange situation? and why is it so? I repeat: the mind that gives the order to will could not give the order if it did not will to do so; but it does not do what it orders. It does not will with its whole being, therefore it does not order with its whole being. The mind orders in so far as it wills, and its orders are not obeyed in so far as it does not will them; for it is the will and nothing else that gives the order that the will should exist. If the will were a full will, it would not give the order that the will should exist, since it would already exist. It is not, therefore, such a strange situation, that one should will and not will; it is a sickness of the mind, which, even when uplifted by the truth, does not fully arise, being weighed down by its habit.

8.10.22 *Let them perish from before your face* (Ps. 68.2 [Ps. 67.3]), O God, as perish they do; those *vain talkers and seducers* of men's minds (Tit. 1.10), who, having perceived in their contemplation the existence of two wills, assert that these two minds belong to two Principles,[10] one good, the other evil. They themselves are truly evil, as long as they hold these evil opinions, but these same people would assuredly be good, if they were to perceive the truth and assent to it. Then your Apostle could say to them: *You were once darkness, but now you are light in the Lord* (Eph. 5.8). As long as they have wished to be light not in the

10 '... two wills ... two Principles'. Augustine here returns to his critique of Manichee dualism, which also focused on the problem of the imperfect correspondence between conscious will and action. The word translated here as 'Principle' is *natura*, which can mean 'substance', but which suggests also 'coming into being'; whereas *substantia*, the word used earlier in this book for the divine substance, suggests 'continuous underlying being'. In ch. 24 Augustine reverts to *substantia* and uses also *principium* to describe the Manichees' false doctrine.

Lord but in themselves, thinking that the soul-principle is the
same as God, they have become all the more dense darkness; in
their horrendous arrogance they have departed from you, the
true light that lights every man that comes into the world (Jn 1.9).
Take heed what you say; *blush for shame, go to him, and be
enlightened, and your countenances will not be ashamed* (Ps. 35.4
[Ps. 34.5]). It was I, when I contemplated *serving my Lord God*
(Jer. 30.9), as I had long intended – it was I who willed and
I who did not will; it was I. I neither fully willed nor did I fully
not will. Thus I contended with myself and was rent in pieces
from myself, and even this rending came about without my
willing it, nor was it evidence of some mind-principle not my
own, but of my own punishment. Therefore it was *no longer
I that did this, but the sin that dwelt in me* (Rom. 7.17, 20) – that
sin itself being part of the punishment for a sin more willingly
committed, since I was a son of Adam.

8.10.23 For if there are as many opposing Principles as there
are mutually resisting wills, it follows that there are not two
Principles, but many. If one were to consider either going to a
Manichee conventicle or to the theatre, the Manichees would
exclaim: 'See! There are two natures, one leading him this way,
the other leading him back the other way. What other origin
could there be for this hesitation between two mutually antag-
onistic wills?' I, however, say that both wills are evil, both the
one that leads him towards the Manichees and the one that
leads back towards the theatre. But they believe it is only a
good one which leads people to themselves. Well; suppose
some Catholic were to ponder and hesitate, caught in a conflict
between two opposing wills, whether he should go to the
theatre or the Catholic church. Would the Manichees also not
hesitate before replying? They will either acknowledge – as they
are unwilling to do – that it is out of a good will that one goes
to the Catholic church, as people do who have been steeped in
its sacraments and abide in them; or suppose that there are two
evil Principles and two evil minds in conflict within one man –
in which case their usual teaching that there is one nature that
is good and another that is evil, cannot be true; or they will be

converted to the truth and not deny that when a man ponders a course of action, then his one soul wavers between various wills.

8.10.24 Let them not say, therefore, when they perceive that in one man there are two wills at war with each other, that there is a conflict between two opposing minds, one good and one bad, springing from opposing substances and opposing Principles. For you, God of truth, rebuke them and refute them. You show that they are wrong in cases where there are two wills, both of which are evil; as when one ponders whether he should kill a man with poison or a dagger, or which of his neighbours' lands he should annex, seeing as he cannot annex both; or whether he should purchase pleasure at the cost of extravagance, or save his money at the cost of avarice; or, to add a third possibility, whether he should burgle a house, if he gets the chance; or, to add a fourth, whether he should commit adultery, if the opportunity arises of doing this too, if all these possibilities coincide at a single moment in time, and all are equally desirable but cannot all be done at once. Where there are so many appetible courses of action, the mind is torn by four or even more different wills, but the Manichees do not, as a rule, state that there is an equally large number of substances. So also in the case of good wills. If I ask them whether it is good to take delight in the reading of the works of the Apostle or the singing of a sober psalm, or whether it is good to proclaim the Gospel, they will reply that each of these is good. Well: if all of these things are equally delectable at once, is not the human heart distended with different wills, while it ponders which of these it should choose for itself? All these wills are good, and yet they strive against each other, until one course of action is chosen, and the whole will, which had been divided into several wills, is channelled into it. So too, although eternity has a delight that draws us upwards, and pleasure in temporal good draws us back downwards, there is no one soul that wills with all its will either one or the other. It is torn in two by the weight of its troubles, as long as it prefers the former for truth's sake, but for familiarity's sake does not put aside the latter.

8.11.25 Such was the sickness and torment that I knew as I charged myself even more bitterly than my wont, twisting and turning in my bonds until such time as they should be broken utterly; for now they held me only by a thread. But hold me they did. You, moreover, pressed hard on me in the secret places of my being. In your severe mercy you redoubled the scourgings that fear and shame were giving me, to keep me from yielding before the last thin thread that remained was broken, and to stop it from regaining its strength and binding me all the more strongly. For I was repeatedly saying in myself, 'One minute more, and let it happen; just one minute more'; and with those words I was already *entering a covenant with you* (Ezek. 16.8). I was on the point of doing it yet not doing it; not slipping back into my former life, but standing from my next life, catching my breath. I strove, and was ever less far from it, and was on the point of touching it and seizing it; but I was not in it, and did not touch it or seize it, hesitant as I was to die to death and live to life. The time-worn course of life, for all its faults, counted with me more than the unfamiliar, for all its merits; and the closer the moment became when I was to be something new, the more horror it instilled in me. But it did not drive me off or turn me aside, but kept me dangling.

8.11.26 I was held back by those supreme frivolities, those *vanities of vanities* (Ecclesiastes 1.2, 12.8), that were my old friends. They plucked at my carnal clothing and whispered, 'Are you dismissing us?' 'From that moment on, we will not be with you – not for eternity!' 'From that moment on, you will not be allowed to do such and such a thing – not for eternity!' And what thoughts they put into my mind, my God, with their 'such and such a thing's! What thoughts! Let your mercy turn them aside from the soul of your servant! What sordid and shameful thoughts! But it was now much less than half my being that listened to them. They did not block my path and speak out openly against me, but whispered behind my back and pinched furtively at me as I left them behind, to make me look back. Nevertheless, they did delay my progress, and I was slow to tear myself away from them, shake them off, and hasten where I was summoned, as long as Habit, with all its force, said to me, 'Do you think you can do without these?'

8.11.27 But now its words were no more than lukewarm. For, from the direction in which I had set my face, and towards which I hesitated to go, Continence was now revealed to me in all her chaste beauty. Serene she was, not full of dissolute mirth, and nor was there anything dishonourable in her alluring voice as she bade me to come and not to doubt, and her pious hands, as she stretched them out to welcome me and fold me to herself, were full of sheep of your flock, good examples for me. There were many boys and girls there, men and women newly come to adulthood and of every age, grave widows and aged virgins; and in not one of them was Continence barren, but a *mother of children* (Ps. 113.9 [Ps. 112.9]) that are her joy; children she has borne to you, O Lord, her bridegroom. She smiled at me with an encouraging smile, as if saying: 'Can you not do what these men and women have done? Or do you think that they have power to do it in themselves, and not in the Lord their God? The Lord their God it was who gave them to me. Why do you stand back, trusting in yourself, and not stand firm? Cast yourself on him, and do not be afraid. He will not draw back and let you fall. Put away your cares and cast yourself upon him; he will take you up and heal you.' And I blushed all the more, for I could still hear the murmurs of my frivolous pursuits, and I kept dangling in hesitation. Again I thought I heard her speak: 'Close your ears to those impure *limbs of yours upon earth* (Col. 3.5), and let them be put to death. *They speak to you of delights, but not as the Law of the Lord your God*' (Ps. 119.85 [Ps. 118.85]). This debate took place in my own heart, about myself and against myself. Alypius remained firmly at my side, silently waiting the outcome of this unprecedented access of emotion.

8.12.28 But when my meditation had dredged the hidden depths of my being and heaped up in the sight of my heart all the unhappiness I had known, immediately there arose a mighty squall of wind, bearing with it a mighty storm of tears. To pour out this flood of tears, with all the sounds proper to it, I arose and left Alypius; solitude seemed to me more appropriate for the business of weeping. I took myself off to a more secluded spot, where I would be oppressed by no one's presence, not even his. This was my state of mind, and he perceived it; I do not know what words I spoke, but from them it was clear that my voice was pregnant with tears. This was my state of mind as I arose. Alypius, therefore, remained where we had been sitting together, in utter bewilderment. I threw myself down at random on the ground (it happened to be beneath a fig tree), and gave my tears free rein. The rivers of my eyes, an *acceptable sacrifice* (Ps. 51.17 [Ps. 50.19]), burst their banks, and I spoke at length to you, in this strain if not in these words: '*How long, O Lord?* (Ps. 6.3 [Ps. 6.4]). *How long, O Lord, will you be angry with us? For ever? Remember not our iniquities that are of old*' (Ps. 79.5, 8 [Ps. 78.5, 8]). I felt myself held by those iniquities, and cried miserably: 'How long, how long, will this "tomorrow, tomorrow" continue? Why not "now"? Why do I not put an end to my shameful conduct from this hour forward?'

8.12.29 So saying, I wept, my heart crushed with very bitterness. And behold, suddenly I heard a voice from the house next door; the sound, as it might be, of a boy or a girl, repeating in a sing-song voice a refrain unknown to me: 'Pick it up and read it, pick it up and read it.'[11] Immediately my countenance was changed, and I began to ponder most intensely whether children were in

---

11 ' "Pick it up and read it".' Why the child should be singing this is uncertain, and Augustine is in any case more concerned with the use God put these words to than with what the child meant by them. But the word translated 'read' can also mean 'pick'; it may be that the child's song referred to figs from the tree, or other fruit. The story of the child's words that are interpreted as marking divine will appears in various forms, but two in particular may well be in Augustine's mind. Ambrose's consecration to the bishopric of Milan is said to have occurred after he, in his capacity as secular official, quelled a riot between the supporters of two opposing candidates for the episcopal see. In the silence that ensued, a child's voice was heard to cry, 'Bishop Ambrose!' So also in the *Aeneid*, Aeneas has received a prophecy (3.255–7) that he will not found his city of Rome until he has been forced by hunger to eat the plates from which he is eating. After his arrival in Italy, his men eat a type of pitta-bread meal, lastly eating the bread itself. At this Aeneas's young son Ascanius observes, as a joke, that they are 'eating their plates'. This is taken as a fulfilment of the prophecy (*Aen.* 7.107ff).

the habit of singing a chant of this sort as part of a game of some kind, but I had no recollection at all of having heard it anywhere. I checked my outburst of tears and arose, taking this to be nothing other than a God-sent command that I should open the Bible and read the first chapter I found, whatever it might be. For I had heard that Antony, on chancing to enter church in the middle of the Gospel reading, had taken heed of what was being read as if it were addressed to himself: *Go and sell all that you have; give it to the poor, and you will have treasure in heaven; and come and follow me* (Matt. 19.21).[12] By this divine utterance, I had heard, he was immediately converted to you. In high excitement, therefore, I returned to the place where Alypius was sitting; for I had left my copy of the Apostle Paul there when I had risen to go aside. I seized it, opened it, and read in silence the first heading I cast my eyes upon: *Not in riotousness and drunkenness, not in lewdness and wantonness, not in strife and rivalry; but put on the Lord Jesus Christ, and make no provision for the flesh and its lusts* (Rom. 13.13–14). I neither wished nor needed to read more. No sooner had I finished the sentence than it was as if the light of steadfast trust poured into my heart, and all the shadows of hesitation fled away.

8 12.30 I placed my finger or some other marker in the book and closed it; the new-found tranquillity of my features gave Alypius to understand what had happened. He then gave me to understand his own inner state – for of that I was ignorant – in the following way. He asked if he could see what I had been reading. I showed him the passage, and he read attentively, beyond the point to which I had read. I did not know what came next; but it was the words: *Welcome the weak in faith* (Rom. 14.1). This he took to refer to himself, and showed it to me. Strengthened by this admonition, and without any of my troubled hesitation, he joined me in a resolve and purpose that was both good and wholly in accord with his character – a character that had now long differed for the better from my own. Then we went indoors to my mother, and told her what

12 'For I had heard ... *follow me*'. A summary of events described in the *Life of Antony* ch. 2.

had happened. She rejoiced. We told her how it had happened. She was exultant and triumphant, and blessed you, who *can do more than we ask or understand* (Eph. 3.20); for she saw that in my case you had granted her so much more than she was accustomed to ask with pitiable tears and groans. You had turned me back to yourself; I would seek neither a wife nor any worldly ambition, but stand fast in the rule of faith, where you had revealed to her all those years before that I would be. You *turned her grief into gladness* (Ps. 30.11 [Ps. 29.12]) a gladness much more fruitful than the one she had wanted, and much more full of true love and chastity than she had hoped to gain from any grandchildren, the offspring of my flesh.

BOOK NINE

9.1.1 O Lord, I am your servant; I am your servant, and the son of your handmaid. *You have burst my bonds; I will offer you the sacrifice of praise* (Ps. 116.14–15 [Ps. 115.16–17]). Let my heart and tongue praise you, and *let all my bones say, 'Lord, who is like unto you?'* (Ps. 35.10 [Ps. 34.10]). Let them say this, and answer me. *Tell my soul, 'I am your salvation'* (Ps. 35.3 [Ps. 34.3]). Who am I, and what sort of 'I'? What manner of evil did I not do; or if I did not do, did I say; or if I did not say, did I will? *But you, O Lord, are good and merciful* (Ex. 34.6, Ps. 86.15 [Ps. 85.15], Ps. 103.8 [Ps. 102.8]). With your right hand you had regard for the depth of my deadness, and from the lowest places in my heart you drained away the abyss of corruption, so that I should not will at all what I willed, but will what you willed. But where, throughout that space of years, had my free will been, and from what deep and secret place was it called forth at a moment's notice, – the free will to submit my neck to your *easy yoke*, and my shoulders to your *light burden* (Matt. 11.30), Christ Jesus, *my Helper and my Redeemer* (Ps. 19.15 [Ps. 18.15])? How sweet it suddenly was to me to be deprived of all the sweets of frivolity, and what a joy to throw away what I had feared to lose! For you cast those sweetnesses out of me, you, my true and highest Sweetness; you cast them out, and entered in their stead; you who are sweeter than every pleasure (but not to flesh and blood), brighter than any light (but deeper than any secret place), exalted above all rank (but not to those who exalt in themselves). Now my mind was free from the 'gnawing cares'[1] of politicking, of getting, of wallowing, of scratching the mange of my lusts, and I spoke openly to you, my radiance, my riches, and my salvation, O Lord my God.

9.2.2 It seemed good to me in your sight not to make a sudden break with my routine, but quietly to withdraw the offices of my tongue from the fairs where verbal fluency is bought and sold.

---

1 '"gnawing cares"'. Horace, *Odes* 1.18.4.

No more would boys, *meditating* not *on your Law* (Ps. 119.70 [Ps. 118.70]) and your peace but on the madness and the lies and the warfare of the law courts, purchase from my lips the weapons for their mad passion. By happy coincidence, there were now only very few days left over until the Vintage Vacation,[2] and I decided to bear them out, and retire at the end of the year in the regular way; and, having been redeemed by you at a price, not return to offer myself for sale. My counsel, therefore, was open before you; but not open to men, except to our band of friends. We agreed among ourselves not to publish the matter abroad to anyone; albeit you had given us, as we *climbed out of the valley of weeping* (Ps. 84.6 [Ps. 83.6–7]) and sang the Song of Ascents,[3] sharp arrows and burning coals against the deceitful tongue (Ps. 120.2–3 [Ps. 119.2–3]), which, pretending to give counsel, speaks for the accuser, and which gobbles up like meat and drink what it pretends to love.

9.2.3 You had *pierced my heart with the arrows* (Ps. 11.2 [Ps. 10.3], Prov. 7.23) of your love, and I carried fixed deep in my vital organs your words, and the examples of your servants; those whom, once stained black, you have made radiant, and, once dead, you have made alive. These words and those examples, heaped up on my pondering heart, burnt and took away the slumber that oppressed me. They kept me from falling over the brink into the abyss, and set me so fiercely ablaze that every breath of accusation from the *deceitful tongue* (Ps. 120.2–3 [Ps. 119.2–3]) could only inflame me more, and not put out the fire. But since there would be those who *for your Name's sake, which you have sanctified throughout the earth* (Ezek. 36.23), would praise my avowed purpose, it seemed like self-glory not to wait for the vacation, which was so near, and to abandon my public profession, exposed as it was for all to see. Then everyone would turn their heads towards me, and reflect how I had

2 'Vintage Vacation'. A legal vacation, between 23 August and 15 October. Augustine's fellow-African Christians Minucius Felix (fl. c. A.D. 200–40) and Cyprian of Carthage (A.D. 200–58) see the Vintage Vacation as a suitable time for conversion; the heat of the summer is past, and it is time for the harvest.
3 'the Song of Ascents'. The title of the Pilgrim Psalms 120–34.

wished to anticipate the beginning of the Vacation, which was
so near at hand; and it would be noised abroad that I had been
avid to make a show of greatness. And what business of mine
was it to have my state of mind so publicly dissected, and for
our good to be blasphemed (Rom. 14.16)?

9.2.4 Moreover, that summer my lungs had begun to give way
under all the pressure of my literary work; I had difficulty catching my breath, and the pains in my chest were evidence that it
was damaged, no longer capable of producing a clear, full-toned
voice. This circumstance had at first unsettled me greatly, since
I was now in effect compelled by necessity to lay down the
burden of my teaching duties, or at any rate to take a break from
them, to see if I could be cured or recover my strength. But
when the full will to leave myself free and to see that *you are
Lord* (Ps. 46.10 [Ps. 45.11]) arose and was confirmed in me (Lord,
you know these things), I began to rejoice, since this gave me a
pretext (and not a spurious one) for my actions, which would
lessen the offence that men took at it – men who, for their own
children's sake, would have me never be free. Therefore I was
full of joy, and bore with the space of time until the end of term
(there might have been some twenty days or so). But it needed
strength to bear with them, for the greed that had always been
my partner in bearing the burden of my professional business
had now departed from me, and I remained alone with the
burden – or would have done, had Patience not come to my aid.
Let some servant of yours and brother of mine say I was wrong
to do so; to have suffered myself to sit, even for one day, *in the
seat of falsehood* (Ps. 1.1), now that my heart was full of the
thought of serving you. I offer no defence. But you, most merciful Lord, did you not forgive and pardon me this sin also in the
holy water of baptism?

9.3.5 Verecundus, however, was racked with anxiety at our good
purpose; he saw that because of the bonds that bound him so
tightly, he was being left behind by those of us who had thrown
our lot in together. Not yet a Christian, he had a wife who was
baptized, and this hindrance hobbled him more tightly than the
rest of us, and kept him from the journey which we others were

undertaking; the only way in which he wanted to be a Christian, he said, was the way in which he could *not* be. But out of friendship he offered to support us out of his own resources, so long as we lived there. *You will repay him, O Lord, at the resurrection of the righteous* (Lk 14.14), since even now you have repaid him for his expenses. For while we were away, being now at Rome, he was seized by an illness of the body, and, having become a Christian and been baptized in this life, he left it for a better. Thus you had mercy not only on him but on us also, lest we, reflecting on his kindness towards us and unable to reckon him one of your flock, should be tormented by a pain too great to bear. Thanks be to you, O God! We are your own. Your words of encouragement and consolation proclaim it; you who are faithful to your promise to repay Verecundus for the use of his country estate at Cassiciacum, where we found rest from the heat of the world in you, with the ever-flourishing verdure of your Garden, for you have *forgiven him his sins on earth* (Matt. 9.5–6, Mk 2.5, 9, Lk 5.23) on *the mountain flowing with milk, your mountain, the fertile mountain* (Ps. 68.15–16 [Ps. 67.16]).

9.3.6 Thus Verecundus was filled with anxiety, Nebridius with rejoicing. Although he too, while not a Christian, had *fallen into the pit* (Ps. 7.16 [Ps. 7.16], Ps. 57.7 [Ps. 56.7]) of that most pernicious error of believing that the flesh of your Son, the Truth, was an illusion, he was in the process of emerging from that pit; and though not yet steeped in any of the sacraments of your Church, he was a most ardent seeker after the Truth. Not long after my conversion and regeneration through baptism in you, he, a baptized Catholic also, serving you in perfect chastity and continence in Africa, among his own people, his whole house having now become Christian through him, was released by you from the flesh. And now he lives in the *bosom of Abraham* (Lk 16.22); for whatever is signified by that 'bosom of Abraham', there lives my beloved Nebridius, my sweet friend, whom from being a freedman you have made your adoptive son. There he lives; for what other place is there for a soul such as his? There he lives, in the place concerning which he asked so many questions of me, a mere man and unversed in such matters. No longer does he put his ear to my mouth, but puts his spiritual mouth to your fountain and drinks all the wisdom he desires or can, endlessly blessed. Nor do I think he is so drunk with that wisdom that he forgets us, seeing as you, whom he drinks in, *are mindful of us* (Ps. 136.23 [Ps. 135.23]). Such was our state; Verecundus we consoled, sad as he was despite our friendship at our conversion, and exhorted him to be faithful in his own degree, that of conjugal life, and Nebridius we awaited, until such time as he should follow us, as he could and would do very shortly. At last those days had unfolded. Long and many they seemed to us, in our longing for the freedom and leisure to sing from the depths of my heart: *My heart has said to you, I will seek your face; your face, Lord, will I seek* (Ps. 27.9 [Ps. 26.8]).

9.4.7 The day came for me to be freed in practice from my profession of rhetoric, from which I had already been freed in thought. And it came to pass that you rescued my tongue from the pit from which you had already rescued my heart, and I gave thanks to you as I set off, rejoicing, with all my friends, for Nebridius's estate. My literary activity there (which, indeed, was now in your service, but still breathing all the pride of the schools, like a boxer in a break between bouts) is attested by the books I wrote – dialogues with those present, or with myself alone before you; my dialogues with Nebridius, who was absent, are attested by my letters. When could there be time enough to recall all your great benefits towards us at that time, especially as I press on to record other and greater benefits? For my memory calls me back, and it is sweet to me to confess to you the inner scourges with which you mastered me, and how you flattened me out, *bringing down the mountains and hills* of my thoughts, and how you *made straight* my winding paths, and my *rough places smooth* (Is. 40.4, Lk 3.4–5); and how you brought my heart's brother, Alypius himself, into subjection to the Name of your only-begotten Son, *our Lord and Saviour Jesus Christ* (2Pet. 3.18), which at first he had thought unworthy to be engrafted into our writings. He had wanted them to be redolent more of the cedarwood tablets of the schoolroom (those cedars which the Lord had now laid low) (Ps. 28.5 [Ps. 27.5]), than the health-giving herbs of the Church, simples against serpents (cf Mk 16.18).

9.4.8 And how I cried out to you, my God, when I read the Psalms of David, those songs of faith, whose pious music will not admit the haughty spirit, while yet untutored in your true love and a catechumen, taking my vacation on the estate with my fellow-catechumen Alypius. My mother too stayed fast with us, feminine in her attire but masculine in her faith, with the serene assurance of an old woman, a mother's love, and a Christian's piety. How I cried out to you as I read those Psalms, and how they inflamed me for you, and set me ablaze to repeat them, if I could, throughout the world, as a rebuke to human pride! But throughout the world they are indeed sung, and *there is none that can hide from your heat* (Ps. 19.6 [Ps. 18.7]). What bitter pangs of resentment and anger I felt for the Manichees, and what pity too, for they did not know your sacraments, those healing medicines, and were madly opposed to the antidote that could have healed their madness. I wish they could have been by my side then, without my knowing that they were there, and that they could have looked on my face and heard my cries when I read the Fourth Psalm during that period of leisure, and seen how that Psalm affected me: *The God of my righteousness heard me when I called upon him; he delivered me in my tribulation. Have mercy upon me, O Lord, and hear my prayer* (Ps. 4.1 [Ps. 4.2]). I wish they could have listened, without my knowing that they were listening, so that they would not think that it was for their sake that I spoke as I did as I read the Psalm. Nor, indeed, would I have spoken the words I did, nor in the same way, if I had felt myself watched or listened to; nor, if I had, would they have paid attention to how I spoke with myself and to myself before you about my mind's intimate feelings.

9.4.9 I was at once bristling with fear and boiling over with hope and *exultation in your mercy* (Ps. 31.8 [Ps. 30.7–8]), O Father. All this was manifest in my eyes and my voice, when *your good Spirit* (Ps. 143.10 [Ps. 142.10]) turned back towards us and said: *Children of men, how long will you be heavy of heart? Why do you love vanity, and seek after falsehood?* (Ps. 4.2 [Ps. 4.3]).

For I had loved vanity, and sought after falsehood. And all the while you, O Lord, had *glorified your Holy One* (Eph. 1.20), raising him up from the dead and *setting him at your right hand* (Eph. 1.20), from whence he could send forth from on high his promised *Advocate, the spirit of truth* (Lk 24.49, Jn 14.16–17). He had indeed already sent him, but I did not know it. He had already sent him, for he had already been glorified by his resurrection from the dead and his ascension into heaven. Before this, *the Spirit had not yet been given, for Jesus had not yet been glorified* (Jn 7.39). *How long will you be heavy of heart?* the prophetic voice proclaims. *How long will you love vanity, and seek after falsehood? Know that the Lord has glorified his Holy One* (Ps. 4.2–3 [Ps. 4.3–4]). 'How long', it proclaims, and 'know' it proclaims, but for so long had I been ignorant, loving vanity and seeking after falsehood; and therefore I *heard and trembled* (Habbakuk 3.16), for these words were addressed to those such as I remembered that I had been. For in those deceitful doctrines which I had held to be the truth, there was vanity and falsehood; and in the pain of recollection I was full of groans, loud and heavy. If only they could have heard my groans, those who still love vanity and seek after falsehood; perhaps they would be moved, and spew out their doctrines, so that you would *hear their prayer when they cried out to you* (Ps. 4.1, Ps. 31.25 [Ps. 30.23]). For it was a true death of the flesh that our Intercessor died for us.

9.4.10 I read the words. *Be angry, and sin not* (Ps. 4.4 [Ps. 4.5]), and how moved I was, my God! I had now learnt to be angry with myself for my past, so as not to sin in the future; and rightly was I angry, seeing as it was not some other being, belonging to the 'Race of Darkness', which was sinning in me; those who say this *store up wrath for themselves in the day of anger, when your righteous judgement shall be revealed* (Rom. 2.5). No longer did I think my goods external ones, nor did I seek them with the eyes of my flesh, by the light of the physical sun. For those whose wish it is to rejoice in outward things, soon waste away and spend themselves on things visible and temporal, and feed their famished minds by licking at illusions. Would that they

grew weary of hunger, and said *Who will show us good things?*
Let us speak, and let them listen: *The light of your countenance
has been sealed on us, O Lord* (Ps. 4.6 [Ps. 4.6–7]). We are not the
light that lightens every man that comes into the world (Jn 1.9), but
we are enlightened by you; thus *we who were once darkness are
light in you* (Eph. 5.8). Would that they saw that inward Eternity,
having tasted which I gnashed my teeth, being unable to show
it to them if they came to me with their hearts looking outwards,
turned away from you, and said: *Who will show us good things?*
(Ps. 4.6). It was there, where I was angry; there, within my
chamber, where I was filled with compunction, where I had
made my sacrifice to you, *offering my old life* (Eph. 4.22, Col.
3.9), and, putting my hope in you, beginning to meditate on my
renewal – there you cast your sweetness over me, *gave me gladness of heart* (Ps. 4.7). I cried out loud as I read all this outwardly,
and recognized its truth within; nor did I wish to increase in
earthly goods only to consume and be consumed by time, when
I had other *corn and wine and oil* (Ps. 4.8 [Ps. 4.9]) in that eternal
Unity.

9.4.11 And from the depths of my heart I cried out in the words
of the next verse: oh, those words *in peace*, and *in the Same*! Why
does it say: *I will lie down and take my rest* (Ps. 4.7 [Ps. 4.9])?
Because who will stand against us, when the word comes true
that is written: *Death is swallowed up in victory* (1Cor. 15.54)?
And you are indeed the Same,[4] seeing as you are unchanging,
and in you there is rest and forgetfulness of all our labours, since
there is none other with you, nor is there a multitude of other
things to be attained that are not what you are; but *you alone, O
Lord, have stablished me in hope* (Ps. 4.8 [Ps. 4.10]). I read this
Psalm and was filled with ardour, but found nothing that I could
do to those deaf, dead Manichees, of whom I had been one – a
pestilence, one who barked against you, full of bitterness, blind
to the writings honeyed with the honey of heaven, radiant with

4 'the Same'. A word that Augustine uses almost as a title of God. It is not
itself a translation of any Greek technical philosophical term, but is presented
in a context which suggests Neo-Platonic emphasis on the immutability and
transcendence of God.

your radiance; and I was grieved over the enemies of this Scripture.

9.4.12 When shall I recall all that befell during the days of that vacation? But I have not forgotten, nor shall I pass over in silence the sharpness of your lash, nor the wondrous swiftness of your mercy. You tortured me with a toothache, and when it had grown so severe that I could not talk, the thought arose in my heart that I should call on all the friends that were with me to pray for me to you, the God of all manner of salvation. I wrote this request on a wax tablet and gave it to them to read; and as soon as we had set our knees in suppliant posture, the pain fled. But what pain was it? How did it flee? I was afraid, *my Lord and my God* (Jn 20.28), I acknowledge; not since my life began had I known such a thing. By secret ways your commandments crept into my deepest being. Rejoicing in faith, I *praised your name* (Ps. 145.2 [Ps. 144.2], Ecclesiasticus 51.15); but that faith would not leave me free from concern about past sins, which had not yet been forgiven me by washing in your baptism.

9.5.13 The Vintage Vacation over, I sent word back to Milan that her citizens should look for another seller of words for their students, both because I had chosen to serve you, and because I was not strong enough for that profession, in view of my dyspnoea and chest pains. I also wrote to your high priest, that holy man Ambrose, giving him some indication of my past wanderings and of my present resolve, and asking for advice on which portions of your Scriptures I should read first of all, in order to become more fit and ready to receive your great grace. He bade me read the Prophet Isaiah; I suppose because he is the plainest foreteller of the Gospel, and of the calling of the Gentiles. But I, not understanding my first reading from him, and thinking that the whole book was similar, put it off, to be resumed when I was better versed in the language of the Lord.

9.6.14 When the time came for me to put my name forward for baptism, we left the estate in the country and returned to Milan. Alypius, too, chose to be reborn with me in you; he had now *clothed himself with the humility* (Col. 3.12) that befits your sacraments, and, mighty conqueror as he was of the body, had resolved with rare courage to tread even Italy's icy soil barefoot.[5] The young Adeodatus, too, we made one of our company – my son after the flesh, and the child of my sin; but you had shaped him well. He was aged just fifteen in years, but in his abilities he surpassed many a learned sage. It is your gifts that I confess to you, O Lord my God, *creator of all things* (2Macchabees 1.24, Ambrose, *Hymns* 1.2.1), who can in manifold ways refashion our unlovely deeds in loveliness; for I had no part in that boy except the sin. As for his nurturing by us in your discipline, it was you who inspired us, and no other. There is a book of mine, entitled *The Teacher*; in it, it is he who talks with me. You know that the opinions put forward in that book by the person of my interlocutor, were his, when he was aged sixteen in years. I saw other things about him more wondrous still. I was in awe of his abilities; and who but you could be the architect of such wonders? Swiftly you took his life away from the earth, and I recall him with all the more assurance, now that I have nothing to fear for him in boyhood or youth, nor even in full manhood. We had made him one of us, our coeval in your grace, to be brought up in your discipline. We were baptized, and anxiety over our past life fled from us. Nor, during those days, could I be satiated with the wondrous sweetness of contemplating the depth of your counsel for the salvation of mankind. How I wept at the *hymns and sacred songs* (Eph. 5.19) of your Church, how moved was I at its tuneful voices! Those voices flowed in through my ears, and the truth, pressed and strained out of them, entered my heart, and from my heart a pious longing came boiling up and overflowed. My tears ran; I wept, and it was well with me.

9.7.15 It was not long since the Church at Milan had instituted this manner of strengthening and encouraging themselves, with brothers thronging together, full of zeal, singing with voices and

---

5 '... barefoot'. Going barefoot was practised by various Christians at this time, and was not unknown in other religions. It was proscribed by the Council of Saragossa in 380 as typical of the heretical Priscillianist movement, but clearly not universally abandoned. Augustine himself regarded the matter as one of indifference. Alypius, like Augustine, was an African, and would have found North Italy rather cold.

hearts in harmony. There was a year, not much more, during which Justina, mother of the boy king Valentinian, was persecuting Ambrose, the man of God, in the interests of her own heresy; she had been seduced by the Arians. The devout populace mounted watch in the church, ready to die with their bishop, your servant. My mother, your handmaid, was there, and took her stand as one of the foremost in those anxious vigils, living on prayers. I too, though as yet unwarmed by the heat of your Spirit, was none the less excited by the consternation and uproar in the city. It was then that the custom was established of singing hymns and psalms after the Eastern fashion, to keep the people from growing weary and faint-hearted; and the custom then established has been maintained, and many if not all your flocks throughout the rest of the world have imitated it.

9.7.16 Then you revealed to your aforementioned priest in a vision the place where the bodies of the martyrs Protasius and Gervasius lay hidden. These you had kept incorrupt for many long years, hidden away in your secret treasury, from which in due time you would bring them forth to check the madness of a woman, queen though she was. These bodies, once brought to light, were exhumed and transferred with due honour to the Ambrosian Basilica; and as they were being transferred, not only were demoniacs healed, the unclean spirits themselves confessing your power, but also a blind man, a citizen and well known in the city. He, having asked and been told the reason why the populace was in such a tumult of rejoicing, jumped up and asked his guide to take him to the place. He was brought there, and requested and was granted admission to touch with his handkerchief the bier of your saints, whose *death is precious in your sight* (Ps. 116.15 [Ps. 115.15]). He did so; and as soon as he applied the cloth to his eyes, they were opened. Rumour of this deed ran swiftly through the city; fervent and glowing praises were offered up to you for it; and by it the ill intent of that woman, your enemy, if not turned to belief and health, was at least prevented from the madness of persecution. Thanks be to you, my God! From whence and to what purpose have you led my recollection to this point, that I should confess to you these things also – which, great as they are, I might have forgotten, and passed over? Yet even then, when *the scent of your ointments* was heavy in the air, I did not *run after you* (Song of Songs 1.3). All the more, therefore, did I weep as I heard the hymns chanted, long sighing for you and at last breathing you, so far as a breath can fill this house of straw.

9.8.17 You, who *make men dwell in a house in oneness of mind* (Ps. 68.6 [Ps. 647.7]), had also joined to our number Evodius, a young man from my own town. He had *turned back to you* (Ps. 51.13 [Ps. 50.15]) while serving an Officer of Public Affairs in the Imperial Service,[6] had been baptized, and, leaving the service of this world, had girt himself up to serve you. We were constantly together, and intended to live together in a holy pact. We considered which place might most profitably contain your servants, and set off together for Africa. While we were at Ostia-on-Tibur, my mother died. There is much that I pass over, as I am in much haste. Accept my confessions and my thanksgivings, O God, for these countless things, even if they remain unspoken. But I shall pass over nothing concerning that servant of yours over which my soul is in travail – she who travailed for me in her flesh, so that I should be born into this temporal light, and in her heart, that I should be born into the light eternal. It is not her gifts that I shall tell, but yours to her. For she neither made herself nor brought herself up; you created her, and neither her father nor her mother knew what manner of woman was coming into being from them. She was brought up *in the fear of you* (Ps. 5.7 [Ps. 5.8]) by the rod of your Christ, the guidance of your only Son, in a faithful house, a sound member of your Church. Nor would she speak so highly of her own mother's attentiveness towards her upbringing as of a servant of hers, a broken-down old woman who had carried her own father on her back, as older girls often carry little children. For this reason, and because of her old age and excellent character, her master and mistress in that Christian household held her in great honour. For the same reasons too she supervised the daughters of the house, diligently exercising the task entrusted

6 'Officer of Public Affairs in the Imperial Service'. See note on 8.6.15.

to her; when the occasion demanded, she could be forthright, rebuking them with a righteous severity and teaching them in sober prudence. For except for the time when they were fed (with the greatest moderation) at their parents' table, she would not let them drink water, even though they were on fire with thirst, in her anxiety to forestall an evil habit. She would add a salutary saying: 'Now you drink water because you do not have wine in your power. But when you come to your husbands and become mistresses of your own storerooms and cellars, water will seem poor stuff; but the habit of drinking will prove too strong.' Thus by reasoned teaching and stern command she checked the greed of youth, and trained the girls' very thirst to keep within a decent measure, and to take no pleasure in anything unseemly.

9.8.18 Nevertheless, it crept up on her – so your maidservant used to tell me, her son – a love of wine crept up on her nevertheless. For when her parents sent her off like a sober-minded girl to draw some wine from the cask, she would dip the cup through the opening at the top, then, before pouring it neat into the flask, she would take the smallest sip, just enough to wet her lips; her senses rebelled at it, and she could take no more. This was not the result of some craving for drink, but, so to speak, of a superabundance of youthful excesses, which boil up in childish hearts in foolish passions, and are usually suppressed by the weight of one's elders. Therefore by adding one nicely measured quantity to another (for *he who spurns due measure perishes little by little*) (Ecclesiasticus 19.1), she had slipped so far into the habit that she could drink off with relish almost whole ladlesful of neat wine. Where then was that canny old woman and her forthright prohibition? For what could prevail against that latent sickness, did not your medicine, O Lord, keep watch over us? Her father and mother and nurses were away, but you were there; you who created her, who call out, who even through 'back-to-front mortals'[7] work some good for the salvation of

7 '"back-to-front mortals"'. This translation is based on the reading *praeposteros homines* instead of the manuscripts' *praepositos homines* ('mortals who are set over us'); a reading felt to be unsatisfactory because i) Monica is *not*

souls. What good was it you worked then, my God? Whence did you cure her? Whence did you heal her? Did you not of your hidden providence bring forth from another soul a harsh and cutting rebuke, like a surgeon's knife, and at one stroke cut short the gangrenous part? For the maidservant with whom she usually went to the cask quarrelled with her young mistress, as is the way; and the two of them being alone together, she taxed her with this accusation, and uttered the most bitter insult, calling her Little Miss Tipsy. My mother, stung by the lash of these words, contemplated the shamefulness of her habit, and forthwith rejected it and put it away. Just as friends often corrupt by flattering, so enemies often correct by quarrelling. Nor do you repay them for what you have done through them, but for what they themselves have willed. The maidservant in her anger endeavoured to hit at her young mistress, not to heal her; and she spoke in secret, either because their quarrel had overtaken them in that place and at that time, or so as to avoid danger to herself for having been so slow to inform on her mistress. But you, O Lord, ruler of all dwellers in heaven and earth, turn to your uses the course of that deep torrent, the flow of the world whose very turbulence is ordered; with another soul's sickness you healed her. And let none, on reading this, ascribe it to his own power, if another whom he wishes to have corrected be corrected by a word of his.

9.9.19 So it was that my mother was brought up to be modest and sober, rather put by you in subjection to her parents than by her parents to you; and as soon as 'her years were ripe for marriage',[8] she was handed over to a husband, whom she *served as her master* (Eph. 5.22, 1Pet. 3.6). She tried anxiously to *win him*

(Continued from previous page.)
corrected by the nurse set over her but by a maidservant, and ii) the 'even' would be redundant if *praepositos* were the correct reading. The phrase *praeposteri homines* is taken from Sallust, *Jugurthine War* 86; the plebeian solder-turned-politician Gaius Marius is rebuking the ineffectual aristocrats who dominated political life for their reliance on book learning and reputation of their ancestors rather than on their own practical experience.

8 "years were ripe for marriage". From Virgil, *Aeneid* 7.53 (describing the chaste Lavinia, destined bride of Aeneas).

for you (1Pet. 3.1), speaking of you by her very moral character, by which you made her beautiful and worthy of her husband's reverent love and admiration. His affronts to the marital bed she endured, never having a harsh word with him on that score. She *waited for your loving-kindness upon him* (Ps. 86.15 [Ps. 85.13]); believing in you that he might be made chaste. He, for his part, was as quick to boil up in anger as he was to plunge into acts of friendship. But she had learnt not to resist him when he was angry, not only in deed, but even in word. When she saw that his anger was checked and calmed, and that the time was right, she would give him an account of her own actions, if his outburst had been at all ill-considered. Moreover, when several good ladies, whose husbands were gentler than her own, would, in the course of a friendly conversation, blame their husbands' manner of living for the marks of the blows that they bore – sometimes even marring their features – she would blame the women's tongues. She would point out to them, as if in jest but in fact in all earnestness, that from the moment they heard the marriage contracts read out, they should have regarded them as legal instruments by which they were made maidservants. 'Remember the terms and conditions,' she would say. 'You should not be so arrogant with your lords and masters.' And though the womenfolk were astonished at her, knowing how fierce a husband she endured, it was never heard among them nor made known to them by other means that Patricius beat his wife, nor that any domestic dispute between them had lasted for a whole day. When they asked her, as friends do, the reason for this, she would explain her practice, as I have stated it above. Those who followed it, learnt its worth and thanked her; those who did not, were kept down and suffered for it.

9.9.20 Her mother-in-law, who was at first stirred up against her by the whisperings of their wicked serving women, she won round by her compliant attitude; she persisted in tolerance and docility, until her mother-in-law took the lead in reporting to her son the meddling tongues of their servants, who were disturbing the domestic peace between her and her daughter-in-law, and demanding that they be punished. He, therefore, in obedience to his mother, taking care for the discipline of his household and consideration for the harmony of his own, punished with blows those thus delated, to the satisfaction of their delator; who thenceforth promised that any serving women who sought her favour by speaking ill in any way to her of her daughter-in-law, should expect similar rewards of her. Thereafter none ventured to do so, and they dwelt in a sweet agreement distinguished by their mutual goodwill.

9.9.21 This great gift also you had bestowed upon that good servant of yours, in whose womb you created me, *O God, my mercy* (Ps. 59.17 [Ps. 58.18]): whenever she could, she would show herself a peacemaker between any souls in dissension and disharmony; so much so that having heard each one say many a harsh word about another – all the eructations of bloated and bilious discord, when in acidulous colloquy with a friend it brings up great gouts of ill-digested hatred for some absent enemy – she would reveal nothing to one concerning the other, save what might avail to reconcile the two. This would seem a small good to me, had I not had sad experience of countless quarrels; some loathsome, sinful pestilence stalks far and wide, not only disclosing one enemy's angry words to another, but even adding words that were never spoken. It should not be too much for a man, one of human kind, neither to arouse nor increase enmity between men with hard words, if he does not also study to quench this enmity with kind words. Such was my mother, thanks to you, her inner Teacher in the school of her heart.

9.9.22 Last of all she *won for you her husband* (1Pet. 3.1), at the very end of his temporal life; nor, now that he was a baptized believer, did she weep for the conduct which she had tolerated before he believed. She was also the servant of your servants. All of them who knew her praised and glorified and loved you in her, feeling your presence in her heart, attested by the fruits of her holy living (2Pet. 3.11). She had been *the wife of one husband; she had rendered her obligation to her parents; she had kept her house in all piety; her good works bore witness to her. She had brought up her children* (1Tim. 5.4, 9–10), *travailing over them*

(Gal. 4.19) whenever she perceived that they were straying from you. Finally, O Lord – for it is by your gift that I speak – before she fell asleep in you, she tended all of us servants of yours, who were living in fellowship together, having obtained the grace of baptism; she tended us as if she were the mother of all, and served us as if she were the daughter of all.

9.10.23 When the day was at hand when she would leave this life – you knew this day, but we did not – it came about (and this I believe you contrived, working in your hidden ways) that she and I were alone, leaning out of a window that overlooked the courtyard garden of the house that lodged us, there at Ostia-on-Tibur, where after the labours of our long journey we were refreshing ourselves, far from the bustle of the crowds, for our sea voyage. The two of us, then, were alone; and we talked together in all sweetness, forgetful of the past, straining in you, the present Truth, for the things before us. What manner of eternal life awaited the saints, we asked – the life that *eye has not seen nor ear heard, that has not ascended into the heart of man* (1Cor. 2.9)? And in our hearts we thirsted for celestial streams of your fountain, O Fount of Life, the fountain that is in you; that being sprinkled with its waters we might somehow contemplate this great matter, according to our understanding.

9.10.24 When our conversation reached the point at which no pleasure derived from carnal senses, however great, however illumined by bodily light, seemed in respect of the sweetness of that Life worthy not only of comparison, but even of mention, then we raised ourselves up in a more ardent longing for the Same,[9] moving step by step through all things corporeal, even the sky itself, from which sun and moon and stars shine upon the earth. Still higher we went, through inward contemplation and discussion and admiration of your works. We came to our own minds, and passed beyond them to attain the land of *richness unfailing* (Ezek. 34.14), where you *feed Israel* (Ps. 80.1 [Ps. 79.2]) for ever with the food of truth. There, life is the Wisdom through which all things that were and that are to be

9 'the Same'. Cf note on 9.4.11.

come into being; yet it does not itself come into being, but is as it has been and will always be. And more than that; there is neither past nor future in it, but only being, since it is eternal. And as we talked and thirsted for it, we attained it, according to our small degree, for the space of a whole heartbeat; and sighing we left firmly fixed there the *first-fruits of the Spirit* (Rom. 8.23), and made our way back to the clatter of human speech, where words have a beginning and an ending. But what is like your Word, our Lord, that *abides in itself,* not waxing old but *renewing all things* (Ecclesiasticus 7.27)?

9.10.25 We said, therefore: Let us suppose the tumult of one's flesh were to fall silent, that the vain illusions of earth, waters and air were to fall silent, that the sky were to fall silent. Let us suppose that one's very soul were to fall silent, and, by not thinking about itself, were to transcend itself; suppose all dreams and revelatory images, all tongues and symbols, all that comes to be by passing away were to fall silent – for all these things say to whoever listens, '*We did not make ourselves*' (Ps. 100.2 [Ps. 99.3]); 'our Maker is he who *abides for ever*' (Ps. 33.11 [Ps. 32.11], Ps. 117.2 [Ps. 116.2], Is. 40.8, Jn 12.24). Let us suppose that they were to fall silent, having aroused us with these words to listen to their Maker; suppose also that he, the Maker, were to speak – he alone, not through things he has made, but through himself, so that we could hear his word; not through fleshly tongue nor through angel's voice, not through the *sound of the thunder* (Ps. 77.18 [Ps. 76.18]) nor through the riddle of a parable, but suppose we could hear him whom we love for all these things, but without all these things, just as even now we stretched out and with soaring contemplation attained the eternal Wisdom that abides above all things. Let us suppose also that this state were to be prolonged, and that other, far inferior visions were removed, and this one vision were to enrapture and swallow up and hide the beholder in itself, so that life would eternally be as this moment of understanding for which we sighed – would such a state not be what is meant by the words, *Enter into your Master's joy* (Matt. 25.21)? And when shall this be? Will it be when *we all shall rise, but shall not all be transformed* (1Cor. 15.51)?

9.10.26 So we said, if not in this manner and in these words; but *you know, O Lord* (Tobit 8.9, Jn 21.15–16), that as we discussed such matters that day, the world and all its pleasures became to us at our words a thing disprized; and my mother said to me, 'My son, for my part, I no longer take any pleasure in this life. What I am doing here still, and why I am here, I do not know; my hope in this world is spent. There was one thing for which I used to long to remain a while longer in this life – to see you a Catholic Christian, before I died. This my God has bestowed upon me, and more; I see you now his servant, scorning worldly happiness. What am I doing here?'

9.11.27 What I said in reply I cannot recall; for within a mere five days, or not much more, she took to her bed with an attack of fever. One day, as she lay sick, she fell unconscious, and for a short time she was taken away from those present. We all ran into the room, but she was quickly restored to her senses, and catching sight of my brother and me as we stood by her she said, as if puzzled, 'Where was I?' Then, perceiving our grief and consternation, she said, 'You will leave your mother to rest here.' I said nothing, and checked my tears. My brother, however, said something or other, encouraging her to believe that she would die in her homeland and not abroad, as if that were a happier way to die. On hearing this, her face was filled with anxiety, pushing him aside with her eyes for thinking in this way; then, gazing at me, she said, 'See what he says!' Then to both of us she said: 'Leave my body where you will; do not be troubled with any concern on its behalf. One thing only I ask you: that you remember me at the altar of the Lord, wherever you are.' Having framed this sentence in such words as she could, she fell silent, tossed about by the worsening sickness.

9.11.28 I, however, rejoiced as I meditated on your gifts, O God Invisible – the gifts that you put into the hearts of your believers, from which spring such admirable fruits; and I gave thanks to you as I recalled what I knew well – how she had always been in a fever of anxiety about her burial place, which she had appointed and prepared for herself against the time, alongside the body of her husband. For, having lived in great harmony

with him, she wished – so little can the human mind comprehend of things divine! – to add to that happiness; she wished it
to be remembered among men that after her travels across the
seas it had been granted to her that her dust should be mixed
with her husband's, and his with his wife's. When this empty
wish had, by *the fulness of your bounty* (Ps. 104.28 [Ps. 103.28],
2Thess. 1.11), begun to retreat from her heart, I did not know,
and I was full of wonder and rejoicing that she had shown herself thus to me, even though in our conversation at the window,
when she had said, 'What am I doing here?' she had not shown
any longing to die in her homeland. I heard, too, later, that
while we were at Ostia, she talked one day with certain friends
of mine, with the assurance permitted to a mother, on the contempt of this life and benefits of dying. I was not there, but they
were astounded at this woman's courage (which you had given
her), and had asked whether she was not afraid to leave her body
so far from her own city. 'Nothing', she replied, 'is far from God;
nor need I fear that at the end of the world he will not know
where to raise me up.'

On the ninth day, then, of her illness, in the fifty-sixth year
of her life and the thirty-third year of mine, that pious and
devout soul was released from her body.

9.12.29 I pressed her eyes shut, and as I did so a great flood of
grief flowed into my heart and overflowed in tears. Immediately
my eyes, at a forced command of the will, absorbed this fountain
and dried up completely; and it was ill with me in that great
struggle. Then too, as she breathed her last, the child Adeodatus
burst out in lamentation; then, restrained by all the rest of us,
fell silent. In this way something childish in me also – the something that was slipping into tears – was checked by the voice of
that young heart, and fell silent. For we did not think it proper
that her death should be marked with tearful plaints and groans,
these being the usual means of bewailing, as it were, the
unhappy lot of the dead, their complete snuffing out. But there
was nothing unhappy in my mother's death, nor was she dying
utterly. This we held to be true by the testimony of her moral
character, her unfeigned faith, and by irrefutable reasoning.

9.12.30 What was it, then, that ached so deeply within me, if not the fresh wound that came from the sudden breaking of the habit of living together in all sweetness and love? I rejoiced, it is true, in her testimony; how in her last illness itself, by way of compliment to some service of mine, she would call me a dutiful son, and in the greatness of her love recall that she had never heard my lips cast a hard word or insulting sound at her. But what was the honour I did to her compared to the devoted service that she had rendered me? My soul, therefore, being bereft of the great solace that she had given me, was smitten and, so to speak, stripped of its life – the life that had been made one out of her life and mine.

9.12.31 So it was that when we had checked young Adeodatus's tears, Evodius seized a psaltery and began to sing a psalm. The whole household answered him with the response: *Mercy and judgement shall I sing to you, O Lord* (Ps. 101.1 [Ps. 100.1]). Many of the brothers and many female religious, hearing what was happening, came and joined us. Those whose duty it was to arrange the funeral, did so in the customary way; and I went aside, to a place where I could with propriety speak, and before those who accompanied me, thinking that I should not be left alone, I gave a disputation on a theme suitable to the occasion. Thus with the lotion of truth I soothed my agony – an agony known to you, but unknown to them. They listened intently, and thought that I had no sense of grief. But I rebuked my affection in your ears, where none of them could hear, for its lack of toughness, and checked the flood of sorrow; and gradually it receded from me, only to return, driven by its own momentum. It did not succeed in breaking out in tears, or in changing my countenance; but I knew what I was suppressing in my heart. And being sorely displeased at myself to find that these human traits, which according to the due order and lot of our condition must needs befall us, had such power over me, I grieved with fresh grief for my grief, and was torn by a twofold sadness.

9.12.32 Even when the body was taken out for burial, I went and came back without weeping. Not even in the course of the prayers that we poured out to you, when, according to the custom of the place, the sacrifice of our ransom price was offered for my mother as her body lay beside the sepulchre,[10] before being laid to rest in it – not even in the course of those prayers did I weep, but all day long I besought you, as best I could, to heal my grief. But you did not heal me, perhaps wishing to impress on my memory how the chain of every habit is opposed to a mind which feeds on the Word in whom there is deceit. I even thought I should take a bath, as I had heard that the baths were so called for this very reason: the Greeks call them *balanion*, because they drive care from the mind.[11] This too I confess to your Mercifulness, O *father of the orphans* (Ps. 68.5 [Ps. 67.6]): I took a bath, and after my bath was just as I had been before. The bitterness of grief had not been sweated out of my heart. Then *I slept and woke again* (Ps. 3.5 [Ps. 3.6]), and found my grief greatly lessened; and, as I lay alone in my bed, I recalled those true-spoken verses of your servant Ambrose:

> O thou, the All-Creator God,
> Guide of the heavens on their road,
> Who dost the day with glorious light
> Adorn, with grateful sleep the night;
> Sleep that the limbs, from toil once more
> Refreshed, to labour might restore,
> To weary minds might give relief,
> And set the mourner free from grief.[12]

9.12.33 From then on, I regained little by little my former perception of your handmaid and her mode of living; her piety towards you, her holy gentleness towards me, her moral recti-

10 '... the sacrifice ... beside the sepulchre'. A celebration of communion. It is notable, in view of much later controversies about the Funeral Mass, that Augustine describes this in similar terms to Monica's celebratory meals at the tombs of the saints in Book Six; that is, as a local custom not in itself to be either recommended or deplored.

11 'the Greeks ... from the mind'. The Latin word for bath, *balneum*, is an old borrowing from the Greek term *balanion*; Augustine is relying on a false etymology of this term as being derived from the Greek *ballo* 'to cast out' and *ania* 'worry, care'.

12 'O thou ... free from grief'. Ambrose, *Hymns* 1.2.1–8

tude. I was destitute of her, and it was a pleasure to weep in your sight over her and for her, over myself and for myself. The tears that I had held back, I gave leave to flow as much as they wanted, spreading them out where my heart could see them; and I found rest in them, for in them were your ears – not the ears of some man, who might look on my weeping with contempt. Even now, O Lord, I confess to you in these writings. Let him who will, read them, and look on them how he will; and if he should find some sin in my weeping for my mother for the least part of an hour – the mother who was for a while dead in my eyes, who had wept for me for so many years, that I might live in your eyes – let him not laugh at me, but rather, if he is full grown in love, let him also weep for my sins to you, the Father of all brothers of your Christ.

9.13.34 For my part, now that the wound caused by my mother's death had been healed (so far as carnal affection can be held in check), I poured out to you, our God, tears of quite another sort for your handmaid: those that flow from a spirit smitten by the contemplation of the perils that face every soul that *in Adam dies*. Although she had been *brought to life in Christ* (1Cor. 15.22), and although, while still not released from the flesh, her life was such as to bring praise to your name for her faith and moral character, nevertheless I would not venture to say that, from the time that you gave her new life in baptism, not one word passed her lips that was contrary to your teaching. For the Truth, your Son, even said: *If a man should say to his brother, 'You fool!' he will be liable to the fire of hell* (Matt. 5.22). And woe even to men who live a praiseworthy life, if you should sift them without mercy! But as you do not enquire relentlessly into our sins, we hope and trust to have some place in you. But if one should enumerate before you his true good deeds, what is he enumerating but your gifts to him? Would that men would learn that they are men, and that *he who boasts would boast in the Lord!* (1Cor. 1.31, 2Cor. 10.17).

9.13.35 So it is, my Praise and my Life, *God of my heart* (Ps. 73.26 [Ps. 72.26]), that I set aside for a little while her good actions, for which I give thanks to you with rejoicing, and now pray to you for my mother's sins. Hear my prayer, through the Healing of our wounds, who *hung on the Tree* (Deut. 21.23, Gal. 3.13), who, *sitting at the right hand of the Father, intercedes for us* (Ps. 110.1 [Ps. 109.1], Rom. 8.34). I know that she dealt mercifully, and *forgave her debtors from her heart* (Matt. 6.12, 18.35); forgive her also what debts she ran up in all those years after she was washed in the saving waters. *Forgive, Lord, forgive, I pray* (Numbers 14.19); *enter not into judgement* (Ps. 143.2 [Ps. 142.2]) with her. *Let mercy triumph over judgement* (James 2.13), for your sayings are true, and you have promised mercy to the merciful (cf Matt. 5.7). That they are merciful is your gift also; you who have *mercy to those to whom you will have mercy, and are merciful to those to whom you will grant mercy* (Ex. 33.19, Rom. 9.15).

9.13.36 I believe you have indeed already done what I ask of you; but *accept the freewill offerings of my mouth, O Lord* (Ps. 119.108 [Ps. 118.108]). For as the day drew near when she would be released from the flesh, she gave no thought to having her body covered in a sumptuous winding sheet, nor scented with costly perfumes; she did not desire a choice sepulchre, made no provision for burial in her homeland. She placed no such charges upon us, but required only that she should be remembered before your altar, which she had served without letting a day pass. From that altar she knew that the sacred Host was distributed, by which the *record of the debt that stood against us was cancelled* (Col. 2.14–15), by which the Enemy was led captive even as he reckoned up our sins, and sought to make some against him in whom we conquer, and *found no grounds for accusation* (Lk 23.4, Jn 14.30, 18.38, 19.4). Who will repay our Redeemer his innocent blood? Who will restore to him the *price for which he bought us* (1Cor. 6.20, 7.25), to snatch us away from the Enemy? It was to the sacrament of this ransom price that your handmaid bound herself with the bond of faith. Let no one tear her away from your protection. Let not the *lion and the serpent* (Ps. 91.13 [Ps. 90.13]) interpose themselves, be it by force or by guile; for neither will she reply that she owes nothing, and be shown guilty and overcome by the cunning Accuser, but will reply that her *debts have been forgiven* (Matt. 6.12) by him to whom no one will repay what he, though no debtor, paid for us.

9.13.37 Let her be in peace, then, with her husband, *before and after whom she was married to no one* (1Tim. 5.9) whom she served *bringing profit to you by her patience* (Lk 8.15), and *winning him also for you* (1Pet. 3.1). Inspire, O Lord my God, your servants, my brothers, your children, my masters, whom I serve with heart and voice and pen; inspire them, that all who read these words of mine might remember at your altar your handmaid Monica, with Patricius, her sometime spouse, through whose flesh you brought me into this life; how, I do not know. Let them remember with pious respect my parents in this transitory life, and remember also my brothers, with whom I share you as our Father and the Catholic Church our Mother; they are my fellow-citizens in the *eternal Jerusalem* (Gal. 4.26), for whom your people sigh on their pilgrimage, from their setting out till their returning. And let my mother's last request of me be granted to her more abundantly through the prayers and confessions of many than through my prayers alone.

BOOK TEN

10.1.1 *May I know you*, my Knower; *may I know you, even as I also am known* (1Cor. 13.12). Strength of my soul, enter that soul and fit it for yourself, that you may inhabit and dwell therein, and it may be *free from spot or wrinkle* (Eph. 5.27). This is my hope, and therefore I speak, and in that hope I rejoice, whenever I rationally rejoice. As for the other things of this life, the more one weeps for them, the less they should be wept for, and the less they are wept for, the more they should be wept for. *Behold, you have loved truth* (Ps. 51.6 [Ps. 50.8]), since *he that does what is true comes to the light* (Jn 3.21). It is my purpose, in making my confession in my heart, to do what is true before you, and in making my confession in writing, to do what is true before many witnesses.

10.2.2 But what is there in me that could remain hidden from you, O Lord, *to whose eyes the depths of a man's conscience lie bare, even if I refused to confess it to you* (Hebr. 4.13, Ecclesiasticus 42.18, 20)? I would be hiding you from me, not me from you. As things are, however, my groaning is testimony that I take no pleasure in myself. But you shine on me, and I take pleasure in you, whom I love and long for. So may I blush for myself, cast myself aside, and choose you instead, being pleasing neither to you nor to myself, unless that pleasure comes from you. *To you, O Lord, I stand revealed* (1Cor. 5.11), whatever I may be. My profit in confessing to you I have spoken. I do it not with words and utterances of the flesh, but with words of the soul, with the outcry of my thought, that is known to your ears. In so far as I am evil, confessing to you is nothing other than taking no pleasure in myself. In so far as I perform my pious duty, confessing to you is nothing other than not ascribing this fact to myself. *For it is you, O Lord, who bless the just* (Ps. 5.12 [Ps. 5.13]); but first you *make just the impious* (Rom. 4.5). The *confession that I make in your sight* (Ps. 96.6 [Ps. 95.6]), O Lord, is both silent and vocal. It is silent in that it makes no sound; it is vocal in my

215

feelings. I say nothing right before men that you have not heard from me first, nor do you hear any such thing from me that you have not told me first.

10.3.3 What business, then, do I have with men, that they should hear my confessions, as if they were the ones who would *heal all my infirmities* (Ps. 103.3 [Ps. 102.3], Matt. 4.23)? They are an inquisitive breed, eager to learn of other people's lives, full of idleness when it comes to amending their own. Why do they seek to hear from me what I am, when they refuse to hear from you what they are? And when they hear me speaking of myself, how do they know whether what I say is true, seeing as *no man knows what goes on in a man, except the man's spirit that is within him* (1Cor. 2.11)? But if they were to hear about themselves from you, they would not be able to say, 'The Lord is lying.' For what is it to hear about one's self from you if not to recognize one's self? And who could recognize himself and say, 'It is false,' were he not himself lying? But since *love believes all things* (1Cor. 13.4, 7), at least among those whom it makes one, joined together to itself, I too, O Lord, confess even so to you, that men, to whom I cannot show whether I am telling the truth, may hear me. Those whose ears have been opened to me by love will believe me.

10.3.4 But you, O my inner Physician – make clear to me, I pray, my profit in doing all this. As for the confessions of my past wickedness, those that you have *forgiven and covered* (Ps. 32.1 [Ps. 31.1]), blessing me in you, changing my soul by faith and by your sacrament[1] – these confessions, when read and heard, stir up the heart, lest it should slumber in despair and say, 'I cannot'; so that it should rather *wake up in the love* (Song of Songs 5.2) of your mercy and the sweetness of your grace, which makes strong every sick man who through that grace becomes conscious of his own sickness. The good, too, find delight in hearing of those who committed wicked deeds in the past, but are now free from them; nor are they delighted because those deeds were

---

1 'by your sacrament'. 'Sacrament' in the *Confessions*, when not further qualified, is generally to be understood as referring primarily to baptism.

evil, but because they were and are no more. What profit, therefore, my Lord, to whom my conscience daily confesses, more
confident in the hope of your mercy than in its own integrity –
tell me, what profit do I have in confessing before men also, in
your presence and through this writing, what I still am, and not
what I was? I have seen and set down my profit from the latter.
But what I still am, even as I write these confessions – there are
many who would know that, those who have known me and not
known me, and those who have heard something from me or of
me, but whose ear cannot hear my heart, where I am whoever
I am. They wish, therefore, to hear it from my own confession:
what I am within, in the part inaccessible to their eyes and
ears and minds. They wish to do so, however, because they will
believe me; otherwise, what would they learn? The Love
through which they are good tells them that I am not lying in
my confession of myself, and that love in them believes me.

10.4.5 But what profit do they have in wishing to hear of me?
Do they wish to share in my thanksgiving, when they hear what
progress you have granted me to make towards you? Do they
wish to pray for me when they hear how much I have been
slowed down by the burden of myself? To such people I will
make myself known. It is no slight profit, O Lord, if *many give
thanks to you for my sake, and that many pray to you for my sake*
(2Cor. 1.11). Let some brotherly spirit love that in me which you
teach should be loved, and mourn for that in me which you
teach should be mourned. Let it be some brotherly spirit who
does this; not a stranger's, not one of the *foreign children, whose
mouth speaks vanity, and whose right hand is a right hand of iniquity* (Ps. 144.7–8 [Ps. 143.7–8]). Let it be a brotherly spirit, who,
in finding good in me, rejoices over me, and in finding fault in
me, is full of sorrow over me. To such I will make myself known;
let them sigh with relief over my good things, and with sorrow
over my bad things. My good things are your statutes and your
gifts, my bad things are my sins and your judgements. Let them
sigh with relief for the former, with sorrow for the latter; and let
songs of praise and lamentations arise into your presence from
the hearts of my brethren, those vessels full of incense offered

to you (cf Rev. 8.3–4). And you, O Lord, that take delight in the fragrance of your holy temple, *have mercy upon me according to your great mercy* (Ps. 51.1 [Ps. 50.3]), *for your own Name's sake* (Matt. 10.22, 24.9); you who never abandon what you have begun, *bring to fulfilment the things in me that are imperfect* (Phil. 1.6).

10.4.6 This is the profit I have of my confessions: that I should confess not what I was, but what I am, and confess it not only before you with secret *exultation and trembling* (Ps. 2.11, Phil. 2.12), and secret grief and hope, but also in the ears of those children of men who believe. These are my companions in my rejoicing and the sharers of my mortality, my fellow-citizens and fellow-pilgrims; those that have gone before me, those that will come after me, those that come with me. These are your servants, my brethren, those children of yours who, it is your will, should be my masters, whom you have bade me serve, if it is my will to live with you and of you. And it would not be enough that your Word should have given this commandment with speech, had that Word not also shown the way with deeds. Therefore I too follow his teaching with deeds and words; I do so *under your wings* (Ps. 17.8 [Ps. 16.8]), and great indeed would be my peril, but that under your wings *my soul is subdued* (Ps. 60.1 [Ps. 61.2]) and my weakness is known to you. I am a little child, but my Father lives for ever, and my Guardian is sufficient to me; for he who begat me and he who watches over me is *one and the Same* (Ps. 102.27 [Ps. 101.28], Hebr. 1.12).[2] You are all my good things; you are almighty, with me before I am with you. To such, therefore, as you bid me serve, I shall make known not what I was, but who I have now become and who I still am; nor do I judge myself (1Cor. 2.11). This, then, is how I would be heard.

10.5.7 But you, O Lord, judge me. For although *no man knows all about a man except the man's spirit that is within him* (1Cor. 2.11), nevertheless there is a part of a man that is unknown even to the spirit within him. But you, O Lord, who made him, know

---

2 '... *the Same*'. See note on 9.4.11.

everything about him. Even I, although *before your presence
I despise myself and count myself dust and ashes* (Job 42.6, Ecclesiasticus 10.9), nevertheless I know something of you, which I do
not know of myself. Now truly we *see in a glass darkly*, not yet
face to face (1Cor. 13.12); and therefore, as long as I journey away
from you, I am more present with myself than with you. I know
that you are not subject to any manner of corruption; but for
myself, I do not know which temptations I can resist and which
I cannot. Yet there is hope, for *you are faithful*. You *do not let us
be tested more than we can bear, but give us a way out of our testing
so that we might endure* (1Cor. 10.13). I confess, therefore, what
I know of myself; and I confess also what I do not know, for
what I do know, I know because you enlighten me, and what
I do not know, I do not know only so long as it takes for *my
darkness to be like the noon-day in your sight* (Is. 58.10, Ps. 90.8
[Ps. 89.8]).

10.6.8 My consciousness that I love you, O Lord, is not doubtful but sure. You have smitten my heart with your Word, and
I love you. But heaven and earth and all that is in them – these
all tell me from all sides to love you. Indeed they unceasingly
tell all peoples, so that *they might have no excuse* (Rom. 1.20).
You will *have mercy more deeply on whom you will have mercy,
and will show mercy to whom you have shown mercy* (Ex. 33.19,
Rom. 9.15); and even were that not the case, then *heaven and
earth would surely tell out your praise* (Ps. 69.35 [Ps. 68.35]) to deaf
ears. In loving you, what do I love? No physical beauty, no
temporal glory, no radiancy of light that commends itself to
these eyes of mine; no sweet melody of songs tuned to every
mode, no soft scent of flowers or of ointments or of perfumes,
no manna, no honey, no limbs that can receive corporal
embrace; yet I do love some kind of light, some kind of voice,
some kind of fragrance, some kind of food, some kind of
embrace, when I love my God, who is light, voice, fragrance,
food, embrace to my inner man. There it is that a light shines
on my soul that no place can contain, a sound is uttered no
time can take away, a fragrance cast that no breath of wind can
disperse, a savour given forth that eating cannot blunt, and there

clings to me that which cannot be torn away by satiety. This is
what I love in loving my God.

10.6.9 And what is this? I questioned the physical world concerning my God, and it replied to me, '*I am not he, but it is he
that made me*' (Jn 18.25, Ps. 100.2 [Ps. 99.3]). I questioned the
earth, and it said, 'I am not he'; and all that was in it confessed
likewise. *I questioned the sea and the depths* (Job 28.14), and *all
living things that creep* (Gen. 1.20), and they replied, 'We are not
your God; look above us.' I questioned the winds that blow, and
the whole air and all its indwellers said, 'Anaximenes is wrong;
we are not God.'[3] I questioned the sky, the sun, the moon, the
stars: 'Nor are we the God whom you seek,' said they. And I said
to all these things that surround the doors of my flesh, 'Tell me
about my God, that which you are not; tell me something of
him.' They cried out with a great voice, 'It was he that made us.'
My questioning was the concentration of my mind, and their
response was their beauty.[4] And I turned to myself, and said to
myself, 'Who are you?' And I replied, 'A man.' Behold, my body
and the soul in me stood ready for me, one without and the
other within. From which of these was it that I should seek my
God, having now sought him through my body all the way from
earth to heaven, as far as I could cast the rays of my eyes? But
what was within was better. To that all my bodily messengers
brought their reports; it presided over them, and judged the
replies of heaven and earth and all that was in them, when they
said, 'We are not God,' and 'It was he that made us.' My inner
man gained knowledge of this through the ministry of my outer
man. The inner I gained knowledge of this I, I the mind,
through my bodily senses. I questioned the physical world concerning my God, and it replied to me, '*I am not he, but it is he
that made me.*'

3 "Anaximenes ... God". Anaximenes was a Greek philosopher of the sixth
century B.C., one of the earliest of the Greek physicists. In his account of the
universe, air (*aer*) is the primary matter. Air can be condensed or rarefied into
other substances; some of these (fire, wind, cloud, water) are regarded as divine.
4 'beauty'. The Latin word translated here as 'beauty' (*species*) is a key term for
Augustine. It includes ideas of beauty, perceptibility, specific type and divine
order. See the discussion in 12.3.3, and the note there.

10.6.10 Surely this beauty is apparent to all whose senses are whole and unimpaired? Why does it not speak the same to all? The animals see it, from the greatest to the least (cf Ps. 104.25 [Ps. 103.25]), but cannot question it. They have no innate rationality set over them, to judge of the senses and the messages they bring. But men can ask, so that they may *see and understand the hidden things of God through the things that he has made* (Rom. 1.20); but men are subject to these created things through their love of them, and being subject they are unable to judge them. These things neither reply to those that question them but do not judge them, nor do they alter their utterance (that is, their beautiful appearance) if one man only sees them and another sees and questions them, appearing in one way to one man and in another to another. Their beauty appears in the same way to each, but is dumb to the one and speaks to the other – or rather, it speaks to all, but is only understood by those who hear its voice outwardly, and inwardly test it against the Truth. For it is Truth that says to men: 'Your God is not earth and sky, nor any corporeal thing.' This is what their nature says. Do you not see? It is a physical mass, lesser in its parts than in the whole. You, therefore, are better – it is you, my soul, that I address – for you quicken the mass of your body, giving it life, that which no body can give to another. But your God is life to you also, the life of your life.

10.7.11 What, then, do I love, in loving my God? Who is he that is above my soul? Through that soul I shall ascend to him. I shall transcend my own strength, the strength by which I cleave to the body and fill its frame with living force. Not by that strength will I find my God. If I did, then the *horse and mule that have no understanding* (Ps. 32.10 [Ps. 31.9]) would find him also; for they have the same strength, and through it their bodies also are alive. There is another strength, not only that by which I make alive the flesh that the Lord has wrought for me, but also that by which I make it percipient. Thus do I bid *the eye not to hear and the ear not to see* (Rom. 11.8), but assign to the eye and the ear their properties of sight and hearing, and so also with each of my other senses, according to their due place and function. But despite the diverse properties which are assigned to my senses, it is I and I alone who control them. I shall transcend this strength also, for this too is common to horse and mule; they too experience sensation through their bodies.

10.8.12 I shall, therefore, transcend even that innate strength of mine, ascending by degrees to him that made me. I shall come to the plains and broad palaces of memory, where there are hoards of countless images brought in from the things of all kind that the senses perceive. There is the storehouse of all that we ever contemplate, whether by increasing or by diminishing or by altering in some way the objects that our senses have encountered, and of everything else which is entrusted for safe-keeping there and has not yet been swallowed up and buried in oblivion. When I am there, I ask for whatever I want, and some things come forward at once, whereas others take longer to search out, as if they are being dug up from some more remote repository. Some things come swarming out at me, and, while something else is being requested and sought, leap into view as if to say, 'Is it us that you want?' These I swat away from the face of my recollection with the hand of my heart, until the thing I want is revealed and comes into sight from the hidden depths. Some things come to hand easily and in unbroken sequence, just as they are requested; those that come first give way to those that follow on from them, and, having given way, are stored up, to come forth the next time I want them. All this happens when I relate something from memory.

10.8.13 In the palace of Memory is preserved according to its peculiar type all that is brought in by its proper entrance. Light and colour of all kinds and shapes of physical objects are brought in through the eyes, all kinds of sounds through the ears and smells through the entrance-way of the nose, and tastes of all kinds through that of the mouth. Through the senses of the body as a whole we perceive what is hard, what is soft, what is hot and cold, rough and smooth, heavy and light, what is inside and what is outside the body. All these things are taken into the vast recesses of memory, with its hidden and ineffable crannies, and are stored up there, to be recalled and reconsidered when they are needed; they all enter the Memory by their proper doors, and are laid up therein. Nor is it they that enter; but rather there are in the Memory the images of the things perceived by the senses, standing ready for Thought when it recollects them. Who can say how these images are formed? But it is clear by which senses they are apprehended and stored up within. For when I am in darkness and silence, I can, if I wish, bring out in my memory the colours, and distinguish between black and white and any others I wish; nor do sounds burst in and upset the thing I am contemplating, which was brought in through the eyes, although they also are there, lying hidden by themselves. I can summon them too, if I wish, and they are immediately at hand; my tongue can be at rest and my throat silent, and I can sing all I want, nor do the images and colours that are nevertheless present also interpose and interrupt; I am reconsidering another store of treasure, that which flows in through the ears. So also I can remember just as I wish all the other things that are brought in and heaped up by all the other senses. Without smelling, I can tell the scent of lilies from that of violets. Without tasting or touching, I can remember honey and boiled must, smooth and rough, and by recollection prefer the former.

10.8.14 All these things I do within, in the great hall of my memory. There heaven and earth stand ready for me, with everything in them that I have been able to perceive, save that which I have forgotten. There too I often encounter and recall myself; what I have done, when and where I did it, and in what frame of mind. There are all the things that I have remembered, whether I have experienced them myself or taken on trust another's account. From that same store I take the likenesses of things I have experienced or which, by inference from what I have experienced, I believe to have happened; I take various different images of this sort, and, weaving them together with what is past, I envisage actions, consequences and hopes that are to come. Moreover, I contemplate all these things as if they were in the present. 'I shall do this and that,' I say to myself, in that great vault of my mind, full as it is of the images of so many and so various objects, and 'this' and 'that' follow. 'If only this or that were so!' 'God forfend this or that!' These things I say to myself, and as I say them, there come to me from Memory's treasure house the images of all the things to which I refer. Nor could I say them at all, were they not there.

10.8.15 Great is the strength of Memory, great indeed, my God; an inner chamber vast and infinite. Who has ever sounded its depths? This strength belongs to my mind and to my nature, yet I myself cannot comprehend all that I am. Is the mind, then, too narrow to hold itself? And if so, what is the part of itself that it does not contain? Can it be outside itself rather than inside itself? How, then, can it not contain itself? Great wonder rises within me over this question; bewilderment overwhelms me. Men go to marvel at the heights of mountains, at the mighty waves of the sea, at spreading torrents of rivers, at the Ocean's circling stream,[5] at the evolutions of the stars, yet they abandon themselves, and do not marvel that when I say these things, I do not see them with my eyes, nor yet could I say them, if I did not inwardly see in my memory the mountains, the waves, the rivers and the stars, which I have seen, and the Ocean, which I believe on trust to exist, all with as much spatial extension as if I could see them outwardly. It is not that I swallowed up these things by seeing them, when I did see them with my eyes, nor is it they that are within me; it is their images. I know too by which sense each thing was impressed upon me.

10.9.16 But these are not the only things borne by my memory, with its immeasurable capaciousness. In it also are all the elements of the liberal arts that I have acquired and not yet forgotten, as if kept apart in some placeless inner place. Nor is it the images I carry, but the things themselves. The nature of literature, the art of disputation, how many types of question there are – whatever I know of these is in my memory. I do not retain an image, having left the thing itself outside; it has not made itself audible and passed away, as a voice leaves its imprint

5 '… Ocean's circling stream'. In ancient thought, the Ocean was the river that encircled the world. The name is regularly given to the Atlantic.

through the ears, by means of which it can be traced back as if it were still audible, when it is not. Nor is it as a scent; it has not passed away and melted into the winds, as a scent causes an olfactory sensation, whereby it casts on to the memory an image of itself, which by a process of reminiscence we can recall. It is not like food, which, when in the stomach, no longer gives forth a taste, but gives a taste in the memory; or like any thing which is perceived by physical contact and of which, even when not present with us, the memory can form an image. These things are not admitted to the memory; it is their images that are conceived with wondrous quickness, stored up, so to speak, in wondrous chambers, and, by recollection, brought forth in wondrous ways.

10.10.17 It is true that when I hear that there are three sorts of question, 'whether it is, what it is, what sort it is', I retain the images of the sounds of which these words are composed, and I know that these sounds have passed through the air, making a noise, and now no longer exist. But the actual things signified by those sounds I have not touched with any of my corporal senses; I have seen them with my mind only. What I have stored away in my memory are not images, but the things themselves. And let them tell me, if they can, by what means they entered me. For when I run through all the gateways of my flesh, I cannot find the one by which they came in. My eyes say, 'If they had colours, then we must have reported them.' The ears say, 'If they made a noise, then we informed you of them.' The nostrils say, 'If they gave off a smell, then they must have entered through us.' The sense of taste speaks too: 'If there is no flavour, it is no use asking me.' The touch says, 'If it had no body, I did not handle it; if I did not handle it, I did not report it.' Whence and by what route did they enter my memory? I do not know how; for when I learnt them, I did not take on trust somebody else's heart; I recognized them in my own and affirmed that they were true, and put them away, so to speak, into safe-keeping, to bring them out when I wished. They were there, therefore, even before I learnt them.

But, I may be told, they were not in my memory. Where,

then, or why, when they were uttered, did I recognize them and say: 'Yes, it is true,' if they were not already in my memory, albeit in the more recondite cellars, so remote and abstruse that it might have been impossible for me to contemplate them, had someone's reminder not rescued them?

10.11.18 For this reason, we find that 'learning' those things whose images we do not imbibe through our senses but perceive inwardly, through themselves, as they are, without images, is nothing other than by means of thought and reflection to gather together and to arrange the things that are indeed contained within the memory, but which lie far and wide, in no set order. They are positioned ready to hand, so to speak, within the memory, where they had previously lain hidden, scattered and neglected, so that they will come to me promptly when I concentrate. And how many such things does my memory hold which have now been found and, as I said, placed ready to hand, which I am said to have 'learnt' or 'come to know'! If I cease to recall them at measured intervals, they become submerged once more, and slip away into the more remote chambers; with the effect that I must think them up again out of there (for there is no other direction they could have taken) as if for the first time. I must drive them together again, to make them knowable; that is to say, I must herd them together from where they are scattered. Hence the verb 'to think' (*cogito*). The words 'to think' (*cogito*) and 'to herd' (*cogo*) are related, as are 'to act' (*ago*) and 'to shake up' (*agito*), and 'to do' (*facio*) and 'to repeat' (*factito*).[6]

10.12.19 Likewise, my memory contains innumerable proofs and laws concerning numbers and geometry. None of these was

6 'The words … (*factito*)'. Augustine argues on the basis of etymology that 'thinking' (*cogito*) is essentially the same process as 'herding together' (*cogo*); he illustrates this with examples of other pairs of Latin verbs (*ago/agito* and *facio/ factito*) of which one (*ago*, *facio*) is the basic form and the other is a derivative of it, containing the suffix *-ito* originally meaning 'to do something again, to do something with force'. Augustine's derivation is entirely correct, though (as his need for parallel examples shows) the connection may not have been apparent to all readers. The argument that knowledge is recollection goes back to Plato, and (fortunately) rests on other grounds than Latin etymology.

impressed on it by my physical senses. They have neither colour nor sound nor scent; they are neither tasteable nor touchable. I have heard the sound of the words by which they are signified when they are expounded; but the sounds are one thing, the laws and proofs themselves another. The sounds are different in Greek and Latin, but the things belong neither to Greek nor Latin nor any other manner of speech. I have seen lines drawn by artisans that are exceedingly fine, like a spider's thread, but these lines are something else again; they are not images of the laws and proofs themselves, reported to me by the eye of my body. These laws are known to all who, without any physical apprehension, have recognized them within. Numbers too I have perceived with all the physical senses that are themselves countable, but the senses that we use in counting are something else again; they are not images of the numbers themselves, and are all the more existent.[7] Let him who does not see them laugh at me for saying this, and let me grieve for his laughter.

10.13.20 All these laws and proofs I hold in my memory. There I hold also how I learnt them. There are many wholly false arguments which may be deployed against them; these too I have heard and hold in my memory. False as they are, it is not false that I remember them. As for the fact that I have discerned between the aforementioned truths and these false arguments deployed against them, this too I remember: I see in one way that I distinguish them now, and remember in another way that I have discerned between them on many occasions before – all the many occasions on which I have contemplated them. Therefore I both remember that I have understood them on many occasions, and store away in my memory the fact that I now discern and understand, so that hereafter I may remember

7 'Numbers too ... more existent'. Augustine here follows a distinction originally drawn by the Pythagorean school of mathematicians but mediated to him through Neo-Platonism, between numbers as counted in external things (e.g. a hundred and one dalmatians) and numbers proper (One Hundred And One). Allied to this is the well-known Platonic hierarchy of being, in which the intangible concepts or Ideas (here represented by the numbers) are held to be truly existent; the particular tangible examples of them exist only relative to them.

that I understood on this occasion. Therefore also I remember that I remember them, just as, if henceforth I recall that I have been able to remember them on this occasion, I shall recall them by force of memory.

10.14.21 My states of mind also are contained in my memory; not in the same way that the mind itself has them at the time when it experiences them, but in another, far different manner, according to the nature of the force of memory. I can recall without gladness a time when I was glad, and remember without being sad a past sadness. Contrariwise, at times I remember with gladness a past sadness, or with sadness a past gladness. This would not be surprising were it my body; for the mind is one thing, the body is another. If, therefore, I remember with gladness a past physical pain, that is not strange. But in this case, the mind is also the memory; when we commit something to the keeping of memory, we say, 'See that you bear it in mind,' and when we forget, we say, 'It was not in my mind,' or, 'It slipped my mind,' thereby calling memory itself mind. This being so, why is it that when I remember with gladness a past sadness, the mind has the gladness and the memory the sadness, the mind is glad with the gladness that is in it, but the memory is not sad with the sadness that is within it? Is the memory perhaps nothing to do with the mind? Who would venture to say this? The memory, then, is like a stomach to the mind, and gladness and sadness like sweet and bitter foods; when they are committed to memory, they can be stored up there like food that has been passed to the stomach, but cannot be tasted. It is ridiculous to consider these things like each other, nor are they altogether unlike.

10.14.22 Moreover, when I say that there are four things that disturb the mind, namely desire, gladness, fear, and sadness, it is from my memory that I bring them forth; and whatever I may say about them in disputation, dividing and defining each thing according to its genus and species, it is in my memory that I find it and from there that I bring it forth. But I am not disturbed by any of these disturbances, when I recollect and list them. Yet before I retrieved and re-examined them, they were there; that is why by means of recalling them I was able to bring them back to light. Perhaps, then, they are brought forth from the memory by a process of recall, just as food is brought forth from the stomach by a process of rumination. When, then, does the disputant not taste them in his mind's mouth, the sweetness of gladness and the bitterness of grief? Are these two things, which are not alike in all respects, in this respect unlike? Who would be willing to speak of such things, if every time he said the word 'sadness' or 'fear', he were compelled to feel fear or sorrow? Yet we would not speak of them did we not find in our memory not only the sounds of their names, imprinted there by our senses in image form, but also the concepts of the things themselves. They are not taken in through any door of our flesh, but deliberately entrusted to memory by the mind through its experience of these emotions, or even retained by the memory though not entrusted to it.

10.15.23 But who would find it easy to say whether the memory retains them by means of images or not? I can speak the word 'stone' or 'sun', when the things themselves are not present before my senses; their images are readily to hand in my memory. I can speak the words 'physical pain', but as long as I am not in pain, it is not present with me. Yet were its image not in my memory, I would not know what to say when, in the course of a disputation, I distinguished it from pleasure. I can speak the words 'physical health', when I am physically healthy; the thing itself is with me, but were its image also not present in my memory, I could in no way recall what the sound of these words signified. Nor could sick people, when the word 'health' was spoken, recognize what was said, were the same image not held by the force of memory, even though the thing itself was not present in their body. I can speak the names of the numbers that we use in counting – but it is not their images but the numbers themselves that are present in my memory. I can name the image of the sun, and this image is itself present in my memory. It is not the image of an image, but the image itself that I recollect; it is itself ready to hand when I search my memory. I can speak the word 'memory', and recognize what

I speak; and where do I recognize them but in my memory itself? Is my memory also present before itself by means of its image and not through itself?

10.16.24 And what of the times when I speak the word 'forget-fulness' and recognize forthwith the thing whose name I speak? From whence would I recognize it, if I did not remember it? It is not the sound of the name that I mean, but the thing itself that it signifies. If I forgot that, what good would the sound do? There would be no way in which I could recognize it. When, therefore, I remember my memory, that memory is present before itself through itself. When, however, I remember forget-fulness, both memory and forgetfulness are present; memory, by which I remember, forgetfulness, which I remember. But what is forgetfulness if not a loss of memory? How, then, can it be present for me to remember it, seeing as when it is present, I cannot remember it? But if what we remember, we retain in our memory, and if, unless we remembered forgetfulness, we could in no way recognize the thing when we heard the name by which it is signified, it follows that forgetfulness is retained in the memory. Forgetfulness, then, is present, to keep us from forgetting; but when it is present, we forget. Are we to under-stand from this that forgetfulness is not present to the memory through itself but through its image; since if it were present through itself, it would not make us remember, but forget? Who can pursue this argument? Who can comprehend how it is?

10.16.25 For my part, O Lord, I am straining at this question, and straining within myself. I am become a *land of toil and much sweat* (cf Gen. 3.17, 19), I am not now pondering the tracts of heaven, measuring the space between the stars, or seeking the foundations of the earth; it is I who remember, I, the mind. It is not so strange if what I am not is far from me; but what is closer to myself than I am? And yet the stores of my memory are not comprehended within me, since I cannot name myself without it. What, then, am I to say, seeing as it is beyond doubt that I remember forgetfulness? Am I to say that what I remember is not in my memory? Am I to say that forgetfulness is in my memory for this very purpose, that I do not forget? Either is utterly absurd. But what third alternative is there? How am I to say that it is the image of forgetfulness and not forgetfulness itself that my memory holds, when it remembers forgetfulness? How am I to say this also, inasmuch as before the image of any thing is imprinted on the memory, it is first necessary that the thing itself should be present for its image to be imprinted? It is thus that I remember the image of Carthage, and of all the places I have been; it is thus that I remember the faces of people I have seen, and the reports of the other senses; it is thus that I remember physical well-being or pain. When all these things are present, my memory takes images from them for me to consider and turn over in my mind, when I remember the things themselves; the images are present when the things are not.

If, then, it is through its image and not through itself that forgetfulness is held in my memory, then it must have been present for its image to have been taken. When, however, it was present, how did it inscribe its image on my memory, seeing as by its very presence it erases even what it finds already recorded there? But for all this, I have no doubt that in some way, even if that way be incomprehensible and inexplicable, I remember the forgetfulness which buries in oblivion what we remember.

10.17.26 Great is the force of memory; it is something to be shuddered at, my God, a deep and endless multiplicity. My mind is this thing; I am this thing. What, then, am I, my God? What manner of creature am I? A life unconstant, manifold, and utterly unmeasured. In the countless fields and grots and caverns of my memory, full beyond counting with countless kinds of thing, I range through images, as with all physical objects, through presences, as with the liberal arts, through mental concepts and records, as with my states of mind, which memory retains even when the mind is not undergoing them, though whatever is in the memory is also in the mind. Through all these things I range, flitting this way and that. I go as deep in as I can, and nowhere is there an end; such is the force of memory, such is the force of life in a man that lives this mortal life!

What, then, am I to do, my true Life and my God? I shall transcend even this force which is called memory; I shall transcend it, and press on towards you, sweet Light. What are you saying to me? Through my mind I ascend to you who remain above; I transcend even this force of mine which is called memory, willing to attain to you where you may be attained, and cleave to you where you may be cloven to. Beasts and birds also have memory, for otherwise they could not go back time and again to their lairs and nests, nor to the many other things with which they grow familiar. For neither could they grow familiar with any things, if not through memory. I shall, therefore, transcend my memory also, to attain him who *set me apart from the four-footed beasts, and made me wiser than the fowls of the air* (Job 35.11). I shall transcend even my memory – but where shall I find you, the truly Good, sweetness untroubled, where shall I find you? If I find you but through my memory, I forget you. And how shall I find you, if I forget you?

10.18.27 *A woman had lost a silver coin, and she took a lantern and sought for it* (Lk 15.8); but had she not remembered it, she could not have found it. For when she had found it, how would she know whether it was the same one, if she could not remember it? I remember myself losing and seeking and finding many things, and hence I know; for, when I have been looking for something, and people have said to me, 'Is it this one?' or, 'Is it that one?' I have kept saying 'No' until the thing I was seeking was put in front of me. If I could not remember that thing, whatever it may be, I could not find it even if it were put in front of me, as I could not recognize it. This is what always happens when we seek something and find it. But if it happens that something is lost to our eyes but not to our memory, as with any visible body one might mention, an image of it is retained within, and we seek for the thing until it is restored to our sight. Nor do we say that we have *found what was lost* (Lk 15.9) if we do not recognize it, nor can we recognize it, if we do not remember it. The thing in question has been lost to the eyes, but is retained in the memory.

10.19.28 How does one explain the fact that when the memory itself loses something, as it does when we forget, and we seek to remember – where do we seek, if not in the memory? And if in the memory something other than what we seek happens to be put in front of us, we reject it, until the thing we seek comes along. Moreover, when it comes along, we say, 'This is it'; which we could not say if we did not recognize it, nor would we recognize it, if we did not remember it. But there is no doubt that we had forgotten it. Or had it not totally fallen out of our mind, but only in part? Do we on the basis of the part that we have retained seek the missing part? Does our mind perceive that it is not at any given point handling all that it is used to handling, and, hobbling along on the stump of its habit, demand the return of the missing part? It is as when we catch sight of a man whom we know, or think of him, and, having forgotten his name, seek for it; and we do not connect to him anything else that comes along, since we are not in the habit of thinking of it along with him, and therefore we reject it, until the right name comes along; the faculty of recognition is immediately acquainted with it, and accordingly rests content. But from whence does it come to us if not from the memory? For when we are reminded of one thing by another, it is from that thing that the other comes to us; but if it were utterly wiped out of our minds, we would not remember even if reminded. We have not, then, entirely forgotten what we remember we have forgotten. But what we have forgotten altogether, lost as it is, we cannot seek.

10.20.29 How, then, do I seek you, O Lord? When I seek you, I seek the blessed life. *I will seek you that my soul may live* (Ps. 69.33 [Ps. 68.33]). From my soul lives my body, and from you lives my soul. How, then, do I seek the blessed life? It is not mine until I say, 'Enough, there it is.' How should I say that I seek it? By recollection, as if I had forgotten it yet retained the memory of my forgetfulness? Or through a desire to learn something unknown, which I had either never known or had forgotten so completely that I could not remember that I had forgotten it? This blessed life is desired by all; there is no one who would not desire it. But if they want it so much, how have they known it? How have they seen it, that they love it? We must surely have it in some way or other. Those who have the blessed life are blessed in a different way from those who are blessed in their hope. Those who have it through hope have it in a lesser way than those who are blessed in reality, but are in a better condition than those who are blessed neither in reality nor in hope. But even these would not wish as they do to be blessed, if they did not have blessedness in some way; and it is beyond all doubt that they do wish for it. In some way or other they have known it, and retain it in their faculty of recognition, whatever that may be. I am in great perplexity whether it be the memory; for if it were, then surely we would all have been blessed at some time, whether all of us individually, or in the man who first sinned, in whom we have all died and from whom we are all born in misery (cf 1Cor. 15.22). But this I do not seek to know now; I seek to know whether the blessed life is in our memory. For we would not love it, had we not known it. We hear this name, and we all acknowledge that this is the very thing we seek; but it is not the sound that delights us. A Greek, on hearing the name spoken in Latin, takes no delight, for he does not know what is said; but we take delight in it, as he would if he heard it in Greek, for the thing itself is neither Greek nor Latin, though Greek- and Latin-speakers and all speakers of every other language long to gain it. The blessed life, therefore, is known to all; all would without hesitation respond, if they could be asked in one word whether they wished to be blessed, that they wished it indeed. This would not be, unless the thing whose name that word is, were retained in their memory.

10.21.30 Is it, then, remembered in the way that someone who has seen Carthage remembers it? No; the blessed life is not a thing visible to the eyes, not being a physical object. Is it in the way that we remember how to count? No; he that has a recollection of numbers does not seek to gain them, whereas the blessed life is something that we love because we have a recollection of it, and yet we seek still to gain it, so as to be blessed. Is it like the way that we remember the art of rhetoric? No; although in this case also even those who have not yet attained eloquence remember what it is when they hear the name; and although many of them do desire to be eloquent (from which it is clear that they do have a recollection of it), it is nevertheless through their physical senses that they have observed the eloquent – even though they would neither take delight in them had they not some inner recollection, nor would they wish to be eloquent, did they not take delight in them. The blessed life, however, is not something that we experience at second hand, nor through our physical senses.

Is it, then, like the way that we remember times of joy? Perhaps. I can remember being joyful even when I am sorrowful, just as I can remember blessedness when I am in misery. But I have not perceived joy with any physical sense. I have neither seen nor heard nor smelt nor tasted nor touched it, yet some recollection of it has lodged in my memory, and I can recall my times of joy – sometimes with loathing, sometimes with long ing, according to the different objects over which I remember having rejoiced. I have at times been suffused with joy over matters for shame, which I detest and abjure when I recall. At other times I have rejoiced over things good and noble, which I recall with longing, even though they are no longer with me, and hence I am sorrowful when I recall my former joy.

10.21.31 Where, then, or when have I experienced a life of bles-sedness? How is it that I can recall it and love it and long for it? This is not true of me alone, nor me and a few others; everyone wishes to be blessed; and did we not know it with such sure knowledge, we would not will it with such sure will. If we were to ask two people whether they wished to serve in the Imperial Service, one might say that he did and the other that he did not. If, however, we asked them whether they wished to be happy and blessed, each of them would immediately and without hes-itation say that he did – and the only reason why one wished to serve in the Imperial Service and the other did not was so as to be thus happy. So it is that everyone agrees that they wish to be blessed, just as they would agree if asked that they wished to be joyful, and call this same joy 'the blessed life'. It is this one end that all seek to attain, one by one route, another by another, namely joy. This is a thing that no one can say that he has not experienced, because each one finds it in his memory, and recognizes when he hears the words 'blessed life'.

10.22.32 Far be it, Lord, far be it from the heart of your servant, who confesses to you, far be it that whatever joy I joy in, I should think myself blessed. There is a *joy which is not given to the impious* (Is. 48.22) but to those who freely worship you; you are yourself their joy. And even this is the blessed life; to rejoice before you, in you, because of you; even this and none other. As for those who think there is another life, they are chasing after another joy, and not the true one. Nevertheless, their will is not averse at least to some image of joy.

10.23.33 Is it not, therefore, beyond doubt that all wish to be blessed, since those who do not wish to rejoice in you, the only blessed Life, have no wish whatever for the blessed life? Or is it that all do wish to be blessed, but since *the flesh lusts against the spirit and the spirit against the flesh*, so that they *do not what they wish* (Gal. 5.17), they fall off and are content with what they can do, as what they cannot do they do not wish for strongly enough to be able to do it? I ask all people whether they would rather *rejoice in the truth or in falsehood* (1Cor. 13.6); they have no less hesitation in saying that they would rather rejoice in the truth than in saying that they wish to be blessed. And the blessed life is to rejoice in the truth; for this is rejoicing in you, who are the Truth, O God, *my Light* (Ps. 27.1) and *the saving health of my countenance and my God* (Ps. 42.7, 15 [Ps. 41.6–7, Ps. 42.5]). All wish for this blessed life; this life, which alone is blessed, all wish for; all wish to rejoice in the Truth.

I have known many who wished to deceive, but none who wished to be deceived. How, then, do they know the blessed life, if they have not known the Truth also? That too they love, for they do not wish to be deceived; and seeing as they love the blessed life, which is none other than rejoicing in the truth, they must also love the truth; nor would they love it had they not some record of it in their memory. Why, then, do they not rejoice in it? Why are they not blessed? Because they are caught up in other affairs, which make them wretched, rather than what would make them blessed, of which they have only a slight recollection. *For a little while yet the light is among men; let them walk, let them walk, lest the darkness overtake them* (Jn 12.35).

10.23.34 Why, then, is 'truth the mother of hatred',[8] and why does the man of God *become an enemy to those to whom he preached the truth* (Gal. 4.16), seeing as men love the blessed life, which is none other than rejoicing in the truth? Why indeed, if not because they love the truth in such a way that whatever else they love, they define what they love as the truth; and not wishing to be deceived, they do not wish to be shown to have been deceived. It is, therefore, for the sake of the thing that they love in place of the truth that they hate the truth. They love the truth for its radiance; they hate it when it shows them wrong. Not wishing to be deceived but wishing to deceive, they love the truth when it reveals itself, and hate it when it reveals them. It is thus that the truth will repay them; it will expose those who do not wish to be exposed by it, for all their wishing, and will not be exposed to them. Thus, even thus, is the human soul; thus blind and sick, mange-ridden and unsightly, desiring to be hidden, but desiring that nothing be hid from it. But instead its payment shall be that it will not be hidden from the truth, but that the truth shall be hid from it. Nevertheless, despite its wretchedness, it would rather rejoice in truths than in falsehoods. Blessed will it be, if, unperturbed by any outward trouble, it rejoices in the one Truth through which all truths exist.

10.24.35 See how far I have roamed in my memory, searching for you, O Lord, and I have not found you outside it. Nor have I found anything of you which I have not remembered, ever since I came to know you. For since I came to know you, I have not forgotten you; where I have found the truth, I have found my God, the Truth itself; and since coming to know that Truth, I have not forgotten it. Since, then, I came to know you, you have remained in my memory, and when I recall you and take pleasure in you, I find you there. This is my sacred delight, which you have given to me, *having regard in your mercy* (Ps. 31.8 [Ps. 30.8]) for my poverty.

10.25.36 But where in my memory do you abide, O Lord? Where in my memory? What manner of chamber have you

8 ' "truth the mother of hatred" '. Terence, *Andria* 68.

fashioned for yourself? What manner of sanctuary have you built for yourself? You have conferred on my memory the honour of abiding in it, but this I ponder – in what part of it do you abide? I have transcended in recalling you the parts of it that are common to the beasts, for I did not find you there, amid the images of things corporeal. I came to the parts to which I commit my states of mind, nor did I find you there. I entered the very seat of the mind, which is there in my memory (for the mind remembers itself also), nor were you there; for just as you are not the image of a corporeal object nor the mental state of a living creature, such as our feelings when we rejoice, are saddened, desire, fear, remember, forget and so forth, neither are you the mind itself. You are the Lord God of the mind. All these things change, but you abide changeless above all things, and have deigned to dwell in my memory since I came to know you. And why do I ask in what place in it you dwell, as if there were indeed places within it? Surely you dwell in it, for I have remembered you ever since I came to know you; and when I recall you, I find you there.

10.26.37 Where, then, did I find you? How did I come to know you? You were not already in my memory before I came to know you. Where did I find you, that I could come to know you, if not in you and above myself? Not in any place; we *go backward and forward* (Job 23.8), but do not find you in any place. You, O Truth, are set over all who come to you for counsel everywhere; and at one and the same time you give your oracles to all who seek counsel from you, even when their counsels are different. Clear are your oracles, but not clearly do all hear them. All seek counsel on matters they want to know, but they do not always hear what they want to hear. The best servant of you is he who is not more intent on hearing from you what he wants to hear, than on wanting what he hears from you.

10.27.38 Late have I loved you, Beauty so ancient and so new, late have I loved you! Behold, you were within and I was without; and there I sought you, plunging unformed as I was into the fair things that you have formed and made. You were with me, and I was not with you. I was kept far from you by the things that would not have been, were they not in you. You called and cried aloud, and shattered my deafness; you flashed and blazed like lightning, and routed my blindness. You cast your fragrance, and I drew breath, yet pant for you; I tasted, yet hunger and thirst; you touched me, and I was on fire for your peace.

10.28.39 When I cling to you with all my being, I will have no grief or toil; my life will be alive, wholly full of you. But whom you fill, you raise up; and as it stands, I am not full of you, and hence am I a burden to myself. The joys I should weep for contend with the sorrows over which I should rejoice, and I do not know where the victory will fall. The evils I should grieve for contend with the goods I should rejoice over, and I do not know where the victory will fall. Oh, *have pity on me, O Lord* (Ps. 31.10 [Ps. 30.10]) have pity on me! See my wounds; I do not hide them. You are the physician, and I am sick. You are pitiful, and I am pitiable. Surely *a man's life on earth is a testing* (Job 7.1), for who would willingly have its harshnesses and toils? These things you bid us endure, not to love. No one loves what he endures, even if he loves to endure. For however much he may rejoice that he endures, he would rather have nothing to endure. In adversity I yearn for prosperity, in prosperity I fear adversity. What middle ground is there between these two, in which a man's life is not a testing? Woe and woe again to the prosperities of the world, once for the fear of adversity, and woe again for the ruin of happiness! Woe and woe again to the adversities of the world for the yearning for prosperity, and again for the very hardness of adversity, and yet again lest it break our powers of endurance! What is a man's life on earth if not a testing without intermission?

10.29.40 And all my hope is nothing if not in your exceeding great mercy. Give what you command, and command what you will. You enjoin continence upon us. *And knowing* (as it is said) *that no one can be continent unless God give it, and that to know whose gift it is in itself a mark of wisdom* ... (Wisdom 8.21). It is through continence that we are gathered together and restored to that unity from which we were dispersed into multiplicity. For he who loves along with you anything that he does not love for your sake, loves you the less. O Love ever burning and never extinguished, Love, my God, set me ablaze! You command us to be continent; give what you command, and command what you will.

10.30.41 This surely you command: that I should keep myself from *the lust of the flesh and the lust of the eyes, and from worldly ambition* (1Jn 2.16). You commanded me to keep from concubinage, and concerning marriage itself you have counselled a course better than that which you have permitted.[9] And since you granted me continence, it came to pass, even before I became a dispenser of your Sacrament. But there still live in the memory, of which I have spoken so much, images of these things, fixed there by habit. My mind is beset with images that have no power when I am awake, but in my dreams they persuade me not only to take pleasure but also to give way to it; it is just as if these things really happened. The illusion produced by these images works so strongly in the soul in our flesh that false visions persuade me when asleep to do what true visions cannot do when I am awake. Am I, then, not myself when asleep? Does the moment in which I pass from this side to sleep and back again make such a difference between myself and myself? Where at that moment is my reason, which resists such insinuations when waking, and, if the very things themselves were put before it, would remain unmoved? Is it closed off when the eyes close? Does it fall asleep when the corporal senses sleep? And how is it that even in our dreams we often resist these thoughts and, mindful of our purpose and remaining fast in it in all chastity, give no assent to these allurements? And yet is there such a difference that, when things happen otherwise, we should wake up with an easy conscience? Should we consider that our dreams have nothing to do with us, and that we ourselves have done nothing, even though we do regret what somehow or other was done in us?

10.30.42 Surely your hand, O God Almighty, has power to *heal*

9 '. . . counselled a course . . . you have permitted'. Cf 1Cor. 7.38 (Paul's advice that chastity is better than marriage, though marriage is itself permissible).

all my soul's sicknesses (Ps. 103.3 [Ps. 102.3], Matt. 4.23), and by your more abundant grace to extinguish the lascivious stirrings I feel even in my sleep. Increase, O Lord, more and more your gifts in me. Let my soul, freed from the lime of concupiscence, follow me towards you; let it not rebel against itself; even in dreams, let it not only not commit those shameful and corrupting deeds, led by images of living things to the point of carnal emission, but let it not even consent to them. It is no great thing for the Almighty, *who can do more than we ask or understand* (Eph. 3.20), to see that nothing of this sort appeals to us even as much as can be checked at the merest command; not only in this life, but also at this time of my life. What I still am in respect of this manner of evil, I have told my good Lord, *rejoicing with trembling* (Ps. 2.11) for what you have given me, mourning in so far as I am not yet brought to fulfilment, hoping that you will fulfill your mercies towards me, until I gain in its fulness the peace that my inward and outward parts will have with you, when *death has been swallowed up in victory* (1Cor. 15.54).

10.31.43 There is another kind of evil that belongs to this day, and would that it were sufficient to it (cf Matt. 6.34)! In eating and drinking we restore that which daily falls away from our bodies, until such time as you destroy food and the stomach (cf 1Cor. 15.53), when you will slay our need with wondrous satiety, and *clothe the corruptible in eternal incorruption* (1Cor. 15.54). But as it stands, my need is sweet to me, and I fight against that sweetness, lest I be deceived by it; daily I wage war against it, reducing my body time and again to slavery by fasting, driving the pains from it by pleasure. For hunger and thirst are pains, of a sort; they burn and choke us to death like fever, or would do if the medicine of foods did not come to our aid. That this medicine is at hand to help us is in accordance with the consolation afforded us by your gifts, through which earth and sea and sky minister to our weakness; hence the daily ruin of our body is called 'pleasure'.[10]

10 '. . . hence the daily ruin . . . is called pleasure'. That is, our repeated attacks of hunger and thirst, though signs of the body's decay, are the occasion for eating and drinking, which are in themselves pleasurable sensations.

10.31.44 This you have taught me: that I should approach the eating of food like the taking of medicine. I pass over from the unpleasant sensation of want to the ease that comes with satiety; but the snare of concupiscence lies in wait for me even as I pass. The passage is itself a source of pleasure, and there is no other means by which I can pass the way that necessity forces me to pass. And although I eat and drink for my health's sake, a dangerous sweetness tags along at our heels and often attempts to go first, to make me do for pleasure's sake what I say or wish to do for my health's sake. Nor do pleasure and health limit themselves to the same amount; what is enough for my health is not enough for the demands of pleasure, and often it is doubtful whether, driven by need, I seek to sustain my body, or whether, misled by desire, I seek to minister to my concupiscence. My wretched soul is full of glee at this very uncertainty, and uses it in preparing the case for its defence, rejoicing that it is not clear what is the due amount of food to maintain one's physical well-being, and covering the work of pleasure with the pretext of health. These temptations I daily endeavour to resist. I call upon your right hand, and take to you all my hesitation; having as yet no firm policy on this matter.

10.31.45 I hear the voice of my God bidding me: *Let not your hearts be weighted with tipsiness and inebriety* (cf Lk 21.34). Inebriety is far from me; have mercy upon me, lest it come near me. Tipsiness, however, has at times crept up on your servant; have mercy on me, that it be far from me. *No one can be continent, except you give it* (Wisdom 8.21). Many things you bestow upon us when we pray, and whatever good thing we have received before we pray, we have received it from you. From you also we have received the power to recognize that we have received these good gifts from you. I have never been a drunkard, but I have known drunkards made sober by you. It is your doing that those who have never been drunkards are not drunkards, and your doing also that those who were drunkards are so no longer; and your doing also that both should know by whom this was done. And I have heard another saying of yours: *Go not after your lusts, and forbid yourself your pleasure* (Ecclesiasticus 18.50). And by your gift I have heard this saying also: *Neither if we eat shall we have too much, nor if we eat not shall we have too little* (1Cor. 8.8). That is to say, neither will one thing make me rich nor the other poor. I have heard another saying also: *I have learnt to be satisfied with what I have; I have learnt to be rich and to be poor. I can do all things in him who strengthens me* (Phil. 4.11–13). He that said this is a soldier of the heavenly army, not the dust that we are. But remember, O Lord, that *we are but dust* (Ps. 103.14 [Ps. 102.14]), and that of dust you have made man, and that he *was lost and is found* (Lk 15.24, 32). In himself he had no power; Paul also was dust, whom I love for the sake of the words that, prompted by your inspiration, he spoke: *I can do all things in him who strengthens me* (Phil. 4.11–13). Strengthen me, so that I gain this power; give what you command, and command what you will. Paul confesses that he has received this power, and that *what he boasts, he boasts of in the Lord* (1Cor. 1.31, 2Cor. 10.17). And I have heard another man say: *Take from me the lusts of the stomach* (Ecclesiasticus 23.6). Hence it is clear, my holy God, that when what you command be done is done, it is your gift.

10.31.46 You have taught me, good Father, that *to the pure all things are pure, but woe to him who by eating causes offence* (Rom. 14.20); that all your creation is good, and that *nothing should be rejected that is eaten with thanksgiving* (1 Tim. 4.4); and that *it is not food that commends us to God* (1Cor. 8.8); and that *no one should judge us in matters of food or drink* (Col. 2.16); and that *he that eats should not despise him that does not eat, nor should he that does not eat judge him who does* (Rom. 14.3). All this I have learnt, and thanks and praise be to you, my God, my Teacher, who knock at the door of my ears and enlighten my heart. Deliver me from every temptation. It is not unclean food that I fear, but unclean greediness. I know that Noah was permitted to eat all manner of flesh that could serve as food (Gen. 9.2–3), that Elijah was refreshed by eating meat (1Kings 17.6), that John, endowed with wondrous abstinence, was not polluted by the flesh of living creatures, that is, the locusts that served him as food (cf Matt. 3.4). I know too that Esau was deceived by his greed for lentils (cf Gen. 25.34), that David reproached himself for wanting water (2Kings 23.15–17), and that our King was tempted not with meat but with bread (Matt. 4.3). For this reason also the people of Israel merited their reproach in the desert; not because they desired for meat, but because in their desire for meat they murmured against the Lord (cf Numbers 11.1–20).

10.31.47 Set as I am in the midst of these temptations, I strive daily against greed for food and drink. This is not something I can resolve to cut off once and for all and never to touch again, as I could with sexual congress. I must hold the reins of the throat and relax or tighten them in their proper degree. And who is there, O Lord, who is not carried away at least to some extent beyond the bounds of necessity? If there is such a man, he is a great man indeed, and let him *magnify your name* (Ps. 69.30 [Ps. 68.31], Rev. 15.4). I am not such a one; *I am a sinful man* (Lk 5.8). But I also magnify your name. Let him who has *overcome the world* (Jn 16.33) *intercede before you for my sins* (Rom. 8.34), counting me among *the weaker members of his body* (Rom. 12.5, 1Cor. 12.12, 22), since *your eyes have seen my substance yet being unperfect, and in your book will be all my members written* (Ps. 139.16 [Ps. 138.13]).

10.32.48. The allurement of scents, however, does not bother me too much. When they are absent, I do not feel the need of them; when they are present, I do not reject them. I would even be ready to do without them for ever. Or so I think I would; I may be deceived. For here too there is a lamentable darkness, in which the faculty that is within me may hide from me. My mind, when it questions itself about its own powers, cannot readily trust itself, since what is in it is generally hidden, if it has not been revealed by experience, and in this life, which is called 'all testing' (Job 7.1), no one should be sure that one who has been able to pass from a worse state to a better is not passing also from a better state to a worse. Our one hope, one confidence, one firm promise is your mercy.

10.33.49 The pleasures of the ear used to hold me tight in their coils and keep me subject, but you have released and delivered me. Now when I hear your words chanted with a well-trained and melodious voice, I yield to the sounds given life by those words, but only a little way; I am not trapped by them, and can get up and leave them, if I will. But these sounds, along with the verbal expressions by which they have their life, demand a place of some dignity in my heart, and I can scarcely furnish them with one suitable. Sometimes I think I give them more honour than is proper, when I reflect that our minds are more religiously and more ardently disposed towards the flame of piety when these words are sung thus than if they were not; and that all of our spiritual affections have their proper measures in voice and singing, according to their various kinds, and are stirred up by a sort of hidden kinship with them. But it is improper to give the mind over to the pleasure of the flesh; and this pleasure often deceives me, when my emotion is not content merely to accompany my reason and take second place to it, but seeks to outrun it and lead it, for no other reason than that it was for reason's sake that pleasure earned admittance. So it is that in matters of music I sin without perceiving it, and perceive it afterwards.

10.33.50 Sometimes, however – and very occasionally – my concern to avoid this very deceit goes beyond its due measure, and I fall into the error of excessive severity. At such times I would have all the sweet and tuneful chants used in repeating the Psalms of David set far from my ears, and from those of the Church itself. At such times the practice which, as I have heard tell, was followed by Athanasius Bishop of Alexandria seems to me the safest. He would have his reader intone the Psalm with such a measured inflexion of the voice that he sounded more as if he were reciting than chanting. But when I remember the tears I poured out at the sound of the Church's chants in the first days after I had recovered my faith, and how I am moved even now – not by the chanting but by the things chanted, when they are chanted in a clear voice and to a well-suited melody – I acknowledge once more the great benefit of this institution. Thus I waver between the peril that this pleasure can produce, and my own experience of its health-giving power. I am increasingly led to think – which I do not advance as my irrevocable pronouncement − that the practice of singing in church is a good thing. Through the delights of the ear, the weaker soul can rise up and be moved to piety. But when it happens that I am more moved by the chanting than by the thing chanted, I confess that I have sinned punishably, and then I would rather not hear a chanter. So am I placed! Weep with me and weep for me, you who have any good impulse in your heart, from which deeds proceed. As for you without such an impulse − you are not moved by such things. But you, O Lord my God, hear my prayer; behold and see, have mercy on me and heal me.[11] In your sight I have become the object of my own investigation, and this itself is my disease.

10.34.51 There remains the pleasure of the eyes, which belong to my flesh. It is about this pleasure that I utter these confessions. Let the ears of *your temple* hear these confessions, pious and brotherly ears, so that I may conclude my account of the *lusts of the flesh* (1Jn 2.16) which still batter at me demanding admission, much as I *groan and long to be clothed from above with my habitation which is from heaven* (2Cor. 5.2). Beautiful and varied shapes, bright and pleasant colours − these things my eyes love. Let them not hold my soul; let my soul be held by the God who made all these things. They are good indeed, but he is my Good, not they. They touch me throughout each day as I wake, and I am given no rest from them, as I am from the sound of voices singing, and sometimes, in silence, from all sounds. For Light herself, the queen of colours, instils herself in all that we see; wherever I am in the daytime, she falls on me in a thousand ways and caresses me, even when I am occupied with something else and do not notice her. But she creeps in on me so deeply that if she is suddenly taken away, I miss her and long for her; and if she is absent long, my mind is saddened.

10.34.52 O Light seen by Tobias, who, though the eyes of his flesh were closed, showed his son the way of life and with the foot of love went before him without straying![12] O Light seen

11 '... behold and see ... heal me'. A conflation of Ps. 6.2, 9.3, 13.3, 80.14, 103.3 [Ps. 6.3, 9.14, 12.4, 79.15, 102.3] Matt. 4.23.
12 'O Light ... without straying!' See Tobit 4.2.

by Isaac, who, though his fleshly eyes were burdened and filmed with age, was counted worthy not to recognize his children and thereby to bless them, but to bless them and thereby to recognize them![13] O Light seen by Jacob, who, though his sight too was dimmed, cast light from his radiant heart upon the tribes of the future People of Israel foretokened in his sons, and laid his hands crossed in prophetic fashion upon his grandchildren by Joseph! Their father straightened out that cross on the outside, but Jacob placed his hands according to his own inner sight![14] That is the one Light, and all who see and love it are One. As for the corporeal light of which I was speaking, that sweetens earthly life for its blind lovers with an alluring and perilous sweetness. But when they learn to praise you, *the God and Creator of all things* (2Macc. 1.24; Ambrose, *Hymn* 1.2.1), for that light also, then they subsume it into their hymn to you, and are not subsumed by their own slumber. Such would I be. I resist the wandering urges of my eyes, to keep my feet, by which I enter upon your Way, from being ensnared. I lift up my invisible eyes to you (cf Ps. 121.1 [Ps. 120.1]), so that you will *pluck my feet out of the snare* (Ps. 25.25 [Ps. 24.15]). You will pluck them out without delay, for they are ensnared. You do not cease to pluck them out, but I am caught over and over again in the traps that are scattered all around; for you, the *Keeper of Israel, will neither slumber nor sleep* (Ps. 121.4 [Ps. 120.4]).

10.34.53 What countless things men have added to the enticements of the eyes, by skill and by craftsmanship, in clothing and shoes and vessels and all manner of handiwork, in paintings also and divers artefacts! They have far exceeded the measure set by necessity for the use of these things and their meaning in religion; they have pursued outwardly their own works, abandoning inwardly him by whom they were made and disfiguring that which they were made (Matt. 6.16). But for this reason also, my God and my glory, do I sing a hymn to you and *offer the sacrifice of praise* (Ps. 116.17 [Ps. 115.17]) to you that have sanctified me: because the beauties that pass through the souls and into the

13 '... to bless ... and to recognize them!' See Gen. 27.1–40.
14 '... Jacob ... inner sight!' See Gen. 48.1–22.

hands of these artificers come from that Beauty which is above all minds, for which my soul sighs day and night. From that Beauty these craftsmen that pursue outward beauties take the yardstick by which they perceive what is good, but not the yardstick by which they should use it. That Beauty is there and they do not see it; if they did, they would not depart from it, but would *keep their strength safe with you* (Ps. 59.9 [Ps. 58.10]), not dispersing themselves in pleasures that sap the strength. I who speak this and make these distinctions also catch my foot in these beauties, but you pluck my foot out, O Lord; it is you who pluck my foot out, for *your mercy is before my eyes* (Ps. 26.3 [Ps. 25.3]). I am caught most pitiably, and you in pity pluck me out; sometimes without my realizing it, when I am only lightly caught, sometimes with pain, when I have become stuck fast.

10.35.54 Moreover, there is another form of temptation that is perilous in manifold ways. Beyond the lust of the flesh, which is present in all sensory delights and pleasures, and in service of which those who depart from you perish away, there is in the soul a certain vain and inquisitive greed that works through all the senses; not for pleasures of the flesh, but for experience through the flesh. This greed cloaks itself in the name of 'research' and 'knowledge'. As this greed exists in the desire to become acquainted with things, and as the eyes are the sense by which we chiefly gain such acquaintance, it is named in the Word of God the 'lust of the eyes'.[15] It is the faculty of seeing that properly pertains to the eyes, but we use this verb also of other senses, when we refer to their cognitive powers. We do not say, ' "Hear" or "smell" or "taste" or "feel" how bright something is'; in this context, we say 'see'. But we say not only 'See how bright!' but also 'See what a noise!' 'See what a smell!' 'See what a taste!' 'See how hard!'. Thus sensory experience is generically called 'the lust of the eyes', as I have said, because the other senses by analogy also claim for themselves the task of seeing, in which eyes hold the first place, when they seek acquaintance with a thing.

15 '…"the lust of the eyes"'. The so-called 'Triple Concupiscence' of 1Jn 2.16. See note on 2.2.2.

10.35.55 There is greater evidence of the distinction between the working of pleasure and the working of curiosity in the senses. Pleasure pursues things that are beautiful, that sound or smell or taste agreeable, or are smooth to the touch; whereas curiosity seeks both these things and their opposite, wishing only to try them out, not driven by a desire to undergo the unpleasant sensation but by a lust for personal knowledge and acquaintance. What pleasure is there is seeing a mangled corpse, and shuddering at it? But wherever such a corpse lies, people come to be filled with horror and to turn pale. They are even afraid of seeing such things in their dreams — as if someone forced them to see them when awake, or as if they had been induced by some rumour that it was a beautiful sight! The same is true of the other senses, though it would take too long to go through them one by one. It is because of this same morbid desire that freaks of all kinds are exhibited in public spectacles. It is for this reason that men seek to examine the secrets of nature, which are beyond us; it does no good to know them, yet men desire nothing but to know. It is for this same reason, with this same goal of perverse knowledge, that men seek what they do by the magic arts. It is for this reason also in religious matters that God is put to the test, when men *demand signs and wonders* (Lk 11.16, Jn 4.48) not in order to gain salvation, but for the mere experience of them.

10.35.56 In this great wood, full as it is of snares and perils, I have cut back and shaken away many of the brambles from my heart, according as you have given me power to do, *O God of my salvation* (Ps. 18.46 [Ps. 17.47], Ps. 38.22 [Ps. 37.23]). But when, surrounded as I am in my daily life on all sides by temptations of this sort and their clamour — when can I dare to say that I paid no attention to any such things, nor was tempted by them into idle speculation? I am no longer carried away by the theatre, it is true, nor am I concerned to discover the paths of the stars, nor has my soul ever sought oracles from the shades; all sacrilegious rites I detest. But what thoughts the Enemy puts into my mind, how many devices he deploys to get me to seek a sign from you, to whom I owe humble and sincere service! I beseech

you by our King and by our homeland of Jerusalem the sincere
and chaste, let me always be as far and further from acquiescence
to such things as I already am. But when I pray for anyone's
salvation, my attention is directed towards another and far different end; then grant, as you do grant, that I may willingly
follow you as you do what you will.

10.35.57 But who can count the many tiny and insignificant
matters in which our curiosity is tempted every day, and how
often we slip? How many times do we at first tolerate those who
tell us silly tales, so as not to offend the weak, then by degrees
do we give them heed? I no longer watch a hare chased by a
dog, if it happens in the theatre, but if I happen to be crossing a
field, the sight of the chase may distract my attention and turn
it from pondering some deep question to itself. I am not forced
to stray from the path physically, by my ass or donkey, but by
my heart's inclination; and unless, having given me proof of my
weakness, you then admonish me either to lift myself up by
some sort of meditation from that sight to you, or to scorn the
whole thing and pass on, my mind drifts away and my thought
is blunted. Or what of the many times when I am sitting at
home and my attention is captured by a lizard catching flies or
a spider enmeshing them as they fly heedlessly into her nets? Is
it the case that because these are little creatures the same thing
does not take place? From these sights I press on to praise you,
who have wondrously created all things and set them in their
due place. It is one thing to pick one's self up quickly, another
thing not to fall. My life is full of such things, and my one hope
is *your exceeding great mercy* (Ps. 86.13 [Ps. 85.13]). When my
heart becomes a receptacle for this sort of thing and carries great
burdens of vanity, this is also the reason why our prayers are
often interrupted and disturbed, and when in your sight we
turn our heart's voice to your ears, idle thoughts fly at us from
somewhere or other, and our important business is cut short.

10.36.58 Should we not set this down also in the class of things
to be despised? Or what will restore us to hope if not your well-
tried mercy, seeing as you have begun to change me? You know
to what extent you have changed me, having first cured me of

the lust for self-justification, so as to *forgive me all* my other *iniquities, and heal all my diseases*; to *redeem my life from corruption, and to crown me with loving-kindness and mercy*, and *to satisfy my heart's desire with good things* (Ps. 103.3–5 [Ps. 102.3–5]). You checked my pride with the fear of you, and tamed my neck to your yoke. That yoke I still carry and it is light to me, for you have promised that it would be and have made it so; and yet it was light even in the days when I was afraid to submit to it, and I did not know it.

10.36.59 But what, O Lord, who alone are lord without pride, being *the only true Lord* (Is. 37.20), having no lord, what of this third sort of temptation[16] — the will to be feared and loved by men for no other reason than to gain a joy that is no joy? Has that temptation ceased to trouble me, or can it, in this life? This is a wretched life, and that is a shameful sort of pride. This is a reason, perhaps the greatest reason, why we do not love you or fear you as we should. For this reason you *resist the proud, but give grace to the humble* (James 4.6, 1Pet. 5.5). You sound your thunder over the *ambitions of this world* (1Jn 2.16), and the *foundations of the mountains tremble* (Ps. 18.7 [Ps. 17.8]). It is necessary for us, for the performance of certain offices of human society, to be loved and feared by men; and for that reason the Enemy of our true happiness presses upon us, baiting his traps with the words, 'Well done! Well done!' so that in our greed to gather them up we are caught unawares, setting aside our joy that comes from your truth and placing it rather in human deceits. Thus he deceives us into taking pleasure in being loved and feared, not for your sake, but in your place, so that, having made us like himself, he may keep us to share not in the harmony of love, but in the fate of damnation. He has resolved to *set his seat above the North Wind* (Is. 14.13), to gain the obedience of the cold and dark-hearted with his perverse and twisted imitation of you. But as for us, O Lord, behold, we are your *little flock* (Lk 12.32); keep us yourself. Put forth your wings, and we shall run for shelter beneath them. Be yourself our boast;

16 'this third sort of temptation'. The third item of the so-called 'Triple Concupiscence' of 1Jn 2.16. See note on 2.2.2.

may we be loved for your sake, and let your word be feared in us. He who would be praised by men though reproached by you, will not be defended by men when condemned by you. *He who sins not in the desires of his heart is praised, and he shall be blest who bears no iniquities;*[17] but such a man is praised for the gift you have given him. If, however, he rejoices more at being praised than at having the gift for which he is praised, then his praise too runs counter to your reproaches. The one who praises him is better than the one who is praised. The former takes delight at the gift of God in man, whereas the latter has more pleasure in the gift of man than of God.

10.37.60 I am tested by these temptations every day, O Lord; I am tempted incessantly. *The tongue of man is a furnace* (Prov. 27.21) that burns every day. You bid us be continent in respect of this sort of temptation also; give what you command and command what you will. You know my heart's groaning and my eyes' floods over this matter. Nor can I readily infer how far I am cleansed from this pestilence, and I fear greatly my hidden faults, which are known to your eyes but not to my own. In respect of other sorts of temptation I have some power to examine myself; in this, almost none. In the case of carnal pleasures and of curiosity for superfluous knowledge, I can see how far I have managed to curb my mind, when I do without the objects of my desire, either of my own choice or because they are not there. Then I can ask myself how much or how little of an imposition it is not to have them. Even in the case of riches, which are desirable as a means to minister to one or two or all three of these lusts, if the mind cannot decide so long as it has them whether or not it contemns them, it can let go of them, to test itself. But what can we do about going without praise and testing ourselves out in that respect? What a hard life it would be, how savage and inhuman, if no one were to know us who did not detest us! What greater madness can be said or conceived? And if praise is and should be the usual companion of a good life and good works, we should no more abandon its company than we should

---

17 '*He who sins not ... no iniquities*'. An adaptation of Ps. 10.3 (Ps. 9.24); where, however, the sense is the opposite.

abandon a good life. But I cannot perceive how calmly or how badly I do without something unless it is not there.

10.37.61 What is it then, O Lord, that I confess to you in respect of this sort of temptation? What but that I take pleasure in being praised. But I take more pleasure in the truth than in being praised. If I were given the choice of being on the one hand mad or mistaken on all matters and still praised by all men, or on the other hand of being firm in my wits, firmly convinced of the truth, and reviled by all, I know what I would choose. I would not, however, have another man's praise for me increase my pleasure in any good quality of mine; but increase it it does, I confess, whereas criticism diminishes it. When I am troubled over this wretched trait of mine, a justification sidles up to me – what sort of justification, *you know, O Lord* (Ps. 69.5 [Ps. 68.8]), for it makes me uncertain: you have bidden us be continent, that is, to withhold our love from certain things. But you have bidden us also be just, and justice is the standard against which we should measure our love. Nor have you willed it that we should love only you, but that we should love our neighbour also. Often I find myself taking pleasure in my neighbour's progress or prospects of it, when I take pleasure in his intelligent praise of something, and likewise I am saddened by his lack of progress when I hear him criticizing what he does not understand or what is good. Sometimes I am even saddened by praise of myself, either when things which I dislike in myself are praised, or when lesser and lighter goods are valued at more than they are worth. But again, how do I know whether I am thus affected because I do not wish to disagree about myself with one who praises me – not because I am concerned for his benefit, but because those goods which I do like in myself are all the sweeter to me when another likes them as well? There is a sense in which it is not I who am praised, when that praise does not correspond to my own view of myself – when either those things are praised that I dislike, or those things are praised that I like less. Am I thus uncertain of myself in this matter?

10.37.62 In you, O Truth, I see that it is right that I should be moved by praise of myself – not for my own sake, but for my neighbour's benefit. Whether I am so moved, I do not know. In this matter I know myself less than I know you. I beg you, my God, make me also known to myself, so that I may confess to my brothers as they prepare to pray for me what I find wanting in myself. Let me question myself again, more diligently. If it is for my neighbour's benefit that I am moved when I am praised, why am I less moved if another person is unjustly criticized than if I am? Why am I more stung by an insult to myself than to another person, even if it is cast at them no less unjustly in my presence? Do I not know this also? Is it only left for me to deceive myself and live a lie in heart and tongue in your presence? *Put all such madness far from me, O Lord* (Prov. 30.8), lest my own mouth become the *oil of sinners* and *anoint my head* (Ps. 141.5 [Ps. 140.5]).

10.38.63 *I am poor and needy* (Ps. 109.22 [Ps. 108.22]); but better off when I groan in secret, dissatisfied with myself and seeking your mercy, till what is lacking in me be restored and reach its fulfilment in the peace that is unknown to the eye of the proud. But the words that proceed from men's mouths, and the deeds that become known among them, carry a most perilous temptation of their own. This arises out of our love of being praised; we love to beg good opinions of men, then scrape together these opinions to bolster our private sense of our own superiority. When I am tempted by this love of praise, and rebuke it, it glories in the fact – even though I am rebuking it in myself. Often indeed it glories more vainly still in its own contempt of vainglory. Then this love of praise ceases to glory in the very contempt of glory, seeing as it does not contemn what it glories in.

10.39.64 In respect of this sort of testing, there is another evil within me, too much within. Men make fools of themselves when they are pleased with themselves though not pleasing or displeasing to others, or not seeking to please others. Being pleased with themselves they are displeasing to you, not only because they are pleased with their bad qualities as if they were good ones, but also because they are pleased with the good qualities that come from you as if they were their own, or even because they are pleased with the good qualities that come from you as if they had earned them themselves. They might even acknowledge them to come from your grace, but not rejoice and share them, but begrudge them to others. In all these and other such perils and labours you see how my heart trembles, and I perceive more clearly how quickly you heal my wounds than how you keep me from being wounded.

10.40.65 When have you not walked with me, O Truth, teaching me what I should avoid and what I should seek to gain, whenever I have referred to you my visions of lower things, so far as I was capable of seeing them, and sought your counsel? With my senses I surveyed the world outside, so far as I was capable, and took thought for the life of my body and those same senses. Then I went back inside myself, to the caverns of my memory, those vastnesses wondrously full of countless resources; I *pondered and was afraid* (Habakkuk 3.2) and could distinguish between none of them without you, nor did I find any of them to be you. Nor was it I who discovered all the things that I surveyed and endeavoured to value according to their true worth, receiving some things as messages from my senses and questioning them, perceiving other things to be compound of several elements, distinguishing and counting the various messenger senses; and, having gathered them into the wealth of memory, handling some things, storing others away, and casting others out. Nor was it I that did all this – that is, the force that is in me by which I did it. Nor were you that force; for you are the abiding light which I consulted about all of them: whether they existed, what they were, what value should be attached to them. I listened as you taught and commanded me. This I often do. I find pleasure in it, and take refuge in that pleasure during what release I can get from my necessary activities. In all the things that I go over when I go to you for counsel I find no safe place for my soul except in you. There I can gather my scattered pieces, nor is any part of me lost from you. At times you take me inside and admit me to a state of mind far out of the ordinary, to some sensation of sweetness. If this sweetness is ever brought to perfection in me, I do not know what there will be that will not be comprised in that life. But then I fall away, weighed down by these burdens of cares, back to earthly things; I am sucked into everyday affairs and get stuck in them. I weep much, but am stuck fast. The burden of habit deserves no less. I would be with you, but have not the strength; I have the strength to be here, but would not; in both respects, I am miserable.

10.41.66 I have, therefore, pondered my sicknesses that are my sins in respect of these three lusts.[18] I have called on your right hand to save me. With my wounded heart I have seen your radiance, and could not fix my eyes on it, but said, 'Who can do this? I have been cast off from the sight of your eyes' (cf Ps. 31.22 [Ps. 30.23]). You are the Truth that presides over all things. But I in my greed did not want to lose you, but wished to possess both you and falsehood, like one who wished to lie, but not so much that he did not himself know what truth was. In this way I lost you; for you do not deign to let one possess you and falsehood together.

10.42.67 Whom can I find to reconcile me to you? Should I approach the angels? What appeal should I make? What rites perform? Many have attempted to return to you, and, not being able of themselves, have essayed these means and have fallen into a desire for arcane visions, and been accounted worthy to be deluded; or so I have heard. Full of pride in their learning, they have puffed up their chests, not beaten them; they have drawn to themselves the *powers of the air* (Eph. 2.2) attracted by their likeness of heart, as fellows and sharers in their arrogance. Being deceived by their magic powers, they have sought a mediator to purify them, and there was none. Instead there was the Devil, *transforming himself into an angel of light* (2Cor. 11.14). For proud flesh he has a great appeal, not being himself of fleshly body. Those who sought in their pride to be reconciled to you were mortals and sinners; but you, O Lord, are immortal and without sin. It was right that the *Mediator between God and men* (1Tim. 2.5) should be like to God in one respect and like to men in the other. If he were similar to men in both respects, he would

18 'these three lusts'. The so-called 'Triple Concupiscence' of 1Jn 2.16. See note on 2.2.2.

be far from God; if he were like to God in both respects, he would be far from men, and in these ways would not be a mediator. The false mediator, through whom according to your hidden judgements they deserve to be deluded in their pride, has one thing in common with men, namely sin, but wishes to appear to have the other quality in common with God; not being clothed in fleshly mortality, he wishes to flaunt himself as an immortal. But *the wages of sin are death* (Rom. 6.23); and this is what he has in common with men, that with men he might be condemned to death.

10.43.68 But the true mediator, whom you in your hidden mercy sent and made known to the humble, that by his example they might learn the same humility – that *Mediator between God and men, the man Christ Jesus* (1Tim. 2.5), appeared between mortal sinners and the Immortal and Righteous One. Mortality he shared with man, righteousness with God. The wages of righteousness are *life and peace* (Rom. 8.6); and through the righteousness that joined him to God he *made righteous the impious* (Prov. 17.15, Rom. 4.5), and *made void the death* (2Tim. 1.10) that he willingly shared with them. He it was who was revealed to the holy Patriarchs of old, that even as we are saved through faith in his past Passion, so might they also be saved through faith in his future Passion. In so far as he was man, he was Mediator; but in so far as he was the Word, he was no intermediate figure, being *equal to God* (Phil. 2.6), God with God, and at the same time one God.

10.43.69 How you have loved us, good Father, *who did not spare your only Son but gave up for us sinners* (Rom. 8.32)! How you have loved us, for whom your Son *did not think equality with you a thing to be grasped at but was obedient to death, even to death on a cross* (Phil. 2.6–8). He alone was *free among the dead* (Ps. 88.5 [Ps. 87.6]), *having power to lay down his life and power to take it up again* (Jn 10.18). For our sake he was to you both victor and victim, and victor because victim; for our sake he was to you both priest and sacrifice, and priest because sacrifice. He made us sons before you, not servants, being begotten of you yet serving us. With good reason is my hope strong in him, for you will *heal all my diseases* (Ps. 103.3 [Ps. 102.3], Matt. 4.23) through him who *sits at your right hand and intercedes for us* (Rom. 8.34); otherwise, I would despair. Many and great are those diseases, many and great; but your healing is greater. We might think your Word far from union with men and despair, did not *the Word become flesh and dwell among us* (Jn 1.14).

10.43.70   Terrified by my sins and by the greatness of my misery I tossed these things over in my heart and contemplated fleeing to the wilderness, but you forbade me and strengthened me, saying: *For this did Christ die for all, that those who live should live not for themselves, but for him who died for them* (2Cor. 5.15). Behold, O Lord, *I cast on you my care* (Ps. 55.22 [Ps. 54.23]), *that I may live*; I shall meditate on the wonders of your Law (Ps. 119.18–19 [Ps. 118.17–18]). *You know my ignorance and my weakness* (Ps. 69.5 [Ps. 68.6]); teach me, and heal me. Your only son, *in whom the treasure of wisdom and knowledge are hidden* (Col. 2.3), *has redeemed me by his blood* (Rev. 5.9). *Let not the proud heap calumny upon me* (Ps. 119.21 [Ps. 118.22]) because I *think on the price paid for me* (Ps. 62.5 [Ps. 61.5]), and eat and drink and give alms, and in my poverty *long to be satisfied* (Lk 16.21) with him along with those who *eat and are satisfied*. And *those who seek the Lord praise him* (Ps. 22.21 [Ps. 21.27]).

BOOK ELEVEN

11.1.1 Yours is eternity, O Lord. Can you be ignorant of what I tell you, or not know at the time what happens in time? Why, then, do I tell you all these stories of mine? Surely not that you should learn them from me. Rather I raise up towards you my mind and the minds of those who read all this, so that together we may say: *Great is the Lord and worthy of high praise* (Ps. 48.1 [Ps. 47.2]). I have said before what I say now: it is out of love for your love that I do this. We pray, and yet the Truth says, *Your Father knows what you need before you ask* (Matt. 6.8). It is, therefore, our own disposition that we open up to you when we confess to you our miseries and *your mercies upon us* (Ps. 33.21 [Ps. 32.22]), so that you will fulfil the work of deliverance you have begun in us; that we may cease to be miserable and become blessed in you; for you have called us to be *poor in spirit, meek and mourning, hungry and thirsty for righteousness, merciful and pure in heart, peacemakers* (Matt. 5.3–9). Behold, I have told you many things, according to my will and ability; but it was you who first willed that I should *confess to you, O Lord my God, that you are good, and your mercy is everlasting* (Ps. 118.1 [Ps. 117.1]).

11.2.2 When will I have strength to relate in full with the tongue of my pen (cf Ps. 45.2 [Ps. 44.2]) all the ways in which you have encouraged me, terrified me, comforted me and guided me, and brought me to preach your word and administer your Sacrament to your people? Even if I am strong enough to tell all these things, each drop of time is precious to me. I have long burnt to *meditate on your Law* (Ps. 1.2 [Ps. 1.2]) and confess to you my knowledge and my ignorance of it, the beginnings of your enlightenment and the remnants of my darkness, until my weakness is swallowed up in strength. I do not wish the hours to trickle away on anything else; those hours I find free from the need to rest my body or exercise my mind, or to pay the service we owe to men, or which we do not owe and yet pay.

11.2.3 *O Lord my God, give ear to my prayer* (Ps. 61.1 [Ps. 60.2]), and let your mercy *hearken to my desire* (Ps. 10.19 [Ps. 10A.17]). Not for my sake alone is my desire full of hesitation; it wants to be of use to the brothers I love. You see in my heart that this is so. I shall dedicate to you the service of my thought and my tongue; give me something I can offer you. *I am poor and needy* (Ps. 86.1 [Ps. 85.1]), *and you bestow your richness on all who call upon you* (Rom. 10.12), untroubled by care yet caring for us. *Circumcise my lips* (Ex. 6.20) within and without from all folly and all falsehood. Let my pure delights be your Scriptures; let me neither be deceived nor deceive others though them. *O Lord, give ear and have mercy* (Jer. 18.19, Ps. 27.8 [Ps. 26.7]), O Lord my God, light of the blind and strength of the weak; light also of the sighted and strength of the strong, give ear to my soul and hear me as I cry to you from the deep (cf Ps. 130.1 [Ps. 129.1–2]). For if your ears are not there to hear us even in the deep, where will we go (cf Ps. 139.6 [Ps. 138.7])? To whom will we cry? *Yours is the day, and the night is yours* (Ps. 74.17 [Ps. 73.16]); at your command the moments fly away. Grant me a space among them where I can meditate on the secrets of your Law, and do not close it up when I knock for admission (cf Matt. 7.7–8, Lk 11.9–10). Not for nothing was it your will that all those pages of dark mysteries should be written, nor that those *woods* should not have *deer that flee and take refuge* in them, walk and find pasture, rest and ruminate in them (cf Ps. 29.8 [Ps. 28.7]). O Lord, make me complete and reveal them to me. Behold, your voice is my joy, your voice that sounds above the floodtides of pleasure. Grant me what I love; for I do love it, and this love also you have given me. Desert not your gifts, and do not despise the thirsty grass that is yours. I shall confess to you whatever I find in your Scriptures; *I shall hear the sound of praise* (Ps. 26.7 [Ps. 25.7]); I shall drink of you, and *consider the wonders of your Law* (Ps. 119.18 [Ps. 118.18]) right from the beginning, when you *made heaven and earth* (Gen. 1.1), through to the saints' everlasting reign with you in your holy City (cf Rev. 5.10).

11.2.4 Lord, have mercy upon me and *hearken to my desire* (Ps. 10.19 [Ps. 10A.17]). What I am contemplating is not a thing of earth, not gold or silver, not of stone or splendid raiment; not ranks or dignities, not carnal pleasures, nor things needful to the body, nor to this our life of pilgrimage – all those things which stand in our way as we *seek your Kingdom and your righteousness* (Matt. 6.13). See, my God, from whence my desire springs. The unrighteous have indeed told me of delights, but not *according to your Law* (Ps. 119.85 [Ps. 118.85]). Behold from whence my desire springs. *Behold*, Father, *and see* (Lamentations 1.9); see and approve, and *let it be pleasing in your mercy's sight* (Dan. 3.40) that I should find grace before you, and that the inner secrets of your Scriptures be opened to me when I knock (Matt. 7.7–8, Lk 11.9–10). I beseech you through our Lord Jesus Christ, your Son, the *man of your right hand, the Son of Man, whom you have confirmed* (Ps. 80.18 [Ps. 79.18]) as the Mediator between you and us; through whom you have *sought us when we did not seek you* (Rom. 10.10), but sought that we should seek you; your Word, through whom you have *made all things* (Jn 1.3), and among them me; your only Son, through whom you have called your faithful people to be your adopted children, and among them me. I beseech you, through him that *sits at your right hand and intercedes for us* (Rom. 8.34), in whom are the *treasures of wisdom and knowledge hidden* (Col. 2.3). It is these treasures that I seek in your Scriptures. Moses wrote of this Word (Jn 5.46). This is what the Son himself says; this is what the Truth says.[1]

11.3.5 May I hear and understand how *in the beginning you made heaven and earth* (Gen. 1.1). This Moses wrote. He wrote and departed; he passed on from here to you and is not now before me. If he were, I would lay hold of him and ask him and beseech him through you to explain these things to me; I would incline the ears of my body to hear the sounds that burst from his lips. If he spoke Hebrew, his voice would batter against my senses in vain, nor would my mind grasp any of what he said; but if he

---

1 'This is what ... the Truth says'. A programmatic statement for the exposition from Genesis that takes up the remainder of the *Confessions*. Augustine is still counter-attacking the Manichee charge that the Old Testament God was a lesser deity, by asserting that Jesus, the Truth (a term loved by the Manichees), himself acknowledged the authority of Moses.

spoke Latin, I would know what he said. But how would I know whether he spoke the truth? And if I did know this, would it be from Moses that I knew it? It is within me, within the chamber of my meditation that the Truth speaks; not in Hebrew, nor in Greek or Latin or any outlandish speech, without lips, without vocal organs, without sound of syllables he would say, 'Moses speaks true.' Immediately I would say to Moses, the man of God, with full confidence in him, 'You speak true.' Being, therefore, unable to question him, it is you, O Truth, that I ask; you, my God, who inspired Moses to speak, I ask to have mercy on my sins; you who granted him, your servant, to speak, grant me also to understand.

11.4.6 Behold, heaven and earth exist. They cry out that they are created; for they are subject to change and variation. But in anything that exists and was not created, there is nothing that was not previously (for that is change and variation). Heaven and earth cry out that they did not make themselves: 'We exist, because we were made; before we existed, we did not exist, and could not be made by ourselves.' The sound of their voice is itself the evidence. It was you, therefore, O Lord, that made them; you, the beautiful (for they are beautiful); you, the good (for they are good); you, who Are (cf Ex. 3.14); for they are. They are not beautiful nor good nor existent in the way that you are, their Stablisher, compared to whom they are neither beautiful nor good nor existent. We know all this, and thanks be to you; and our knowledge compared to your knowledge is ignorance.

11.5.7 But how did you make heaven and earth, and what was the instrument of this mighty handiwork of yours? You were not like a human craftsman, shaping one physical object out of another according to the judgement of his soul, which has the ability to impose as it will the form that it perceives with the inner eye (and whence would it have this ability, were it not that you had made it?). Moreover, such a craftsman imposes this form on a body that already exists and has the means of existence, such as earth or stone or wood or gold or any thing of this sort. And whence would all these things have existence, had

you not established them? It is you who made the workman's
body; you who made the mind that commands the limbs; you
who made the material from which he makes what he makes;
you who made the intelligence by which he understands his
trade and sees within what he should make without; you who
made the physical sense that acts as intermediary, communi-
cating from mind to material that which he is making, and
bringing in return news of what has been made, so that the
mind may consult inwardly the Truth that reigns over it, to find
out if the thing is well done. All these things praise you, the
creator of all. But as for you – how do you make them? How,
O God, did you make heaven and earth? Assuredly you did not
make heaven and earth in heaven and earth, nor in the air nor
in the waters, for these belong to heaven and earth; nor in the
universe did you make the universe, for before it came to be,
there was nowhere that it could come to be. Nor did you hold
in your hand anything from which to make heaven and earth;
for whence could you have had this material, not made by
yourself, from which to make other things? What exists, but
that you exist? Thus it was, therefore: *you spoke and they were
made*, and by your Word you made them (Ps. 33.9 [Ps. 32.9], Jn
1.1, 1.3).

11.6.8 But how did you speak? Surely not in the way that the
voice came from the cloud saying, *'This is my well-beloved Son'*
(Matt. 3.17, 17.5, Lk 9.35)? That speech was uttered and passed
away; it began, and ended. The syllables rang out and passed
on, the second after the first, the third after the second and so
on in sequence, until the last succeeded the rest, and silence the
last. Hence it is clear and apparent that this speech was uttered
by some movement of your creation, obedient to your eternal
will, yet temporal. These words, made in time, were reported by
the outward ear to the mind that foresaw them, whose inward
ear is inclined to hear your eternal Word. That mind then compared these words, audible and temporal, with your Word that
remains eternally in silence, and says: 'It is not the same; it is
not the same at all. These words are far below me and are not;
for they hasten on and pass away. *But the Word of my God abides*

above me for ever' (Is. 40.8). If, then, you spoke with words that
ring out and pass away when you commanded heaven and earth
to come into existence, and thus made heaven and earth, then
there was already a physical creation before heaven and earth,
by temporal movements of which that utterance ran its temporal
course. But there was nothing physical before heaven and earth;
or if there was, then surely without transitory speech you made
the means by which you made that transitory speech thereby
commanding that heaven and earth should be. For whatever the
means were by which that speech came to be, it would not exist
at all were it not made by you. What word, then, did you speak
when you commanded that there should be a physical entity by
which those words should be?

11.7.9 You call us, then, to understand the Word, the God that
with you is God (Jn 1.1), who is spoken eternally and by whom
all things are spoken eternally. Nor did you finish saying one
thing and say another, so that all things might be spoken; you
spoke them at once and eternally. Otherwise there would be
time and change, and neither true eternity nor true immortality.
This I know, O Lord, and I give thanks. This *I know, and confess
to you* (Matt. 11.25–7, Lk 10.21–2); all who are not ungrateful for
a constant Truth know this, and bless you with me. We know,
O Lord, that in so far as what used to exist does not exist, it
dies, and in so far as what used not to exist does exist, it comes
into being. But no part of your Word either yields place or takes
the place of anything, for it exists truly immortal and eternal.
By your Word, therefore, who is coeternal with you, you say
once and eternally all that you say; and whatever you say should
come into being, comes into being. By speaking alone you make
it; yet not all that you make by speaking comes into being at
once and eternally.

11.8.10 Why is this so, O Lord? I see why after a fashion, but
how to express it I do not know, unless by saying that everything
that begins or ceases to be, begins or ceases to be at just that
moment when it is deemed in the eternal Reason, in which
nothing begins or ceases, that it ought to have begun or ceased.
That Reason is your Word, who is also *the Beginning, for he also*

speaks to us (Jn 8.25). Thus he says in the Gospel through the flesh; he uttered these outward sounds for the ears of men, to the end that they might believe and *seek and find* (Matt. 7.7) him inwardly in the eternal Truth, where the good and only Teacher teaches all his disciples. It is here that I hear your voice, O Lord, as you tell me that he who speaks to us is he who teaches us, and that he who does not teach us, even though he speaks, does not speak to us. And who is our teacher, if not the abiding Truth? Even when we receive intimations through your creation, which is subject to change, it is to the abiding Truth that we are led. There we learn in truth, when we abide and listen to him and *rejoice greatly at the voice of the Bridegroom* (Jn 3.29), and return ourselves to our source. He is the Beginning, for if he did not remain firm while we went astray, there would be no place to which we could return. But when we return from our wandering, it is by coming to know the Truth that we return. In order that we might come to know the Truth, he teaches us, for *he is the Beginning, and he speaks to us* (Jn 8.25).

11.9.11 In this Beginning, O God, you made heaven and earth; in your Word, in your Son, *in your strength, in your wisdom* (1Cor. 1.24), in your Truth, wondrously speaking, wondrously making. Who can understand it? Who can proclaim it? What is it that flashes now and again upon me and pierces my heart without wounding me? I shudder and burn. Inasmuch as I am unlike it, I shudder; inasmuch as I am like it, I burn. It is Wisdom, Wisdom itself, that flashes upon me, rending the cloud that surrounds me. But when its light is cut off from me by the darkness and mass of my punishments, the cloud covers me again. *My strength fails me because of my poverty* (Ps. 31.11 [Ps. 30.11]), and I cannot endure what is good for me, until you, O Lord, who have *forgiven me all my iniquities,* also *heal all my diseases;* for you also will *redeem my life from corruption, and crown me with loving-kindness and mercy,* and *satisfy my heart's desire with good things, renewing my youth like an eagle's* (Ps. 103.3–5 [Ps. 102.3–5]). For *by hope are we saved, and with patience we look for your promises* (Rom. 8.24–5). Let him who can, hear you speak within; I shall confidently proclaim with the

Psalmist, *How manifold are your works, O Lord; in wisdom you have made all things* (Ps. 104.24 [Ps. 103.24]). That Wisdom is the beginning, and in that Beginning you made heaven and earth.

11.10.12 But full of the old ways are those who say to us, 'What was God doing before he made heaven and earth? If he was on leave and not engaged in any work, why did he not continue to postpone his work for ever, as he had always done before? If some impulse arose in God, some new will to establish a creation that he had not established previously, how could his be a true eternity, in which a will arose which had not existed before? For the will of God is not a creation but is before creation, seeing as nothing is created without the creator's prior willing of it. The will of God pertains to his very substance; but if something arose in the substance of God that did not exist previously, that substance could not truly be called eternal. But if God's will that creation should exist were eternal, why was creation also not eternal?'

11.11.13 Those who say such things do not yet understand you, Wisdom of God,[2] light of the mind; they do not yet understand how the things that come about in you and through you do come about. They endeavour to be wise in eternal matters, but their heart still flutters around, concerned with the motions of things past and future; it is still vain. Who will hold it fast and fix it down, that it may abide for a while and grasp for a while the radiance of the ever-abiding Eternity, to compare it with the never-abiding temporalities, and to see that it is beyond comparison? – that no time, however long, may become so except from a multitude of tiny points in time which cannot all be drawn out together at once. But in eternity nothing passes away; the whole is present, whereas no time is fully present. Let them see also that all past time is pushed away from the future, and all future time follows on from the past; and that all time

2 'Wisdom of God'. A title of Christ (cf Eph. 3.10). In Jewish scriptural interpretation, adopted by Christians, Wisdom is seen as the agent or helper of God in the work of creation; cf Prov. 8.22–31.

past and future is created by that which is always present and proceeds from it. Who will hold fast the heart of man, that it may abide and see how the abiding Eternity, neither past nor future, dictates the past and the future? *Can my hand do this* (Gen. 31.29), or the hand of my tongue accomplish by spoken words so great a thing?

11.12.14 This is my reply to those who say, 'What was God doing before he made heaven and earth?' I will not give the reply that someone is said to have given, wittily sidestepping the force of the question: 'He was preparing hell for people who ask questions too deep for them.' Seeing the answer is one thing, laughing at the questioner is another. This is not my reply. I would more readily reply, 'What I don't know, I don't know,' than reply in such a way as to make fun of one who has asked deep questions and give credit to one who has given an untrue response. But you, our God, I call the creator of all creation; and if by the words 'heaven and earth' we are to understand 'all creation', I venture to say this: 'Before God made heaven and earth, he was not doing anything. For if he was doing anything, what was it if not making creation?'[3] And if only I knew all that I wish profitably to know, as well as I know that no created thing was made before any created thing was made.

11.13.15 But should anyone's inconstant mind stray among images of previous periods of time and wonder that you, God all-powerful, all-creating, all-upholding, fashioner of heaven and earth, put off this great work for countless aeons before doing it – he should wake up and pay attention, for he is wondering at things that are untrue. How could those countless

---

3 '"... he was not doing ... making creation"'. The translation here necessarily obscures the original in two ways: first, the same Latin verb means 'to do' and 'to make'; second, Latin does not always distinguish between 'making creation' and 'making some created thing', or between 'all creation' and 'every created thing'. Augustine's argument can be paraphrased thus: before making heaven and earth, God was not doing/making anything. Had he been doing/making anything, that thing would have been a creation. But 'heaven and earth' in the Biblical phrase may be taken to mean 'creation' generally; hence God cannot have been doing anything before he 'made heaven and earth'.

aeons have passed by without your having made them, source and Stablisher of all aeons? What periods of time could there have been that were not established by you? How could they have passed by, if they had never existed? All times are your workmanship; if there was any time before you made heaven and earth, why is it said that you put off your work? It was you who made that very time; nor could any periods of time pass by before you made them. But if no time existed before heaven and earth, why do they ask what you were doing then? There was no 'then' when there was no time.

11.14.16 Nor is it in time that you precede time; otherwise, you would not precede all times. All times past you precede in the loftiness of your ever-present eternity, and all future times you outlast; for they are future, and, having come, will be past, whereas you are the same, and *your years are unfailing* (Ps. 102.27 [Ps. 101.28]). Your years neither come nor go; our years come and go, as all years do. Your years abide together at once, because they abide. They do not pass away when new ones arrive and cut them off, for they do not pass away; whereas our years will all be when they will all not exist.[4] *Your years are but one day* (Ps. 90.4 [Ps. 89.4], 2Pet. 3.8), and your day is not 'every day' but 'today', since your today does not give way to your tomorrow, nor take over from your yesterday. Your today is eternity; therefore him to whom you said, *Today I have begotten you* (Ps. 2.7, Acts 13.33, Heb. 1.5, 5.5), you begat as your coeternal. You are the one who have made all times, and who are before all times, nor at any time was there not time.

11.14.17 At no time, then, had you not made something, seeing as you had made time itself. Nor are any times coeternal with you, seeing as you are abiding; were they abiding, they would not be times. For what is time? Who can explain simply and briefly? Who understands it so well as to be able offer a word on the subject, or understands it even in thought? What in the

---

4 'whereas our years ... will all not exist'. Augustine appears to be arguing that our years will not 'be' [i.e. will not have reached their full sum] until the moment when they cease to exist.

course of conversation do we mention with more easy familiarity than time? Moreover, when we mention it, we understand perfectly what we say; we understand also when we hear someone else mention it. What, then, is time? As long as no one asks me, I know; but if someone asks me and I try to explain, I do not know. But this I do say with confidence; I know that if nothing passed away, there would be no past time; if nothing came round, there would be no future time; and if nothing existed, there would be no present. How, then, do these two times exist, past and future, when the past no longer exists and the future does not yet exist? And the present – if that were always present and not passing in the past, it would no longer be time but eternity. If, then, in order to be a time, the present comes about by passing into the past, how can we say even that the present exists, seeing as its ground of existence is that it will not exist; the result being that we cannot truly say that time exists except because it tends towards non-existence?

11.15.18 We say 'a long time' and 'a short time', but only say this of past or future time. We call a past time long if it was, for example, one hundred years ago, and a future time long if it is one hundred years from now. We call a past time short if it was, say, ten days ago, and a future time short if it is ten days from now. But how can that which does not exist be long or short? What is past no longer exists, what is future does not yet exist. We should not say, 'It is long ago' or 'It is far in the future'; rather we should say, 'It was long ago' or 'It will be far in the future'. My Lord, my Light, will not your Truth laugh at men in this matter also? A time that was long – was it long when it was already past, or while it was still present? It had the means to be long at that time when there was something to be long. But when it was past, it no longer existed; and that which had no existence whatever had no means to be long. We should not, then, say, 'It was a long time past'; for we shall not find anything to have been long, seeing as since it became past, it does not exist. Rather we should say, 'It was a long time present', since it was long while it was present. It had not yet passed on into non-existence; hence it had the means to be long. But when it passed on, it simultaneously ceased to be and hence to be long.

11.15.19 Let us see, then, soul of man, whether the present time has the means to be long. It is given to you to perceive and to measure lapses of time. What answer will you give me? Are a hundred present years a long time? Let us see first whether a hundred years can be present. In the case of the first year, then that year is present, but ninety-nine are in the future, and therefore do not yet exist. In the case of the second year, one year is already past, another is present, the rest are in the future. So also we may say of any intermediate year out of that hundred; before it will be the years in the past, after it the years in the future. The hundred years, therefore, will not have the means to be all present.

Let us see, then, whether any given year is itself present. In the case of its first month, the other months are in the future; in the case of the second month, the first has passed and the rest do not yet exist. Therefore not even the year in question is wholly present; and if the whole year is not present, it is not the year that is present. A year is twelve months, of which any one given month is present, the rest either past or future. Although even the month in question is not present, but one day. If it is the first day, the rest are in the future; if it is the last, the rest are past; if it is any of those that intervene, it is in between past and future days.

11.15.20 So it is that the present, the one time that we found worthy of the name 'long', is contracted to the space of scarcely one day. But let us consider even that space of time. Even one day is not wholly present. It is made of up hours of day and night, twenty-four in all. To the first of these hours, the rest are in the future; to the last, the rest are in the past; to any of the intervening hours, some are in the past and some are in the future. Even that one hour is made up of little fleeting moments; what part of it has flown away is past, whatever remains to it is future. If we comprehend any atom of time that can no longer be divided into the parts of moments, however short, that atom is the only thing that can be called 'the present'. But even this flies so swiftly from the future to the past that it cannot be assigned a fraction of a moment's extension. For if it has extension, it is divided into past and future, whereas the present has no space. Where, then, is there a time that we can call long? Is it the future? We do not say, 'It is long in the future', as there is not yet anything to be long; rather we say, 'It will be long in the future'. When, then, will it be? If even then it will still be in the future, it will not be long, for there will not yet be anything to be long. If, however, it will be long at just that time when out of that non-existent future it comes into being and becomes the present, thereby providing for the possibility of something that could be long – then the present cries out with all the arguments set out above that it is impossible for it to be long

11.16.21 And yet, O Lord, we do perceive intervals of time; we compare them to each other and say that some are longer and others shorter. We can also measure how much longer or shorter one is than another, and say that it is twice as long or three times as long as another, or that one is the same length as the other. But when we perceive and measure periods of time, that time is passing by; and who can measure things past, which no longer exist, or future, which do not yet exist? Or does someone venture to say that it is possible to measure the non-existent? It is as time passes by, then, that it can be perceived and measured; once past, it does not exist, and hence cannot be measured.

11.17.22 I am asking questions, Father, not making assertions; be my ruler and guide me. Who is there that would venture to tell me that there are not three tenses, past, present and future, just as we learnt as boys and as we teach boys, but that there is only the present, as the other two do not exist? Or is it that the past and the future also exist, but when the present comes to be out of the future, it proceeds from something hidden, and into something hidden it returns, when from the present it becomes the past? For when have those who have made prophecies seen these future events, if they do not yet exist? What does not exist, cannot be seen. Nor could those who relate past events relate them truly, if they did not perceive them in their mind; but if they did not exist, they could not be perceived at all. The future and the past, then, exist.

11.18.23 Let me question further, *O Lord, my hope* (Ps. 71.4 [Ps. 70.5]). Let not my concentration be disturbed. For if future and past exist, I wish to know where they exist. If I cannot yet know this, I know at least that wherever they are, they are not future or past there, but present. If they are future there also, they do not yet exist there, and likewise if they are past there, they no longer exist there. Wherever and whatever they are, if they exist, they must be present; although when a true account of the past is given, it is not the past events themselves that are retrieved from the memory, but words conceived of the images of those events, which in passing by they have stamped on the mind through the senses. My boyhood no longer exists; it is in the past, which no longer exists. When I recall it and speak of it, it is the image of it that I contemplate in present time, for that image exists still in my memory. Whether this is why future events can be predicted, whether we have presentiment of the already-existent images of things that are themselves still non-existent, I confess, my God, I do not know. But this I do know: we generally premeditate our future actions, and that premeditation is present, whereas the action which we premeditate does not yet exist, being in the future. When we go about this action and set about doing what we premeditated, it is then the action exists; then it is assuredly not future but present.

11.18.24 By whatever means this secret capacity for presentiment of future events exists, only the existent can be seen. What already exists is not future but present. When we say that we see the future, it is not the non-existent, that is, the future, that we see, but their causes or perhaps tokens of them that we see. These causes or tokens already exist; they are, therefore, not future but already present to those who see them, and from them they conceive the future in their minds and predict it. Moreover, these conceptions already exist and are present to those who make the predictions as they contemplate them within. Let me take one example from all the many. I contemplate the first glow of dawn; I foretell that the sun is going to rise. What I contemplate is present, what I foretell is future; it is not the sun that is in the future, for that already exists, but its rising, which does not yet exist. But if I did not form an image of its rising in my mind, just as I now do as I talk of it, I could not predict it. But neither the glow of dawn that I see in the sky is the sunrise, although one precedes the other, nor is my mental image of it. These two things are present to enable me to predict the sunrise in the future. Things future, then, do not yet exist; and if they do not yet exist, they do not exist; and if they do not exist, they cannot be seen. But they can be predicted from things present, which already exist and can be seen.

11.19.25 Tell me then, Ruler of your creation, what are the means by which you teach souls things in the future? You taught your prophets. By what means do you teach the future, you to whom there is nothing future? Or do you rather teach things present from the future? For what does not exist cannot be taught either. Your means are far beyond my sight; *they are too excellent for me, and of myself I cannot attain them* (Ps. 139.5 [Ps. 138.6]). But with your help I can, for it is you, sweet Light of my secret eyes, that have given me this power.

11.20.26 It is now transparently clear that things future and things past do not exist, and that it is not correct to say that there are three tenses, past, present and future, though it may be true to say that there are three tenses, the present-regarding-the-past, the present-regarding-the-present and the present-regarding-the-future. These three times do exist in some way in the soul, though I do not see them elsewhere: present memory regarding the past, present contemplation regarding the present, and present expectation regarding the future. If it is permissible to say this, then I see and acknowledge that there are three times, past, present and future. Let it even be said, with the customary catachresis, 'There are three sorts of time, past, present and future.' Let it be *said*. I do not mind; I offer no resistance or reproach; but let it be understood that this is a manner of speaking, and that neither the future nor the past now exists. For there are few things that we call by their proper names, and more that we do not, but still recognize what we mean.

11.21.27 I said a little earlier that we measure time as it passes by, and hence we can say that one space of time is twice as long as another, or that two spaces of time are the same length, and make all other such statements on the division of time as we can by a process of measurement. For this reason, as I was saying, it is as time passes by that we measure it. If someone should ask me how I know, I would reply, 'I know that we measure; and that we cannot measure what does not exist; and that things past and future do not exist.' But how do we measure the present, seeing as it has no duration? We measure it as it passes by, and when it has passed by it is not measurable, for there is nothing to be measured. But when it passes, where does it come from and where does it go to, and by what route? From where, if not from the future? By what route, if not by the present? Where to, if not into the past? It passes, then, from what does not yet exist, through what has no extension, into that which no longer exists. But what are we measuring if not some temporal extension? What do we mean when we say that periods of time are twice as long or three times as long or equal and so forth, if we are not referring to temporal extensions? In what space of time, then, do we measure the present? In the future, from which it passes on its way? But what does not yet exist we cannot measure. Is it in the present, by which it passes? But what is without extension we cannot measure. Is it in the past, to which it has passed? But what no longer exists we can- not measure.

11.22.28 My mind is on fire to solve this most complex enigma. Do not close these matters off from me, O Lord my God, good Father; through Christ I pray, do not close them off from my longing, both the familiar and the hidden. Do not keep me from searching their inner depths; let them grow clear with the radiance of your mercy, O Lord. Whom shall I question about these things? And to whom shall I more profitably confess my ignorance than to you, who are not bored by my burning zeal for your Scriptures? Give me what I love; for I do love, and this love is your gift. Give me what I love, Father; for you know truly how to give good gifts to your children (cf Matt. 7.11). Give me this; I have undertaken to learn these things, and *great is the task before me* (Ps. 73.15 [Ps. 72.16]) until you disclose them. Through Christ I pray; for the sake of his name, the name of the Holy One, let none of your holy saints lift up his voice against me. *I too have believed, and therefore I speak* (Ps. 116.10 [Ps. 115.10], 2Cor. 4.15). This is my hope, and for this I live; that I may *contemplate the delight of the Lord* (Ps. 27.4 [Ps. 26.4]). The old days of my life you have put away and they pass by; how, I do not know. We speak of one time and another, one period and another: 'When he said this', 'When he did that', 'How long it is since I saw him', 'This syllable has twice the duration of that short syllable'.[5] We say all this and are understood; we hear it and we understand. These things are wholly straightforward and familiar; yet they hide themselves away from us again, and we discover them anew.

11.23.29 I once heard a learned man say that motions of the sun and the moon and the stars are time, but I did not agree. For why are the motions of *all* physical objects not time instead? Or suppose that the heavenly lights were to cease in their courses, but a potter's wheel were to spin; would there not be time by which we could measure its revolutions and say that it revolved at regular intervals, or that some revolutions were slower and some quicker, some took more time and some less? Or if we did say this, would we not be speaking in time? Or how would some of the syllables of our words be long and some short, were it not because some were pronounced over a longer period of time and some over a shorter? O God, grant men in little things to see the signs that mark things large and small alike. The stars and the heavenly bodies exist over the signs of the zodiac; in periods of time, in days and in years. They exist; but neither would I say that a revolution of my notional little wheel was a day, nor would my learned friend say that for that reason it was not time.

5 '... short syllable'. Classical Latin poetry, such as Augustine learnt at school and later taught himself, relied for its metre on an opposition between long and short syllables. This distinction, though still used in poetry of his day, had effectively broken down in the spoken language, and the length or 'quantity' of individual syllables had to be learnt by heart.

11.23.30 I long to know the force and the nature of time, by which we measure the motions of physical bodies and say that one motion lasts, as it might be, twice as long as another. This is my question; seeing as by 'a day' we mean not only the period of time when the sun is above the earth (according to which definition day is one thing and night is another), but also the sun's whole circuit from east back to east (according to which definition we say 'So many days have passed by', meaning days including their nights, the space of the night not being reckoned a thing apart) – seeing, then, as a day is counted as completed by the sun's moving in a circuit from east back to east, my question is this: is it the motion that is the day, or the period of time over which it is completed, or both? If it is the former, then it would be a day if the sun completed its course in a space of time equal to one hour. If it is the latter, it would not be a day even if the time elapsed from one sunrise to another were equal to no more than one hour; the sun would have to perform twenty-four revolutions to complete a single day. If it is both, we would not say it was a day if the sun were to complete its circuit in the space of one hour, nor if the sun were to stand still and a space of time were to pass by equivalent to that in which the sun regularly completes its course from morning to morning. I am not, therefore, asking 'What is a day?' but 'What is time?'. It is by measuring the sun's circuit with time that we would say it had been completed in half the usual space, if it had been completed in a space of time equivalent to twelve hours; we would compare the two times and say that one was twice as long as the other, even though on some occasions the sun completed its circuit from east to east in one period, and on other occasions in twice that period. Let no one tell me, then, that the motions of the heavenly bodies are time. For once the sun stood still in answer to a man's prayer, so that a battle could be completed and won (cf Joshua 10.12–13); the sun stood still, but time went on. It was in a space of time sufficient for the purpose that the battle was fought and finished. I see, then, that time is a species of distension.[6] But do I see it, or do I think I see it? You will make it plain, O Light and Truth.

6 *(See footnote on opposite page.)*

11.24.31 Do you bid me agree with anyone who says that time is the motion of a physical body? You do not. That no body moves except in time I allow; it is you who tell me this. That the motion of a body is time I do not grant; you do not tell me this. When a body moves, I measure the duration of its motion in time, from the point when it begins to move until the point when it stops. If I have not seen when it began, and if it carries on moving, so that I cannot see when it stops, I cannot measure it, except perhaps between the point when I begin to watch and the point at which I stop. If I watch it for long, I can at least report that it was moving for a long time, but not how long; for when we say how long something is, we do so by comparison, as in. 'Such-and-such was as long as so and-so,' or, 'Such-and-such was twice as long as so-and-so,' and so forth. If, however, we have been able to observe the distance between the points from which and to which the body in question has moved (or the parts of it, if the body is turning as on a lathe), we can say how much time it took the body (or part of it) to complete its motion from one place to another. Seeing, then, as the motion of a physical body is not the same as the means by which we measure the duration of this motion, who fails to perceive which of the two should be called 'time' in preference to the other? And if a body should alternate between periods of motion and periods of being stationary, it is in time that we measure not only the periods of motion but also the stationary periods: 'It stood still for as long as it had moved,' we say, or, 'It stood still two or three times as long as it moved.' The same is true of whatever our capacity for measurement grasps or guesses at; that is why we habitually talk of 'more' and 'less'. Time, then, is not physical motion.

6 '... a species of distension'. The translation here preserves Augustine's word (*distentio*) rather than glossing it as 'extension'. This is because *distentio* is a far more unusual and arresting word in Latin than *extensio*, and its interpretation has given rise to some debate. It has been suggested that a suitable translation is 'distraction causing anxiety'. Some reference to the psychology of the perception of time may be intended, though this translation seems over-precise. Perhaps Augustine uses *distentio* as a deliberately obscure word, meaning that time is more than a point or series of points, but without committing himself further.

11.25.32 *I confess to you, O Lord* (Ps. 9.2 [Ps. 9.2], Matt. 11.25, Lk 10.21), that I still do not know what time is; and I confess moreover that I know that it is in time that I say this; that I have been talking about time for a long time, and that that time is only long because of the lapse of time. How, then, do I know this, seeing as I do not know what time is? Or is it perhaps that I do not know how I say what I know? Pity my case, for I do not know even what I do not know! *Behold, my God, I am before you. I do not lie* (Gal. 1.20); my heart is even as I speak. It is you who will *light my lantern, O Lord, my God; you will lighten my darkness* (Ps. 18.28 [Ps. 17.29]).

11.26.33 Surely my soul confesses with true confession to you that I measure time? So it is, my God; I measure, and do not know what I measure. I measure in time the motion of a physical body. Surely I measure time itself in similar manner? Or could I measure physical motion, how long it lasts and how long it takes to get from one point to another, were I not measuring time in which it moves? How, then, do I measure time? Do I measure a longer time in terms of shorter units, as we measure the length of a cross-beam in cubits? It is thus that we suppose we measure the length of a long syllable in terms of the length of a short syllable, and say that it is twice as long.[7] It is thus that we measure the length of poems in terms of the number of lines, and the length of lines in terms of the number of feet, and the length of feet in terms of the number of syllables, and the length of long syllables in terms of the length of short syllables; it is thus that we measure poems, not in pages, for that is a measure of place, not of time. As we speak, our voices pass on, and we say, 'It is a long poem, being composed of so many lines; the lines are long, consisting as they do of so many feet; the feet are long, extending over so many syllables; this is a long syllable, being twice as long as a short.' But even so we have not wrapped it all up according to some fixed measure of time; for it is possible that a shorter line might be pronounced over a longer time, if the pronunciation were drawled out, than a longer verse pronounced in a clipped manner. The same is true of the poem, its feet, and

7 '. . . twice as long'. See note on 11.22.28 above.

its syllables. For this reason it seems to me that time is nothing other than distension; but of what? I do not know; but it would be wondrous were it not of the mind itself. For tell me, I beseech you, my God: what do I measure when I say either imprecisely, 'This time is longer than that time', or even when I say precisely, 'This time is twice as long as that time'? It is time that I am measuring, I know. But it is not future time, which does not yet exist, nor the present, which has no extension, nor the past, which no longer exists. What, then, am I measuring? Is it time as it passes but before it is past? This is what I said before.

11.27.34 Go further, my mind; concentrate mightily on this. *God is our helper* (Ps. 62.8 [Ps. 61.9]); *it is he that made us, and not we ourselves* (Ps. 100.2 [Ps. 99.3]). Concentrate on where the truth is dawning. Consider something that belongs to a physical body, such as the sound of a voice. It begins to sound, sounds, goes on sounding, and then – stops. Then there is silence, and that sound is past; there is no more sound. Before it sounded, it was in the future, and could not be measured, since it did not yet exist. Now also it cannot be measured, since it no longer exists. The time at which it could be measured was that at which it was sounding, seeing as then there was a sound capable of being measured. But even then, it was not standing still; it was moving and passing away. Or does that not make it more measurable? As it passed away, it was being extended over some temporal space by which it could be measured, whereas the present has no spatial extension. If it was then that it could be measured, let us consider another physical sound. It begins to sound, goes on sounding on a constant and unvaried note. While it sounds, let us measure it, for when it stops sounding it will be past and there will be nothing to measure. Let us measure it, then, and say how long it is. But it goes on sounding, and can only be measured from its beginning, the point at which it begins to sound, to the end, at which it ceases to sound. It is the intervening space, then, that we measure; the interval between some beginning and some ending. Therefore it is impossible to measure an utterance that is not yet completed, and say how long or short it is, or whether it is equal to any other voice, the same

length or twice the length, and so forth. But when it is completed, it will not exist. How, then, can it be measured? Yet we
do measure periods of time; not those that do not yet exist, nor
those that no longer exist, nor those that have no extension, nor
those that have neither beginning nor end. It is neither future
time, then, that we measure, nor past time nor present nor
passing; and yet we do measure periods of time.

11.27.35 *Deus creator omnium* ('O thou, the all-creator God').[8]
This line has eight syllables, alternately long and short. The four
short syllables, the first, third, fifth and seventh, are half the
long syllables, the second, fourth, sixth and eighth. Each of
these long syllables takes twice the time of each of the shorts.
I pronounce the line and can report that it is so, as long as
I perceive it through my immediate perception. So long as the
immediate perception lasts, I measure the long syllables by the
short and perceive that they are twice as long. But how, seeing
as the long and short syllables alternate with each other, if the
first is short and the second long, how can I keep the short
in my mind and put it alongside the long as my standard of
measurement, so as to discover that it is twice as long; inasmuch
as the long syllable sounds out only when the short syllable has
stopped? And the long syllable itself – can I measure that when
it is present, seeing as I cannot measure anything unless it is
finished? But its finish is its passing away. What is it, then, that
I measure? Where is the short syllable by which I measure?
Where is the long syllable that I measure? Both have sounded,
flown away, passed on, no longer exist. Yet measure I do, and
answer with confidence that so far as I can trust my senses and
my training, one is one length and the other twice as long in
temporal extension. Nor could I do so, were it not that they
have passed away and are finished. It is not the syllables themselves, then, that I measure (for they no longer exist), but something that remains fixed firm in my memory.

11.27.36 It is in you, my mind, that I measure time. Do not try to
hinder me, for this is so; do not hinder yourself or be distracted

8 '*Deus creator omnium*'. See 2Macc. 1.24; also Ambrose, *Hymns* 1.2.1 (quoted at
9.12.32).

by your own sensations. It is the sensation made on you by things as they pass by, which remains when they have passed by, that I measure, not the things that have passed on in order to bring about this sensation. It is this that I measure when I measure periods of time. It follows that either this sensation is time, or that I do not measure time. And what of when I measure periods of silence, and say that one silence lasted for as much time as another sound? Surely then I stretch out my thought to the measure of that sound as if it were still sounding, and thus am able to report in terms of temporal extension on periods of silence. Even when voice and mouth are at rest, we can go over poems and lines and any other form of speech in our thought, and indeed the measurement of movements of all kinds; we can report on their temporal extension and say how long this or that thing is, in precisely the same way that we could were we to pronounce them aloud. – Suppose someone were to choose to utter a sound slightly longer than usual. He thinks first and decides how long it is to be; he goes over the space of time in silence, commits it to memory, and begins his utterance. That utterance then sounds, until such time as it is brought to the end determined for it. But no; it has sounded and will sound, for that part of it which is complete has indeed sounded, and that part which remains will sound and thus goes on being completed, as long as the present intention draws the future into the past. The future diminishes as the past grows, until the future be consumed and all be past.

11.28.37 But how is the future either diminished or consumed, seeing as it does not yet exist, and how does the past grow, seeing as it no longer exists? In the mind, however, that brings all this about, there are three things: expectancy, attention and memory. What the mind expects passes though what it gives attention to into what it remembers. Who would deny that the future does not yet exist? But there is in the mind the expectancy of things future. Who would deny that the past no longer exists? But the memory of things past continues to exist in the mind. Who would deny that the present has no temporal extension, passing away as it does in a moment? But the attention, through which what arrives hastens to depart, endures and remains. There is no such thing, then, as a long future time, seeing as it does not exist; a long future is a long expectation of the future. Nor is there any long past, seeing as that no longer exists; a long past is a long memory of the past.

11.28.38 Suppose I am about to recite a familiar poem. Before I begin, my expectation extends to cover the whole poem. When I have begun, my memory extends to cover the portion that I have already plucked and garnered in the past. The life-span of this action of mine distends over my memory, on account of what I have already recited, and over my expectation, on account of what I have yet to recite. Then there is my attention, which is present to draw what was future into the past. The more this process is repeated and repeated, the shorter my expectation and the longer my memory, until all my expectation is consumed, the action is complete and wholly passed into my memory. What holds good in the case of the poem as a whole, the same holds good also in all its several parts and syllables. The same holds good in some longer action, of which that poem might be a part. The same holds good of a man's life as a whole, the parts of which are all that man's actions. The same holds good also of the whole generation of the children of men, the parts of this generation being the lives of all men.

11.29.30 But *your loving-kindness is better than lives* (Ps. 63.3 [Ps. 62.4]); and behold, my life is a distension, and yet *your right hand has upheld me* (Ps. 18.35 [Ps. 17.36], Ps. 63.9 [Ps. 62.9]) in my Lord, the Son of Man, the *Mediator between you* the One, *and us* (1Tim. 2.5), the many. Through many things and in many ways your right hand has upheld me, so that *through him I may understand in whom I also am understood*; and, gathered up from my former days, pursue the One. *I forget the past*, and do not distend in various directions. Rather I stretch out, not for things future and transitory, but for that which is before me; not distended in various directions but with intent and purpose I *pursue the palm of my high calling* (Phil. 3.12–14), where I shall *hear the voice of praise* (Ps. 26.7 [Ps. 25.7]) and *contemplate your delight* (Ps. 27.4 [Ps. 26.4]), that neither comes nor passes away. As it is, *my years pass by in groaning* (Ps. 31.10 [Ps. 30.11]), but you are my solace, O Lord, my eternal Father. I have torn myself between one time and another, not knowing the due order of these times; and my thoughts, the inmost bowels of my being, are riven with these clamorous diversities, until I flow back together into you, refined and purified by the fire of your love.

11.30.40 *I shall abide and stand fast in you* (Phil. 4.1, 1Thess. 3.8), in my form and in your truth, nor shall I suffer the questions of men who are punished with a sickness that makes them thirst for more than they can hold; who say, 'What was God doing before he made heaven and earth?' or 'Why did it occur to him to make something, seeing as he had never before made anything?' Grant them, O Lord, to consider well what they say, and to learn that 'never' is not sayable where there is no time. If someone is said never to have done something, what is being said if not that he had at no time done such a thing? Let them see, then, that there is no time without creation, and cease *speaking vanity* (Ps. 144.8 [Ps. 143.8]). Let them *stretch out for what is before them* (Phil. 3.13), and understand that you are the creator of all times and eternal before all times; and that there are neither times coeternal with you nor any created thing, even if it is before time.

11.31.41 O Lord my God, in what deep recess is your secret hidden, and how far from there have the consequences of my sins cast me? Heal my eyes, that I may rejoice in your light. If there is some mighty mind so knowing and foreknowing that it knows all things past and future as thoroughly as I know that one song, it is a mind truly wondrous and amazing, a thing astonishing and terrible. From it nothing is hidden in all time past and remaining, just as no part of that song is hidden from me; it knows what and how much has passed since its first beginning, and what and how much remains until the end. But far be it that you, creator of the universe, creator of souls and bodies, should have such knowledge of all things future and past. Far be it; you are far more wondrous and far more hidden. It is not so with you as with the singer of a song and his audience, whose senses are distended and whose feelings alternate between the expectation of sounds to come and the memory of sounds past; no such thing happens to you, the unchangingly eternal one, the truly eternal creator of men's minds. Just as in the beginning you knew heaven and earth without alteration in your knowledge, so in the beginning you made heaven and earth without distension in your activity. Let him who understands this confess to you, and let him that does not understand confess to you also. *Oh how exalted you are, yet the humble in heart are your home* (Ps. 139.5 [Ps. 138.6], Dan. 3.87)! You *raise up them that are laid low* (Ps. 145.14 [Ps. 144.14], Ps. 146.8 [Ps. 145.7–8]), nor do they fall whose exaltation you are.

BOOK TWELVE

12.1.1 My heart is anxious over many things, O Lord, battered as it is in this poor life of mine by the words of your holy Scripture. Men mostly lack understanding when they speak; they speak more of seeking than of finding, their petition is longer than its granting, their hand more ready to knock than to take up the task (cf Matt. 7.7–8, Lk 11.9–10). I hold to your promise – for what can break it? – : *If God is for us, who is against us?* (Rom. 8.31). *Ask, and you will receive; seek, and you will find; knock, and the door will be opened to you. For all who ask, receive; he who seeks, will find; to him that knocks will the door be opened* (Jn 16.24, Matt. 7.7–8, Lk 11.9–10). These are your promises, and who would be afraid of being disappointed in them, seeing as it is the Truth that promises them?

12.2.2 Let my tongue in all humility confess to your Sublimity that it is you who made heaven and earth. The heaven that I see, the earth I tread, from which comes the clay that I carry around – it is you who made all this. But where is the 'heaven of heaven' that we read of in the words of the Psalmist: *The heaven of heaven is the Lord's, and the earth he has given to the children of men* (Ps. 115.16 [Ps. 113.24])? Where is that heaven which we cannot see, compared to which all the perceptible heavens are earth? For all the perceptible heavens, though corporeal and not entire throughout, nevertheless contain form and beauty right down to their lowest parts, their foundations being the earth; yet compared to the 'heaven of heaven', even the heavens which belong to our earth are earth. These two physical things, heaven and earth, great as they are, may rightly be called 'earth' compared to that heaven, whatever it may be, which belongs to the Lord and not to the children of men.

12.3.3 This earth, moreover, was *invisible and without order* (Gen. 1.2); there was a deep abyss of some sort, over which there was no light, there being no distinct form to it;[1] for which reason you commanded that it be written that *there was darkness over the abyss* (Gen. 1.2). For what is darkness but absence of light? And if there had been light, how would that light have existed, if not by shining over the abyss and illuminating it? And seeing as there was not yet light, what does it mean to say that there was darkness but to say there was no light? There was, then, darkness over the abyss, there being no light above it, just as where there is no sound there is silence. And what does it mean to say that there is silence in a place if not to say that there is no sound there? Surely it is you, O Lord, that have taught this soul that confesses to you. Surely it is you that have taught me that before you gave form and distinct shape to this formless mass, there was nothing; neither colour nor figure, nor body nor spirit. Yet there was not absolute nothingness; there was a kind of formlessness, lacking distinct shape.

12.4.4 How could this be expressed so as to give at least some suggestion of its meaning even to the slower-witted, but by some everyday word? And what in the whole world could be found more akin to utter formlessness than 'earth and abyss'? For in accordance with their degree, the lowest of all, they are less fair and shapely than all other, higher things, bright and radiant as they are. Why, then, should I not take these words to refer to this formless mass, which you made without distinct shape to be the material from which you formed this shapely earth; and that it was in order to suggest this in terms suitable

---

1 Augustine uses repeatedly in this passage the word *species*, here translated 'distinct form'. The etymology of the word, as Augustine would certainly have known, lies in a root meaning 'to see' (as in *spectacle*). In classical Latin it often means 'beauty'; it is also used by Latin philosophical writers to translate the Greek *idea*, as in Plato's Theory of Ideas or Forms – the doctrine that objects perceived by the senses exist in virtue of their participation in supreme archetypes or Forms. In later Latin a sense 'special, distinct type' seems to have developed. Augustine's use of the term evokes all this range of meanings. Thus to say that the earth was 'without *species*' is to gloss both parts of the description 'invisible and without order'. It also looks forward to the work of God as the Beauty from which all beauty proceeds; God's creative work makes the earth visible, gives it its distinctive forms [in their due order], and hence gives it beauty.

for human understanding that it is written that *the earth was invisible and without order* (Gen. 1.2)?

12.5.5 When we meditate on these things and ask what it is that the senses apprehend, our mind speaks to us: 'This does not refer to any apprehensible form, such as life or justice; it is the raw matter from which physical things are shaped and not itself perceptible to the senses, seeing as the visible and perceptible do not exist in the invisible and orderless.' In so saying, human meditation seeks either to come to knowledge of that invisible and orderless earth through very ignorance, or to come to ignorance through its very knowledge.[2]

12.6.6 But as for me, O Lord, if I am to confess to you with lips and pen all that you have taught me concerning this raw matter – the name of which I heard so long ago and did not understand, hearing it from those who themselves did not understand. I meditated upon it and invested it with countless changing shapes, and hence did not meditate on it at all. My mind imagined foul and loathsome forms, their natural order twisted out of shape – but forms they were. I used the word 'formless'[3] to describe not that which lacks all form, but that which had a form such that if it were to become perceptible to me, my senses would shrink from it as from something monstrous and at odds with itself, and my human weakness would be thrown into confusion. But what I meditated upon was not an utter lack of form, but something formless in comparison to things fairer in form. True reason urged me that I should strip it of all vestiges of form of whatever kind, if I willed to meditate on utter formlessness, but I could not. I was more apt to think that which lacks all form to be non-existent than to meditate on something between form and nothing, being neither unformed nor nothing, a formless near-nothing.

2 'In so saying ... very knowledge'. See note on 1.6.10. Augustine is arguing that in interpreting the Scriptures, it may be more beneficial to entertain a variety of exegetical possibilities [provided none of them is *per se* wrong] than to commit one's self to a single interpretation [however correct] at the expense of others.

3 ' "formless" '. The Latin word *informis*, literally 'without form, without beauty', usually means 'ugly'; here Augustine uses it in its etymological sense.

At this point my mind ceased to question my spirit, full as it was with images of physical objects endowed with form and interchanging and altering them at whim; I applied myself intently to those physical objects themselves and looked more deeply into their mutability, the means by which they ceased to be what they were and become what they were not. I formed the notion that their passage from form to form came about through a certain formlessness, not through absolute nothingness. But I wanted knowledge, not notions; and were my tongue and pen to confess to you how far you have unravelled this question for me, which of my readers would last out long enough to take it in? Not that my heart will cease for that reason to pay you honour and to offer a song of praise for the things it has not the strength to tell in full. The very mutability of things itself contains all the forms into which things mutable can change. And what is this mutability? Is it mind? Is it body? Is it some special form of mind or body? If it were possible to say 'a something/nothing' or 'an is/is-not', that is what I would call it. But it already existed in some sort, in order to contain those visible and ordered forms with their distinct shapes.

12.7.7 And what could be the source of its being in any sort, were it not you, from whom all things exist, in so far as they exist? But its distance from you is proportionate to its dissimilarity to you; it is not a matter of spatial distance. It is you, then, O Lord, who are not one thing in one place and another in another, but the same and the same and the Same,[4] *holy, holy, holy, Lord God almighty* (Is. 6.3, Rev. 4.8), who in the beginning (which is from you), in your Wisdom (which is born of your substance), made something from nothing. You made heaven and earth not of yourself, for then there would be something equal to your only-begotten Son and hence to you; and it would be in no way right that there should be something equal to you but not of you. Moreover, there was nothing apart from yourself from which to make heaven and earth, O God, one Trinity and threefold Unity; hence it was from nothing that you made heaven and earth, a great something and a little something. For

4 '... the Same'. See the note on 9.4.11.

you are almighty and good in making all good things, the great heaven and the little earth. You existed, and nothing else from which you made heaven and earth; two somethings, one close to you, one close to nothingness; one, than which only you were higher, one, than which nothing was lower.

12.8.8 But the *heaven of heaven is yours*, O Lord; whereas *the earth*, which you have *given to the children of men* (Ps. 115.16 [Ps. 113.24]) to see and touch, was not such as we now see and touch. It was invisible and without order; there was an abyss, over which there was no light; there was darkness over the abyss, that is to say, more so than in the abyss. That abyss, now composed of visible waters, has even in its lowest depths a light proper to its kind, perceptible in some sort to the *fish and living things that creep* (Gen. 1.20–6) on its bed. But the world as first created was a near-nothing, being as yet utterly without form. Nevertheless, it did exist, for it was capable of being formed. You, O Lord, *made the world from formless matter* (Wisdom 11.18), a near-nothing which you made from nothing, and from this matter you made the mighty works at which we children of men marvel. Marvellous indeed is this corporeal heaven, the *firmament between water and water* that you made on the second day after the creation of light (cf Gen. 1.6–9); 'Let there be ...,' you said, and it was so. This firmament you called 'heaven'; but it is the heaven that belongs to this earth and sea, the things you made on the third day, giving visible shape to the formless matter which you made before all days. Heaven, too, you had made before all days – the heaven of this earthly heaven; for it was in the beginning that you made heaven and earth. But as for the earth that you had made, that was formless matter, being invisible and without order; and there was darkness over the abyss. From this invisible and orderless earth, from this formlessness, from this near-nothing, you made all the things that constitute and do not constitute this inconstant world. Mutability itself is apparent in this world; it is through mutability that we are able to perceive and measure time, since it is by change in things that time comes into being; through alteration and metamorphosis in the outward shape that is fashioned from material that is the invisible earth of which I have spoken.

12.9.9 Therefore, in his account of how in the beginning you made heaven and earth, the Spirit, your servant Moses's teacher, says nothing of 'days' or of other periods of time. This is because the 'heaven of heaven', which you made in the beginning, is, though a created thing, apprehensible only to the mind; and although it is in no way coeternal with you, the Trinity, nevertheless it shares in your eternity. Rapt in the most blessed sweetness of contemplating you, it holds in check completely its capacity for change. It has not fallen away from you since it was made; but rather by cleaving to you it outlasts all periods of time, which fly away as one succeeds to the next. But as for the 'formlessness' – 'earth invisible and without order' – that too is not numbered in days. For where there is no distinct form and no order, and where nothing comes or goes, there are no such things as days, nor does one space of time succeed to the next.

12.10.10 O Truth, Light of my heart, let not my darkness speak to me! I spent myself on these earthly things and clouded my being, but even in this darkness I began to love you. I strayed, yet remembered you. I *heard your voice behind me* (Ezekiel 3.12) calling on me to return, and could scarcely hear for the tumult of those who know no peace. And now, behold, I return fevered and panting to you, the Source. Let none forbid me; let me drink from this stream and from it let me live (cf Jn 4.13–14). I would not be my own life; of myself I have lived wretchedly, and been death to myself. In you I live again. Speak words of consolation to me, and talk gently with me. I have put my faith in your Scriptures, and their words are hidden indeed.

12.11.11 You have spoken to me already, O Lord, and said aloud in my inner ear that you are eternal, *alone having immortality* (1Tim. 6.16); that you change neither in form nor in motion; that your will does not vary according to the times, for it is no immortal will that is one thing at one time and another at another. All this is clear to me in your sight; let it grow clearer and clearer, I pray, and in this revelation let me abide in all soberness of mind beneath your wings. Likewise, O Lord, you have spoken aloud in my inner ear and told me that all beings and substances that exist and yet are not what you are, are your making. Only the non-existent is not from you. As for motions of the will away from you, the Existent, towards the less existent – such a motion is a breach of duty and a sin; yet no man's sin either harms you or disturbs the order that your command has decreed, in the greatest part or the least. All this is clear to me in your sight; let it grow clearer and clearer, I pray, and in this revelation let me abide in all soberness of mind beneath your wings.

12.11.12 Likewise you have spoken aloud in my inner ear and told me that no created thing is coeternal with you, even if you are its sole pleasure, even if by drawing on you in all steadfastness and chastity it never avails itself of its mutability in any way; even if you are ever present with it and it holds fast to you with all its heart, having neither a future to look forward to nor a past to remember; even if at no point does it alter, nor is it distended over any period of time. Happy indeed is that creature, if any such there is, that cleaves to your blessedness; blessed to have you as its eternal indweller and enlightener! I can think of nothing I would more readily call 'the heaven of heavens that is the Lord's' than a *dwelling place* of yours, which *contemplates your joy* (Ps. 27.4 [Ps. 26.4]) without any falling off or departure in pursuit of other things; a pure mind, in harmony and at one with the sure bond of peace that exists between those holy spirits, the citizens of your City in the heaven above these heavens.

12.11.13 Hence let the soul which has travelled far abroad[5] understand, if it now *thirsts for you*, if its *tears are become its bread, while day by day men say to it, where is your God?* (Ps. 42.1–3 [Ps. 41.1–3]) – if it now *seeks from you one thing that it requires of you; that it may dwell in your house all the days of its life* (Ps. 27.4

5 '... the soul which has travelled far abroad'. Here Augustine takes up the imagery of the Prodigal Son, which is prominent in the early books of the *Confessions*. The Prodigal Son likewise 'travels to a far country' (cf Lk 15.13).

[Ps. 26.4]) – and what is its life if not you? – and what are your days if not your eternity, even as *your years are unfailing* (Ps. 102.27 [Ps. 101.28], Hebr. 1.12)? Hence let the soul understand, I say, if it can, how far your eternity is above all time, inasmuch as your heaven, though not coeternal with you, has not journeyed abroad, but through cleaving incessantly and unfailingly to you knows no successive sequences of time. All this is clear to me in your sight; let it grow clearer and clearer, I pray, and in this revelation let me abide in all soberness of mind beneath your wings.

12.11.14 There is, then, a formless something between the changing forms of these least and lowest objects. Only someone who through vanity of heart strayed and wallowed in illusions of his own making would tell me that, if all outward shape were destroyed and consumed, so that there remained only the formlessness through which objects change and are metamorphosed from one shape to another, this formlessness could show change over time. It could not; for time only exists through variety of motion; and where there is no outward form, there is no variety.

12.12.15 I have considered these matters in accordance with your gift to me – as far as you stir me up to knock at the door, and as far as you open to me when I knock (cf Matt. 7.7–8, Lk 11.9–10). Having done so, I find that there are two of your creations which, though neither is coeternal with you, do not experience time. One is so formed that it contemplates you unfailingly and without changing for a moment; although capable of change, it none the less enjoys unchanged your eternity and unchangingness. The other is formless, and has not the wherewithal to change from one form to another, whether moving or standing still, and hence cannot be subject to time. But this you did not leave formless; for before all days you made in the beginning heaven and earth, the two things of which I was speaking.

The earth was invisible and without order, and there was darkness over the abyss (Gen. 1.1–2). These words suggest formlessness; they are intended to win over by degrees those who are able to conceive an utter lack of outward form but cannot bring

themselves to conceive of nothingness.[6] According to this interpretation, from this formlessness another heaven and earth, visible and ordered, were made, along with water that has outward
form and all the other things which were made thereafter at the
foundation of the world. Moreover, it is recorded that they were
not made without 'days'. Their nature was such that in them one
period of time succeeds to another, as they change in ordered
sequence from one movement and form to another.

12.13.16 This is what I provisionally understand when I hear your
Scriptures speaking to me and saying, *In the beginning God made
heaven and earth, and the earth was invisible and without order,
and there was darkness over the abyss*, but not saying on what day
you made all these things. I understand it provisionally with
reference to the heaven of heaven, the heaven that is perceptible
only to the intellect. In that heaven intellectual perception means
simultaneous knowledge, *not in part, not in riddles, not in a mirror*, but in full, plainly, *face to face* (1Cor. 13.12). It is not now this
and now that, but, as I said, simultaneous knowledge, without
successive sequences of time. I understand it also with reference
to the invisible and orderless earth, which likewise was without
successive sequences of time, which cause things to be now this
way and now that; for where there is no distinct form, there is
no 'this' and no 'that'. My provisional view of why the Scripture
says, *In the beginning God made heaven and earth* without any
mention of days rests on these two premises: 'heaven' refers to
the 'heaven of heaven', the first-formed thing, whereas 'earth'
refers to 'earth invisible and without order', the utterly formless.
The Scripture immediately goes on to state which earth is
meant; and by stating that on the second day a firmament was
made and was called 'heaven', it suggests which heaven it had
spoken of previously, without mention of days.

6 '... they are intended ... of nothingness'. Here I have read *cogitare possunt*
instead of the manuscripts' *cogitare non possunt*. The manuscript reading is good
Latin but the sense is doubtful; the Scripture, in Augustine's exegesis, could
not recommend itself to anyone who did not believe in the possibility of formlessness. The extra *non*, if it was not in Augustine's own text, may have arisen
out of the general complexity of the passage, and a desire for what was felt to
be a good rhythm for the end of a clause.

12.14.17 Wondrous is the depth of your sayings! Behold, before our eyes is only the surface of them, a blandishment to entice the little ones; but wondrous is the depth, my God, wondrous is the depth! To look into that depth is to shudder; to shudder at the privilege, and to tremble with love. Its *enemies I hate sorely* (Ps. 139.21 [Ps. 138.21–2]); would that you would slay them with your two-edged sword,[7] that it might have no enemies! I would have them thus be slain to themselves, that they might live for you.

And there are others who do not condemn but praise the Book of Genesis, but say, 'The way in which the Spirit of God, who wrote all this through his servant Moses, meant it to be understood, was not what you say it was, but as we say.' To these I reply as follows: you judge the issue between us, O God of us all.

12.15.18 'Will you say that they are false, then, the things that the Truth speaks in my inner ear; that the eternity that belongs to the Creator is true indeed, and that his substance does not vary in any way over time, and that his will does not extend beyond his substance? This is why he does not will now one thing, now another, but once and simultaneously and for ever wills all that he wills; not willing them repeatedly, nor willing now one thing, now another, nor willing later what he had not willed earlier, nor not willing later what he had willed earlier. For such a will is mutable, whereas all that is mutable is not eternal; but our God is eternal.

'Will you deny also what the Truth says aloud to my inner ear; that expectation of things to come becomes contemplation when they do come, and that contemplation becomes memory when they have passed away; and that all mental vision which changes in this way is mutable; and all that is mutable is not eternal; whereas our God is eternal?

'These inferences I draw, these links I make, and I discover that it was not out of any change of will that my God, the eternal God, established the created world, nor is his knowledge subject to what is transitory.

7 '... two-edged sword'. A common metaphor for the Scriptures; cf Ps. 149.6, Ecclesiasticus 21.4, Prov. 5.4, Rev. 1.16.

12.15.19 'What then will you say, you opponents of mine? Is what I say false? "No," they reply. Well then: is it false that every formed being or every matter capable of being formed exists only because it is of him who is supremely good, because he supremely exists? "This too we do not deny," they say. Well then: do you deny that there is a sublime creation that cleaves with such chaste love to the true and truly eternal God that it does not loosen its hold of him and disperse itself on any change or sequence of time, but rests in true contemplation of him and him alone? For you, O God, as you teach us, *reveal yourself to those who love you, and satisfy them* (Jn 14.8, 21); and for that reason it does not decline from you towards itself. This is the house of God, not earthly, not corporeal, even with the stuff of heaven, but spiritual, sharing in your eternity, being eternally without stain. *You have established* that house *for ever and ever; you have made fast your commandment, and it will not pass away* (Ps. 148.6). Nor, however, is that house coeternal with you, for it is not without beginning; it was made.

12.15.20 'For even though we have not discovered any time which existed before that "house", and even though *wisdom was first of all created things* (Ecclesiasticus 1.4), that wisdom was not coeternal with you, our God, its Father, nor is it equal to you. *Through it were all things created* (Col. 1.16), and in the beginning you made heaven and earth; but the wisdom that was created, namely a being perceptible only to the intellect, was light through contemplation of the Light.[8] For though it is created, it too is called wisdom. But the difference between the Wisdom that creates and the wisdom that is created is as great as that between the *Light that enlightens* (Jn 1.9) and the light that is enlightened, or the difference between the Righteousness that makes righteous, and the righteousness that is made righteous thereby – for we too are called your righteousness; one of your

8 '"but the wisdom ... of the Light"'. Augustine here fuses Ecclesiasticus 1.4 ('Wisdom was first of all created things') with an anticipation of Gen. 1.3 ['And God said, Let there be light']. Wisdom and Light are both seen in Christian tradition as attributes or titles of Christ; Augustine stresses that although wisdom and light are the first-created things, they are to be distinguished from the uncreated Wisdom and Light in which they participate.

servants says, *We are the righteousness of God in him* (2Cor. 5.21). It follows, then, the first of all created things was the wisdom which was created, the rational and intellectual mind of your chaste City, our mother on high, free and *eternal in the heavens* (2Cor. 5.21). And what heavens are they, if not the *heavens of heavens that praise you* (Ps. 148.4) – these being also *the heaven of heaven, which is the Lord's* (Ps. 115.16 [Ps. 113.24])? This being so, even if we have not discovered any time that existed before wisdom (since wisdom was first of all created things, and precedes the creation of time), nevertheless it follows that before wisdom is the eternity of its Creator, from whom wisdom took her beginning when she was made – not her beginning in time, for as yet there was no time, but the beginning of her creation.

12.15.21 'Hence this house is of you, our God, but is something other than you; it is not the Same.[9] Not only have we discovered no time that was before it, but not even any time within it, worthy as it is to *see your face* (Matt. 18.10) always, without turning aside from it in the least; for which reason it knows no alteration or change. Yet there is in it the capacity for change; it could *be darkened and chilled*, were it not that by cleaving to you by force of love it *shines like the noonday* (Is. 58.10), having its heat from you. O house of light and beauty, how I love your fair honour, and the habitation of the glory of my Lord, your Mason and Indweller! For you I sigh on my pilgrimage, begging your Maker to dwell in me through you, as he is my Maker also. *I have strayed like a lost sheep*, but on the shoulders of my Shepherd (Ps. 119.176 [Ps. 118.176], Lk 15.4–5), your Builder, I hope to be brought back to you.

12.15.22 'What do you say to me, you opponents whom I was addressing, who nevertheless believe that Moses was a pious servant of God and that his books are the oracles of the Holy Spirit? Is not the house of God as I have described it? Not coeternal with God, but nevertheless according to its proper measure eternal in the heavens, where it is vain for you to seek for temporal sequences, since you will find none; for whatsoever

9 ' "... the Same" '. See 12.7.7, 9.4.10 (with note), and 9.10.24.

has cleaving to God as its good transcends all distension and all fleeting space of time. "It is so," they say. Which, then, do you argue is false out of the things that my heart has cried out to my God, hearing the inner voice that glorifies him? Is it that there was formless matter where, because there was no form, there was no order? But where there was no order, there could be no successive sequences of time; and yet that near-nothing, in so far as it was not wholly nothing, was of him from whom all things exist that exist in any degree. "This too," they say, "we do not deny." '

12.16.23 It is with these that I would debate somewhat before you, my God – these who grant the truth of all that the Truth speaks inwardly, in my mind, and does not keep silent. Let those who deny it yelp and howl at themselves all they will; I shall endeavour to persuade them to be quiet and open a path for your Word to come to them. If they should reject me and refuse to do so, then do not you, my God, cease speaking to me, I beseech you. Speak *truly in my heart* (Ps. 15.2 [Ps. 14.3]). You alone speak thus; those others I shall leave outside to blow in the dust and raise up a cloud of it, and get the dirt in their eyes, while I *enter my inner chamber* (Matt. 6.6) and sing songs of love to you, groaning *groans beyond telling* (Rom. 8.26) as I travel on my pilgrimage, remembering Jerusalem, my heart stretching out for her, Jerusalem my fatherland, Jerusalem my mother, and you who are ruler over her, her enlightener, father, guardian, husband, all joys chaste and strong, all gladness unalloyed, all good things beyond saying; who are at once all good things, being the one supreme and true Good. Nor shall I turn aside until you, my God, take all that I am, dispersed and deformed as it now is, and gather it into peace of her who is my most beloved Mother,[10] in whom are the *first-fruits of my spirit* (Gal. 4.26), restoring me to my proper form and strengthening me for eternity.

10 '. . . most beloved Mother'. The Catholic Church. As is clear from the early books of the *Confessions*, Augustine's earliest love of the Catholic Church was passed on to him from his mother, and he continues to use such maternal language to describe it.

This is how I speak with those who do not call truths false-hoods, who join with us in honouring the sacred Scripture that you have proclaimed through your holy servant Moses and in setting it up as the supreme authority to be followed, yet who oppose us on other matters. You, our God, be the judge between my confessions and their objections.

12.17.24 These are the ones who say, 'Although what you say is true, it was not these two things that Moses had in mind when, by revelation of the Spirit, he said, *In the beginning God made heaven and earth*. By the name "heaven" he did not mean that spiritual or intellectual creation which *contemplates the face of God for ever* (Matt. 18.10), nor by the name "earth" did he mean formless matter.' – Well then, what did he mean? – 'In using these words, our hero Moses meant what we say he meant.' – And what is that? – 'By the names "heaven" and earth" he meant to indicate in a short but all-encompassing expression the entire visible world, so that thereafter, in his list of days, he could give as it were a catalogue of each individual created thing that it pleased the Spirit to utter in this way. The men he spoke to were a people so uneducated and carnal-minded that he judged it right to entrust them only with such works of God as were visible.' But as for the earth's being invisible and without order, and the darkness over the abyss, from which, as is shown by what follows, on the days of creation God made and ordered all the visible things that are known to all people – this they agree it is not improper to interpret as being formless matter.

12.17.25 Well now: suppose someone else were to say that by the names 'heaven' and 'earth' Moses meant to suggest first that same formlessness and confusion, because out of it this visible world and all created things that are clear and apparent in it, which together are generally called 'heaven and earth', were established and perfected? Or suppose someone else again were to say that the phrase 'heaven and earth' might reasonably be taken to mean created things visible and invisible; and that for this reason the whole of creation, which God made in wisdom (that is, in the beginning), is summed up in two such words? But, this commentator might say, they are not of the very substance of God, not being the Same as God. Moreover, there is in all of them a capacity for change, whether they abide, like the eternal house of God, or whether they change, like the human soul and body. It was (says our commentator) the common material of all things invisible and visible that is indicated by these words *the earth was invisible and without order, and there was darkness over the abyss*. This material was formless, it is true, but capable of being formed. From it heaven and earth, that is to say, all created things visible and invisible, both now given form, could come into being. Such an interpretation distinguishes between *the earth invisible and without order*, which it takes to mean the physical material being receiving any formal quality, and the *darkness over the abyss*, which it takes to mean the spiritual material before its unmoderated flux was checked and it was enlightened with wisdom.

12.17.26 Someone else again may choose to take it another way: that in the passage *In the beginning God made heaven and earth*, it is indeed created things visible and invisible that are meant by the words 'heaven and earth', not yet brought to full perfection and form, but rather the raw material of creation, the formless and inchoate mass from which things are formed; their grounds for this being that in the formless mass there already existed, albeit intermingled with one another and not yet distinguished by their formal qualities, those things that when divided and set in their due order are called 'heaven' and 'earth', the one a spiritual creation, the other a physical.

12.18.27 Having heard and pondered all this, I have no wish to *contend in words; that is no good for anything except undermining its hearers* (2Tim. 2.14). But *the law is good for upbuilding, if it is used lawfully* (Eph. 4.29, 1Tim. 1.8), its purpose being love that proceeds from a pure heart, a good conscience, and an unfeigned faith. I know on which commandments, according to our Teacher, *hang all the Law and the prophets* (Matt. 22.40). What hindrance is it to me, my God, light that lightens my eyes in secret, what hindrance is it to me as I make my ardent confession, that these words may be understood in such diverse senses, seeing as they are none the less true for it? What hindrance is it if I take them to mean something other than Moses took them to mean? All of us who read him are striving to hunt down and comprehend his meaning, and, believing him to speak truly, we dare not suppose him to have said anything that we know or think is false. As long, therefore, as each of us endeavours to get from the Holy Scriptures the same meaning as the writer's, what harm does it do if someone takes it to mean something that you, light of all true-speaking minds, show him is true – even if this was not the meaning of the writer whom he is reading, seeing as Moses too meant something true, even though it was not the same thing?

12.19.28 It is true, O Lord, that you made heaven and earth. It is true also that the 'beginning' is your wisdom, in which you *made all things* (Ps. 104.24 [Ps. 103.24]). Likewise it is true that the names of the two great parts of this visible world – namely 'heaven' and 'earth' – may serve to sum up all beings established and made. It is true that every mutable thing suggests to our mind the formless state from which it takes its form, and through which it is changed and transformed. It is true that what clings so tightly to the Formable Immutable that, though mutable, it is unchanged, is not subject to time. It is that the formlessness, being next to nothing, is not subject to the process of time by which one thing succeeds to another. It is true that the material from which something is made can, by a figure of speech, bear the name of the thing made from it; hence the names 'heaven' and 'earth' can be given to the undefined state of formlessness from which heaven and earth were made. It is true that of all formed things nothing is closer to formlessness than 'earth' and 'abyss'. It is true that you are the maker of all things; not only what is created and formed, but also what is creatable and formable. For *all things come from you* (Rom. 11.36, 1Cor. 8.6). It is true that whatever is formed from formlessness is at first formless, and only afterwards formed.

12.20.29 All these are truths; no one has any hesitation in saying as much, if you have given his inner eye sight of such matters, and if it is his fixed belief that your servant Moses spoke *in the Spirit of truth* (Jn 14.17). But one commentator will say: ' "*In the beginning God made heaven and earth*." This means that through his Word, coeternal with himself, God made the world that is perceptible to the intellect and the senses, that is to say, the spiritual and physical world.' Such a commentator is taking as his own just one out of all these truths.

Another will say: '"*In the beginning God made heaven and earth*." This means that through his Word, coeternal with himself, God made the entire mass of this physical world, along with all the beings in it that are perceptible and familiar to us.' This commentator, too, is taking for himself another truth from among many.

Another will say: '"*In the beginning God made heaven and earth*." This means that through his Word, coeternal with himself, God made the formless matter from which to make his spiritual and physical creation.' This is another truth, again chosen from among many.

Another will say: '"*In the beginning God made heaven and earth*." This means that through his Word, coeternal with himself, God made the formless matter from which to make his physical creation, in which heaven and earth, which now we perceive as entities with their own distinct form within the physical mass of the world, were intermingled.' This commentator, too, is taking one truth from among many

Another will say: '"*In the beginning God made heaven and earth*." This means that at the very outset of the work of creation, God made the formless matter which contained heaven and earth intermingled. From this they were formed, and now stand out and are visible along with all things that are in them.' He, too, is taking one truth from among many.

12.21.30 So also with the interpretation of the words which come next: *The earth was invisible and without order, and there was darkness over the abyss.*[11] One commentator will say: 'This means that the physical object which God made was the raw matter from which physical things were to be constructed, but was itself

11 'So also ... *the abyss*.' O'Donnell in his commentary points out that each of the interpretations advanced in 12.21.30 corresponds closely to one interpretation in 12.20.29, the first corresponding to the first, the second to the second, and so on.

formless, without order and without light.' Such a commentator is taking as his own one out of all the possible truths.

Another will say: ' "*The earth was invisible and without order, and there was darkness over the abyss.*" This means that everything described as "heaven and earth" was a dark matter, still without form, from which the physical heaven and earth could come into being, along with all the physically perceptible objects that are in them.' This commentator, too, is taking for himself another truth from among many.

Another will say: ' "*The earth was invisible and without order, and there was darkness over the abyss.*" This means that the whole of what is called "heaven and earth" was a still formless and dark matter. From it was made the heaven which is perceptible only to the intellect (otherwise called "the heaven of heaven"), and the earth, by which is meant every physical being. The name of "earth" implies also the physical heaven, from which every creature visible and invisible comes into being.' This is another truth, again chosen from among many.

Another will say: ' "*The earth was invisible and without order, and there was darkness over the abyss.*" It is not formlessness that the Scripture is referring to under the name of "heaven and earth". The formlessness itself, which Scripture calls "the earth invisible and without order" and "the dark abyss", already existed. It is from this formlessness that, according as the Scripture says earlier, God made heaven and earth, that is, the spiritual and the physical creation.' This commentator, too, is taking one truth from among many.

Another will say: ' "*The earth was invisible and without order, and there was darkness over the abyss.*" This means that formlessness was, so to speak, the material from which, as the Scripture says earlier, God made heaven and earth. As for "heaven and earth", that means the whole physical mass of the world divided into its two main parts, the higher and the lower, along with all the familiar and everyday creatures in them.' He, too, is taking one truth from among many.

12.22.31 In response to these last two opinions, one might attempt to answer as follows: 'If you do not take the words "heaven and earth" to refer to this formless matter, then there must have been something not made by God, namely the material from which he made heaven and earth. For the Scripture did not relate how God made this material; unless we are to understand that it is symbolized by the words "heaven and earth", or by the word "earth" alone, in the verse *in the beginning God made heaven and earth*. In that case, we may decide to take the following words (*the earth was invisible and without order*) to refer to formless matter; but if so, we should take it to be the same formless matter that God is described as having made in the preceding verse (*God made heaven and earth*).'

But those who assert either of the last two opinions cited above will, on hearing this, reply: 'As for the formless matter, we do not deny that it was made by God, from whom all good things come (cf Gen. 1.31). For just as we say that the created and formed are more good, so we grant that the creatable and formable are less good – but still good. As for the Scripture's not recording that God made this formlessness, no more did it record God's making many other things, such as the Cherubim and Seraphim, which the Apostle divides into Thrones, Dominations, Principalities and Powers (cf Col. 1.16); but it is clear that God did make them.

'Or if the words *God made heaven and earth* cover all things, what are we to say of the waters over which *the Spirit of God was moving* (Gen. 1.2)? If these are to be understood under the heading of "earth", how can we take the word "earth" to refer to the formless matter? We can plainly see that the waters have fairness and form.

'Or if we do take the words "heaven and earth" to mean "all things", why is it written that from the same formlessness a firmament was made and called "heaven" (cf Gen. 1.7–8), and not that waters were made? For the waters are no longer formless and invisible; we see the fairness of their forms as they flow.

'Or if they only received their form when God said, *Let the water that is beneath the firmament be gathered into one* (Gen. 1.7–9), and if that gathering were the act of formation, what are we to say of the waters that are above the firmament, which, were they formless, would not have merited such an exalted place; but nor is it written at what word they were formed? If, then, the Book of Genesis says nothing of God's making something that no sound faith nor sure understanding doubts that he made, and if no sober teaching dare to say that those waters are coeternal with God on the grounds that in the Book of Genesis we hear them mentioned but do not find it related where they were made, why in the case of the formless matter which the Scripture describes, calling it *earth invisible and without order*, and *dark abyss*, should we, taught by the Truth, not understand that it was made by God out of nothing, and for that reason is not coeternal with him – even though the Biblical narrative omits to tell us where it was made?'

12.23.32 Having heard and examined all this, so far as my weakness of understanding allows (a weakness I confess to you, my God, who know it already), I see that two sorts of dissent can arise when a messenger proclaims a true message using symbols. The first is over the truth of the matters reported, the second over the messenger's intended meaning. We go about our enquiry into the establishment of creation, asking what is true, in one way; but it is in another way that we go about asking what Moses, the great servant in the household of your faith (cf Gal. 6.10), intended his reader and hearer to understand by those words.

As far as the first sort of dissent is concerned, let them all depart from me who think they know things that are false. As far as the second sort is concerned, let them all depart from me who think that Moses said things that are false. But let me be joined in you, O Lord, to those who in the breadth of love feed on your truth; with them let me take delight in you. Let us together approach the words of your Scripture, and seek your meaning through the meaning of him by whose pen you dispensed those words.

12.24.33 Surrounded as we are by the many truths contained in these words, which strike one seeker in one way and another in another, who among us has discovered what you meant by these words? Who can say that in his narrative Moses meant this or that as confidently as he can say this or that interpretation is

true, whether Moses meant it or something else? Behold, my
God, how confidently I, your servant, who have vowed to offer
the sacrifice of confession to you in these writings, and who
prayed that in return for your mercy I may *perform my vows to
you* (Ps. 116.16 [Ps. 115.18]) – behold how confidently I say that
through your immutable Word you made all things, both visible
and invisible. Would I say with the same confidence that this
was what Moses made in mind when he wrote *in the beginning
God made heaven and earth*? Through your truth I see that this
is certainly true; but I cannot see what Moses had in mind when
he wrote these words. It is possible that when he said *in the
beginning*, he was thinking of the very outset of creation; it is
possible that he meant us to understand 'heaven and earth' in
this passage as an entity not yet formed and perfected, but that
each of them, whether a physical or spiritual entity, was inchoate
and formless. In short, I see that he could have meant any of
these things, and still spoken the truth. I do not see what Moses,
that great and holy man, beheld in his mind when he uttered
these words; but whether it was one of these things or something else I have not listed, I do not doubt that he saw what was
true, and expressed it in fitting terms.

12.25.34 *Let no one make any more trouble for me* (Gal. 6.17),
saying: 'Moses did not mean what you say he meant; he meant
what I say.' For if such a person were to say to me, 'How do you
know that Moses meant what you understand by his words?'
I might have to bear it patiently and answer as I did above, or
perhaps at greater length, if my questioner were obdurate. But
when he says, 'Moses did not mean what you say; he meant
what I say,' without denying that both what he says and what
I say is true – then, O God, life of the poor, in whose breast
there is no contradiction, rain down your tender influences on
my heart, and let me endure with patience such people, who do
not speak to me in this way because they are divinely inspired
and have seen what they say in the heart of your servant. Rather
they are proud and know not Moses's meaning, but love their
own, not because it is true but because it is theirs. If they did
not, they would love the other true interpretation no less, just as

I love what they say when it is true; not because it is theirs, but because it is true. If, however, they do indeed love it because it is true, then it is both theirs and mine, for it is the common property of all truth-lovers. But as for their asserting that Moses did not mean what I say but what they say – that I reject. I can show no love for that attitude; for even if their interpretation is true, nevertheless it shows a hasty judgement which comes not from knowledge but from brashness; it is not the fruit of vision but of pride. But fearful are your judgements, O Lord, since your truth belongs not to me nor to this person or that, but to all of us whom you openly call to share in it, with the terrible warning that we should *not consider it our private property, lest we be deprived of it* (1Tim. 6.5). For whoever claims as his own that which you have set out for the enjoyment of all, and wants for his own what belongs to everyone, is driven away from what belongs to all and back to what belongs to himself; that is, from truth to falsehood. For *he who speaks falsehood speaks of his own falsehood* (Jn 8.44).

12.25.35 *Give ear, O God, Judge supreme and very Truth, and hear what I say to this opponent* (Jer. 18.19). Give ear and listen; it is before you that I speak and before my brothers, those who *use the law lawfully* to achieve the *goal of love* (1Tim. 1.5–8). *Behold and see* (Lam. 1.9–12) what I say to him, if it pleases you. The answer I give him is fraternal and irenic: 'If we both see that what you say is true, and if we both see that what I say is true, tell me where we see it. I do not see it in you, nor you in me; we both see it in the unchangeable Truth itself, that is above our understanding. Seeing, then, as we are not arguing over the light that comes from our Lord and God, why should we argue over our neighbour's thoughts, which we cannot see in the way that we can see the unchangeable Truth? Even if Moses himself were to appear and say "This is what I meant", we would still not see the Truth in the same way, and yet we would believe. Let no one, then, be *filled with pride against his brother over what is written* (1Cor. 4.6). Let us *love the Lord our God with all our heart, with all our soul and with all our mind, and our neighbour as ourselves* (Deut. 6.5, Matt. 22.37–9, Mk 12.30–1, Lk 10.27).

Unless we believe that whatever Moses meant in the Scriptures, he meant it for the sake of these two commandments, that we should love God and our neighbour, we *make the Lord a liar* (Jn 5.10), if our attitude towards our fellow-servant's views is not what Moses taught us it should be. There are so many true meanings to be extracted from these words; see how foolish it is, then, to be in a hurry to assert which of them Moses really meant, and with destructive controversies to offend against the spirit of love – when it was for the sake of love that Moses said all the things we are trying to elucidate!

12.26.36 And yet, my God, Exaltation of my humility, Rest from my labour, you who hear my confessions and *forgive my sins* (Matt. 6.15, Mk 11.25), it is you who teach me to love my neighbour as myself; for my part, I cannot believe you would give Moses, your faithful servant, less of a gift than I would hope and pray that you give me, if I were born when he was born, and if you had set me in his position and charged me with the same task: to dispense, by service of heart and tongue, the writings that so much later would profit all peoples, and, from the high peak of authority they command throughout the whole earth, put down the words of all false and proud teachings. And what would I wish, were I born then as Moses? – for we all come *from the one lump* (Rom. 9.21), and *what is a man*, unless you *are mindful of him* (Ps. 8.4 [Ps. 8.5])? If I were he, and if I were charged by you with the task of writing the Book of Genesis, I would want you to give me such ready eloquence, such skill at weaving language, that those who cannot yet understand how God creates, would not reject my words as going beyond their own powers, nor would those who can understand find that I, your servant, had in the course of my few words overlooked any notion that they had themselves formed in the course of their own meditations, so long as that notion were true; and that if any one of them had by the light of Truth come upon any other notion, it would not be impossible to take that meaning also from my words.

12.27.37 For just as a spring that rises in a small place is more fertile and with its various rivulets supplies a flow of water to a wider area than any one of those rivulets which, however far they flow, can be traced back to the one source, so the tale told by your appointed Dispenser, destined as it was to benefit so many later commentators, rises in low and measured language and bubbles up into trickles of pure truth. From those streams each of these commentators takes what meaning he is capable of forming in these matters, some one meaning, some another, extracting it through various complicated twists of language. Some, when they read or hear these words, think that God is like a man, or like some physical object endowed with immense power; and that he formed the sudden and unprecedented resolution to make two great physical objects, heaven and earth, one higher, one lower. These objects were to be outside himself and, so to speak, at some spatial distance from himself; and that within them all things were to be contained. And when they hear the words, *God said, Let there be* ... this or that, they think that his words had beginning and ending, that they were pronounced over a period of time and then passed away; and that immediately after their passing away there existed what was commanded to exist, and so on in this vein, in accordance with the things familiar to us in our fleshly life. While such souls are still childish and weak, they are nursed at the bosom of this low style of speaking as at their mother's breast. Their faith is built up in the healthiest way, enabling them to have a sure and fixed belief that it was God who made all the living things their senses can behold as they look about themselves, in all their wondrous variety. But should some soul disdain what it sees as the low style of Moses's words, and in pride and weakness reach out beyond the cradle in which it was nursed, then, poor soul! a sad tumble it will have. Then, Lord God, have mercy, and let not *them that pass by* (Lam. 1.12) trample on that unfledged chick, but let it live, till it can fly.

12.28.38 Others, no longer using these words as a nest, but treating them rather as spreading orchard, spy hidden fruit in them and flap happily down, chattering as they search out and tear at the fruit. They see, when they read or hear these words, that your abiding permanence, O God eternal, surpasses all time, whether past or future; that there is nothing in your temporal creation that you have not made; that your will, being the same as you are, is in no way changing, nor is it now what it was not before. It was by prompting of this will that you made everything; not out of yourself, making your likeness the form of all things, but out of nothing, making a formless unlikeness which, according to the level of understanding appointed for and given to each thing according to its kind, could, by returning to you, the One, be formed through your likeness. Thus all things came to be and are exceeding good (cf Gen. 1.31), whether they remain round about you or whether by slowly distancing themselves in time or place they make or undergo beauteous variations. This is what such people see and rejoice to see in the light of your truth, as much as they can here.

12.28.39 One of them concentrates on the words, *in the beginning God made . . .* , and by 'beginning' he understands 'wisdom', for that too *speaks to us* (Jn 8.25).[12] Another one likewise concentrates on the same words, and takes 'beginning' to mean the outset of creation, understanding *in the beginning God made . . .* as meaning 'first God made . . .'. And of those who understand *in the beginning* to mean that in wisdom you made heaven and earth, one takes the phrase 'heaven and earth' itself to be a name given to the matter from which heaven and earth were created, while another regards them as beings each with their own distinct form, and another takes one, called 'heaven', to be a formed, spiritual entity, and 'earth' to another entity, a formless being composed of corporeal matter. Even those who understand the words 'heaven and earth' to mean still formless matter from which heaven and earth were to be formed, do not all understand it the same way; one understands it to be the material from which the creation perceptible to the intellect and senses was brought to perfection, another takes it to be the material only, for the physical and sensible world contains in her ample lap all beings visible and perceptible. And even those commentators who think that in this passage 'heaven and earth' means created things divided into their proper forms and set in

12 *'speaks to us'*. For Augustine's exegesis of this obscure phrase, see 11.8.10.

their proper place, do not understand all in the same way. One thinks it means all creation visible and invisible, another that it means only the visible creation, in which we can look up and see the heaven in all its radiance, or look down and see the earth in all its darkness, and all things that are in heaven and earth.

12.39.40 But a commentator who takes the words *In the beginning God made . . .* to mean 'First God made . . .' cannot give a true interpretation of the words 'heaven and earth', except by taking them to mean the material for the making of heaven and earth – the whole creation, that is, the creation perceptible only to the intellect, and the physical creation. If he takes it to mean that the universe was already formed, then we may reasonably ask him what, if God made the universe thus, did God do thereafter? Our commentator will find that once the whole universe is created, there is nothing left to be created, and will be reluctant to hear the question, 'How can it be that God created the world first, if thereafter he did nothing?'

But if our commentator says that creation was at first formless, he is not guilty of self-contradiction, provided he can understand the difference between precedence in eternity, precedence in time, precedence in preferability, and precedence in origin. Precedence in eternity is how God precedes all things; precedence in time is how the flower precedes the fruit; precedence in preferability is how the fruit precedes the flower; precedence in origin is how the sound precedes the singing. Of these four that I have listed, the first and the last are very hard to understand, the middle two very easy. It is no common thing, O Lord, to behold your eternity which, without changing, makes all changeable things and thereby precedes them; it is a thing exceeding hard to contemplate. And whose mental perception is so sharp that without great difficulty he can tell how sound precedes singing – singing being formed sound, and it being possible for something not formed to exist, but not for the non-existent to be formed? Thus the material precedes what is made from it. Material does not precede what is made from it through having made it, being itself the object of the action of making; nor does material precede what is made in temporal distance. We do not at some earlier time utter formless, unsung sounds, which at some later time we join or mould into the form of a song, as we fashion wood into a chest or silver into a vase; all materials of this sort precede the things formed of them in time also, but in the case of singing this is not so. When we sing, we hear the sound of the song; we do not first hear the formless sound and later the sound formed into song. The initial sound, whatever it is, passes away; nothing of it is left to be found, recovered, and by cunning skill put back together. Song, therefore, is transformed in the course of its sound, that sound being the material from which it is made. In short, sound is formed into shape so that the song might exist. So also, as I was saying, the material of sound precedes the form of song. It does not precede it through having power to make it, nor is the sound the craftsman of the song, but is subject to the will of the singer, coming as it does from the body which makes the song. Nor does it precede in time, being uttered simultaneously with the song; nor in preferability, as the sound is not more desirable than the song, inasmuch as the song is not only sound but sound given a beautiful form. But it does precede the song in origin; the song is not formed that sound might exist, but the sound is formed that the song might exist.

Let him who can pursue this analogy, and interpret the passage to mean that what was made first was the raw material of the universe; and that it was called 'heaven and earth' because from it heaven and earth were made. It was not made first in time, seeing as it is things with form that make use of time, whereas the primal material was without form. Nor can anything be said of it except that, although it is, so to speak, prior in time, it is far lower in preferability, since all things with form are better than those without; and that it is preceded in eternity by the Creator, who from nothing made the material from which something could be made.

12.30.41 Given this diversity of true interpretations, 'truth gives birth to harmony'.[13] *God have mercy upon us* (Ps. 67.1 [Ps. 66.2]),

13 ' "truth gives birth to harmony" '. An adaptation of Terence, *Andria* 68, 'truth gives birth to hatred'.

and grant us to *use the Law lawfully* (2Tim. 1.8), holding on to
the purpose for which the commandments were given, and in
pure love. And if anyone asks me which of these things your
servant Moses meant by those words, then this is not the voice
of my confessions if I do not confess to you that I do not know.
Yet I know that all those interpretations are true. Of the carnal-
minded I say nothing – I have said as much of them as I judged
proper; they are little children, but promising ones, and are not
deterred by the words of your Scriptures which, few and lowly
as they are in style, speak so eloquently and so profoundly. But
let all of us whom I acknowledge to perceive truths in those
Scriptures and to utter them, *love one another, and likewise love
you, our God* (Deut. 6.5, Matt. 22.37–9, Mk 12.30–1, Lk 10.27, 1Jn
4.7), the fount of truth, if we are indeed thirsty for the Truth,
and not for vanities. And let us honour your servant, the Dispenser of your sacred Scripture, full of your Spirit, and believe
that by your revelation he had in mind when writing these words
what is most excellent in the light of truth, and most salutary
and beneficial.

12.31.42 When, therefore, someone says, 'Moses meant what
I understand by this passage,' and someone else says, 'No, he
meant what I understand by it,' I think I show more proper
caution in saying: Why not both, if both are true? And if someone sees a third meaning in these words, or a fourth, or any
truth at all, why should we not believe that Moses, through
whom the one God tempered the Holy Scriptures to the minds
of the many readers who would see various truths in them, himself saw them all? For my part, I am bold to avow that my
own attitude is thus: if I were to write something of Scriptural
authority, I would rather write in such a way that whatever truth
one could comprehend about those matters, it would be echoed
in my words, rather than write one true opinion so plainly as to
exclude other opinions whose falsity could not offend me. I am
reluctant, therefore, my God, to rush into believing that Moses
did not receive a similar gift from you. In writing these words,
Moses perceived and considered every truth that we have been
able to find in them and every truth we have not been able to

find, or have not yet been able to find but which nevertheless can be found in them.

12.32.43 Finally, O Lord, you who are God and not flesh and blood, if there is something that a man cannot fully see, surely it cannot be hidden to your good Spirit, which *leads me also into the land of righteousness* (Ps. 143.10 [Ps. 142.10]), whatever you were intent on revealing to future readers through those words, if even he through whom they were spoken did have in mind only one of the many true interpretations? If this is so, let the interpretation that he had in mind be exalted over all the rest. As for us, O Lord, show us either that meaning or whichever one you will, so long as it is true. Whether you reveal to us what you revealed to Moses or whether you reveal something else that arises from the same words, let it be you that feed us; let no error deceive us.

Behold, O Lord, how many words I have written, how many about how few! What strength of mine could suffice to explain every book of your Scripture in this way, what time would be enough? Let me, then, make my brief confession to you through them; let me choose one interpretation inspired by you; let it be true and sure and good. Even if many spring to mind in passages where many meanings might spring to mind, let this be my confession of faith: if what I say is what your servant meant, so much the better – that is what I should endeavour to do. But if I do not achieve this end, then let what I say be what your Truth means to me through those words – that Truth which spoke to Moses also what it meant to speak.

BOOK THIRTEEN

13.1.1 I call on you, my *God, my Mercy* (Ps. 59.17 [Ps. 58.18]), who made me and did not forget me when I forgot you. I call on you to enter my soul; the soul you make ready to receive you with the longing you inspire in it. Desert me not as I call upon you; you who anticipated me before I called upon you, who pressed on me with manifold and diverse voices, that I should hear you from afar and turn back to you, and call upon you as you called out to me. It is you, O Lord, who wiped clean the record of my ill deserts, not *paying me back at my own hands* (Ps. 18.20 [Ps. 17.21]), with which I rebelled against you; you anticipated my good deserts, paying me back with your hands, with which you made me (cf Ps. 119.72 [Ps. 118.73]). Before I was, you were; I did not exist for you to give me existence; but behold, I am. Your goodness anticipated both your making of me and the material from which you made me. You did not need me, nor am I so good that you, my Lord and my God, should find me any help. I do not serve you as if you would grow weary of your work without me, nor is your authority any the less if I do not obey you. When I worship you, it is not as if I am tending a field, which would be untended without me; you are not unworshipped. Rather I serve you and worship you so that because of you it may be well with me; for it is you who gave me existence, so that it might be well with me.

13.2.2 It is of the fulness of your goodness that your creation exists. Good as it is, it is of no benefit at all to you, nor is it equal with you; but because it was you who enabled it to come to be, it is a good that does not fail.[1] For what were the prior deserts of heaven and earth, which you made in the beginning? Let them declare what were the prior deserts of this spiritual

1 'Good as it is ... that does not fail.' Augustine alludes here to the doctrine of evil as absence of good, steering a path between the Manichaean doctrine of the created world as evil and its creator as a lesser god, and any suggestion that God's goodness would be diminished without the existence of the world.

and this physical entity, which you made in wisdom; why it is that all things, even in their inchoate and formless state, should be dependent on these entities. All created things, according to their kind, whether spiritual or physical, exceed their appointed measure and depart for the distant Land of Unlikeness. What is spiritual but without form is better than any physical object with form, and what is physical and without form is better than utter non-being; yet all would be left hanging formless by your word, were they not called back through that same Word to your unity, given form, and through you, the one highest Good, became all *exceeding good* (Gen. 1.31).

13.2.3 What prior service did physical matter do you, that it should earn the right to exist at all, even in an invisible and formless state? It would not even have existed, even in an invisible and formless state, had you not made it. It could have done you no prior service for just that reason – it did not exist.

Or what prior service did your spiritual creation do you in its inchoate state that it should earn the right to exist, even in a state of flux and darkness like the abyss and unlike you, had it not been turned back through your Word to that Word by which it was made, and being enlightened by it should become light (cf Gen. 1.3, Jn 1.9), not equally with you but conformable to a form equal with you?[2] Just as for a physical object, 'being' is not the same as 'being beautiful' (otherwise it could not be ugly), so for a created spirit 'living' is not the same as 'wise living' (otherwise it would

2 'Or what prior service ... equal to you?' O'Donnell on this passage observes that Book 13 of the *Confessions* deals with the concept of *conversion* ('turning back'), which is seen as metaphysically a similar process to that of *formation*, discussed in Book 12. Central to an understanding of this passage is Rom. 8.29: 'For those whom (God) foreknew he also predestined to be conformed to the image of his Son.' Thus the spiritual creation, on being converted or turned back towards God, begins to reassume the likeness of the Son (who is equal to the Father) through whom it was made. But the whole passage is rich in allusions to earlier parts of the *Confessions*, without which also it is highly opaque. These allusions include references to 'the abyss', the condition of having abandoned God which Augustine introduces at 1.2.2; and the notion of dissimilarity as characteristic of the soul which has abandoned God (contrast 'the Same' at 1.6.10 and elsewhere, a description of God amounting almost to a title).

be unchangeably wise).[3] It is good for it, therefore, to cleave to you always. Having gained the light by turning back to you, it should not by turning away from you lose that light, and slide away into the life which is like the darkness of the abyss. We too, we who are spiritual creatures as regards our soul, had turned from you, our Light, and in that life we *were once darkness* (Eph. 5.8). Even now we labour in the remnants of our time in the dark, until in your only-begotten Son we become the *righteousness that is as the mountains of God*; we who were *your judgements as the great abyss.*[4]

13.3.4 As for the words that you spoke to the first of your created works, *Let there be light* (and there was light) (Gen. 1.3), these I believe can be taken without self-contradiction to be addressed to your spiritual creation; there was by now a life of some sort for you to enlighten. But neither had such a life done you any prior service deserving of existence, to be capable of enlightenment, nor even when it did exist had it done you any prior service, deserving of enlightenment. You would have had no pleasure in it had it remained formless and not become light – which it did, not by existing, but by contemplating the light that enlightens and by cleaving to it. That it had life at all, that it lived a blessed life, it owed only to your grace; it was changed for the better and turned back to that which cannot change either for better or for worse – to that which you alone are, since you alone exist without complexity. For you it is not one thing to live and another to live a blessed life; you *are* blessedness.

13.4.5 What, then, would have been lacking to complete your good even if those things had either not existed at all, or had

3 'Just as ... unchangeably wise'. Another difficult passage. Augustine's meaning is that the mere fact that a spiritual creation exists (i.e., is alive) does not mean that it is wise/philosophical. This good condition it only achieves by adherence to its Creator.

4 '... we who were ... *the great abyss*'. Augustine here fuses 2Cor. 5.21 ('For our sake he made him to be sin who knew no sin, so that in him we might become the righteousness of God') with Ps. 36.6 [Ps. 35.7] ('thy judgements are like the great abyss'). The overall sense is that mankind, *qua* spiritual creature turned away from God, is under the judgement of God; and is comparable to 'the sea' in the creation story of Genesis, inasmuch as both are formless – the sea through being yet unformed, mankind through having lost the form given it at creation.

remained formless? You are yourself that Good. It was not out of need that you made those things; out of the fulness of your goodness you restrained them and turned them back into form, not so as to complete your joy through them. You are perfect, and their imperfection was unpleasing to you; it is from you that they are perfected and become pleasing to you, not as if you were imperfect and needed to be made perfect by their perfection. Your *good Spirit* was *moving over the face of the waters* (Ps. 143.10 [Ps. 142.10], Gen. 1.2), but it was not borne up by the waters, as if resting on them; for when your Spirit is said to rest in something, then your Spirit is making that thing rest in itself. It was your will, incorruptible and unchangeable, sufficient in itself for itself, that was moving on the face of the waters, the life that you had made. 'Living' for that life is not the same as 'living blessedly', for though it lives, it is in flux and clouded by its own darkness. It remains for that life to be turned back to him by whom it was made, and to become more and more alive at the *fount of life*, and *in its light to see light* (Ps. 36.10 [Ps. 35.10]); to be brought to perfection, enlightened, blest.

13.5.6 Behold, my God, I now see *in a riddle* (1Cor. 13.12) the Trinity that you are. You, the Father, in the beginning of our Wisdom, that is, your Wisdom, born of you, equal to you and coeternal with you, namely your Son, made heaven and earth. I have spoken much of the heaven of heaven, of the earth's being invisible and without order, and of the abyss darkened as the spiritual mass, still without form, wandered and would have been cut off from you, had it not been turned back to him from whom came all life of any kind; how being enlightened by him it gained distinct and fair form and became life; and how there came to be the heaven of heaven, which was later made between water and water. By the word 'God' I understood the Father, who made all these things; by the words 'in the beginning' I understood the Son, in whom he made them; and believing as I did that my God was a Trinity, I sought in his holy oracles, and lo! I found the Spirit moving above the waters. Behold the Trinity that is my God – Father, Son and Holy Spirit, the Creator of the whole creation.

13.5.7 But for what reason, O Light that speaks the truth – for it is to you that I apply my heart, lest it teach me vanities; dispel the darkness from my heart and tell me, I beseech you through our mother Love; tell me, I beseech you, for what reason does the Scripture wait until it has mentioned heaven and earth invisible and orderless, and the darkness above the abyss, before speaking of your Spirit? Was it because it was appropriate to hint at it in these terms, saying that it 'was moving over' something? This could not be said unless it were first stated what your Spirit could be understood to be moving over. It was not moving over the Father, nor yet the Son; nor could it rightly be said to be 'moving over' unless it was said *what* it was moving over. First, therefore, the Scripture had to speak of the thing the Spirit was moving over, then the Spirit itself, which could not be described in any other terms than those of 'moving over'.

Why, then, is it inappropriate to indicate the Spirit in any terms other than those of 'moving over'?

13.7.8 Let him whose understanding permits him, pursue the words of your Apostle: *Love has been poured out in our hearts through the Holy Spirit, who has been given to us* (Rom. 5.3). Let him follow the Apostle as he teaches us about spiritual gifts, and *shows us the more excellent way* of love (1Cor. 13.31), *bending the knee before you* (Eph. 3.14) for our sake, that we may *learn the more excellent knowledge of the love of Christ* (Eph. 3.19).

From the very outset, then, the More Excellent was moving over the waters. To whom and how shall I explain how the burden of concupiscence drags us down into this sheer abyss, and how we are raised up by the love which comes through your Spirit, who moved over the waters? To whom and how shall I tell it? It is no physical place in which we are drowned and undrowned. What is more like, and what is more unlike?[5] It is our own attitudes, it is our loves, it is our uncleanness of spirit,

5 'What is more like, and what is more unlike?' An obscure phrase. By 'like' Augustine probably means that excessive human desire (concupiscence) is supremely 'like' the formless abyss, in that they distort the proper form of the human will. By 'unlike', Augustine is probably appealing to his doctrine of God as 'identity' (see note on 9.4.11), the opposite of which being 'unlikeness' (cf 7.10.16).

that flow downwards in their love for the anxieties of life. It is
your holiness that lifts us up with a love for a life free from
anxiety, so that we may *lift up our hearts* (Col. 3.1–2), where your
Spirit moves over the waters; that we may come to that more
excellent rest, when our soul has crossed the *waters that are
without substance* (Ps. 124.5 [Ps. 123.5]).

13.8.9 Angels would surely have been carried away by this
downward flux; man's very soul would surely have been carried
away. Between them they would have revealed the abyss into
which the entire spiritual creation had fallen, in all its darkness.
But from the first you had said, *Let there be light*, and there was
light, and everything in your heavenly City that had understanding obeyed and clung to you, resting in your Spirit which
moves unchangingly over all that is changeable. Had you not
done so, the very heaven of heaven would, in itself, have been a
dark abyss; but *now it is light in the Lord* (Eph. 5.8). Wretched
and restless indeed are those spirits which are carried away by
this downward flux, revealing the depths of their darkness,
stripped as it is of the raiment of your light; but through that
very restlessness you give abundant proof of the greatness of
your rational creation, which is unsatisfied and cannot know
blessedness and rest in anything less than you, and hence not
even in itself. *For it is you, O Lord, who will lighten our darkness*
(Ps. 18.28 [Ps. 17.28]); *from you arise our raiment, and our darkness
shall be as the noonday.*[6] Give yourself to me, my God; restore
yourself to me. Behold, I love you; if that is not enough, let me
love you more strongly. I cannot measure and know how much
love I lack; how much more would be enough to make my life
run to your embraces and not turn aside until it was *hidden in
the hidden depth of your countenance* (Ps. 31.28 [Ps. 30.28]). This
alone I know: that without you it is not well with me, not only
outwardly but also within myself, and that all my wealth that is
not my God, is poverty.

6 '... *from you* ... *as the noonday*'. Is. 58.10. Augustine's rather curious text is
based on a misreading of the Greek; at some point, either a Greek or a Latin
scribe has misread the correct reading *iamata* ('healings') as (*h*)*imatia* ('clothing'). Augustine would presumably be at least as concerned with deriving a true
exegesis as with establishing the true reading.

13.9.10 Was not the Father or the Son moving over the waters?
If these words are understood as referring to physical place, then
neither was the Spirit moving over the waters. If, however, the
words are taken to mean that the Godhead stood out unchangeable over all that is changeable, then all three – the Father and
the Son and the Holy Spirit – were moving over the waters.
Why, then, is it said only of the Spirit? Why is it said of him
only, seeing as it seems to refer to the place where he was? The
Spirit is not place; it is said of him only that he is your gift. It is
in your gift that we rest, and there that we enjoy you. Our rest
is our proper place. It is love that takes us there, and your good
Spirit that *lifts us up from the gates of death* (Ps. 9.13 [Ps. 9.14–15]).
In your good will is our peace (cf Lk 2.14). Physical objects tend
by their weight towards their proper place. Weight does not
only tend towards the lowest point; it tends towards its proper
place. Fire tends upwards, a pebble downwards. It is in accordance with their weight that they act, and it is their own places
that they seek. Oil poured underneath water rises up on top of
the water; water poured on top of oil sinks under the oil. It is in
accordance with their weight that they act, and it is their own
places that they seek. Things disordered are restless; when they
are put in order, they find their rest. My weight is my love; by
that love I move in whatever direction I move. By your gift we
are set on fire and borne upwards; we are set ablaze and start to
move. We climb the upward path in our hearts, and sing the
Song of Ascents.[7] By your fire, by your good fire we are set
ablaze and begin to move, going upwards towards *the peace of
Jerusalem*; for *I rejoiced with those who said to me, We will go into
the house of the Lord* (Ps. 122.1, 6 [Ps. 121.1, 6]). There will your
good will find a place for us, and we shall wish for nothing other
than to *remain there for eternity* (Ps. 61.6 [Ps. 60.8]).

13.10.11 Blessed is that created thing which has known no other
state of being, even though it would itself have been something else, had not your Gift, which moves over everything

7 '... Song of Ascents'. A reference to Ps. 84.7 [Ps. 83.6], combined with a
reference to the name 'Song of Ascents' given to Ps. 120–34 [Ps. 119–33], the
psalms of the pilgrims going up to Jerusalem.

changeable, taken it up as soon as it was made, letting no time intervene between its creation and the moment when you called it, saying, *Let there be light*, and it was light![8] In our case, there is a distinction of time; we *were darkness, and have been made light* (Eph. 5.8). But it was declared what this created thing should be, in case it were not enlightened; and it was so declared as if this created thing were at some previous time dark and subject to flux, in order to make clear the reason why it was made. It was made in order to be something else; to turn back towards the unfailing light, and to be light. Let him who can, understand this, and let him seek understanding from you. Why should he trouble me, as if I could *enlighten any man that comes into the world* (Jn 1.9)?

13.11.12 Who can understand the omnipotent Trinity? And yet who does not speak of the Trinity, if he does indeed speak of a trinity? Rare is the soul that, in speaking of a trinity, knows what it is saying. Men struggle and contend, but without peace no one sees that vision.[9] I would have men consider three things which are within themselves. These three things are far different from the Trinity, but I say this so that men should exert themselves over this analogy, find it good, and perceive how far short it falls. The three things I have in mind are: being, knowing and willing. I am and I know and I will. I am knowing and willing, I know that I am and that I will, I will to be and know. Let him who can, see through these three things how impossible it is to separate a life, a life that is one, a mind that is one, a being that is one; and how impossible it is to make a distinction – yet a distinction there is. It is open to any man to do this; all he need

8 'Blessed ... it was light'. O'Donnell follows Knauer in taking the 'created thing' to be 'the heaven of heavens', the object of so much exegesis in Book 12. It seems preferable to take it to refer to light; Augustine has by now arrived at Gen. 1.3. The point seems to be that although light owes its light-ness to its reflection of God, the true Light, none the less it has never fallen away from that Light, even though it is a created thing and hence mutable.

9 '... peace ... vision'. A phrase unexplained in itself, but perhaps another allusion to Jerusalem (as in the references to Ps. 122 in 13.9.10). Augustine elsewhere cites the gloss of Jerusalem as 'vision of peace' (e.g. *Literal Commentary on Genesis* 28).

do is to consider himself and see it, and tell me. But when he has found some meaning in this analogy and acknowledged it, let him not think that he has discovered what is unchangeably above all such things, which unchangeably is and unchangeably knows and unchangeably wills. Whether it is because of these three things there is a Trinity, or whether in each of them all three are present, or whether in some wondrous way, simple and complex, bound within its own boundless borders, in which the Same is both known to itself and sufficient to itself in its rich store of unity, who can readily contemplate? Who can in any way tell? Who can pronounce on it in any way, however rash?

13.12.13 Go on with your confession, O faith of mine. Say to the Lord your God: *Holy, Holy, Holy, Lord* (Ps. 55.5 [Ps. 54.6]), my God, in your name were we baptized, O Father, Son and Holy Spirit; in your name we baptize, O Father, Son and Holy Spirit. For in us also has our God through his Christ made heaven and earth, his spiritual and his physical churches. Before it received form from your instruction, the earth of which we are made was invisible and without order; *we were covered with the darkness* (Ps. 55.5 [Ps. 54.6]) of ignorance, for *according to man's wickedness do you instruct him* (Ps. 39.13 [Ps. 38.12]), and *your judgements are as the great abyss* (Ps. 36.6 [Ps. 35.7]). But your Spirit was moving over the waters; pitiable as we were, your pity did not abandon us. You said, *Let there be light. Repent, for the kingdom of heaven is at hand* (Matt. 3.2, 4.17). *Repent, and let there be light. Our soul was sore troubled within us, and we remembered you, O Lord, and the land of Jordan and the hill* (Ps. 42.8 [Ps. 41.6-7]) which is *equal to you*,[10] but which for our sake became low. We were unhappy at our darkness; we turned back to you, and there was light. And so, behold, *we were once darkness and now we are light in the Lord* (Eph. 5.8).

13.13.14 But this is still so *by faith, not yet by sight* (2Cor. 3.7). *It is by hope that we are saved; but if we see what we hope for, it is not hope* (Rom. 8.24). *Abyss* still *calls upon abyss*, but still *with the*

10 '... *the land of Jordan ... equal to you*'. Augustine is here interpreting the 'hill' of the Psalm as referring to Jesus. For the equality of Jesus with the Father, see Phil. 2.6, alluded to here.

voice of your waterfloods (Ps. 42.9 [Ps. 41.8]). Even he who says, *I could not speak to you as if to spiritual people, but as to carnal* (1Cor. 3.1) — even he does not yet *think that he has understood, but forgetful of what is past stretches out for what is before* (Phil. 3.13), *burdened with groaning* (2Cor. 5.4), and his *soul thirsts for the living God, as harts desire the water brooks, saying 'When shall I come before him?'* (Ps. 42.1–2 [Ps. 41.2–3]). He *longs to be clothed with his dwelling place which is from heaven* (2Cor. 5.2), and calls upon the lower abyss, saying, *Be not conformed to this world, but be reformed in newness of mind* (Rom. 12.2), and: *Do not be children in your mind, but in wickedness be children, that you may be made perfect in mind* (1Cor. 14.20) and: *O foolish Galatians, who has bewitched you?* (Gal. 3.1). But all this he says no longer in his own voice; it is in the voice of you who *sent down your Spirit from on high* (Wisdom 9.17) through him who *went up on high* (Ps. 68.18 [Ps. 67.19]) and *opened the floodgates of his gifts* (Malachi 3.10), so that *the waters of the flood should make glad your City* (Ps. 46.4 [Ps. 45.5]). For him *the friend of the bridegroom sighs* (Jn 3.29), having now the *first-fruits of the Spirit within him, but yet groaning inwardly, waiting for his adoption, the redemption of his body* (Rom. 8.22–3). It is for him that he sighs, being a part of the Bride's body; it is for him that he is jealous, being the friend of the Bridegroom. For the Bridegroom, not for himself, is he jealous; it is in the voice of your waterfloods, not in his own voice, that he calls upon the other abyss. For that abyss he is in his jealousy *afraid, lest just as the serpent deceived Eve through his guile, so also their minds may be corrupted and fall away from the chastity that is in* the Bridegroom (2Cor. 11.3), *your Only-begotten Son* (Jn 1.18). What is that Light of our sight? When we *see him as he is* (1Jn 3.2), that will be an end of the *tears that are become my food day and night, while continually men say to me, Where is your God?* (Ps. 42.3 [Ps. 41.4]).

13.14.15 I too say, 'Where are you, my God?' See where he is. *I rest a little while in you* (Job 32.20), *pouring out my soul in the voice of exultation and confession, the sound of one that keeps the feast day* (Ps. 42.4–5 [Ps. 41.5]). And yet my heart is still full of sorrow because it slips away and becomes 'abyss', or rather because it perceives that it is still abyss. My faith, the faith you have kindled in the night to light my way, says, *Why are you so sorrowful, O my soul, and why do you trouble me so sorely? Hope in the Lord* (Ps. 42.6–7, 14–15 [Ps. 41.6, 12]); *his word is a lantern to your feet* (Ps. 119.105 [Ps. 118.105]). Hope and persevere, until the night, the mother of the wicked, be past, and an end come to the anger of the Lord. *We were once children of that anger* (Eph. 2.3); *we were once darkness* (Eph. 5.8), and the residue of that darkness we drag around in our bodies, dead as they are because of sin, *till the day breaks and the shadows vanish* (Song of Songs 2.17). Hope in the Lord; *in the morning I shall arise and meditate; I shall always make my confession to him. In the morning I shall arise and see the salvation of my countenance, even my God,*[11] who *by the Spirit that dwells in us will give life even to our mortal bodies* (Rom. 8.11); for that Spirit moves in mercy over the inner darkness and flux of our hearts. Through him we have received the pledge (cf 2Cor. 1.22, 5.5) that we are 'light', even while we are still on this pilgrimage; even while it is still by hope that we are saved and made *children of the light and children of the day, not children of the night nor of the darkness* (1Thess. 5.5); though we were once darkness. To human minds there is no clear distinction between us and the children of the darkness; you alone, you who *try our hearts* (Ps. 17.3 [Ps. 16.3], Prov. 17.3), who call the light 'day' and the darkness 'night', divide us from them. Who but you could distinguish between us? *What do we have that we have not received* (1Cor. 4.7) from you, we who are *vessels all shaped from the same metal, some for honour, some for disgrace* (Rom. 9.21)?

13.15.16 And who but you, our God, made us the 'firmament' (cf Gen. 1.7) of authority that is above us in the divine Scriptures? *Heaven will be rolled up like a scroll* (Is. 3.4), and even now is *stretched out like the skin of a tent* (Ps. 104.2 [Ps. 103.2]) above us.[12] Your divine Scriptures are all the more highly exalted in

11 '*in the morning ... even my God.*' A complex of references to Ps. 5.3 [Ps. 5.5], and Ps. 42–3 [Ps. 41–2]

12 '*Heaven will be rolled up ... above us.*' Augustine in this passage plays on the double sense of *pellis* ('skin') as 'tent' (made of leather in antiquity) and 'hide' (as below). There may also be a third sense; in late antiquity parchment, made of animal skin, increasingly displaced papyrus as a writing material.

their authority inasmuch as the mortals through whom you dispensed them to us have died the mortal death. And you know, O Lord, you know how you clothed mankind in skins when as a result of sin they became mortal (cf Gen. 3.21). Hence you have stretched out like a skin the firmament of your Scriptures, those words of yours that chime out in harmony, which by the ministry of mortals you have set over us. By the very death of the dispensers of your Word, you have stretched out and made fast the authority of the oracles you published through them, till it reaches over all things that are below; not so was their authority made fast and stretched out on high while they were alive. You had not yet stretched out the heaven like a skin; you had not yet spread abroad the report of their death.

13.15.17 Let us see, O Lord, those heavens, the *works of your fingers* (Ps. 8.3 [Ps. 8.4]). Disperse from our eyes the mists with which you have clouded them. In those heavens is your testimony, that *gives wisdom to little children* (Ps. 19.7 [Ps. 18.8]). *Bring forth*, my God, *perfect praise from the mouth of infants and sucking babes* (Ps. 8.2 [Ps. 8.3]). No other books have I known that can so *bring down the proud* (Ezek. 10.6), and so bring down *the enemy and the defender* (Ecclesiasticus 30.6) – him who, by defending his own sins, refuses the reconciliation you offer. No other oracles have I known, O Lord, no others have I known so pure, that urge me to confess to you, that soothe me into *submitting my neck to your yoke* (Matt. 11.29–30), and which bid me worship you without seeking a reward. May I understand these oracles, good Father. I am one of those set under your heavens. Give me this gift of understanding; it is for the sake of us under those heavens that you have made them fast.

13.15.18 There are other *waters that are above this firmament* (Gen. 1.7), I believe; waters that are immortal and hidden from earthly corruption. Let them praise your name; *let the peoples of your angels that are above the heavens praise you* (Ps. 148.2–5). They have no need to look up to this firmament and to read in order to know your word. They see your face for ever, and in it read without syllables of temporal duration the will of your eternal Will. They read, they choose, they love;[13] they are for ever reading, and what they read never passes away. In choosing and loving, they read the very immutability of your counsel. Their book is not closed, neither is their scroll rolled up; you are their book and scroll, and are so for eternity. You have set them in their due place above the firmament. That firmament you have made firm, so that the peoples under it can, in their infirmity, look up to it and recognize your mercy, which makes you, the maker of time, known in time. For in heaven, O Lord, *your mercy and your truth reach to the clouds* (Ps. 36.5 [Ps. 35.6]). *The clouds pass away* (Ps. 18.12 [Ps. 17.13]), heaven remains. Those who preach your word pass from this to another life, whereas your Scripture stretches out over all peoples until the end of time. *Heaven and earth also shall pass away, but your words shall not pass away* (Matt. 24.35). The skin will be rolled up and the *grass* over which it is stretched out will *perish with all its glory, but your word abides for eternity* (Is. 40.6–8). This word now *appears to us not as it is, but in the riddle of the clouds and in the mirror of heaven* (1Cor. 13.12). For though we also are beloved of your Son, *it is not yet apparent what we shall be* (1Jn 3.2). Your Son *waited with nets of the flesh* (Song of Songs 2.9), he spoke lovingly to us, and set us on fire, and we *run after his fragrance* (Song of Songs 1.3, 11). But *when he appears, we shall be like him, for we shall see him as he is* (1Jn 3.2). It will be ours to see him as he is, but it is not yet.

13.16.19 For just as you entirely *are*, so you alone *know*; you unchangeably *are*, you unchangeably *know*, you unchangeably *will*. Your being knows and wills unchangeably; your knowledge is and wills unchangeably; your will is and knows unchangeably. Nor does it seem righteous before you that a changeable creature should know the unchangeable Light which enlightens it, in the same way that the Light knows itself. Therefore my soul is *as a waterless land before you* (Ps. 143.6 [Ps. 142.6]), being as unable

---

13 'They read, they choose, they love'. Latin *legunt, eligunt, diligunt*; the second and third verbs are compounds of the first, which can mean 'to pick' or 'to read'. It is not clear in what sense the angels 'choose' the words they read, and Augustine does not follow up the idea; the suspicion is that he is led into this phrase by his fondness for rhetorical flourishes.

by itself to slake its own thirst as it is unable by itself to enlighten itself. For *with you is the fount of life, in your light shall we see light* (Ps. 36.9 [Ps. 35.10]).

13.17.20 Who is it that has gathered bitter men[14] together into one community? They have the one end and purpose, namely temporal and earthly felicity, to which end they do all they do, however much they are tossed by a tide of countless different concerns. Who is it but you, O Lord, who gave the word that *the waters should be gathered together in one, and that the dry land should appear* (Gen. 1.9), thirsty for you? *The sea also is yours, and you made it, and your hands shaped the dry land* (Ps. 95.5 [Ps. 94.5]). The word 'sea' does not here refer to the bitterness of our wills,[15] but the gathering together of the waters. For you constrain even the evil desires of men's souls and set limits for them, allowing them to proceed only *so far and no further, and making the waves break upon each other* (Job 38.10–11). Thus you make the sea, ordered by your governance that is above all things.

13.17.21 But the *souls that thirst for you* and which *appear before you* (Ps. 42.1–2 [Ps. 41.2–3]) have nothing in common with 'the sea', being set apart from it by their different end and goal. These you water with your hidden sweet spring, so that *the land*

14 Augustine in this passage continues with his interpretation of the creation myth in Genesis, turning now to Gen. 1.9, 'And God said, "Let the water under the heaven be gathered together into one place, and let the dry land appear".' A. here uses the word 'seas' (*mare*, plural *maria*) interchangeably with 'waters', and plays on the similarity between *mare* and the verb *amaricare* (to make/be bitter); with the important distinction that although God made the sea, this does not mean he made human bitterness. The emphasis is instead on the 'gathering together' of humans, bitter as they are.

15 '. . . the bitterness of our wills'. God is repeatedly characterized as 'Sweetness' (first at 1.4.4). Sweet things are intrinsically desirable, as (for Augustine) is God; it is natural that we should find pleasure in them. Some of our actions, those not truly directed towards God, leave a bitter aftertaste; but it was their sweetness that initially attracted us to them. The human condition is repeatedly compared to the sea, usually with reference to its instability rather than its lack of sweetness. Augustine is not suggesting that it is inappropriate to compare human wills to the sea in point of bitterness, but is simply not advancing that interpretation here.

may give its fruit (Ps. 85.12 [Ps. 84.12]). At your command, O Lord God, the land does give its fruit, and our soul brings forth works of mercy *according to its kind* (Gen. 1.12), *loving her neighbour* (Matt. 22.39, Mk 12.31), assisting him in his physical needs, *having in herself seed according to her likeness* (Gen. 1.12). That is to say, so far as lies within our weak nature's power, we sympathize with those in need and help them in the way that we would wish to be helped, if we were in similar need; not only in easy matters, as it were in the green blade, but in sheltering them and aiding them like a strong oak, or like a fruitful tree, willing to do good and to rescue the wronged from the hand of the mighty, providing the sturdy stock of righteous judgement, and sheltering them in its shade.

13.18.22 Even so, O Lord, I beseech you, even so *let truth arise from the earth, and let righteousness look down from heaven* (Ps. 85.11 [Ps. 84.12]), just as you make and give joy and riches. *Let there be lights in the firmament* (Gen. 1.14). *Let us break our bread with the hungry, and let us bring the homeless beggar into our homes; let us clothe the naked, and not despise the servants that are of our kind* (Is. 58.7–8). When these fruits spring from the earth, *see that this is good* (Gen. 1.25), and let temporal light break forth upon us. From this lower fruit of action let us reach for the joys of contemplation, and gain the higher Word of Life. Let us appear like lights in the world, cleaving to the firmament of your Scripture. In that Scripture you reason with us, teaching us to distinguish between things perceptible to the intellect and things perceptible to the senses as it were between day and night; or between souls given over to things perceptible only to the intellect and those given over to things perceptible to the senses. Let it not be you alone who divide light from darkness in the secret place of your discernment, as it was before the firmament came into being; let your spiritual creatures also, whom you have set in the firmament and distinguished by your grace that is made manifest throughout the world, *shine over the earth and divide day from night, and mark the seasons* (Gen. 1.14–18). For *the old times have passed, and behold the new times have come* (2Cor. 5.17); and *our salvation is nearer than when we first believed. The night is far gone, and the day is at hand* (Rom. 13.11–12). You *bless the crown of your year* (Ps. 65.12 [Ps. 64.12]), *sending out the labourers into your harvest* (Matt. 9.38), where *others have laboured* (Jn 4.38) in the sowing. You *send them also into another field, whose harvest is in the end* (Matt. 13.19). To him who prays you grant his prayer; you *bless the years* (Ps. 65.12 [Ps. 64.12]) of the righteous, but you are yourself the Same, and in your own unfailing years (cf Ps. 102.27 [Ps. 101.28], Hebr. 1.12) you prepare a garner for the years that pass away. By your eternal counsel you give heavenly goods to the earth in their due seasons.

13.18.23 *To one man is given through the Spirit a word of wisdom,* as it were a greater light, given for the sake of those who rejoice in the pure radiance of Truth as in the day's beginning. *To another is given by the same Spirit a word of knowledge,* as it were a lesser light. *To another is given faith, to another the gift of curing illnesses, to another the power to work miracles; to another, prophecy; to another, the discernment of spirits; to another, diverse tongues;* all these things are like stars. *It is the one Spirit that does all these things, dividing its gifts as it wills,* and making the lights of heaven clear and manifest, *for the good of all* (1Cor. 12.7–11). As for the 'word of knowledge' – that knowledge contains all the sacred mysteries which, like the moon, alter over time, and the signs by which the other gifts can be recognized, listed in sequence like the stars. And how different are they from the radiance that belongs to wisdom, in which the aforementioned 'day' rejoices, being as they are the *rulers of the night* (Ps. 136.9 [Ps. 135.9])! They are necessary for those to whom your servant wisely foresaw that he *could not speak as if to spiritual men, but as to carnal* (1Cor. 3.2) – even he who *speaks wisdom among the perfect.* But *man in his natural state* (1Cor. 2.6, 14) is *like a little child in Christ, like an unweaned infant* (1Cor. 3.1–2, Hebr. 5.12–14) who, until he is strong enough to take solid food, and his eyes can bear the sight of sunlight, does not leave the night and is content with the light of the moon and the stars. All this you debate most wisely with us, our God, in the Book that is your firmament, reasoning with us and teaching us through wondrous contemplation to discern all things, though they be still spoken of in terms of constellations and seasons and days and years.

13.19.24 But first *wash yourselves, be clean, and remove the wickedness from your souls and from the sight of my eyes,* and *let the dry land appear. Learn to do good, judge for the orphan and do justice to the widow; let the earth bring forth herbs that give sustenance and trees that bear fruit,* and *come, let us reason together, says the Lord* (Is. 1.16–18, Gen. 1.9, 11). *Let there be lights in the firmament of heaven, and let them shine above the earth* (Gen. 1.14–17). The rich man in the Gospel asked the Good Teacher what he should do to gain eternal life (cf Matt. 19.16–22, Mk 10.17–22, Lk 18.18–23). Let the Good Teacher, whom he thought to be a man and no more (though good he is, being God) – let the Good Teacher tell him that if he wishes to come to life, he should keep the Commandments and put aside the bitterness of malice and wickedness; that he should not kill, not commit adultery, not steal, not bear false witness; that the dry land should appear, and that he should bring forth the fruit of honouring his mother and father, and of loving his neighbour. 'All this', said the man, 'I have done.' Whence, then, come all these thorns, if your land is so fruitful? Go and root out those wild brambles of avarice; sell what you own. Give to the poor, and in giving be filled with fruits; you will have treasure in heaven. Follow the Lord, if you wish to be perfect; join yourself to those among whom he who knows what he divides between day and night speaks wisdom. Thus will there be lights for you also in the firmament of heaven. This will only be, if your heart is there; and that will only be if your treasure is there, as you have heard from your Teacher. But the earth is barren and full of sorrow; *the thorns have choked the Word* (Matt. 13.7, 22).

13.19.25 But as for you, *chosen race, the weak of the world* (1Cor. 1.27), who have *left everything to follow the Lord* (Matt. 19.27, Mk 10.28, Lk 18.28), go after him and *confound the strong* (1Cor. 1.27). Go after him, you *lovely feet* (Is. 52.7, Rom. 10.11), and shine in the firmament. *Let the heavens declare his glory* (Ps. 19.1 [Ps. 18.2]), the heavens that divide the light that belongs to those that are perfect, though not yet like the angels, from the darkness that belongs to those that are little children, though not without hope. Shine over all the earth, and let day radiant with the sun proclaim the word of wisdom to day, and night gleaming with the moon declare the word of knowledge to night (Ps. 19.2 [Ps. 18.3], 1Cor. 12.8). The moon and the stars shine for the night, but are not darkened by it; they themselves illuminate it according to their lesser degree. It is as if God says, *Let there be lights in the firmament of heaven* (Gen. 1.18); there is a *sudden sound from heaven, like the onset of a rushing mighty wind*, and there *appear divided up between them tongues as it were of flame, resting above each of them* (Acts 2.2–3); and there are lights in the firmament of heaven, *having the word of life* (Phil 2.15–16). Run in all directions, you holy fires, you lovely fires. *You are the light of the world*, nor are you *under a bushel* (Matt. 5.14–15). Exalted is he to whom you have cloven, and he has exalted you. Run in all directions, and *make him known to all peoples* (Ps. 79.10 [Ps. 78.10]).

13.20.26 Let the sea also conceive and bear your works. *Let the waters bring forth living things that creep* (Gen. 1.20–2). You have become the mouth of God, *separating the costly vessel from the cheap* (Jer. 15.19); through you he says, *Let the waters bring forth* not a *living soul* (Gen. 1.20) – for that the earth will bring forth – but 'living things that creep, and birds that fly above the earth'. For through the works of your saints your sacred mysteries have 'crept in' among the waves of worldly temptations, through baptism steeping the nations in your Name. Among these sacred mysteries are the mighty wonders you work, which are like the 'mighty whales'. There are also the voices of your messengers that fly above the earth, in accordance with the 'firmament' that is your Scriptures. Those Scriptures are set out as the authority under which they fly wherever they go. *There is neither speech nor language where their voices are not heard; their sound is gone out into every land, and their words to the ends of the earth* (Ps. 19.4 [Ps. 18.4–5]). For you, O Lord, have *blessed them and multiplied them* (Gen. 1.22).

13.20.27 Am I speaking falsely? Am I confusing these things as they are in the firmament of heaven, radiant and accessible only to the mind, with their physical outworkings in this turbulent sea under the firmament of heaven? Am I mixing up one and the other? There are some things, like the lights of wisdom and knowledge, of which we have knowledge that is fixed and defined within certain limits, not reproducing or increasing. These things work themselves out in many and various physical ways. One thing grows from another; you have blessed them, and they multiply, O God; you have had pity on our mortal senses with their fussy tastes, and arranged things so that what, when considered by the mind, is one object, can be expressed and symbolized through physical motions in many ways. These things have been brought forth by the waters, but they have done so at your word. These things have been brought forth by the needs of those people who are estranged from your eternal truth, but in accordance with your Gospel; the very waters that cast them up were those whose bitterness and sickness were the reason why they came forth at your word.

13.20.28 All things are beautiful, you being their maker; and behold, you, the Maker of all things, are ineffably more beautiful. Had Adam not fallen away from you, there would not have poured forth from his womb the sea brine that is the human race, with its depths of curiosity, its storms of pride, its unceasing ebb and flow. There would have been no need for your ministers to perform in physical and perceptible fashion their mystical deeds and sayings in its many waters. This is how the 'creeping things and flying things' have now come to appear to me; and even if men are steeped and initiated in them and are subject to these physical sacraments, they will make no further progress unless their soul in its different degree is revived, and having heard the word that marks the initiation, looks to its fulfilment.

13.21.29 So it is that by your Word it was not the deeps of the sea but the land, now separated from the bitterness of the waters, which brought forth not 'living things that creep and fly', but a 'living soul'. Nor does this soul have any more need of baptism, as the gentiles do, as it did when covered by the waters; for since you laid it down that baptism is the way to enter the

Kingdom of Heaven, there is no other way to enter it. Nor does this soul seek *mighty works and wonders* (Ps. 106.22 [Ps. 105.21–2]) to produce faith; it is not one who *does not believe unless he see signs and portents* (Jn 4.48). The faithful land is now distinct from the sea, with its bitter waters of unfaithfulness, and *tongues are a sign not for the faithful, but for the unfaithful* (1Cor. 14.22).

Nor does the land you have 'established above the waters' need that race of flying things which the waters brought forth at your Word. *Send upon that land your Word* (Ps. 147.15) through your messengers. It is their works I am relating, but *you are the one that works in them* (Phil. 2.13); and they are the ones who work out the living soul. It is the land that brings forth this soul; it is for the sake of the 'land' they do these things on it, just as it was for the sake of the sea that they made 'living things that creep and that fly in the firmament of heaven'. The earth has no need of these creatures, even though it does draw fish from the deep and eat it[16] at the *table you have prepared in the sight* (Ps. 23.5 [Ps. 22.5]) of the believers; it was in order to feed the dry land that it was drawn up from the deep. Birds, too, are the offspring of the sea, but are multiplied upon earth. The faithlessness of men was the reason for the utterances of the first tellers of the gospel; but they encourage the faithful also, and are blessed by them in manifold ways from day to day. But the living soul takes its first beginning from the earth; it can only benefit those already faithful, helping them to *keep themselves from the love of this world* (James 1.27), that their soul might *be alive to you* (2Cor. 5.15). That soul which was *dead while it lived for pleasures* (1Tim. 5.6), for those pleasures, O Lord, bring death; but *you are the life and pleasure of the pure in heart* (2Tim. 2.22).

13.21.30 Let your ministers now work on the earth; not, as they do in the waters of faithlessness, proclaiming and speaking through wonders and sacraments and mystic utterances, where ignorance, in paying attention to them, gives birth to astonishment, and is frightened at your hidden signs – for such is the

---

16 '... draw fish from the deep and eat it'. A reference to the Eucharist; see note on 13.23.34.

first approach to faith for the children of Adam who have forgotten you, *hiding themselves from your face* (Gen. 3.8) and
becoming the abyss. Let your ministers work also in the dry
land, distinct as it now is from the sucking waves of the abyss;
let them be a *form and pattern for the faithful* (1Thess. 1.7), living
before them and stirring them up to imitate them. Let them not
hear and hear only, but hear and do: *Seek the Lord, and your soul
will live* (Ps. 69.33 [Ps. 68.33]), and let the earth bring forth a
living soul. *Be not conformed to this world* (Rom. 12.2), but keep
yourselves from it. The soul lives by avoiding the things in quest
of which it dies. *Keep yourselves from the wildness and bestiality of
pride, from the sloth and pleasure of luxury, and from knowledge
falsely so called* (1Tim. 6.20), that your wild beasts may be gentle,
your flocks tame, your serpents harmless. These are an allegory
of the emotions of the soul; but all loftiness of pride, all delight
in lust, and all venom of curiosity – these are the emotions of a
dead soul. For a dead soul is not so dead that it is utterly without
movement; it is by *falling away from the source of life* (Jer. 2.13)
that it dies, and by so doing it is taken up by the passing world
and is made to conform to it.

13.21.31 But your Word, O God, is the *source of eternal life* (Jn
4.14), and does not pass away. Your Word checks our falling
away, saying to us, *Be not conformed to this world*, but let the
earth bring forth at the source of life a soul that lives, a soul
that in accordance with your Word spoken by your Evangelists
practises continence, *imitating the imitators of your Christ* (1Cor.
11.1). This is the meaning of the words 'according to its kind';
that *a man strives to be like his friend* (Ecclesiasticus 4.4). *Be like
me*, says the Apostle, *for I am like you* (Gal. 4.12). Thus in the
living soul will there be beasts that are good and gentle in their
actions. For you have commanded us, saying, *In gentleness perform your works, and you will be loved by all men* (Ecclesiasticus
3.19). Your flocks too will be tame if, *having eaten, they do not
have too much, nor, having not eaten, do they have too little* (1Cor.
8.8). Your serpents also will be good, not skilled in hurting, but
cunning at avoiding what should be avoided, and seeking to
know the temporal world only so far as is enough for them to

gain through things created an intellectual glimpse of eternity.
For all these animals are obedient to reason, when being checked
from their progress towards death they live and are good.

13.22.32 There will come a point, O Lord our God, our Creator, when our inclinations towards love of the world, through
which we were dying in our ill-living, are checked; when our
soul has come alive by living a good life, and has embraced the
word that you spoke through your Apostle, '*Be not conformed to
this world.*' At that point, the words you added immediately
afterwards will come true: *Be reformed in newness of mind* (Rom.
12.2). No longer shall we live 'according to our kind', as if
imitating whoever happens to have gone immediately before
us, and rather than living according to the example of a man
who is better than us. You did not say, 'Let there be man
according to his kind,' but, *Let us make men in our image and
likeness* (Gen. 1.26), so that we should prove what is your will.
For this reason your minister, having *begotten children by your
Gospel* (1Cor. 4.12), and, not wishing to have them for ever
infants to be fed on milk (1Cor. 3.1–2) and tended as if by a wet-
nurse, said, *Be reformed in newness of mind, that you may prove
what is the will of God, what is good and well-pleasing and perfect*
(Rom. 12.2). Hence you do not say, 'Let there be man', but 'Let
us make man'; nor do you say, 'according to his kind', but 'in
our image and likeness'. He that is renewed in mind and has
gained an intellectual glimpse of the truth does not need
another human to show him the way, nor to imitate his own
kind; but with you showing him the way he proves for himself
what is your will, what is good and well-pleasing and perfect.
You teach him – for he is now capable of perceiving it – to see
the trinity of the Unity, and the unity of the Trinity. Hence it
is said in the plural, 'Let us make man', then it proceeds in the
singular, 'And God made man'; then, having said in the plural,
'in our image', it proceeds in the singular, 'in the image of God'.
Thus *a man is renewed in recognizing according to his image the
God who created him* (Col. 3.10); and having becoming a spiritual man, he judges all things that are to be judged, but is
himself judged by no one.

13.23.33 But this 'judging all things' – what does it mean? That he *has authority over the fishes of the sea and the birds of the air and all flocks and beasts, over all the earth and all things that creep upon the earth* (Gen. 1.26). This he does through his mental understanding, through which he *perceives the things that are of the Spirit of God* (1Cor. 2.14). Otherwise, *man being in honour is without understanding; he is compared and likened to the brute beasts* (Ps. 49.13, 20 [Ps. 48.13, 21]). So it is in your Church, our God; according to the grace you have given her (for *we are your handiwork, created for good works*) (Eph. 2.10), there are some who are set in spiritual authority, and some who are subject to those in authority. It was only in spiritual grace that *you made mankind male and female* (Gen. 1.27),[17] there being *neither male nor female* in physical gender, just as *there is neither Jew nor Greek, neither slave nor free* (Gal. 3.28). But the spiritual, whether they are in authority or whether they are subject to it, judge spiritually. They judge not of the spiritual intelligences that shine in the firmament; it would not be right for them to judge of such an exalted authority. Nor do they judge of your Scripture itself, even if there are things in it that are not radiantly clear; we submit our intellect to that Scripture, and hold it as certain that what is written there is right and true, even if it is closed to our sight. For a man, even one that is *spiritual, renewed in recognizing according to his image the God who created him* (Col. 3.9–10), should be *a doer of the Law and not a judge of it* (James 4.11). Nor does the spiritual judge of the difference between spiritual and carnal men; these are known to your eyes, our God, but to us their nature has not yet been revealed by the works, so that *by their fruits we might know them* (Matt. 7.20). You, O Lord, know them already, and have divided and called them in

---

17 '... *male and female*'. The precise meaning is unclear, but at least two interpretations are possible. Augustine *may* be suggesting that women are spiritually inferior to men, and that the essential difference between the sexes is this spiritual one. But it is more in keeping with his exegetical technique to take the phrase 'men and women' allegorically. Women *are* created physically weaker than men; but the fact that not all of humankind are equally strong physically is no more than a metaphor for the fact that some members of the Church are *spiritually* stronger than others. This does not mean, of course, that Augustine's views are going to correspond with modern views on gender relations.

secret, before the firmament came into being. Nor yet does a man, spiritual though he be, judge of the turbulent peoples of this world; for what business is it of his to judge of those outside, ignorant as he is of who will come from there into the sweetness of your grace, and who will remain in the perpetual bitterness that is impiety?

13.23.34 Man, then, whom you 'made in your image', has not received authority over the lights of heaven, nor over the hidden heaven itself, nor over day and night, which you named before the establishing of heaven, nor over the gathered waters, that is, the sea.

But he has received authority over the fishes of the sea and the birds of the air, over all flocks and all the earth, and over all things that creep upon the earth. He judges and approves whatever he finds right, and rebukes whatever he finds wrong. He does so both through those solemn sacraments in which those whom your mercy tracks down amid the many waters are initiated, and through the solemn sacrament symbolized by the fish raised up from the deep for 'the land' to eat in all due piety. He does so through verbal symbols and expressions subject to the authority of your Scripture, which are like the birds flitting beneath the firmament. He does so in interpreting, explaining, expatiating and debating these symbols; he does so in blessing you and calling upon you.[18] The signs burst forth from their lips

18 'He judges and approves ... calling upon you.' This sentence is, in effect, a summary of the work of the priest. The 'solemn sacraments' are baptism (the 'many waters' derive from Song of Songs 8.7, 'Many waters cannot quench love'). The 'fish' is a symbol of the Eucharist; the starting point for this is probably the fish prepared by the risen Jesus for his disciples at Jn 21.9–14, which comes to be identified with Jesus himself through the famous ICHTHYS acrostic (Iesous CHristos THeo (h)Yios Soter, 'Jesus Christ, Son of God, Saviour). The other activities of the priest are as preacher and exegete (the 'firmament' being the firm truth of the Scriptures), and as leader in worship. What is remarkable about the final catalogue of activities is the legitimation given to various forms of linguistic usage. Augustine, having started out as a schoolboy doing rhetorical exercises on pagan themes, having renounced the profession of rhetoric at the time of his conversion, here reaffirms the value of knowing how to use language, provided his new linguistic expert practises within a Christian context.

and resound, that *the people may answer Amen* (Deut. 27.15). He utters all these physical sounds for the sake of the 'abyss' that is the world, and of the flesh in its blindness; the things he speaks of are invisible to the fleshly mind, and they must be dinned into his ears. Thus although the birds multiply on the land, they take their beginning from the waters. The spiritual man judges by approving what he finds right and rebuking what he finds wrong in the works and habits of the faithful; in almsgiving that is like the 'fruitful earth', in the taming of the emotions that is like the 'living soul', *in chastity, in fasting* (2Cor. 6.3–6), in pious thoughts of the things perceptible to the physical senses. These are the things of which he is now said to 'judge', which he has authority also to correct.

13.24.35 But what is this, what manner of prophetic mystery? You bless men, O Lord, and bid them *increase and multiply and fill the earth* (Gen. 1.28). Do you give us no indication of its meaning, so that we can understand it at least to some extent? Why did you not likewise bless the light that you called day, nor the firmament of heaven, nor the sun and moon, nor the stars, nor the land and sea? I would say, O our God, who created us in your image, that it was your will to bestow the gift of this blessing upon mankind to be his own, were it not that you have also blessed fish and sea monsters in this way; they too increase and multiply and fill the waters, and birds also multiply on land. Likewise I would say that this blessing applied to those kinds of creature which reproduce from within themselves, if I found it resting on trees and bushes and on land animals. But as it is, the words *increase and multiply* were not spoken either to plants or trees, nor to beasts and serpents, although all of these, like fish and birds and men, increase and maintain their race by reproduction.

13.24.36 What, then, am I to say, O Truth, my Light? That all this is empty and idly spoken? Heaven forbid, O Father of piety! Heaven forbid that the servant entrusted with your Word should speak so. Even if I do not understand what you mean by this saying, let better men – that is, men with more understanding than I – make proportionately better use of it, *each one according to the wisdom you have given him* (Rom. 12.3, 1Cor. 3.5). But let my confession be pleasing in your eyes, when I confess to you, O Lord, that I believe that you did not speak in this way for nothing. And as I am reading this passage, I shall not leave unsaid the meaning that it suggests to me; for what it suggests is true, and I do not see anything to prevent me from understanding the words of your Scriptures in a figurative sense. I know that what the mind takes in in a single way can be expressed through a multitude of physical signs, and that what the mind takes in in a multitude of ways can be expressed through a single physical sign. Consider the simple command to love God and one's neighbour; in what a multitude of sacred mysteries does that find physical expression, in how many countless tongues, and in each tongue how many countless modes of speech! So it is that the offspring of the waters increase and multiply. Consider, then, reader, whoever you are: the Scripture proclaims to us in one way and in a single voice, that 'in the beginning God made heaven and earth'. Can we not understand this in a multitude of ways, not deceived by fallacies but pursuing interpretations which may differ but still be true? So it is that offspring of men increase and multiply.

13.24.37 If, then, we consider the nature of things not allegorically but in their proper sense, then the words 'Go forth and multiply' are appropriate to all creatures which reproduce by seed. If, however, we treat them as have been spoken figuratively – and this I think rather to have been what the Scripture intended, for surely it was not for nothing that it bestows that blessing only on the offspring of sea creatures and men – then indeed we do find multiplicities of meaning: your spiritual and physical creatures are like the 'heaven and earth'; righteous and unrighteous souls are like the 'light and darkness'; the holy writers through whom the Law was administered are like the 'firmament that is set between water and water'. Human society and its bitterness is like the 'sea', the zeal of pious souls is like the 'dry land'; *works of mercy in this present life* (1Tim. 4.8) are like 'the plants which cast their seed and the fruitful trees'; the *spiritual gifts manifested for upbuilding* (1Cor. 12.7) are like the 'lights of heaven'; the natural inclinations, when trained in self-restraint, are like the 'living soul'.

In every one of these interpretations, we find the ideas of 'multiplicity' and 'richness' and 'increase'. But what increases and multiplies so that one thing is expressed in many ways, and so that one expression may be understood in many ways, we find only in the physical utterance and the intellectual understanding of symbols. Symbols physically expressed we take to be signified by the 'generations of the waters'; they are necessary to us because of the depths to which our flesh has fallen. Actual things intellectually understood we take to be signified by the 'generations of mankind'; this is because of the fertility of our powers of reason. This, I believe, is why the words 'Go forth and multiply' were spoken by you, O Lord, to each of those two races. In the blessing you granted to us, I see our faculty and power of expressing in many ways what we understand in a single way, and of understanding in many ways what we find written in a single way, and that obscure. In this way the waters of the sea, which can only be stirred by different meanings, are filled. The land also is filled with the offspring of men; its 'dryness' consists in zeal governed by reason.

13.25.38 I wish to say also, O Lord my God, the thoughts that the next verse of your Scripture suggests to me; I shall speak out and not be afraid. You inspire, and I speak truths, for I speak of the words you have willed me to speak. Nor do I believe that I speak the truth if inspired by anything other than you; you are Truth, but *every man a liar* (Ps. 116.10 [Ps. 115.11], Rom. 3.4). Hence *he who speaks falsehood, speaks of his own falsehood* (Jn 8.44). If, then, I speak truth, I speak of your Truth. Behold, you have given us *for food every plant that casts its seed that is upon earth, and every tree that has in itself the fruit of its seed* (Gen. 1.29–30). Nor have you given this to us alone, but also to all the birds of heaven and beasts and creeping things of the earth; to the fish and the great sea monsters you have not given them. I said earlier that these fruits of the earth are allegorical signs and types that point to the works of mercy provided out of the fruitful earth, according to the needs of this life. Such 'earth' was the pious Onesiphorus, *to whose house you gave mercy, because he had often refreshed your servant Paul, and not been ashamed of his chains* (2Tim. 1.16). The *brothers who supplied from Macedon what Paul lacked* (2Cor. 11.9) did likewise, and gave their 'fruit' in this way. But how grieved was Paul at those who did not give him the fruit they owed to him! As he says, *At my first defence no one stood by me, but all deserted me; let it not be held against them* (2Tim. 4.16). For those who minister rational teaching and give their interpretations of divine mysteries, are due their fruit as being like 'men'.[19] They are due their fruit as being like the 'living soul', giving themselves as examples in all manner of self-restraint. So also they are due their fruit as being like the birds of the air in respect of the blessings they bring, which are multiplied upon earth; for *their sound is gone out into every land* (Ps. 19.4 [Ps. 18.5]).

31.26.39 But these things are food for those who rejoice in them; and *those whose god is their stomach* (Phil. 3.19) do not rejoice in them. Nor does the 'fruit' lie in those who provide them, but in the spirit in which they give what they give. In the case of Paul, who was serving God, I see clearly why he rejoiced; I see and share greatly in his rejoicing. He had received from the Philippians what they had sent through Epaphroditus (Phil. 4.18); but I see why he rejoiced. What he rejoiced in was also what he fed on; for he says truly, *I rejoiced greatly in the Lord, that at length revived the concern that you felt for me, for you had grown weary of it.* They had long grown weary of the fruit of that good work; they had drooped and almost shrivelled, yet Paul rejoices for them, because they had revived; he does not rejoice for himself, because they had helped him in his time of need. For this he goes on to say: *I speak not because I lack anything; I have learnt to be content with what I am. I know how to have too little, and I know how to have too much; in any and all circumstances I have been steeped in hunger and thirst, in being rich, in being poor; I can do all things through him that strengthens me* (Phil. 4.10–15).

---

19 'For those who minister ... as being like "men"'. That is, as rational human beings, capable of understanding symbolic expressions (including allegories) and commanded to enjoy the fruits of the earth.

13.26.40 Why, then, great Paul, do you rejoice? What is the source of your joy, and what is the source of your sustenance; you, *man renewed in recognizing according to his image the God who created him* (Col. 3.9–10); 'living soul' full of self-restraint, tongue that soars like a bird as it *speaks sacred mysteries* (1Cor. 14.2)? It is to such living creatures that this food is owed. What is it that sustains you? It is joy. Let me hear what comes next: *But you did well in sharing in my tribulation* (Phil. 4.14). This is the source of his joy and of his sustenance – that they have done well, not that his plight is eased. To you he says, *In my tribulation you have been bountiful to me* (Ps. 4.1 [Ps. 4.2]), for he has *learnt to be rich and to be poor in you, who strengthen him. You know,* he says, *you also, O Philippians, that when I first preached the Gospel, when I left Macedon, no church shared with me and balanced its account between things given and things received, but only you, for you not once but repeatedly sent to help me in my needs* (Phil. 4.12–16). He rejoices that they have now revived and returned to these good works, like a field that regains its life and fertility.

13.26.41 Is it, then, because they had helped him in his time of need – as he writes, 'You sent to help me in my needs' – that he rejoices? Not for that. How do we know? Because he himself goes on to say: *not that I seek a gift, but because I demand the fruit of my work.*[20] I have learnt from you, my God, to distinguish between a gift given and fruit returned. A gift is the actual thing that is given by the one who provides what is needful, such as money, food, drink, clothing, shelter, assistance. The fruit is the good and honest intention of the giver. For the Good Teacher does not say only, *He who receives a prophet,* but adds, *in the name of a prophet;* nor does he say only, *He who receives a righteous man,* but adds, *in the name of a righteous man* – such a person, he says, will receive a prophet's reward or a righteous man's reward. Nor

---

20 '... *I demand the fruit of my work*'. Phil. 4.17. The Latin word *fructus* can be translated 'fruit' (as is necessary in order to preserve the link with Augustine's exegesis of Gen. 1.19–30), or as 'return, interest'. The same is true of the Greek word *karpos* in Phil. 4.15–18, where the prominent sense is the commercial metaphor (seen also in the previous chapter).

does he say only, *He who gives a cup of cold water to one of these little ones of mine*, but adds, *simply because he is my disciple*; and he goes on to say, *Amen I tell you, he shall not lose his reward* (Matt. 10.41–2). Receiving a prophet, receiving a righteous man, offering a cup of cold water to a disciple – these are 'gifts'. 'Fruit' consists in doing all this in the name of a prophet, in the name of a righteous man, in the name of a disciple. It was with such 'fruit' that Elijah was fed by the widow who knew he was a man of God, and for that reason fed him. But when he was fed by means of the raven, that was a gift; nor was it the inner Elijah that was fed, but the outer, who could be harmed by the lack even of such food as he was given. (cf 1Kings 17.1–16 [3Kings. 1–16).

13.27.42 Thus I speak what is true in your sight, O Lord. Outsiders and unbelievers, who, in order to be initiated and won for you, need the sacred mysteries of initiation and the mighty wonders which we believe to be signified by the words 'fishes and sea monsters' (Gen. 1.9–12), take these words to refer to the obligation to refresh your servants physically, or help them by providing for the needs of this present life. But, in their ignorance of why they should do this or what it all means, they fail to feed your servants, nor do your servants get any sustenance from them. The outsiders and unbelievers do not perform these works with holy and honest intent, nor do your servants rejoice in their gifts; they do not as yet see any 'fruit'. For this same reason the 'fishes and sea monsters' feed on the foods that do not spring only from the dry land, set apart and separate as it now is from the bitter waves of the sea.[21]

13.28.43 And *you saw*, O Lord, *all the things that you had made, and behold, they were very good* (Gen. 1.4–31). We too see them, and behold, they are very good. For each race of creatures that you made, when you had given the word that it should be and it

21 'For this reason ... of the sea'. Augustine here picks up his interpretation of the phrase 'fishes and sea monsters' to refer to objects in the physical, rather than the intellectual or spiritual world. Those on the fringe of the Christian community, who support it physically but do not adopt its values, are seen as being creatures of 'the deep', as opposed to the 'dry land' of true believers.

had come into being, you saw that they were severally good. Seven times I have counted it written that you saw that what you made was good; and the eighth time, when you saw all that you had made, you saw not only that it was good, but that it was 'very good', as being all together. The individual creations were good, but when all together at once they are both 'good' and 'very good'. Every beautiful physical body declares as much; a body that consists of beautiful parts is much more beautiful than each of the individual parts which, when united in perfect order, complete the whole, though they are also beautiful even individually.

13.29.44 I have concentrated on the question of whether it was seven times or eight that you saw that your works were good, seeing as they pleased you, but I have not found that any time existed when you saw them – any time that would enable me to understand how many times you saw what you have made. I have said: 'O Lord, surely your Scripture is true, seeing as you are truthful, and it was Truth that proclaimed it? Why then do you tell me that no time existed when you saw them, yet your Scripture tells me that you saw on each individual day that what you had made was good, and when I count them, I find how many times you said this?' You in return say to me that you are my God. You speak in your servant's inner ear, shattering my deafness and crying, 'O man, what my Scripture says, I say; Scripture speaks in temporal terms, but my Word is not subject to time, but stands fast with me in an equal eternity. What you see through my Spirit, I see; just as what you say through my Spirit, I say. And just as when you say them temporally, I do not say them temporally, so when you see them temporally, I do not see them temporally.'

13.30.45 I have listened, O Lord my God, and I have lapped up a drop of your sweetness. I have come to understand that there are some who take no pleasure in your works,[22] and who say that you made many of them, such as the vaults of the sky, under necessity and compulsion. Moreover, they say that you did not

---

22 '. . . some who take no pleasure in your works'. i.e., the Manichees.

make them of yourself; they already existed, having been created in another place from another source, and were brought together, assembled and made fast by you, when you were piling up the ramparts of the world against your defeated enemies, so that they would be cowed by its heaped mass and be unable to rebel against you again. Other things, such as all living flesh, down to the smallest creatures, and all that hold the earth with its roots, they say you neither made nor even fastened together; they are begotten and shaped by the Hostile Mind, another Being not created by you, but the opposite of you. Those who say these things are mad; they neither see your works through your Spirit, nor recognize you in them.

13.31.46 But as for those who do see through your Spirit, it is you who see in them. When they see that your works are good, it is you who see that they are good, and whatever things please them for your sake, it is you who please them in those things; and what pleases us through your Spirit, pleases you in us. For *who among men knows what belongs to a man, except a man's spirit that is within him? But we* – says Paul – *have not received the spirit of this world, but the Spirit that is from God, that we may know the things that God has given us.* And I am admonished to say: *surely no one knows the things that belong to God, except the Spirit of God* (1Cor. 2.11–12). How, then, do we know the things God has given us? The answer comes that the things we know through his spirit are the things that no one knows except the Spirit of God. For just as those who speak through the Spirit of God are rightly told, *It is not you who speak* (Matt. 10.10), so those who know through the Spirit of God may rightly be told, 'It is not you who know.' Therefore those who see through the Spirit may no less rightly be told, 'It is not you who see'; thus whatever through the Spirit of God they see to be good, it is not they who see it, but God. It is one thing, then, for someone to think that something is bad when it is good, as the afore-mentioned persons do. It is another thing for a man to see that something that is good, is good, in the way of the many who take pleasure in your creation, but do not take pleasure in you in it, and hence wish to enjoy the creation more than they enjoy you. It is another thing again when a man sees that something is good, and it is God who sees in him that it is good, to the end that he might be loved in what he has made; – God, who can be loved only through the Spirit he has given; for *love has been poured out in our hearts through the Holy Spirit that has been given to us* (Rom. 5.5). Through that Spirit we see that a thing is good, if in some degree it is good; it has existence from him who does exist 'in some degree', but who is the Is.[23]

13.32.47 Thanks be to you, O Lord! We see heaven and earth, whether this means the higher and lower physical parts or whether it means the spiritual and physical parts of your creation; and in the cosmos constituted by these parts, whether together they make up the physical world or the whole of creation, we see that light has been made and set apart from darkness. We see the 'firmament of heaven'. This may mean what is between the spiritual waters above and the physical waters below, the physical mass from which the world was first made; or it may mean the area bounded by the sky. This too is called 'heaven', and through it the 'birds of heaven' roam between the waters that move over the deep in the form of vapour and which drop down in the form of dew even on clear nights, and the heavier waters that flow on the earth. We see these waters gathered together in distinct form in the plains of the sea, and we see the dry land, whether that means land left uncovered by the waters or whether it means land given form, made visible and ordered, the mother of plants and trees. We see lights which shine down from above, the sun that is *sufficient for the day* (Matt. 6.34) and moon and stars that comfort the night; we see that they all mark and signify the passing of time. We see all around us moisture teeming with fish and monsters and birds; for the physical mass of the air, that bears up birds in flight, takes its density from the vapour that rises from the waters. We see the face of the earth made fair with land animals, and with man, 'made in your image and likeness', set over the irrational animals by reason of his bearing your image and like-

23 '... who is the Is'. Compare the name of God given Ex. 3.14 ('I AM WHO I AM'). Again, Augustine is equating goodness with being and evil with unbeing.

ness – that is, in virtue of his rationality and understanding. And just as there is one thing in his soul that by its rational capacity dominates and another that is subject and obedient to it, so was woman made physically subject to man; she has indeed an equal nature in terms of her mental capacity for reason and understanding, but is subject to the male in respect of her body in the same way that the desire for activity is subject to the skill of acting rightly in accordance with the rational processes of the mind. We see all these things; they are good individually, and collectively very good.

13.33.48 *All your works praise you* (Prov. 31.31, Dan. 3.57), to the end that we should love you; and we do love you, to the end that all your works should praise you. Your works have a beginning and an end in time; they have a rising and a setting, a waxing and a waning, an outward form and a loss of that form. They have sequence, morning and evening, in part hidden, in part plain and open. They were made by you from nothing, not made from you, not from anything that was not you or that existed previously, but from matter that was concreated, that is created by you along with them, for you imposed form on its form-lessness without any time having intervened. For though the matter of heaven and earth is one thing and the form of heaven and earth another, and although you made the matter from nothing and the form from the formless matter, nevertheless you made both at once, so that there should be no interval or lapse of time between the matter and the form that followed it.

13.31.49 We have considered the allegorical reasons why it was your will either that these things should be made or be written in this order, and we have seen that they are good individually and collectively very good – heaven and earth, the head and body of the Church, predestined before all time, having neither morning nor evening, in your only-begotten Word. But when you began to pursue in time what you had predestined, to reveal what was hidden and to impose order on our disordered state – for *our sins were above us* (Ezek. 33.10), and we had departed from you for the depths of the abyss, yet your good Spirit was moving over us and helping us in due season – then you both *justified the unrighteous* (Prov. 17.15, Rom. 4.5), and set them apart from the unjust. You consolidated the authority of your Scripture between those 'above' (that is, those obedient to you), and those 'below' (that is, those subject to them). You gathered together the unfaithful in one compact and alliance, so that the zeal of the faithful might be made manifest, and that they might be obedient to you in the labour of mercy, *distributing even to the poor their earthly wealth* (1Cor. 13.3) to gain the things celestial. Then you kindled the lights in the firmament, your holy ones that *possess the Word of life*, ennobled with spiritual gifts, radiant with sublime authority. Then you brought forth from this physical matter the sacraments in which to steep the faithless nations, along with the visible miracles and audible words, according to the firmament of your Scripture, by which the faithful too were blessed. Then you formed the living soul of the faithful, strong in continence, its emotions set in due order; then you renewed its mind in your image and likeness, making it subject to you alone and needing no human authority as its pattern. You made its rational action subject to its supreme understanding as the woman is subject to the man, and willed that your ministers, necessary as they are in this life for bringing the faithful to perfection, should receive from the faithful such good works as would provide for their temporal needs, and would prove fruitful for the future. All these things we see, and they are 'very good', for it is you who see them in us, having given the Spirit by which we see them and in them love you.

13.35.50 O Lord God, give us peace; for you have given us all things. Give us the peace that comes from rest, the Sabbath peace, and peace that has no evening. All the beautiful and ordered sequence of created things, 'very good' as they are, will complete its due measure and pass away; for in them were morning and evening made (cf Gen. 1.5–31).

13.36.51 But the seventh day is without evening or setting. You have hallowed it, and it abides for ever. Your Scripture tells us that after your works ('very good', as they are described) you rested on the seventh day – even though you were at rest when you performed them. This is a prophecy to us that we too will, after our works (and 'very good' they will be also, seeing as it is you who have given them to us), rest in you in the Sabbath of eternal life.

13.37.52 Then also will you rest in us, even as now you work in us, and your rest will exist through us, even as now your works exist through us. But you, O Lord, are always working and always at rest. You do not see in time, nor do you move in time or rest in time; yet you make both what we see in time, time itself, and rest out of time.

13.38.53 We, then, see the things that you have made because they exist; but for you these things exist because you see them. We see outwardly that they exist, and inwardly that they are good; but you saw them made at just that moment when you saw they were to be made. We are moved to do good at one time, after our heart has conceived by your Spirit; but earlier in time we were moved to do evil, as we abandoned you. But you, O one good God, have never ceased to do good. There exist, indeed, certain works of ours that by your gift are good, but they are not eternal; we hope that after those works we will rest in the great Sabbath you have hallowed. But you, the Good that lacks no good thing, are always at rest, for you are yourself your rest. And who among men will grant a man to understand this? Who among angels will grant an angel to understand it? Who among angels a man? Let them ask this understanding of you; let them seek it in you, let them knock at your door. Thus and not otherwise will they receive, thus will they find, and thus will the door be opened to them (cf Matt. 7.7–8, Lk 11.9–10).

APPENDIX

ON TRANSLATING
AUGUSTINE

Language and Effability

Great are you, O Lord, and worthy of high praise. Great is your strength, and of your wisdom there is no counting (1.1.1). In these words Augustine sets out the leitmotif of the *Confessions*; the nature of God, and the human response to it. These two issues lead him immediately into paradox: Can one have false ideas about God, seeing as any falsehoods are by definition the contrary of God, who is the truth? Can human response be said to be human at all, seeing as it is God who has created humans to respond in the way they do? And how can any truth about God be expressed?

The last question is of particular importance if we are considering how the *Confessions* should be translated, as it is inseparable from Augustine's attitude towards language, which is in turn inseparable from his use of it. Many people have observed how the various stages of Augustine's life are marked by his encounters with language – his bawling inarticulacy as a baby, his involvement with the all-talking Manichees, his renunciation of the profession of rhetoric, to name only a few instances; and it is true he remains acutely conscious of the potentialities and limitations of language as a means of theology, or discourse about God.

On the one hand, Augustine comes very close to asserting the absolute ineffability of God, the logical consequence of which is the absolute impossibility of theology. Any given language is an arbitrary, human system, subject to variations of time and place, and radically unsuited to expressing the transcendent and immutable Deity. On the other hand, Augustine stresses that any statement about God is true *in so far as it is a statement about God at all.* That is to say, if he has indeed made any statement about God, it must by definition be true. The tension between these two positions is clearly seen in Augustine's language. The mere fact that Augustine writes his

359

Confessions at all must mean that he acknowledges the possibility of using language to and about God, for the verb *confess* expresses (more transparently in Latin than in English) an act of speech. But what Augustine is trying to express is a truth which transcends the limits of any given language: 'the blessed life itself is neither Greek nor Latin, though Greek- and Latin-speakers and all speakers of every other language long to gain it' (10.20.29). Often indeed Augustine finds ordinary linguistic usage inadequate to express a truth about God. Thus early in Book One he asks: 'What, then, are you, my God? What indeed, if not the Lord God? For who is lord besides the Lord; who is God besides our God? Highest and best, most mighty, most almighty; most full of mercy and justice, most hidden and most present with us, most lovely and most strong ...' (1.4.4). All the predicates that can truly be ascribed to God are found in him in their highest and best form; it is a tautology to describe God as 'God', but no less so to describe him as 'just' or 'merciful'. This does not lead Augustine to conclude that God is simply ineffable (the statement that God is merciful is, after all, true), but it does lead him to stretch language beyond its usual limits: to describe God as 'most almighty' is simply not logical, as omnipotence does not admit of degrees. Augustine uses paradox to remind himself of the inadequacy of language for his purpose. Nor is this the only such paradox in the *Confessions.* Elsewhere in Book One, again addressing God, he says, 'before anything that can even be called "before", you exist' (1.6.9); towards the end of the work he again describes God as him 'who is the Is' (13.31.46).[1]

---

1 A specialized problem is posed by Augustine's frequent use of titles such as 'Truth' or 'Sweetness' in addressing God, or various persons of the Trinity. So at 10.23.33–4, where Augustine argues that, since nobody likes to be deceived, everybody loves the truth; and that the truth is to be found in its truest form in Jesus, who is the Truth. Modern English conventionally uses capital letters in such titles, but (i) this convention is not found in Latin, and (ii) Augustine would not in any case distinguish between truth as an abstract quality and truth as found in Jesus – they are the same. The translator has attempted to use the conventions of capitalization which will be most familiar to the modern reader; but the reader should be aware that this use of capitalization is not original to Augustine, and is inevitably arbitrary in its application.

All this does not make for easy reading. It would be tempting to dismiss such linguistic turns as mere rhetorical aberrations of taste, which must be stripped away to reveal Augustine's true thought. Rhetoric is, as we will see, certainly important to Augustine. But in these cases, he is using paradox because it reflects exactly his thought; and any attempt to smooth it over will necessarily obscure the arresting quality of the original. If, to take the first example, we were to represent Augustine as calling God 'most powerful and mighty', we would not be saying anything repugnant to his theology, but we would be missing the point, and making him out to be a mere windbag. I have not considered it any part of the translator's task to make Augustine appear less challenging than in fact he is.

Biblical Citations

Augustine's use of biblical citations may also present the reader with some difficulty. In this translation, these citations are printed in italics; but some general observations may also be helpful.

Augustine's biblical citations are, of course, all in translation; and the Old Testament citations are translations of a translation – the Greek translation known as the Septuagint, dating back to the second century BC. Both the Septuagint and the Latin translations used by Augustine can fairly be described as literal translations, and it is possible to talk of a style of 'biblical Greek' or 'biblical Latin' not unlike the biblical English of the Authorized Version. The idioms may be different from those used in ordinary speech; a special vocabulary may be created, in which words have different meanings. The word *confession* is itself a good example of this. To the English reader, the title of the *Confessions* suggests a catalogue of indiscretions. To the average Latin-speaker, the title *Confessiones* would suggest something similar. But to understand the term correctly, we have to go back to the Sepuagint, in which a Hebrew word meaning 'praise' is rendered *homologesis*, from a verb normally meaning 'to agree, acknowledge'. This in turn is rendered into Latin as *confessio*, which thus gains (in Christian usage) the sense 'praise' alongside its inherited meaning. Augustine himself explains in his *Commentary on the Psalms* 141.19: ' "Confession" can be understood in two ways: with reference to our sins, or as praise of God. But the word is generally familiar in reference to sins; and in that sense is so familar to the populace at large that as soon as the word "confession" is heard in the course of a reading, whether with reference to praise or to sins, the fists fly to the breast.'

This is a key point for our understanding of the *Confessions* as a whole: that they are primarily an act of praise, and only a list of Augustine's sins in so far as that conduces towards the glory of God. But it is also an illustration of the sort of specialized biblical Latin that Augustine can appeal to. Numerous other terms in the *Confessions* have acquired this extra charge of meaning, which is not always close to the original sense: for instance *virtus*, usually 'courage, strength', but also 'miracle'; *sacramentum*, usually 'oath of allegiance', but also 'sacrament, allegory'. The list could be extended at great length.

It is not always easy for us to appreciate the massive familiarity Augustine has with the Scriptures, the result not only of the hours spent every day in the liturgy and in private study but also of an educational technique in which memory-training played a key part. A single word of the *Confessions* may be enough to recall a whole passage.[1] So in the list of paradoxes in Book One discussed above, he says: 'For you we perform works beyond our duty, to put you in our debt; but who has anything that is not your own?' (1.4.4). Now the first eight words here represent, very clumsily, just two words of Latin, *supererogatur tibi*; and the first of these is a very rare word, notably found in the words of the Good Samaritan to the innkeeper at Luke 10.35: 'Whatever more you spend (*supererogaveris*), I will repay you when I come back.' One can read a lot of Latin and not encounter this verb; so when one does, it is difficult not to recall the biblical passage.

1 It follows that not all commentators are agreed on whether Augustine is quoting from the Scriptures at any given point. Some of the citations adduced in this version may be disputed, and others not adduced might be added. Sometimes Augustine is clearly alluding to a passage without citing it; such cases are generally signalled in a footnote, or with the direction 'cf'.

Even though there is nothing so substantial as a citation here, we are invited to think about the parable in question and to consider its relevance here.

This technique of allusion could easily be understood as the pious equivalent of a sort of stale classicism, merely substituting Christian motifs for pagan motifs. But this would be a misunderstanding. In the first place, the mere concept of the Bible as a corpus of sacred scripture itself opens up new hermeneutical possibilities. Once these originally disparate documents are seen as forming a divinely ordained canon, it follows that nothing within it can be coincidental; the use of one word at one place is sufficient to evoke its use in another, quite different place. Thus Augustine begins his *Confessions* by calling God, in the words of the Psalmist, 'worthy of high praise', *laudabilis valde*, literally 'very praiseworthy'. He concludes them with a reflection on Genesis 1.31: '*You saw, O Lord, all the things that you had made, and behold, they were very good* ... The individual creations were good, but when all together at once they are both "good" and "very good"' (*valde bona*). Should we put this down to coincidence, or should we hear an echo of the one passage in the other? Certainly the creation as a whole necessarily reflects the character of its Creator.

We have also to consider what Augustine does with his biblical citations; that is to say, how he understands them. In his exegetical technique Augustine often appears remarkably close to those modern literary critics who stress (and often overstress) the difficulty of recovering the author's original meaning in any given passage, and who rather emphasize the role of the reader in generating meaning; and who consequently leave open the possibility of a range of valid interpretations. Augustine does all these things. The fact that so many biblical citations are opaque, and more so in translation, makes this approach both easier and more necessary.

It follows that any translation of the biblical citations in the *Confessions* needs to be close to the original. A periphrastic rendering of a particular verse might be elegant and eminently suitable in one context, but what if the same verse appears a page or two later, with a different construction put upon it? So in Book

Twelve Augustine discusses at some length Psalm 115.16, translated (literally) as *The heaven of heaven is the Lord's*; his purpose being to see what light it sheds on the statement in Genesis 1.1, *In the beginning God made heaven and earth*. Now the traditional English translation is *All the whole heavens are the Lord's*, which is acceptable as paraphrase, but which if used consistently throughout Augustine's exegesis would make nonsense of it. To the objection that a phrase such as *the heaven of heavens* is not good English, one need only reply that *caelum caeli* is no more idiomatic Latin. I have felt, therefore, that a literal translation of the biblical passages not only captures something of the feel of the original, but also enables the reader to see better how Augustine's exegesis works.

We have not, therefore, attempted simply to paste in quotations from any existing biblical translation, where this does not correspond closely to the Latin. None the less, the reader may on occasion be disconcerted to find the translation looks little like anything in the English tradition. In such cases, it may be that Augustine is following a different form of text from that familiar to us. To take one example: at 13.8.9 Augustine cites Isaiah 58.10 in the form 'from you arise our raiment', which is quite unlike anything found in modern translations. Augustine's text of Isaiah seems to be following a Greek variant reading *(h)imatia* ('clothing, vestments'), rather than the better *iamata* ('healings'). This is a particularly striking instance and is noted as such; most other variants are much less significant and are passed by in silence.[1]

I have drawn a parallel here between the language of the Latin Bible and the language of the historic English Bibles. A further parallel may be drawn between the language of the *Confessions* and the language of historic English liturgies, such as the Church of England's *Book of Common Prayer* of 1662. Augustine, like the English liturgists, not only makes extensive use of biblical citations and allusions, but often writes in a generically 'biblical' style even where it is difficult to identify any

[1] In the Books of Psalms, the traditional numbering of the Latin and English Psalms do not usually coincide. I have given the English numbering first, followed by the Latin in square brackets.

specific reference. There is, of course, a continuum between the two. Many of the passages printed in italics in this version may not seem to everyone to qualify as biblical allusions at all; some readers may feel that other passages should have been printed in italics when they are not.

There is one other important parallel to draw between Augustine and the English liturgists. The English liturgists were, to a man, wholly versed in classical rhetoric, and able to deploy it to brilliant effect. One need look no further than the famous Bidding Prayer for an example of their controlled mastery of what, in the language of the day, would be called the 'copy' of English: 'Dearly beloved brethren, the Scripture moveth us in sundry places to acknowledge and confess our manifold sins and wickedness; and that we should not dissemble nor cloke them before the face of Almighty God our heavenly Father; but confess them with an humble, lowly, penitent, and obedient heart; to the end that we may obtain forgiveness of the same, by his infinite goodness and mercy.' The classical rhetorician will easily tick off the various figures of speech: *acknowledge and confess*, synonymy; *confess/dissemble*, antithesis; *humble, lowly, penitent and obedient*, crescendo, and so forth. This is not the place for a disquisition on the classical education of the English liturgists; but the passage serves as an illustration of the way biblical motifs and generically biblical language can be allied to the traditions of Ciceronian oratory. It is time to consider this aspect of Augustine's style.

Rhetoric

Augustine is a rhetorician by training. Although within the course of the *Confessions* he renounces the profession of rhetoric, this is not to say he renounces rhetoric itself – if by 'rhetoric' we mean not empty phrase-making, but the careful selection and arrangement of language. Augustine makes many criticisms of the rhetorical curriculum in which he had been taught, and which he taught himself. It relies heavily on the teaching of myth, that is, of untruths which are also impractical; it fails to make its own teachers objects of virtue; it is geared towards wholly worldly goods, which are not goods in themselves; it reduces learning to a mere commercial transaction. But none of these criticisms is in itself a criticism of rhetoric. Indeed, while Augustine was working on the *Confessions*, he was also breaking the ground for his later work *On Christian Education*, in which he defends the correct use of rhetoric in Christian apologetic: '... who could dare maintain that truth, which depends on us for its defence, should stand unarmed in the fight against false-hood' (*On Christian Eduation* 4.3.4, trans. Green). And the *Confessions* themselves exemplify this position. I am thinking not only of the great rhetorical set-pieces, such as the famous 'Late have I loved you' invocation of Book Ten, the grief over the anonymous friend from Thagaste in Book Four, and so forth. Throughout the work, Augustine shows an attention to the choice and arrangement of language far beyond what we expect from a modern prose author (or indeed most modern poets). At least some of his word-music can be appreciated by readers with no special knowledge of Latin:

(i) Habebant et illa studia quae honesta vocabantur ductum suum intuentem fora litigiosa, ut excellerem in eis, hoc laudabilior quo fraudulentior. (ii) tanta est caecitas hominum de caecitate etiam gloriantium. (iii) et maior etiam eram in schola rhetoris, et gaudebam superbe et tumebam typho, quamquam longe sedatior (domine, tu scis) et remotus omnino ab eversionibus quas faciebant eversores (hoc enim nomen scaevum et diabolicum velut insigne urbanitatis est), inter quos vivebam pudore impudenti, quia talis non eram. (iv) et cum eis eram et amicitiis eorum delectabatur aliquando, a quorum semper factis abhorrebam, hoc est ab eversionibus quibus proterve insectabantur ignotorum verecundiam, quam proturbarent gratis inludendo atque inde pascendo malivolas laetitias suas. (v) nihil est illo actu similius actibus daemoniorum. (vi) quid itaque verius quam eversores vocarentur, eversi plane prius ipsi atque perversi, deridentibus eos et seducentibus fallacibus occulte spiritibus in eo ipso quod alios inridere amant et fallere. (3.3.6)

(i) My studies, too – 'the liberal arts', as they were called – were leading me in a direction of their own; they led me towards 'the brawling law-courts', intending me to excel in them; for the better I could deceive, the more I would be praised. (ii) Such is the blindness of men that they boast even of their own blindness. (iii) I was now a senior pupil in the school of my teacher of rhetoric, rejoicing in my pride, puffed up with my conceit – though much more subdued, *Lord, you know* (Tobit 8.9, Jn 21.15–16), than the Destroyers, and wholly absent from their destructive activities. It was among these Destroyers (an inauspicious, diabolical name that they wore as if it were a badge of sophistication) that I spent all my time, ashamed, in a shameless way, that I was not like them. (iv) I would pass my time with them, and enjoy, at times, the pleasure of their friendship, though their deeds – their destructive activities – always filled me with abhorrence, for they took a reckless delight in affronting the modesty of perfect strangers, harassing them and mocking them without provocation, and so satisfying their greed for the pleasures that come from malice. (v) Nothing is more typically demonic than this activity. (vi) What truer name, therefore, could they have than 'Destroyers', seeing as it is they whom the spirits that deceive in secret had plainly twisted and destroyed first of all, mocking them and seducing them through their very love of mockery and deceit?

The *Confessions* are meant to be read out loud – the reader will remember Augustine's perplexity at Ambrose's habit of silent reading (6.3.3) – and so read, such rhymes and echoes as *laudabilior/fraudulentior* (i), *caecitas/caecitate* (ii), *gaudebam/tumebam* (iii), *inludendo/puscendo* (iv), and *deridentibus/seducentibus* (vi) are easy to make out. Nor is it too difficult to discern such word-plays as *pudore impudenti* (iii) and *eversi/perversi* (vi). Other features of the style are less obvious; for instance, the passage contains an unusual concentration of Greek words (*schola, rhetoris, typho, diabolicum, daemoniorum*), the last three of which certainly have negative denotations. The hardened specialist might note also some unusual vocabulary. *Ductum* (i), for instance, has semi-technical senses which include 'aquaduct, water conduit' and 'plot, structure of a literary work'. Neither would be out of place here – Augustine's literary studies may be carrying him powerless in one direction, like a drop of water in a pipe, or they may be transforming him into a character in *their* narrative. The truly inveterate Latinist might note the hyperbaton or strained word-order of *a quorum semper factis* (iv), emphasizing the *semper*, 'always'; or the unusual plural *laetitiae* (iv), which has a biblical ring to it; or might detect in the bold metaphor of *pascendo* (iv) 'feeding' a reference to the Prodigal Son feeding the swine (Lk 15.15) – a key image in the early books of the *Confessions*. Even now we have not exhausted the list of linguistic features that might summon our attention – and it will be remembered that we chose this passage as a typical specimen of Augustine *not* in high rhetorical mode.

Having considered these various aspects of Augustine's use of language we may now ask: how can all this be rendered satisfactorily into English?

Translation

This question is impossible to anwer without some consideration of what is generally seen as a satisfactory translation. English readers have over the last four hundred years come to expect translations to be a colourless, odourless medium in which the crystallized 'meaning' of the original is held suspended. This approach is characterized on the formal level by a preference for free and fluent translation over literal; and on the cultural level, by the appropriateness of the text in question to the values of its new audience – a feature which one recent scholar has aptly described as 'domestication'. One of the great English translators, John Dryden, gave this approach a classic formulation: 'I have endeavour'd to make *Virgil* speak such English, as he wou'd himself have spoken, if he had been born in England and in this present Age.' It is true that classical texts – and, to a greater extent, the Bible – have enjoyed something of an exemption to this principle; but even this privilege has not lasted to our day. The publication of E. V. Rieu's *Odyssey* of 1946, and of the *New English Bible* of 1961, represent the high-water mark of this fluent, domesticating approach.

The translation offered here does not aspire to this now traditional discourse of fluency. It is true that Augustine can be one of the most fluent story-tellers in Latin; one thinks of Alypius's summary arrest in Book Six, or Victorinus's profession of faith in Book Eight, or the conversion of Ponticianus in the same book. In such passages, fluency is entirely the right approach. But in other, meditative or confessional passages, Augustine should not be made merely to gossip with his reader, or Creator.

It should, perhaps, be stressed that it has been no aim of the translator to produce a wilfully crabbed or archaizing translation. Like every other translator, I began with a pleasant sense of my own special qualification to render Augustine accurately into clear, contemporary prose. In the course of this translation, I have come to see not only that I possess no such qualification, but also that clear, contemporary prose is not always what is required. The sort of stretching of language that we have seen cannot by definition be accurately reproduced in fluent discourse. The highly-wrought artistic prose cannot be reproduced in the language of a daily paper. The attempt to offer what Augustine would say were he writing today in English is sure to fail. It is certain that if Augustine were writing today, he would refer to Darwin, Freud and Einstein, to name but three – but no translator yet has seen fit to update the *Confessions* by supplying these deficiencies. Any translation of a work written 1600 years ago is bound to dehistoricize, but that should be an unfortunate side-effect, not the object of the exercise.

'All of us who read Augustine fail him in many ways', according to James O'Donnell, whose commentary is by far the best guide to reading the *Confessions*. Perhaps the translator fails him more than the commentator; compelled to translate every word (and not only to comment on points of special interest to him), compelled to offer a single formula of words for each sentence, with only the rarest explanatory note to justify a rendering or offer an alternative, he can only hope that his reader will recognize (though through a glass, darkly) some reflection of Augustine in his work; and that where they do not, their conception of Augustine may prove to be more faithful than his own.

Philip Burton

ABOUT THE TRANSLATOR

PHILIP BURTON is lecturer in Greek and Latin at the University of St Andrews. He is the author of *The Old Latin Gospels: A Study of their Texts and Language* and has translated Hugo Grotius' *Commentarius in Theses XI*.

ABOUT THE INTRODUCER

ROBIN LANE FOX is Reader in Ancient History and Fellow of New College, Oxford. His books include *Alexander the Great* and *Pagans and Christians*.